D1481896

DISTRIBUTED DATA BASES

International Symposium on
Distributed Data Bases
March 12-14, 1980

Organized by
Institut National de Recherche en Informatique et en Automatique (INRIA)

under the sponsorship of
ACM, AFCET, AICA, ASAB, DRET, ECI, GI,
IEEE Region 8, IFIP TC-6, IGDD

Symposium Chairman
Louis Pouzin

Program Committee
C. Delobel (Chairman), G. Bucci,
R. Davenport, E. Holler, J. Le Bihan,
G. Le Lann, E. Neuhold, A. Pirotte,
F. Schreiber, S. Spaccapietra, H. Weber

Organizer
W. Litwin

NORTH-HOLLAND PUBLISHING COMPANY
AMSTERDAM • NEW YORK • OXFORD

DISTRIBUTED DATA BASES

Proceedings of the International Symposium on
Distributed Data Bases
Paris, France, March 12-14, 1980

edited by

C. DELOBEL

and

W. LITWIN

1980

NORTH-HOLLAND PUBLISHING COMPANY
AMSTERDAM•NEW YORK•OXFORD

ISBN: 0 444 85471 1

Published by:
NORTH-HOLLAND PUBLISHING COMPANY—AMSTERDAM • NEW YORK • OXFORD

Sole distributors for the U.S.A. and Canada
ELSEVIER NORTH-HOLLAND, INC.
52 Vanderbilt Avenue
New York, N.Y. 10017

PRINTED IN THE NETHERLANDS

PREFACE

One of the major directions in computer science in the years 70-80 was the development of computer networks. It became possible to manipulate an even very distant data base, or to replicate certain information for the creation of a local data base or, finally, to link several local data bases through a local network. More and more often, the search of certain information concerns not only one but several data bases and it may be the same for an update. This creates an interdependency between a number of data bases and one may consider that these data bases constitute, in fact, a new larger data base. Such a data base is usually called a Distributed Data Base (DDB).

All facts indicate that the development of DDB's will be one of the major directions in computer science in the next decade. An increasing number of researchers are investigating this new domain and several prototypes of a DDB management system are being implemented. The goal of this International Symposium on Distributed Data Bases was to review the state-of-art in the domain and to determine future trends.

The Program Committee received approximately fifty papers. Twenty-one of them have been selected with the help of an international group of referees for the oral presentation. The book contains these papers and short descriptions of the four prototype systems which were demonstrated during the Symposium.

Some of the papers deal with the architecture and the implementation of a DDB. Others deal with the decomposition of a query to a DDB into a set of queries to its constituent data bases. Finally, solutions to the problem to maintain the integrity and security of a DDB and for the optimization of performance are proposed. We think that the Symposium has met its goal and that this book will not only interest researchers, but also all professionals and users concerned about DDB's.

Claude DELOBEL
and
Witold LITWIN
Editors

INTRODUCTION

L'un des traits majeurs du développement de l'informatique des années 70-80 a été l'avènement de réseaux d'ordinateurs. Il est devenu possible de manipuler une base de données même très éloignée, ou de copier certaines informations pour en créer une base locale ou, enfin, de relier par un réseau local plusieurs bases locales. De plus en plus souvent, la recherche d'une information concerne dès lors non plus une, mais plusieurs bases et il peut en être de même pour une mise à jour. Une interdépendence entre un certain nombre de bases apparaît et on peut considérer que ces bases constituent, en fait, une nouvelle base, plus large. Une telle base est habituellement appelée Base de Données Répartie (BDR).

Tout indique que la mise en place des BDR sera l'un des traits majeurs de l'informatique de la prochaine décenie. Un nombre croissant de chercheurs est en train d'investiguer ce nouveau domaine et plusieurs prototypes d'un système de gestion d'une BDR sont en chantier. Le Colloque International sur les Bases de Données Réparties avait pour but de faire le point sur ce domaine et d'en déduire les tendances futures.

Le Comité de Programme a reçu approximativement cinquante communications. Avec l'aide d'un ensemble international de lecteurs, vingt et une communications ont été sèlectionnées pour la présentation orale. Le livre contient ces communications et les descriptions brèves de quatre prototypes qui ont été en démonstration lors du Colloque.

Les communications traitent d'une part de l'architecture et de l'implémentation d'une BDR. Elles traitent d'autre part de la décomposition d'une rêqete à une BDR en un ensemble de rêqetes aux bases constituantes. Enfin, des solutions sont proposées en ce qui concerne le maintien de l'intégrité et de la sécurité d'une BDR et l'optimisation de performances. Nous pensons que le Colloque a atteint son objectif et que ce livre intéressera non seulement les chercheurs, mais, également, tout informaticien ou utilisateur concerné par une BDR.

Claude DELOBEL
et
Witold LITWIN
Editeurs

REFEREES / LECTEURS

Nous remercions sincèrement les lecteurs suivants.

The assistance of the following referees is gratefully acknowledged.

ABIDA M.	U.S.A.	LEE E.	U.S.A.
ANDRE E.	France	LE LANN G.	France
BAUM D.	F.R. Germany	LEMKE J.	F.R. Germany
BERNSTEIN P.A.	U.S.A.	LEPAPE B.	France
BIEBER J.	F.R. Germany	LINDSAY B.	U.S.A.
BILLER H.	F.R. Germany	LITWIN W.	France
BOCHMANN G.V.	U.S.A.	MAC DONALD I.G.	U.K.
BOYD D.	U.S.A.	MACHGEELS M.	Belgium
BRACCHI G.	Italy	MAIO D.	Italy
BROWN A.P.G.	U.K.	MARINI G.	Italy
BUCCI G.	Italy	MIRANDA S.	France
BUTSCHER B.	F.R. Germany	MUNZ R.	F.R. Germany
CABANES A.	France	MURRAY P.A.	U.K.
CHABRIER J.	France	NEUHOLD E.	F.R. Germany
DAVENPORT R.	U.K.	NGUYEN GIA TOAN	France
DECITRE P.	France	PALMER J.R.	U.K.
DELOBEL C.	France	PAOLINI P.	Italy
DEMOLOMBE R.	France	PARENT C.	France
DEMUYNCK	France	PEEBLES R.	U.S.A.
DEVOR C.	U.S.A.	PIROTTE A.	Belgium
DOUGLAS A.S.	U.K.	POPESCU-ZELETIN R.	F.R. Germany
FRASSON C.	Tunisie	POUZIN L.	France
GALLOGHEN L.	U.S.A.	PROWSE P.H.	U.K.
GARCIA MOLINA H.	U.S.A.	ROTHNIE J.B.	U.S.A.
GELENBE E.	France	SCHNEIDER H.J.	F.R. Germany
GIRAULT C.	France	SCHREIBER F.	Italy
GOUDA M.G.	U.S.A.	SELINGER P.	U.S.A.
HAINAUT J.L.	Belgium	SINTZOFF M.	Belgium
HANNAFORD D.	U.K.	SPACCAPIETRA S.	France
HARDGRAVE W.T.	U.S.A.	STONEBRAKER M.	U.S.A.
HEATH I.J.	U.K.	SVOBODOVA L.	U.S.A.
HOLLER E.	F.R. Germany	TAGG R.	U.K.
JOUVE M.	France	THANOS C.	Italy
LACROIX M.	Belgium	TIBERIO P.	Italy
LAMPORT L.	U.S.A.	WEBER H.	F.R. Germany
LE BIHAN J.	France	WONG E.	U.S.A.

TABLE OF CONTENTS

SYSTEMS ON DEMONSTRATION

DISTRIBUTED DATA BASES
C. Delobel and W. Litwin (eds.)
North-Holland Publishing Company

SOME CONSIDERATIONS ABOUT DISTRIBUTED DATA BASES ON PUBLIC NETWORKS

R. Popescu-Zeletin, H. Weber

Hahn-Meitner-Institut
Berlin

The paper investigates the feasibility of distributed data bases on public networks as defined in the ISO "open systems architecture". It identifies a number of drawbacks of this architecture from a data base point of view. An architecture for a distributed data base system on public networks -- the ESA System -- is proposed and evaluated.

1. INTRODUCTION

Computer networks have been designed and are getting operational now at an accelerated rate. They increasingly offer more application-oriented services, and thus free the user from concerns about the system's architecture and its internal workings. Early systems were meant to be dedicated to a certain type of application and were meant to connect a fixed number of computer systems of only one type or of a usually small number of different types. Based on the work of a great number of national and international standardization bodies this concept has been extended into a so-called "Open Systems Interconnection" network architecture for the connection of a great number of different types of computers to the communications network in an open-ended fashion. The open systems concept relies on the existence of accepted standards for the connection and communication between different computer systems via the open system interconnection network. A number of countries --especially European-- have adopted those standards proposals and now provide public networks usually operated by the national PTT's. It is obvious now that one of the most important applications of computer networks, the access of remotely stored data in distributed files and distributed data bases, will become one of the main applications for public networks.

Quite a number of services have been identified in the architecture proposals for open systems /1/ for rather different applications of those systems. No special service, however, has been defined so far to support the access and modification of distributed data bases. It will be shown in this paper that the availability of those services is a prerequisite for the development of Distributed Data Base Management Systems (DDBMS) on public networks.

The paper then analyzes the services proposed so far in the ISO standardization proposal with respect to their use as a basis for the development of a DDBMS which meets the aforementioned requirements.

In its third part the paper proposes an architecture for a DDBMS on a public network called ESA (Evolutionary System Architecture) part of which has already been implemented or is being implemented at the Hahn-Meitner Institut in Berlin.

2. CHARACTERISTICS OF DISTRIBUTED DATA BASE SYSTEMS ON PUBLIC NETWORKS

From our study of the German situation we may conclude that a rather great variety of different types of DDBMS on public networks will be suitable for different applications. The types of systems will have different characteristics in three different dimensions.

(1) Applications may vary with respect to the dispersion of data in a distributed data base, and also with respect to the degree of dispersion of access requests to different sites for the execution of queries and modification requests. Some applications require primarily local access to data and almost no access to remote data, while others require as much access to remote data as to local data.

Examples:

At one extreme one may think of an enterprise whose factories are located at distant places. Because of their independent operation, access to remote data bases will be rather infrequent.

A distributed data base connecting all libraries, on the other extreme, may require frequent remote document searches at almost all sites connected to the network.

(2) Distributed data bases on public networks may also vary with respect to the homogenity/heterogenity of the data base systems on the various host computer systems connected to the network. One may find applications which remain totally homogeneous since all data bases of interest to this application are manipulated by the same data base management system. Other applications may spread out over a number of data bases all managed by a different data base management system.

Examples:

One can assume on the one hand that an enterprise whose data bases are located at different sites are all managed by the same type of data base management system. Data base in the federative German public administration, on the other hand, although designed for the same purpose, are frequently managed by totally different data base management systems.

(3) The "Open Systems Architecture" has been proposed to support the communication between computer systems of different types over the public network. Distributed data bases on public networks may therefore also vary with respect to the internal representation of data, data allocation schemes, and access patterns. One may therefore distinguish between homogeneous or heterogeneous distributed data bases on simimlar or different computer systems.

Examples:

The same examples as above may illustrate the two extremes with respect to the similarity/difference of computer systems for some applications of distributed data bases on public networks: Most enterprises maintain similar computer services, even though their applications are rather different at different locations, to minimize the cost of the computer services for the whole company. Rather similar applications which require access to remote data on the other hand are being performed on totally different computer systems in the federative public administration in Germany.

3. OPEN SYSTEMS' CHARACTERISTICS

It is intended in this section of the paper to focus on only a few characteristics which, however, are of particular importance from a distributed data base point of view.

(1) The communication regime has been defined in the architecture proposal to support communication between only two partners in the network. This kind of communication discipline is usually called point-to-point communication. This means, in essence, that data base retrieval or modification requests can only be directed in the network to one other partner at a time. For the execution of retrievals and modications, the architecture supports only consecutive communication with all computer systems addressed in the course of the desired retrieval or modification.

In general, however, one cannot assume that distributed data base are organized in a way that only two partners need to communicate for the execution of a retrieval or modification request. The consecutive execution of the communication between the requesting host computer and a number of other host computers will then be necessary. At the present time no broadcasting mechanism is supported at the session layer or below. Additional software has to be implemented at the DDBMS level, and additional overhead has to be taken into account in the operation of the DDBMS.

For the given network technology with its rather low-band width communication channels, any communication necessary in the course of a query execution will be much slower than the communication between processes in the same computer system. Our experience with centralized data base management systems indicates, however, that response times for retrieval and modification requests in an interactive data base application on a centralized system have almost reached their point of intolerability. Any further delay for the consecutive execution of internetwork communications would be unacceptable.

One may therefore conclude that applications leading to a high degree of dispersion for data and retrieval/modification requests will be primarily communication channel bound. Only those data base applications which exhibit a low degree of dispersion may be executed on public communication networks.

(2) The ISO open systems architecture has been proposed to support a rather wide variety of applications of computer networks. This leads to the definition of a rather rate number of services ordered in a hierarchic fashion over seven layers /1/.

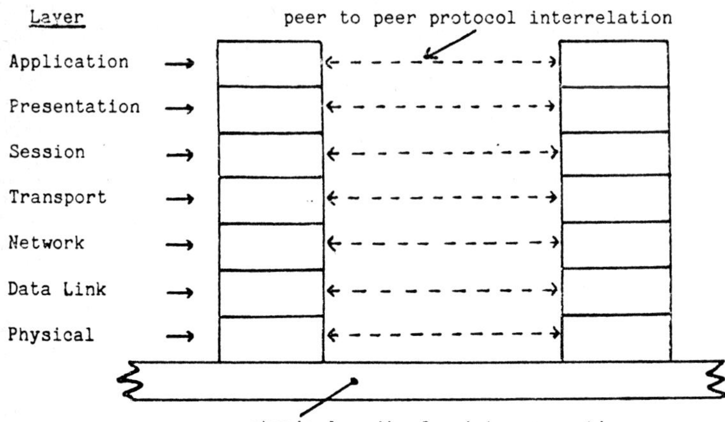

The communication regime is accordingly defined by a seven layer protocol hierarchy. Services for the conversion and translation of different formats and data structures seem to be located at level 6 (presentation layer). Any distributed data base system over a number of different local data base systems, or any distributed data base system located at host computers of different types is expected to use the services supplied by layers 1 to 6. All the services provided by these layers will therefore be permanently supported at any host in the open system, even though a great number of them will not be needed in distributed data base management. The resulting overhead will cause both an increased CPU load at each of the host computers and an increased communciation load. This in turn will lead to delays in the execution of retrieval and modification requests which do not seem to be tolerable in interactive data base applications.

One may therefore conclude that applications leading to a high degree of heterogenity in both data base systems and host computer systems will be primarily CPU bound. Only those data base applications which exhibit a low degree of heterogenity in both data base systems and host computer systems may be executed on public networks.

This does not seem to be a new observation since current trends in distributed data base management development indicate that the mentioned difficulties have been discovered and architectures have been chosen which are supposed to avoid them, e.g.,

(1) If the data are not user-specific and cannot be located at the site of its "main user", they will usually be located centrally to avoid a high degree of dispersion of retrieval and modification requests. A simple data communications systems is usually supplied with the centralized data base to support accesses from remote location (e.g., the so-called "Fach-Informations-Systeme" in Germany providing access to subject specific bibliographies).

(2) If the distributed data base system is heterogeneous with respect to the local data base system or with respect to the host computer system, the system will be designed rather as a dedicated distributed data base management system to avoid unnecessary overhead. Only those systems seem to provide an acceptable performance despite the additional computation load for the conversion and translation for data.

(3) The experienced difficulties with highly heterogeneous distributed data base systems have even led to the decision to redevelop those systems in a homogeneous form.

In summary one may then recommend the following boundaries for the aforementioned system characteristics as depicted in the following graph.

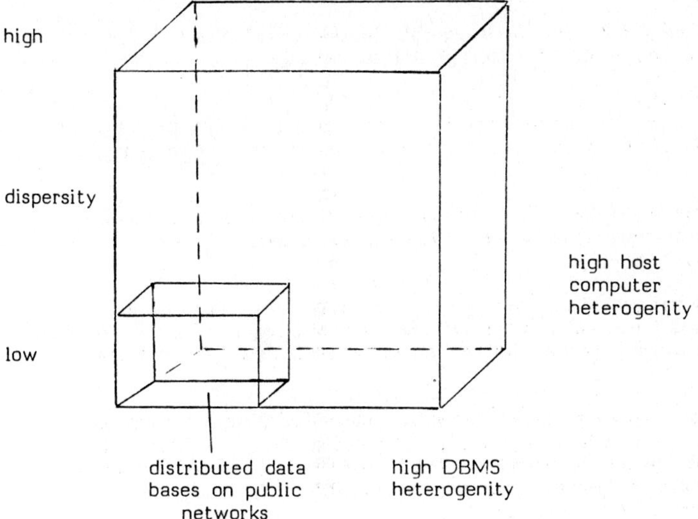

4. DESIGN PARAMETERS FOR DISTRIBUTED DATA BASE SYSTEMS ON PUBLIC NETWORKS

The previous chapters of this paper outlined some of the difficulties encountered in distributed data base management on public networks. It was concluded there that only systems with certain characteristics were feasible. It is our goal now to explore opportunities to design systems which remain within the feasibility boundaries. We will therefore identify some parameters of distributed data base systems whose value may have a great impact on the feasibility of the system and should therefore be properly chosen. Since the degree of heterogenity is generally not influenced by the data base designer, we concentrate here on parameters which determine the degree of dispersity in retrieval and modification requests; data location strategies; directory location strategies; and access and integrity control strategies.

1) In general purpose distributed data base management systems, as they are being developed in many projects, it is assumed that data may be stored in different ways, e.g.,

(i) All data may be duplicated and located at each node of the computer network (i.e., the fully redundant case). Only changes of the data base have to be reported to all other nodes whenever they occur.

(ii) Only parts of the data of the entire data base will be duplicated and located in some of the nodes of the computer network (i.e., the partially redundant case). The retrieval access to nonredundant remotely stored data and changes of redundantly stored data require communication over the network.

(iii) None of the data are duplicated. Disjointed subsets of the data are located at all nodes (i,.e., the nonredundant case). The retrieval and modication access to remotely stored data requires communication over the network.

Depending on the data base use, all three data location strategies may lead to a high or a low degree of dispersion of access requests, e.g.,

(i) a low degree of dispersion may be achieved for a fully redundant data base for arbitrary retrieval requests and almost no change requests.

(ii) a low degree of dispersion may also be achieved for a nonredundant data base with predominantly local retrieval and update requests.

(iii) a high degree of dispersion seems to be unavoidable for partially redundant data bases with rather frequent retrieval requests to nonredundant remote data or with rather frequent modification requests for redundant data.

2) A similar effect may be achieved in the application of different strategies for the location of directories. Directories will be maintained in a distributed data base to allow the access to data stored in the network. They themselves may be centralized or distributed and may contain entries for all or part of the data in the distributed data base,

(i) the directory is maintained at one host in the computer network and accesses to data are provided through this "centrally" located directory only.

(ii) the directory containing entries for all data in the data base is duplicated and located at each host.

(iii) a number of directories contain entries for --not necessarily disjointed-- parts of the data base and are distributed to different hosts in the computer network.

One may observe again that different strategies imply a very different degree of dispersion of access requests for different kinds of applications.

(i) A high degree of dispersion is unavoidable if the directory is maintained once, and located at one host (i.e., centralized directory).

(ii) A low degree of dispersion may be achieved if each directory containing entries for almost only local data is located on only one host.

3) Of similar importance for the degree of request dispersion are the strategies adopted for the access and integrity control in a distributed data base system with duplicated data. The locking necessary to preserve the integrity of duplicated data requires the communication of locking requests to all duplicated data. Different locking strategies may be adopted, e.g.,

(i) each modification request requires the immediate locking of all copies of the requested data for the preservation of the integrity of the data base at each instance in time.

(ii) modification will be performed on one copy of the data leading to temporary inconsistencies of the data base since the modification of the duplicated data will be delayed over a certain period of time.

The first integrity control strategy obviously leads to a high degree of dispersity which may be reduced if the second strategy is applied. This analysis of the impact of some design parameters for distributed data base systems leads us to the following conclusions.

(1) A suitable architecture should provide means for the selection of different data location strategies, directory location strategies, and access and integrity control strategies.

(2) A suitable architecture should encompass two basic components, a front-end system which may be flexibly adjusted to the particular needs of different applications, and a kernel system which provides a number of standard services to support the interface system.

(3) A suitable kernel system should provide interfaces to different services with similar functions but different performance characteristics to support the efficient execution of data base retrieval and modification requests.

An architecture which meets these goals has been developed and will be presented in the next chapter.

5. ARCHITECTURE OF A DISTRIBUTED DATA BASE SYSTEM ON PUBLIC NETWORKS (ESA)

The architecture of a distributed data base system called ESA (Evolutionary System Architecture) is briefly presented and its suitability for public network data base systems is justified. The distributed data base systems consists of two components: a number of front-end systems which may be flexibly designed to meet the requirements of particular applications, and a general purpose kernel system. The system has been designed this way (1) to provide means for the evolution of the whole system over time upon changes of user requirements, (2) for simplicity of the system structure, and (3) to provide the best possible system performance. The gross architecture of the system will be described and depicted in the sequel.

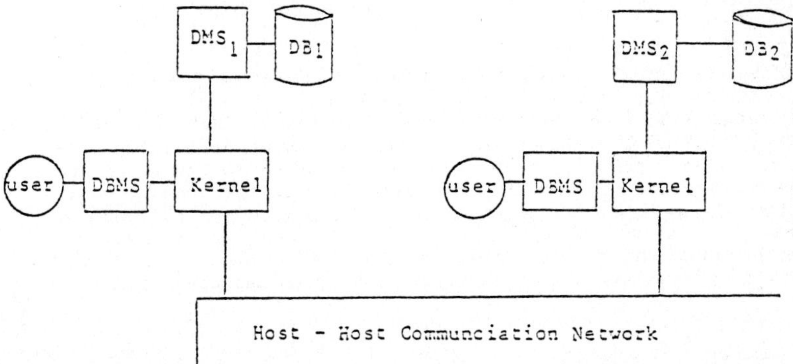

A user initates the execution of retrieval or modification requests at his local DDBMS front-end-system. The front-end system uses the services provided by the kernel system to get access to local data via a local data management system or to remote data via the communication network and the services provided by the remote kernel system.

5.1 ESA Front-End System

The front-end-system has been designed to support the flexible location and relocation of directories and data to achieve the lowest possible degree of dispersity of retrieval and modification requests in the applications associated with this front-end system. The necessary flexibility will be facilitated by composing the front-end system of a number of quasistandardized modules which are designed according to a uniform generic module design concept. The concept provides means for modifications by adding and removing modules /3/. According to this concept modules are defined to exhibit clear and simple interfaces and internal structures which make them function the same way in all possible environments. Thus, modules may be connected to other modules and connections may be removed without any effect whatsoever on the functioning of any other module.

To guarantee this invariance of a module's functionality, a module is defined to exhibit the following characteristic:

Modules identify a particular type of data and all the operations applicable to data of that type. Data and operations defined in a module must fit together properly.

A module design methodology which imposes the necessary discipline is therefore developed along the following guidelines:

(i) Each individual type of data object and all the permissible operations on data objects of this type will be defined together in a module.

The data object will be manipulated by those operations only. Different users may manipulate the data object by invoking one of the predefined operations. This makes the module a self-contained entity which will display the same time invariant characteristics in all environments. The data are called encapsuled by the permissible operations within the module.

(ii) A module definition encompasses the definition of rules for the preservation of the semantic integrity of the type of data defined in the module.

Changes of data are constrained by restrictions which are to be obeyed in order to preserve the semantic meaning of the data. For example: An inventory department's data repository may contain data about parts on hand. The order department is consequently not allowed to change the data in this repository after an order of new parts has been issued, but only after the new parts arrive. Thus, data changes may be tolerated if the preservation of the semantic integrity of the data is guaranteed.

(iii) A module definition encompasses the definition of rules for the execution of concurrent execution requests for its operations.

Changes of data are also constrained by restrictions for the concurrent execution of operations on common data repositories. It is necessary in this case to guarantee that the outcome of the execution of an operation is the same as it would be if the operation were not interleafed with any other operation. Thus, concurrently performed data changes may be tolerated if the preservation of the consistency of data is guaranteed.

Front-end systems, when designed with the aforementioned methodology allow changes of the system by additions and removals of modules as desired.

The concept is applied in the design of a front-end system in ESA in the following way:

The front-end system is constructed in a hierarchic fashion by the composition of modules out of other lower level modules. As a consequence, a front-end systems is built as a hierarchic composition of directories (representing a hierarchic structuring of data types) and of associated operations (representing the hierarchical structuring of application programs). Modules in the hierarchy are related to one another by a so-called "use-relationship" indicating that higher level modules use the services of lower level modules to complete their task. This hierarchic composition may be illustrated with the sample front-end system in the following way.

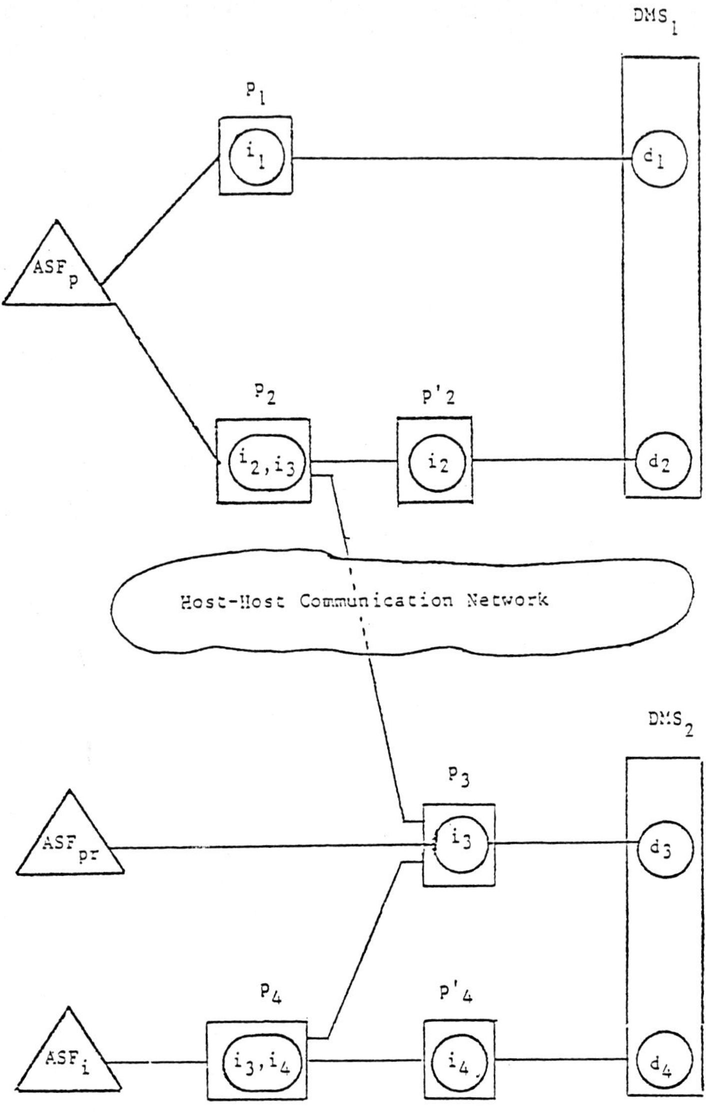

For system changes, arbitrary modules may be added to the hierarchy or removed from the hierarchy if the modules are not referenced anymore in any other modules.

5.2 ESA Kernel System

The kernel system has been designed to encompass a number of general purpose services which are independent of particular data base applications /2/. These services will be provided by a number of system components which will be called:

(i) DATS (Data Access and Transfer Service)
(ii) DDBAC (Distributed Data Base Access Control)
(iii) DDBRS (Distributed Data Base Restructuring Service)
(iv) DDBRCS (Distributed Data Base Recovery Service)

The structure of ESA may then be depicted as follows.

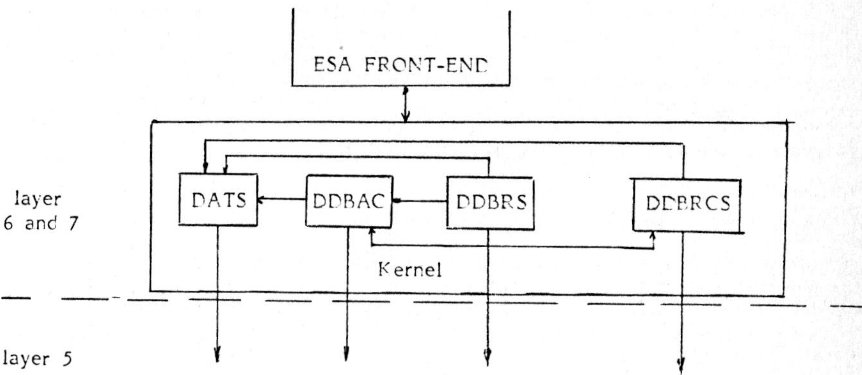

The services provided by each of these components will be briefly described in the following section.

(1) Access Control Component (DDBAC)

A request for the modification of duplicated data has to be signalled to each host where the data resides. In general this involves the transmission of the locking request to quite a number of other host computers. A broadcast mechanism which may support the concurrent transmission of the request does not exist in the open systems architecture and must now be provided on the kernel level. The Access Control Component has been designed to take over this task. It therefore incorporates functions for

- the initialization of communication lines between host;
- the administration of the communication channels; and
- the synchronization between different sessions

in each modification request.

A protocol designed to support the communication between two data access control components provides primitives to support these functions.

(2) Restructuring Component (DDBRS)

The feasibility of distributed data base managment on public networks has been shown to strongly depend on the degree of dispersity. An increasing dispersion of data or a change in the usage pattern may lead to unacceptable performance losses. The restructuring component is designed to record aloud and access statistics which may afterwards be used by the DDBRS to relocate data or to lower the degree of dispersity to an acceptable minimum. A protocol designed to support the communication between two Restructuring Components provide the primitives to support these functions.

(3) Recovery Component (DDBRCS)

A modification request generally requires modifications at a number of different hosts. If a transaction executing a modification request cannot be executed in total because of system failures, the data base may be left incompletely modified. Incomplete modifications generally lead to inconsistencies in the data base. the recovery component has been designed to reinstall the state of the data base as it was before the initialization of the incomplete execution of a transaction. A protocol designed to support communication between two recovery components provides primitives to support this function.

(4) Data Access Component (DATS)

DATS consists of four components with a somewhat overlapping function: Remote File Transfer (RFT), Remote Data Access (RDA), Virtual File (VF) and Remote Execution Request (RER). All four of them are composed of two processes residing on different hosts and they communicate in accordance to a specified protocol. The function of these components may be explained as follows.

Remote File Transfer:

RFT may be initiated by a user process UP and

- it establishes a connection between a local RFT process called FTM (File Transfer Master) and a remote RFT process called FTS (File Transfer Slave);
- it transfers a remote file transfer request;
- it performs an access to the requested file;
- it transfers a message containing the requested file to the requesting host;
- it converts data formats of the transferred data into the formats of the requesting host;
- it stores the transferred copy at the requesting host.

This communication pattern may be depicted in the following graph.

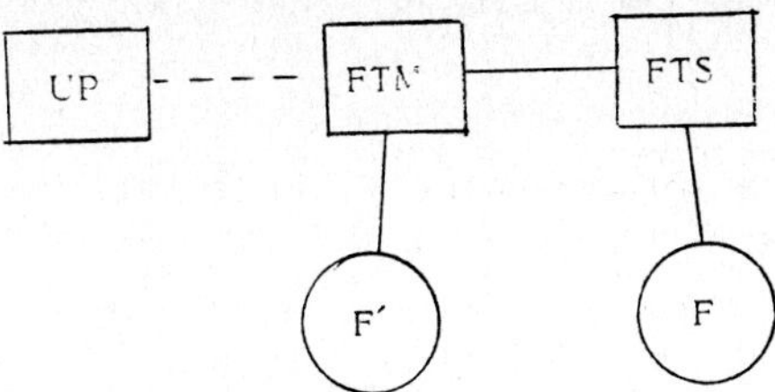

After the initialization of RFT by UP the two processes may continue to execute in an asynchronous fashion.

Remote Data Access:

RDA may be initiated in a user process UP and

- it establishes a connection between a local RDA process RFA, and a remote RDA process AFR;
- it transfers a remote data access request;
- it performs an access to the requested record of a remote file;
- it transfers a message containing the requested record to the requesting host;
- it converts data formats of the transferred data into the format of the requesting host;
- it provides the transferred copy of the requested record to the requesting program.

The communication pattern may now be depicted as follows.

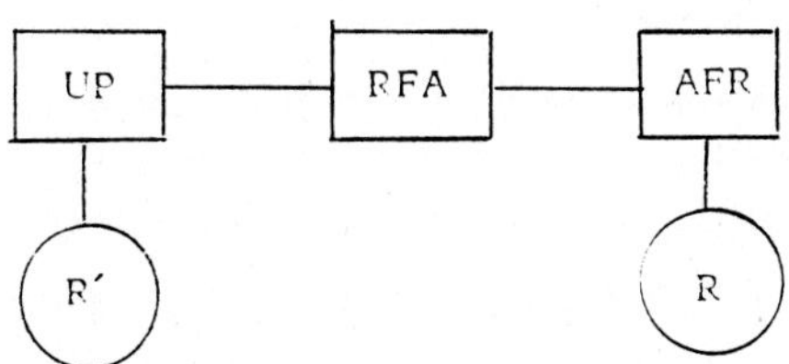

After the initialization of RDA by UP the user process halts until the termination of the remote data access.

Virtual File

VF may be initiated in a user process UP and

- it establishes a connection between a local VF process VFL, and a remote VF process VFR;

- it transfers a virtual file request;

- it maps an access request on a virtual file into an access request on a local file;

- it performs an access to the requested file or records on the remote host;

- it maps the format of the accessed data into the virtual format;

- it transfers the requested data to the requesting host;

- it stores the transferred data in a data repository on the requesting host.

This communication pattern may then be depicted as follows.

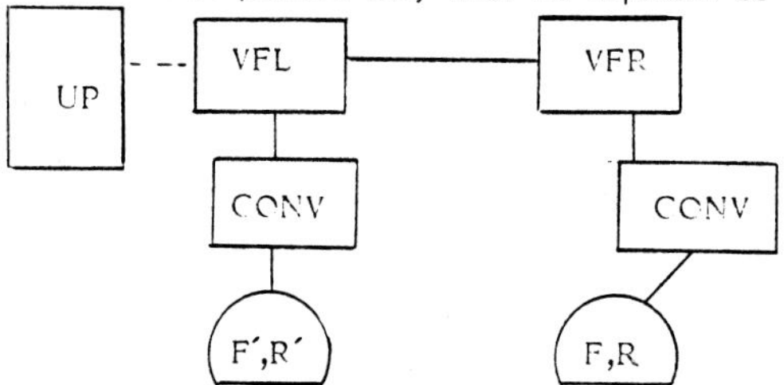

After the initialization of VF by UP the two processes may continue to execute in an asynchronous fashion.

Remote Execution Request (not fully designed yet)

RER may be initiated in a user process UP and

- it establishes a connection between a local RER process RERL and a remote RER process RERR;

- it transfers a remote execution request;

- it performs manipulation on data identified in the remote execution request;

- the results of the remote execution are transferred to the user process (UP)

This RER communication pattern may be depicted as follows.

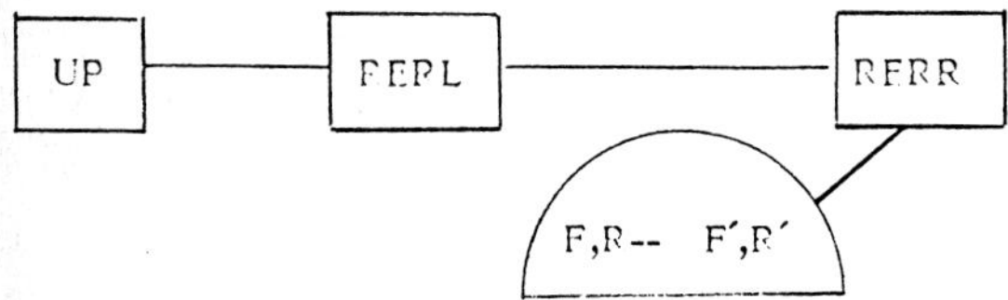

After the initialization of RER by UP the two processes may continue to execute in an asynchronous fashion.

The first three components RFT, RDA and VF may all be used to perform similar tasks. The decision of which component will be used in the execution of a certain user transaction will be based on performance and availability criteria. These criteria have been determined in system modeling, protocol modeling and system simulation studies /5, 6/. A selector component of the Kernel System decides during the execution of user transactions on the selection of one of the aforementioned components.

6. CONCLUSIONS

The paper presents an analysis of some application scenarios for distributed data bases on public networks. It analyzes some important characteristics of the open system architecture from a data base point of view and determines some feasibility boundaries for distributed data bases on public networks. It then presents a proposal for an architecture of a distributed data base system on the given open systems architecture. It may be concluded that the reference model does not meet some of the most important requirements to support DDBMS's efficiently at the present time. We conclude from our experience in public network design that additional services and mechanisms will be necessary to implement DDBMS's.

REFERENCES

1. ISO/TC 97/SC 16 N 227
Reference Model of Open System Interconnection
(Version 4 as of June 1979)

2 Peebles, R., and Manning, E.
"System Architecture for Distributed Data Management"
Computer Vol. 11 (1978) No. 1

3 Weber, H.
"Modularity in Data Base System Design:
A Software Engineering View of Data Base Systems" in
Weber, H., Wasserman, A. (eds)
Issues in Data Base Management
North Holland (1979)

4 Weber, H., Baum, D., Popescu-Zeletin, R.
The Design of a Distributed Data Management System
on a Heterogeneous Computer Network
Infotech State of the Art Report on Distributed Databases Vol. 2 1979

5 Popescu-Zeletin, R., and Butscher, B.
"A Study of Efficiency and Overhead of Data Access and
Transfer Systems in the Heterogeneous Computer Networks"
German Chapter of ACM-Workshop on Communication Networks,
Wiesbaden, Germany, June 1978

6 Baum, D., L.-Bauerfeld, W., Popescu-Zeletin, R.,
K. Ullmann
"End-to-end level data flow analysis for communication networks"
Proceedings of the International Symposium on Flow
Control in Computer Networks, Versailles, France,
Feb. 1979
North-Holland.

DISTRIBUTED DATA BASES
C. Delobel and W. Litwin (eds.)
North-Holland Publishing Company

A DATA DICTIONARY FOR DISTRIBUTED DATABASES

by

G. Martella and F.A. Schreiber

Istituto di Elettrotecnica ed Elettronica,
Politecnico di Milano, P.za L. da Vinci,32
20133 MILANO

The Distributed System Dictionary DSD is presented as a tool for designing, maintaining, and running distributed computing systems, and application programs and data working on them. The DSD functions toward users, system designers, and DB administrators are surveyed; then its role toward the computer network is examined. A logical architecture is then proposed for the DSD, partitioned into several levels which are parallel to those proposed by ANSI/SPARC for DBMS. Finally an architecture for a Data Dictionary Management System is outlined.

INTRODUCTION

Distributed Databases (DDB), which have been for many years the object of researches and experiments, are reaching now a more precise role in the world of Informatics. Among the aims of a DDB system the following seem to have a major relevance :

. to put data closer to their users;
. to avoid too much centralization of resources, which could cause a worstening of system efficiency and efficacy;
. to enhance system reliability;
. to ease Database maintenance and restructuring operations while maintaining a high availability rate;
. to tailor the EDP structure to the functional and organizational structure of the organization;
. to increase the utilization factor of EDP systems.

Reaching these objectives entails the solution of a number of technical problems. Among them we mention :

. an integrated DDB access capability;
. the transparency to the user of the physical data allocation;
. the logical, physical and "distributive" data independence;
. the software portability;
. an efficient cataloguing system.

To most of these problems, solutions have been already given for centralized DB, e.g. the data independence problem /1/. However, in the DDB environment the solution to this problem as well as to others, can be much more difficult and, even if many proposals have been made by different researchers /2/, in many cases it has not yet been attained satisfactorily. Data independence, in fact, must be assured not only at a local level, but also with respect to a possible data reallocation among the nodes of the information network.

In distributed systems however, we find also some problems which, even if already present in the centralized environment, assume a particular relevance since they are critical to the development and use of the DDB. In particular :

. prevention of non-planned data redundancy and of possible data inconsistencies when developing new applications;
. statement of standards for data definition and utilization;
. efficient query management;
. efficient use of the telecommunication resources (computer networks);
and others.

Solutions have been proposed for particular problems. As an example, a good documentation technique for data and programs can afford a development time reduction for new applications /3/; data redundancy can be avoided by suitable cataloguing techniques /4/. However, up-to-day, no integrated tool has been proposed for the design and the management of a DDB. Such a tool, hereafter called Distributed System Dictionary (DSD), should consist in a set of automated procedures for performing a set of functions, and in data relevant to them.

These functions can be either part of a Distributed Database Management System (DDBMS), or part of a Network Operating System (NOS), or should be implemented "ad hoc". They will be described in section 2. In section 3, data associated to these functions will be examined, and they will be considered as constituting a Distributed Database Dictionary (DD), and a logical architecture for the DD will be proposed. Finally in section 4 an architecture for the DD management system will be discussed (DDMS).

In the following we suppose that the Distributed Database is constituted by the aggregation of several autonomous local DB each having its DBMS. This hypothesis has been made for giving a reference structure to the examples, but it does not limit in any respect the general validity of the exposition.

FUNCTIONS OF THE DSD

Like in centralized systems, a DSD is called to perform its functions at different moments of the life of an Information System.

These phases can be listed as follows:
a - design and implementation of the system;
b - updating and maintenance of the system;
c - design and implementation of applications;
d - updating and maintenance of applications;
e - "Run-time" operation of the system;
f - "Run-time" operation of the applications.

While phases a) to d) are peculiar functions which are often implemented "ad hoc", phases e) and f) are related to functions which are usually embedded in other components of the system's software, such as the DBMS and the OS. However also the data necessary to these functions can be mostly stored in the DD and maintained by the DDMS.

Therefore many are the users interested in the DSD:
. the information system designers;
. the information system administrators;
. the DDB users, meaning as "users" all the access requests coming as well from on-line transactions expressed in a conversational language, as from application programs written in a self-contained or in a host programming language.

Fig. 1 shows the different functions of the DSD with respect to each of the above mentioned entities. This partitioning, however, must be considered only a conceptual one, since practically all the functions are heavily interdependent.

In the following, the different functions of the DSD will be examined.

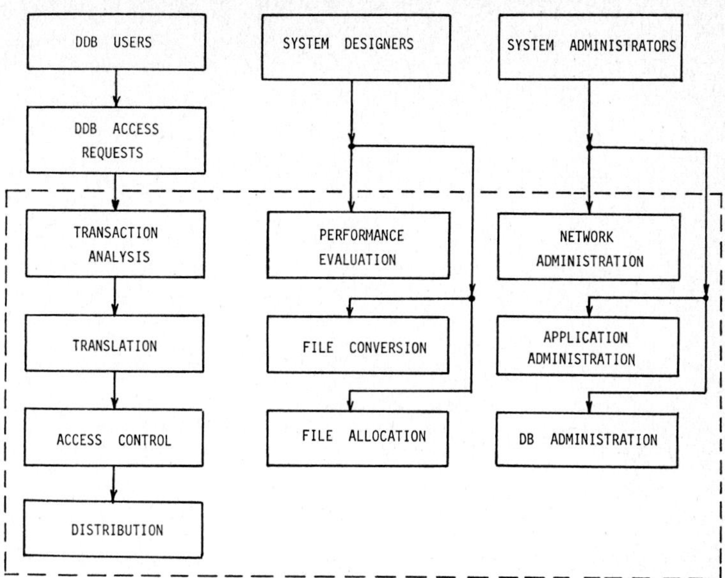

Fig. 1 - Functions of the DSD

2.1 - Functions toward the DDB users

In this class we put the following functions :
. transaction analysis;
. translation;
. control;
. distribution.

2.1.1 - Transaction analysis

After a syntactic check at the high-level DML, a complex transaction must be decomposed into a set of simpler, one parameter, transactions. This operation has already been considered for centralized systems and does not bother with data distribution /5/. However the logical decomposition can be made in different ways and the selection of the best decomposition technique can be made considering that the subsequent operations must be performed into a distributed environment. Therefore an evaluation must be made of how to distribute the simple operations on the nodes of the computer network and, if redundant copies of some file exist in the system, an evaluation must be made also of the transmission parameters (cost, delay, etc.) in order to get the optimal solution /6,7/. The DSD therefore helps the designer by giving him all the information about the network relevant features and about the DDB parameters.

When a suitable set of execution nodes has been selected for the processing of the transaction, possibly a call must be issued to the translation function before starting the actual processing.

2.1.2 - Translation

Usually a DDBMS offers the user two kinds of languages: a conversational language (for queries from on-line terminals), and a high-level procedural language (for application programs acceding to the DDB).

The translation function consists in precompiling or interpreting the user's requests, in such a way as to obtain an instruction set in a language internal to the DDBMS, including calls to modules which define the access procedures. In this phase the DSD will make available maps allowing the translation of complex instructions in the high level language into simple commands. These maps depend on the physical distribution of data, on the local files structure, on the local OS and DBMS and on the network software (fig. 2). We can notice that the translation function entails the passage through different levels of the DDBMS architecture /8/.

The main problem encountered in translating transactions into an internal language consists in choosing the target language itself. In fact this decision has influence both on the number of required translators and on that of the translation operations /9/. Moreover, also the moment to perform translation at influences the number of distribution modules (see section 2.1.4) and the number of translations which are required.

It will be the task of the DSD to suggest the designer, possibly by mean of built-in CAD programs, the solution which minimizes both the number of translators and distribution modules and that of translation operations, on the basis of the "state" of the DDB and of the peculiar transaction.

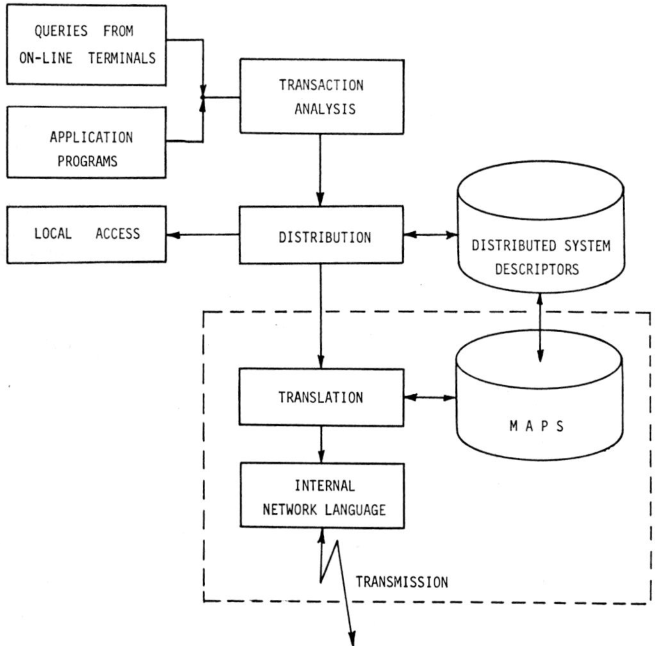

Fig. 2 - Translation function by DSD

2.1.3 - Access control

The access control function has to assure the consistency of a DDB. This means:
. to check for formal correctness of DDB data (integrity):
. to control concurrent access from process to the DDB (locking);
. to grant access permission only to authorized users (privacy);
. to protect the DDB from malfunctionments or failures (recovery).

In fig. 3 the procedures and the information needed by these functions are shown.

We see that for the integrity assurance the DSD must supply the tables of the constraints. The set of constraints, which are defined at the conceptual level in the DDB, can either be the union set of the constraints for the local DB's or a new defined set at the network level /10/. Moreover each application programmer can add other constraints at the external schema level /11/.

Constraints can be as well of static type (i.e. aimed at the control of the present state of data) as of dynamic type (i.e. aimed at the control of a semantically correct evolution from a state to the next-one).

A typical problem in a DDB is often encountered when the access request is made at a node different from that data are stored at. In this case the DSD must choose where to do the control, possibly by means of an "optimizer" looking for the solution entailing the smallest network traffic.

A possible solution, for example, performs control before transmission, that is at the access node if the request is for an insertion operation and at the storage node in the other case. If data are stored at several different nodes the set of constraints is to be examined at all of them and the existence of the DSD can greatly ease the operation.

As to locking (fig. 3), the DSD has to manage the compatibility tables for the resources assignment algorithms. Compatibility tables specify if a process P_1 can be assigned to a resource R_1 even if R_1 has already been assigned to another pro-

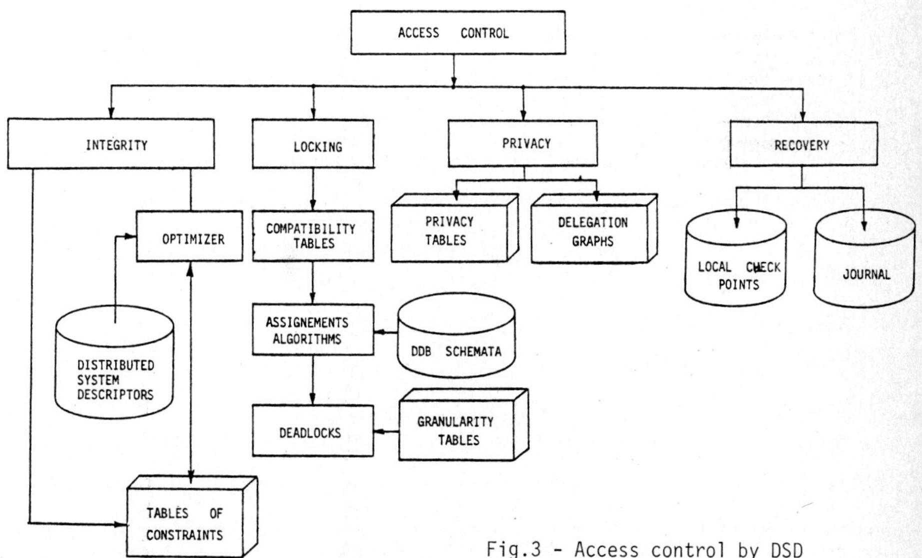

Fig.3 - Access control by DSD

cess P_2 in a given mode. An example of such a table can be found in /12/. It must be noticed that, in a distributed environment, different compatibility tables can coexist reflecting different architectures of local DBMS in the network. The DSD must manage the tables on the basis of the origin and target nodes of the transactions. Moreover the DSD has to find a proper solution to the problem of the locking granularity in accord with the peculiarities of each local DBMS. This solution will define the assignment of the system's resource to the different requests. The assignment algorithm utilizes information coming from the DDB schema and information automatically attached to the request by the DSD, at the area opening time, concerning the opened area name, the opening mode, the request order number and its origin. These data are to be used by the remote assignment routine to reply the requesting computer. The answers (area currently opened, or area not opened, and why) will be analyzed by local assignment routines which will optimize the management of the request queues /13/.

For example, the knowledge of DDB schemata(e.g. the relations hiearchy in a relational system) allows the DSD to prevent deadlocks /14/. It must use two tables: the first, T_1, containing the network global resources in a predefined order,the other, T_2, recording the resources needed to satisfy each request. The latter is ordered following the defined hierarchy and the DSD has the task to lock all the hierarchically lower resources which have not yet been locked when considering each resource request.

As to the control of data access, the DSD has to manage the privacy tables and relations which must have been defined when building the DDB. Privacy tables and relations can represent different control phylosophies, since they depend on the local DBMSs. Usually tables identify several classes (subjects, objects, etc.). which can be differently defined /15/. Relations for instances could be tuples (s, o, t, p, e) where "s" is the subject, "o" is the object, "t" the access mode which is granted iff predicate "p" is TRUE, and "e" is the action to be taken if "p" is FALSE /16/. This relational approach makes DSD's functions easier since it allows considering the access laws as system data, avoiding their extraction at table reading time.

Moreover the DSD has the task of giving data to the authorization mechanism for user access.

These data can be either in the form of many-to-many relations or of tables relating the different classes into which data are subdivided to the local data responsibles. Since one of the main actions to be taken is the delegation or the revocation of the authorization to new responsibles for the control of the classes or of their subsets, task of the DSD is to manage the time sequence of delegations and revocations e.g. by means of "delegation graphs" /17/

As to the recovery/restart function, the DSD has to manage information about DDB checkpoints, forward and backward images, and several levels of journals to follow as well operations performed by each process as those performed on each local DB, in order to be able to recover the DDB whenever a failure has occurred.

2.1.4 - Distribution

The distribution function has to optimize the distribution of the elementary requests, following predefined criteria. This means, for instance, to separate "local" requests from those requiring remote data, to choose the execution order of the elementary requests, to choose the optimum routing, in order to optimize some merit factors such as access time, processing time, network traffic, etc. It is clear that this function is tightly bound to the transaction decomposition function. The latter needsinformation about data (e.g. locality, accessibility, availability, files cardinality, statistical properties, etc.) and system resources, the former needs information about the network "response" to the different decomposition hypotheses. Task of the DSD is to coordinate these functions,

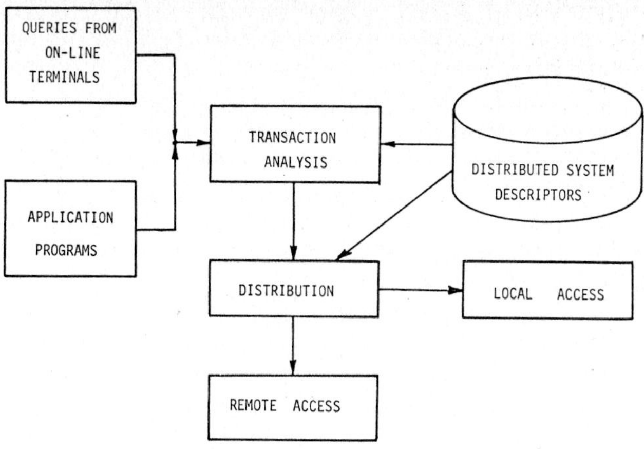

Fig. 4 - Distribution function by DSD

(fig. 4) and to give them all the required data.

2.2 - Functions toward the system designer

The DSD is also a tool for easing the design of the system. In fact by means of DSD the designer will be able to evaluate the system performance corresponding to the different possible choices of hardware/software components and of different architectures. For instance the DSD can be used as a support tool in choosing a local DBMS, to simulate different access methods for selecting those with the highest performance, in choosing report updating and generating procedures. Moreover the DSD can ease the conversion of conventional files into a Database System. In this case a reallocation of files can be convenient and the DSD can provide all the data needed by the assignment algorithms. If multiple copies of files exist in the system and their updating is made by means of broadcasted messages, then also the best routing toward each copy has to be choosen on the basis of data stored in the DSD /18/.

2.3 - Functions toward DDB administrators

In a DDB, different administration functions can be identified. In the case of aggregation of several autonomous DB we find the following functions (fig. 5):

a) Network administration: it is the function which has the task of creating and maintaining the network conceptual schema, the aim of which is to give an integrated view of data in the network's different computers;

b) Network global applications administration: it is the function which has the task of creating and maintaining the external schemata for those applications which actually use the facilities of the DDB, requesting data from different locations;

c) Local application administration: it is coincident with standard application

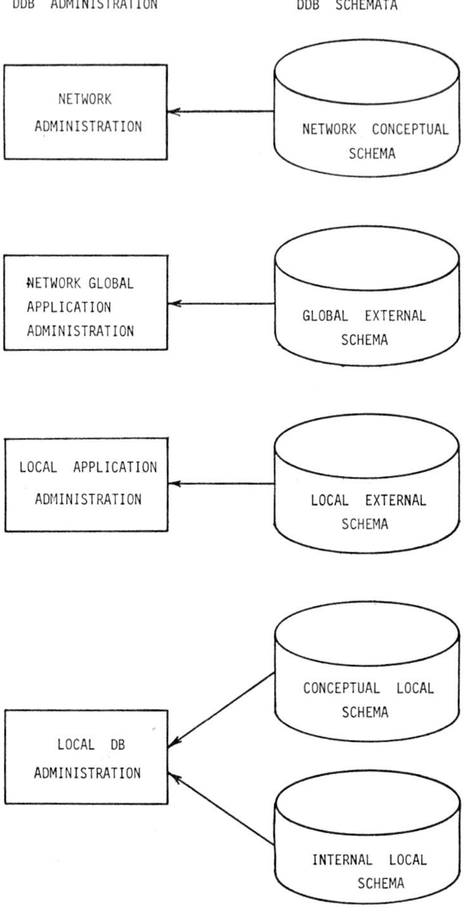

Fig. 5 - Administration functions in a DDB

administration of a centralized DB.

d) Local DB administration: it is coincident with DBA function of a centralized DB.

Relevant to functions a) and b) is the new applications identification, security and consistency control of the DDB, authorization levels definition for data access, data allocation among local DB following efficiency criteria, identification of the network technical features and of network software availability. Relevant fo functions c) and d), besides all the functions concerning the local operation of the DB, is the creation and maintenance of the interface between the local and the network DB schemata. The existence of a DSD can greatly improve and facilitate these activities. In fact, as we saw in section 2.1, the DSD manages all the information related to existing applications, security constraints, data allocation, distributed system descriptors and so on.

All the examined functions require a relevant amount of data. These data have to

be used at different times and in different ways. Moreover they must be structured in such a way as to allow their efficient sharing among the different users. Therefore they constitute a real Database supporting all the activities.
A possible structure for this Database, hencefore called Data Dictionary (DD), is presented in section 4.

ROLE OF DSD TOWARD THE NETWORK

As we saw, the DD must supply system procedures and system users (Database administrators, Network Administrator, Application Administrators) with information about stored data. The information can be classified as follows :

a) information about data "location";
b) information about data "structure";
c) information about data "availability";
d) information about data "usage".

Information of class a) is constituted of files names, their storage nodes, fragmentation criteria, possible redundant copies, etc. Information of class b) consists of name and formats of attributes for each entity or relation, statistical data about them, cardinalities of files, etc.
Information of class c) is related to data items access frequency and mode.

All the information is managed by procedures which are part of the DD. It constitutes the information base of the DD as well to the functions it must performs, as to an efficient "external" management of the DDB.

Very important are the interfacing functions the DSD performs among the network, users, designers, and system programmers. These functions are :
. automatic generation of macros to interface different Operating Systems;
. automatic call to DML translators;
. automatic generation of macros for the different access methods, by means of a catalog of nodes, names and of addressing methods of local data;
. interfacing,by means of correspondence maps,possible different transmission protocols.

Fig. 6 shows a possible use of the DSD as a network interface. User requests are translated into simple queries by means of the DSD in connection with the DDBMS (see section 2.1). Then DSD coordinates distribution and control on execution of requests in the network in connection with the Network Operating System; as we saw in Section 2.1.4.

LOGICAL ARCHITECTURE OF THE DSD

The complexity of management functions in a system with a DDB, and the characteristics of data relevant to them have been introduced in the preceeding sections. We saw, for instance, that the DSD contains information on the DDB description, i.e. on data formats, relations, logical structure, physical allocation, accessibility availability, "responsibility", origin, usage, access and updating frequencies, etc.

On the other hand, the many different uses characterizing this information lead to consider it as a true Database - the Data Dictionary - which supports the DDB, as we saw in section 2.3.

Aim of this section is the description of a logical structure of the DD, which is shown in fig. 7.

The DD has been partitioned into different views, each characterized either by in-

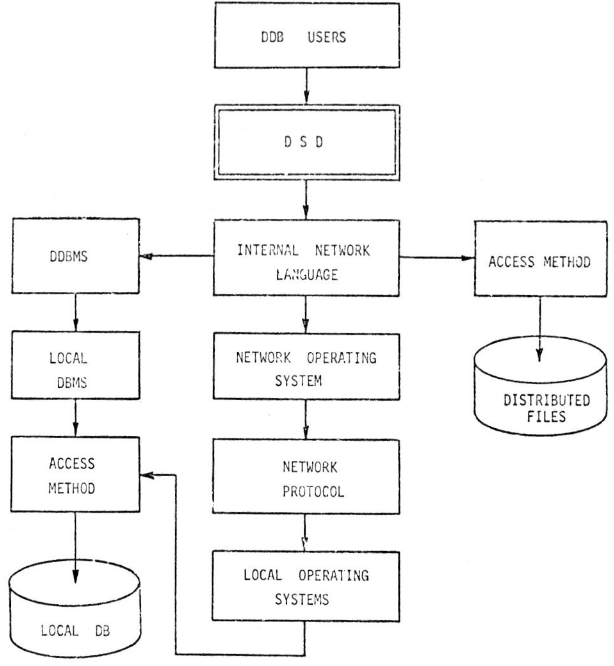

Fig. 6 - DSD as a network interface

formation contained in it, or by its aggregation state, or by its differentiated use, or by users it is relevant to.

In the proposed structure the following levels can be identified :
. NETWORK
. EXTERNAL
. CONCEPTUAL
. INTERNAL

Each of these levels is in correspondence with one or more dictionaries.
In particular :
- one Network Dictionary;
- one Global External Dictionary and as many Local External Dictionaries as the network nodes;
- one Global Conceptual Dictionary and as many Local Conceptual Dictionaries as the network nodes;
- as many Internal Dictionaries as the network nodes.

It must be noticed that, as to the physical storage structure and storage devices involved with the DD, they differ following the type of data (dynamic or static), its use (in real time or off-line), access frequency, etc.

Network Dictionary
The Network Dictionary is the nucleus around which all the management functions of the DDB are centered. It contains information to start every management process of the DDB. In particular:

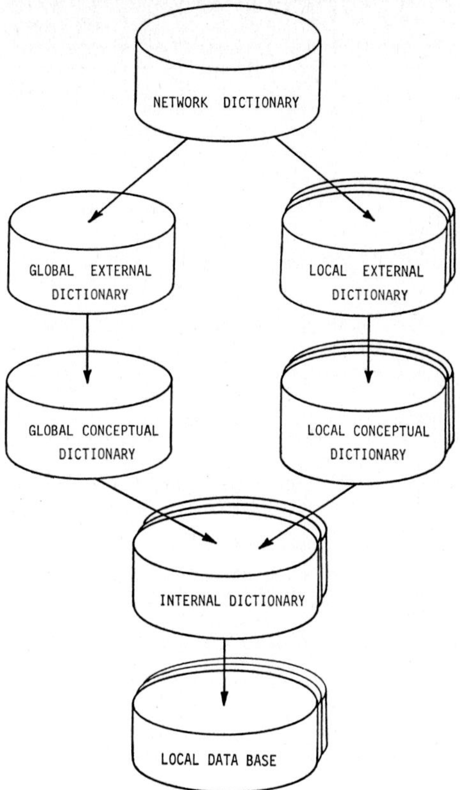

Fig. 7 - Logical architecture of the DD

a) Information for the DDB design :
   . files access programs;
   . total volumes of queries for each file;
   . total volumes of updates for each file;
   From this information, for instance, one could evaluate the optimal number of redundant copies.

b) Information for the distribution function:
   . number and types of transmission links, their unit costs, their mean utilization factor;
   . routing tables;
   . CPU's workloads;
   . Disks occupations;
   This information, together with that listed at a), may for instance, lead to determine the optimal allocation of redundant file copies and of possible operation parallelism.

c) General information about data sharing (whether it belongs to a single application or it is shared among different users), how many copies of it exist in the network and their location, wether an application requires data involving either one or more DB.

d) Information about data availability such as the existence of privacy constraints and possible constraints due to system components failure.
This information is therefore of aggregated or statistical type. It has the task either of preparing all the relevant specific information for the subsequent processing steps or of giving all the necessary elements for the design and administration of the DDB. For instance it may be useful in finding the allocation for redundant data, with respect to the query/update rate and to the consistency properties.

e) Information about data transportability.

The Network Dictionary, besides of being used by the distribution algorithms and module and by the translator, can be used by the network administration function, particularly for those actions related to data "distribution" inside the DDB.

From the Network Dictionary one goes to the Global External Dictionary or to a Local External Dictionary respectively in the case the required data belong to several different DB or to a single DB.

Global External Dictionary

The Global External Dictionary (GED) is constituted by information related to data which are used by global applications, i.e. those applications which work on data belonging to different local DB, and to data which are redundantly stored. As an example, data about component parts of a larger machine can be stored at different warehouses or production plants.

However assembly information has to be obtained at the assembly site and administrative information about them has to be processed by the application programs in the administration computer. Therefore, in order to design and run the application or retrieval programs the following information has to be stored in the GED:

a) data structures;
b) data location;
c) data availability (owing to integrity, consistency, etc.);
d) data accessiblity (owing to security, compatibility, etc.);
e) data translation maps, access paths.

Information in a) is constituted, in the case of a relational model, by the names and formats of the relation's domains, the name of the key domains, statistical quantitative semantical data about domain's values, etc.

Information in b) is constituted by location tables containing relations names, their storage site, partition criteria, cardinalities, etc.

Information in c) is related to both constraints tables and dynamic authorization tables (locking prevention (see section 2.1.3)). In the case that a very tight consistency of different global copies of data is not required, information about last update time has to be provided too.

Information in d) concerns DBMSs, system software, and hardware characteristics of the local computing systems involved in the data distribution.

The GED has therefore to supply information which, together with that found in the Network Dictionary, can determine which local DB and DBMS are interested in the transaction and how the last has to be formulated to obtain the most efficient result.

Global Conceptual Dictionary

The Global Conceptual Dictionary (GCD) contains mainly information about :
. data entities;

. common procedures;
. events;
. their interrelations.

For instance, entities will be described in terms of their attributes and relationships, of the access and identification keys, etc. in a terminlogy which avoids as much as possible any reference to the data model actually used in the conceptual schema of the DDBMS. Moreover, since this information is dynamically evolving, the GCD must contain details on the different versions which are recognized as valid in different environments. The GCD eventually has to contain information about data which possibly are not part of a structured DB, but which exist as conventional file structures.

Local External Dictionaries

Local External Dictionaries (LED) are constituted by the information related to data which are used by the local applications, i.e. which concern data stored at a single network node.

This information concerns:
a) Data structures
b) Data availability
c) Data accessiblity

Information in a) is the same as that referred to in GED, but for it concerns only the data of a single node.
Information b) and c) are related to the local privacy and security constraints and to the integrity requirements imposed by the data shareability.

LED are used also by local application administrators in designing and maintaining local applications.

Local Conceptual Dictionaries

The local Conceptual Dictionaries (LCD) contain mainly information about :
a. local data entities
b. local procedures
c. their interrelations

Information in a) describes entities in terms of their attributes and relationships as in the conceptual schema of the DB it refers to, but prescinding from the particular data model used in the DB schema.

Information in b) describes the elementary procedures related to local data which can be used to build different local applications.

Internal Dictionaries

Internal Dictionaries (ID) contain mainly information about :

a) physical storage structures of local data;
b) access methods and possibly access paths;
c) physical storage devices;
d) redundancy of elementary data items.

As a final remark we can notice that information contained in LED, LCD, and ID is that actually given by currently available Data Dictionaries for Centralized DB.

AN ARCHITECTURE FOR A DATA DICTIONARY MANAGEMENT SYSTEM

The many different data in the DD, the different functions they are used for,the different user requirements, make the use of an automatic management tool for the DD necessary. This tool is constituted by a set of languages and of programs, which are integrated in a Data Dictionary Management System (DDMS), and it is useful for creating, updating and maintaining the DD itself.

The DDMS has to cooperate with the Network Operating System and the Distributed Database Management System, as shown in fig. 8.

This cooperation, besides what discussed in section 2, consists in a continuous exchange of dynamical data concerning the instantaneous "state" of the Network and of the Database.

In particular the N.O.S. has to supply data concerning the network traffic, the occupancy level of each node, the features and the availability of the local hardware and software, etc. The DDBMS has to supply data about the network Schema, about Local External and Conceptual Schemata, about Local Data Dictionaries, about access frequencies, etc.

These data, which in section 2 have been called "System Descriptors" are supplied by means of an interface (fig.9) which has the task of extracting, analyzing and "filtering" them and of putting them in a format directly loadable into the DD.

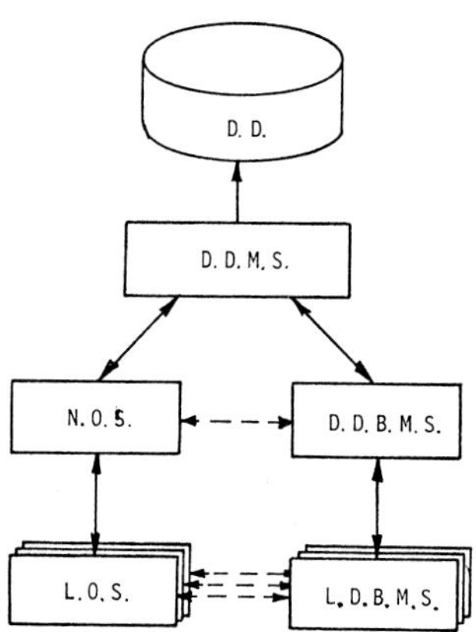

Fig. 8 - DDMS relations toward NOS and DDBMS

The other data constituting the DD, which have been examined in section 3, are loaded and managed, in turn, by means of other programs shown in fig. 9.

The definition procedures allow to specify, for each data-item, the level of the involved Dictionary (EGD, LCD, etc.), the data type, its features, etc., by means of a simple Definition Language. This information describing the logical structure of the Data Dictionary is stored in the system (see "Description of DD" in Fig. 9) and represents the schema of the DD.

The Loading procedures accept the data input and store data in DD files.

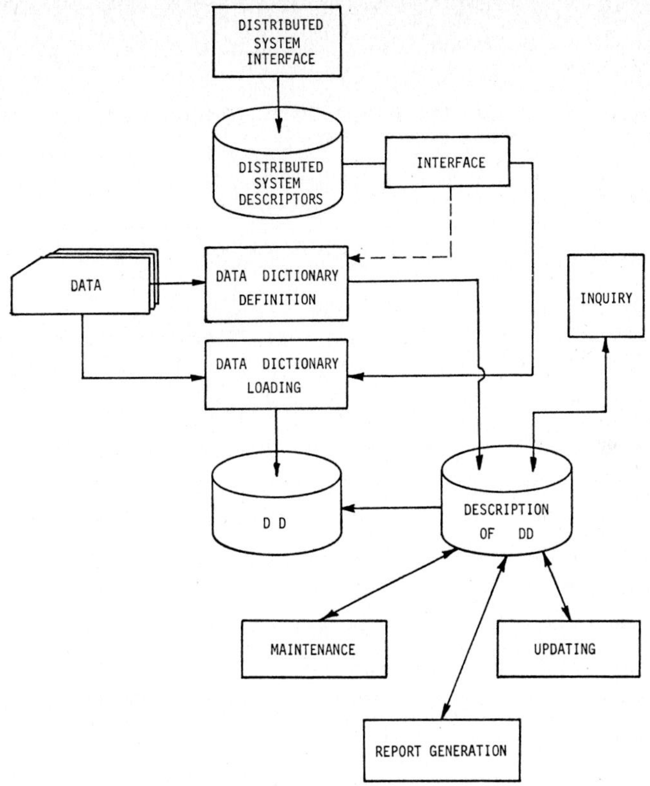

Fig. 9 - DDMS functions

The Inquiry procedures interpret users queries expressed in a User Query Language. The user asks values of one or more data-items, often selecting them by logical operations, he can specify arithmetical and statistical processing (e.g. totals, data comparison, searches of minimum or maximum values, means, variance, etc.).

The maintenance procedures allow data merging, sorting, restructuring, linking, etc.

The updating procedures allow to modify already loaded data, taking into account also the side effects that these changes have on the remaining part of the DD.

The Composition and Production procedures are essentially a Report generator, i.e. they allow the specification of the data to be printed and their formats.

SUMMARY AND CONCLUSIONS

The many problems encountered in designing, maintaining and operating distributed computing systems need, for their solution, a large number of support data which are common to many of them.

These data must be organized and maintained like a true Database. Therefore, in this paper, we tried to identify data needed by the different functions of the distributed system, and to outline a logical architecture for the Distributed Data Dictionary itself and for the system to manage it.

BIBLIOGRAPHY

/1/ ANSI/S3/SPARC, Study Group on Database Management Systems, Interim Report, 1977.

/2/ M. Adiba et Al. "Issues in Distributed Data Base Management Systems: a Technical Overview", in H. Weber, A.I. Wasserman (Ed.) - Issues in "Data Base Management", Proc. IV VLDB Conference, North Holland, 1979

/3/ D. Teichroew, E.A. Hershey "PSL/PSA: A computer Analysis Technique for Structured Documentation and Analysis of Information Processing System" IEEE Trans. on Software Engineering, Jan 1977.

/4/ E.J. Neuhold, H. Biller "Distributed Data Bases on a Network of Minicomputer", Journées "Bases de Données Réparties", Paris, March 1977.

/5/ E. Wong, K. Youssefi "Decomposition - A Strategy for Query Processing", ACM-TODS, Vol. 1, n. 3, Sept. 76.

/6/ A.R. Hevner, S. Bing Yao "Query Processing in Distributed Database Systems" IEEE Trans. on Software Engineering, Vol. S.E.5, n. 3, May 1979

/7/ G. Pelagatti, F.A. Schreiber "A model of an Access Strategy in a Distributed Database" in G. Bracchi; G.M. Nijssen (Ed.) Data Base Architecture - IFIP-TC2 Working Conference, North-Holland 1979

/8/ C. Baldissera, S. Ceri, F.A. Schreiber "Basi di dati distribuite" - Rivista di Informatica, Vol. IX, n. 3, Sept. 1979.

/9/ G. Bracchi, C. Baldissera, S. Ceri "Query Processing Strategies for Distributed Data Base Systems", EEC-CREST Advanced Course on Distributed Data Bases, Sheffield City Polytechnic, July 1979.

/10/ G. Gardarin, S. Spaccapietra "Concurrency in Distributed Data Base" IFIP W.G. 2.6 Meeting, Brussels, 1976.

/11/ K.P. Eswaran, D.D. Chamberlin "Functional specification of a Subsystem for Data Base Integrity", Proc. Int. Conf. on Very Large Data Bases, ACM, New York, 1975.

/12/ C. Parent "Integrity in Distributed Data Bases", Proc. AICA 77, 1977

/13/ J.N. Gray, R.A. Lorie, G.R. Putzolu 'Granularity of Locks in a Large Shared Data Base", Proc. Very Large Data Base, Boston, 1975.

/14/ G.L. Everest "Concurrent Update Control and Database Integrity", Data Base Management, J.W. Klimbie and K.L. Koffeman (Eds.), IFIP 1974.

/15/ G. Martella, G. Nannini "Security Techniques in Information Systems: an overview", Proc. Convention Informatique, SICOB, Paris, 1975.

/16/ M.W. Blasgen et al. "System R.: A Relational Database Management System", IBM Research Laboratory, San José, California, 1976.

/17/ P.P. Griffits, B.W. Wade "An Authorization Mechanism for a Relational Data Base System", IBM Research Laboratory, San José, California, 1976.

/18/ F.A. Schreiber "Problemi posti dal progetto di Data Base Distribuiti: i problemi di allocazione", Rivista di Informatica, Vol. V, n. 2, 1974.

/19/ G. Martella, F.A. Schreiber - "A Data Dictionary for Distributed Databases" (first draft) - ACM Database, Summer 1979.

DISTRIBUTED DATA BASES
C. Delobel and W. Litwin (eds.)
North-Holland Publishing Company

ON THE DEGREE OF CONCURRENCY PROVIDED BY CONCURRENCY CONTROL MECHANISMS FOR DISTRIBUTED DATABASES+

D. Z. Badal*

University of California at Los Angeles
Computer Science Department
Los Angeles, California 90024
U.S.A.

In this paper we shortly review the concurrency control mechanisms for distributed databases and we suggest a number of criteria for their evaluation. The main part of the paper deals with the analysis of the degree of concurrency provided by concurrency control mechanisms based on the mutual exclusion by two-phase locking and on the synchronization by time stamps.

1. INTRODUCTION

The pressure to distribute databases, already strong, can be expected to grow. Many large, geographically distributed organizations find a centralized database system nonresponsive or too costly, or both. Military and computer control systems require the reliability and the availability that centralized database systems cannot provide. Moreover, the centralized database system does not allow system extensibility and modularity nearly to the degree characteristic of distributed database systems. Further, communications costs are increasing relative to the cost of processing equipment. Thus, distributed database systems, which place computing power and data close to the users who require them, are increasingly perceived as more responsive, more reliable, and more economical than centralized alternatives.

However, if the benefits of distributed databases are to be had, several problems inherent to such distributed systems must be satisfactorily solved first. These problems are due to the long transmission delay and narrow bandwidth of most communication networks relative to the internal system delays that result from secondary storage, main memory and CPU characteristics. Reasonable solutions to some general problems of database systems, for example, database integrity, concurrency control or recovery, are often available for centralized database systems. However, such solutions frequently work poorly in a distributed environment because of the significantly different underlying hardware performance parameters mentioned above. Moreover, the distributed database systems pose new problems which do not occur in centralized systems. Partially

---

+This research was supported in part by the Rome Air Development Center, under contract F30602-79-C-0191.

*The author's present address: Computer Corporation of America, 575 Technology Square, Cambridge, Massachusetts 02139, U.S.A.

replicating some portions of a database at several sites of a distributed database system leads to significant consistency issues. Site or communication link failures and network partitions need to be handled in a fashion that permits gracefully degraded service. The transaction processing strategy in a distributed environment permits (and requires) careful optimization. And, of course, the concurrency control problem becomes especially complex in a distributed database system because communications delays prohibit traditional locking strategies. In this paper, we review the approaches to concurrency control in distributed databases and we analyze the degree of concurrency provided by the mutual exclusion and synchronization based concurrency control mechanisms.

2. ISSUES IN CONCURRENCY CONTROL

Although the concurrency control problem is, in principle, the same for centralized and distributed databases systems, it is less complex in centralized database systems because the knowledge of the transaction's activity is localized to one site, i.e., communication delays, lost messages and site failures do not, in general, occur. The primary purpose of concurrency control is to permit exploitation of the multiple parallel execution facilities, i.e., to allow concurrent interleaved execution of transactions, while preserving database integrity. In other words, the concurrent execution of transactions should not result in an inconsistent database state that does not satisfy all of its semantic integrity assertions. The usual view taken requires the concurrency control mechanism to guarantee that the visible states of the database be exactly those which could have been reached if all of the transactions had been executed sequentially, one at a time. This property is called serializability or serial reproducibility of concurrent execution. The concept has been used as a correctness criterion for concurrency control by several researchers (see [ESW78, GRA78, BER678, PAP77, BAD79b]), and it seems to have been universally adopted for commercial systems.

However, in our view, there are also other criteria by which concurrency control proposals for distributed databases must be judged:

- (a) support of dynamic validation of single transaction execution with respect to a set of integrity constraints that relate the data values being altered to other data in the database (internal consistency);
- (b) multiple copy consistency (external consistency);
- (c) transaction conflict resolution;
- (d) robustness (or reliability) of concurrency control in the presence of component failures;
- (e) concurrency control performance.

Below, we briefly survey current work in these areas.

Recently there has been considerable activity directed toward concurrency control for distributed database systems (see [THO76, THO78, BER78, BER77, ALS76, MEN77, STO78, BAD78, ELL77, LAM77, LIN79, KUN79, MEN78, REE78, RIE79, MOL79, BAD79b, KAN79, LEL78, HER79]). However, relatively few deal with distributed (as opposed to centralized) concurrency control (see [ELL77, BER77, ROS78, GRA78, KAN79, STO78, BAD78, BAD79b]) or with the reliability aspects of concurrency control (see [MEN78, STO78, BAD78, MOL79]). In most cases, the facilities for ensuring reliability of distributed databases are built on top of mechanisms for concurrency control, i.e., the concurrency control mechanisms are made reliable by additional layers of software.

It appears that the correct operation of distributed database systems in the presence of site failures is not a particularly difficult problem until one faces the desire to support, in a graceful way, systems that have been partitioned through various unplanned failures. Otherwise, the database segment at a failed site can merely be brought to a consistent state after the site becomes active. We are aware only of two proposals which deal with the network partition problem (see [MEN77, BAD78]). An important part of reliability is the communication protocol for the reliable delivery of messages among the sites. There have been several proposals, most of which are based on the concept of a two-phase commit protocol (see [GRA78]).

The problem of multiple copy updates, sometimes called external consistency, has been addressed explicitly or implicitly in most published papers on concurrency control. It is inevitable that the increased reliability and the locality of data processing which results from several copies of portions of the database at different sites has the negative side effect of increased communication overhead and, in some cases, decreased system throughput. [THO76, THO78, ELL77, KAN79, MOL79, and HER79] consider the external consistency problem in fully replicated databases, and [STO78, BAD78] consider the problem in partially replicated distributed databases.

Assuring that transaction execution satisfies integrity constraints is usually referred to as internal consistency or semantic integrity. While there is little work which deals with integrity constraint checking in the distributed database environment (see [BAD79c]), the centralized database environment received more attention (see [STO75, ESW77, BAD79, HAM78, BAD79a]).

The problem of deadlock handling in distributed database systems is another area which has received increased attention recently (see [GRA78, MEN78, GOL77]).

The last problem of crucial importance is the performance of concurrency control mechanisms. Unfortunately, there seem to be just three studies of performance analysis of different concurrency control mechanisms (see [MOL79, RIE79, KAN79]). However, there seems to be no published work on the degree of concurrency allowed by different concurrency control mechanisms except brief mention of it in [MIN78, BER79, PAP79], nor does there seem to be any conclusive comparative performance analysis or robustness evaluation of different concurrency control methods.

3. CLASSIFICATION OF CONCURRENCY CONTROL MECHANISMS

There are a number of possible classifications of concurrency control mechanisms and it is not a simple matter to select one. We consider here the classification introduced in [BAD79a] which is quite consistent with the traditional operating system terminology. We distinguish three basic classes of consistent concurrency control mechanisms, i.e., those which are serializable or, equivalently, those which allow consistent database states only. The MES or mutual exclusion set class which includes any concurrency control mechanism that operates on the principle of mutual exclusion over the set of data objects accessed by one transaction.

Two usual techniques to achieve mutual exclusion over the set of data objects are two-phase locking (see [ESW78, GRA78, STO78, ELL77]), or sequence numbers (see [THO76 THO78, ROS78]). Another characteristic of the MES class is that the serialization order is always determined at execution time and it cannot be a priori determined or guaranteed. The typical examples of MES class include [STO78, GRA78, ROS78, ELL77, ALS76, MOL79, KUN79, THO78].

The second class of concurrency control mechanisms is the S or synchronization class. The usual technique to achieve synchronization involves the use of a unique sequence number (often called a timestamp) assigned to each transaction. The distinct property of S class concurrency control mechanisms is that the transactions have to execute in the order of their timestamps and thus, if necessary, an a priori ordering of transaction execution can be guaranteed. One could further classify S class according to the way the sequence numbers are generated, according to whether the transaction can have its sequence number changed, etc. The typical examples of S class concurrency control mechanisms include [LAM76, BAD78, LEL78, BER78, REE78, KAN79, and HER79].

The S class of concurrency control can be divided into two subclasses. We call them strong and weak S subclasses. The strong S subclass, or SS subclass, (see [BAD78, KAN79, LAM76]) requires that transactions execute in the order of their original sequence numbers. We believe that there is a demand for a type of concurrency control mechanism which can guarantee an a priori ordering of transaction execution. For example, most real time DBS, such as air traffic control, command and control, would require strong synchronization. The weak S subclass (see [BER77, LIN79]), or weak synchronization (WS subclass) still requires the execution of transactions in the order of their sequence numbers but the sequence numbers can be reassigned and, therefore, the order of transaction execution cannot be guaranteed.

The SS subclass requires that the data objects are known a priori before transaction execution; otherwise, the SS subclass of concurrency control mechanisms will cause serial execution of all transactions. The WS subclass allows run time claiming of data objects, but then it requires one additional mechanism for ensuring the execution in a sequence number order. The required mechanism is the stamping of the data with transaction sequence numbers as orignially proposed in [THO76] and later utilized in [BER77], so that the incoming transaction can decide whether it would execute out of sequence number order. If indeed it would, i.e., the data sequence number is larger, then the transaction with the smaller sequence number is rejected and restarted with the new sequence number.

The important design issue in the S class is how long the transaction has to wait in order to know that transactions with smaller sequence numbers have been executed. Two techniques to decrease such waiting time are as follows. In general case, a transaction executing under S class concurrency control can expect the access with a smaller sequence number from any site of a distributed DBS (DDBS). Thus, if one restricts the number of the sites from which a given transaction can possibly receive an interfering access, then one reduces the delay. Second, if one restricts the communication protocol in such a way that it guarantees that if any message with sequence number i arrives, then any message with sequence number k, k < i, must have already arrived (so called pipeline or FIFO communication rule), then this again reduces the delay. Incidently, both techniques are used by the SDD-1, a distributed database system built by the Computer Corporation of America (see [BER77]).

The third class of concurrency control mechanisms, which we call MEO or mutual exclusion over one data object, is not based on the mutual exclusion over the set of data objects as is the MES class, but only on the mutual exclusion of one data object at a time. An example of the MEO class of concurrency control mechanism can be found in [BAD79b].

Despite some recent results on the effect of concurrency control mechanisms on distributed DBS performance (see [MOL79], [RIE79], [KAN79]), it is not possible to draw any conclusions because the results are based on different assumptions and, therefore, they are inconclusive and partially contradictory. Besides, we do not think that it is meaningful to talk about a particular concurrency control mechanism as the best one because some of them are more suitable for certain applications and system parameter environments, while other concurrency control mechanisms are more suitable for other applications. For example, if the transactions rarely interfere, then the MEO class of concurrency control mechanisms is very likely to outperform other concurrency control classes. Or, if most of the transactions need to access most of the sites of the DDBS, then it is likely that the centralized concurrency control mechanism will perform better than the decentralized concurrency control mechanisms, and vice versa. Or, if the system load is high, then the number of synchronization messages required by a given concurrency control mechanism might become quite important. The comparative analysis of concurrency control mechanisms can be found in [BAD80].

4. ON THE DEGREE OF CONCURRENCY

There are two definitions of "degree of concurrency" to be found in the literature. The first definition is set theoretical and it seems to have been introduced, although in a slightly different context, in [KEL73]. It has reappeared recently in [MIN78], and [BER79]. The degree of concurrency as defined in these papers is a cardinality of the set of all consistent schedules a given concurrency control mechanism can produce. Actually, the classification of most concurrency control mechanisms according to this set theoretical definition of the degree of concurrency appears in [PAP79], and [BER79]. As a matter of interest, the concurrency control mechanism with the highest degree of concurrency, according to the set theoretical definition, has appeared recently in [BAD79b]. The second, and admittedly less formal, definition of the degree of concurrency appeared in [GRA78] where the degree of concurrency is defined as an extent to which the concurrency control mechanism can utilize the system provided concurrent execution facilities. This definition is very intuitive and certainly very practical, but we feel that, although the degree of concurrency may be easily measured in the actual DDBS implementation, it may not be easily estimated or predicted analytically or by simulation. Nevertheless, we feel that this definition of the degree of concurrency provided by a given concurrency control mechanism is the most intimately related to the DDBS performance. The third definition of degree of concurrency is introduced in this paper and we would place it, as far as its theoretical and practical value, between the two already mentioned definitions. By that we mean that it is intuitively related to the DDBS performance and it is also amenable to analysis and prediction. The degree of concurrency is defined here in terms of an average number of data objects blocked by one transaction, i.e., the number of data objects which are not available to any other transaction. The motivation for this definition is the observation that the more data objects are blocked by the transaction, then there is a higher probability that more transactions will interfere. Since any concurrency control mechanism generating consistent databases has to execute interfering transactions serially [BAD79b], then more interference implies more serial execution and therefore less concurrency. Thus the smaller number of data objects blocked by the transaction implies a higher degree of concurrency.

We must admit that, at the time of writing this paper, the equivalence of these three definitions has not been investigated. However, we believe that all three of them are closely related because the concurrency control mechanism proposed in [BAD79b] has the highest degree of concurrency according to the first and third definitions.

In order to derive the degree of concurrency, we assume that it is possible to determine from the syntax of each transaction (T) and before T execution, a set of data objects (DO) which T might need to access. We call such DO virtual DO. The set of DO which the transaction must access in order to execute is called a set of actual DO. We assume that some of the actual objects can be determined only during run time, but in any case, the actual DO are a subset of the virtual DO.

We first analyze the degree of concurrency for the two-phase locking as the representative example of the MES class of concurrency control mechanisms. Depending on the way in which the resources are locked and released by the concurrency control, there are four possible ways in which the transaction can own resources, i.e., have exclusive access to them. (We assume here that all locks are exclusive. Similar considerations would apply to the shared locks.) These four cases are the combination of two ways the consistent concurrency control can lock and unlock resources. Each T can lock the resources in two ways, as follows:

(a) T locks all resources it might require before T execution (i.e., it locks virtual data objects).
(b) T locks resources as needed during T execution (i.e., T locks only actual data objects).

Similarly, the condsistent concurrency control can unlock resources in two ways:

(a) T unlocks all its locked resources only after it terminates its execution.
(b) T unlocks any of its locked resources only after it locked all needed resources and if they are not needed by the executing T any more.

Let m[T] be the average number of data objects held by the transaction, m[TV] be the average number of virtual data objects per transaction and m[TA] the average number of actual data ojects per transaction, and t an average transaction time. Then each of the combinations ac, bc, ad, and bd can be represented as shown in Figure 1.

Each of these cases has its advantages and disadvantages and we will discuss them. Assume that the control, i.e. lock-unlock or synchronization, messages are to be delivered by some communication protocol which requires x messages to lock or unlock one data object.

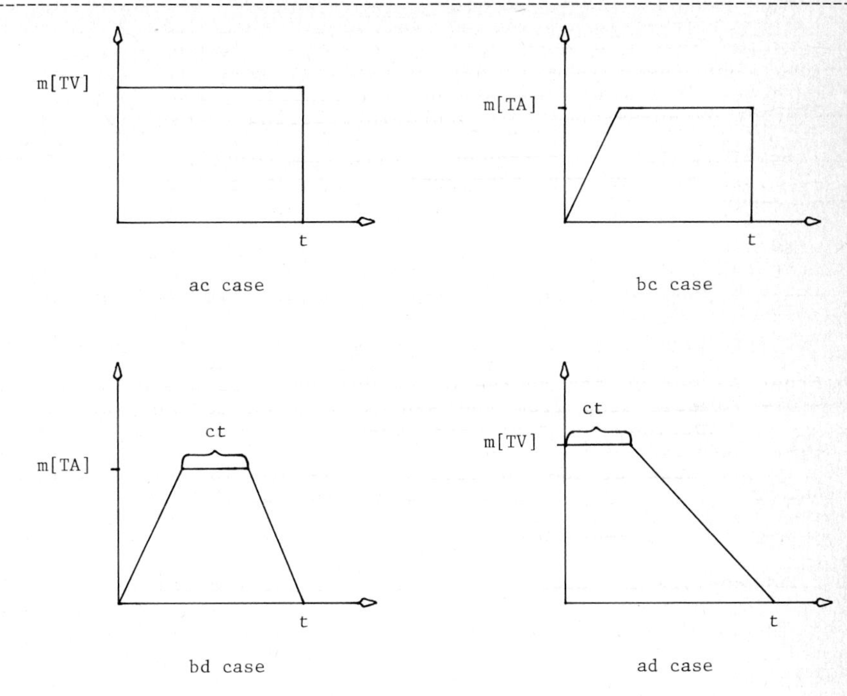

FIGURE 1

ac case:

The disadvantage here is that any data dependent T must lock all potential (i.e., virtual) data objects it might need. The advantage of this method is that deadlocks can be either avoided or prevented, i.e., the deadlock treatment is quite simple. The second advantage is that the execution of transactions can be optimally scheduled. The third advantage is that the locks are released only after the transaction is terminated and, therefore, the rollback of the just executed transaction does not involve any other transactions. The fourth advantage is that the delay introduced by the control messages is more or less independent of the number of objects to be locked. In other words, if we assume some communication protocol with x messages per object, then the delay due to locking and unlocking is directly proportional to 2x and not the number of virtual data objects being locked (i.e., m[TV]).

bc case:

The advantage here is that T locks only the resources it actually needs and, moreover, it locks them when it needs them. The second advantage is that no other transactions are affected when the executed transaction is rolled back.

The bc method has three disadvantages. First, the method must use a deadlock detection and resolution scheme which in distributed systems is more complicated than deadlock avoidance or prevention. Second, it is not possible to schedule transactions optimally. The third disadvantage is that the delay introduced by the communication protocol which set locks is proportional to xm[TA] where m[TA] is the number of actual data objects to be locked. However, the delay due to the release of locks is proportional to x only.

bd case:

The advantage of this method is that T locks the resources only when it needs them and releases them when they are not needed any more. This means that the resources are locked for the shortest possible time. This method has four disadvantages. First, rollback of the just executed transaction could involve rollback of any other transaction which accessed the data objects released by the transaction to be rolled back. Secondly, it is not possible to schedule the transaction execution optimally. Third, deadlock free execution must be accomplished by deadlock detection and resolution. The fourth disadvantage is that the delay due to locking and unlocking is proportional to 2xm[TA], i.e., to the number of control messages.

ad case:

The main disadvantage here is that the number of locked objects is larger than actually needed. Three other disadvantages are that the resources are locked for a longer period than necessary and that the transaction rollback exhibits a domino effect, i.e., potentially, several subsequent transactions must be rolled back as well. The last disadvantage is that although the locking introduces a delay proportional to x, the unlocking delay is proportional to xm[TV]. The advantages of this method are that the transaction can be optimally scheduled and that the deadlocks can be handled by avoidance or prevention.

Let's assume that $m[TA] = k\, m[TV]$, where $k < 1$ and that the average transaction processing time at each locked data object is ct where $c < 1$. Then the average number of objects locked during the average execution time t in each of the above cases (neglecting any potential transaction restarts) is:

$$m[T_{ac}] = m[TV]$$

$$m[T_{bd}] = ((1 + c)/2)m[TA] = (k/2)(1 + c)m[TV]$$

$$m[T_{bc}] = ((3 + c)/4)m[TA] = (k/4)(3 + c)m[TV]$$

$$m[T_{ad}] = ((1 + c)/2)m[TV]$$

Thus since $k < 1$ and $c < 1$, then $m[T_{ac}] > m[T_{ad}] > m[T_{bc}] > m[T_{bd}]$.

An intuitive conclusion one could formulate is that the locking method which results in the smallest number of locked data objects per t should provide the highest degree of concurrency and, therefore, the best system throughput. However, it is not obvious whether optimal scheduling which presumes the locking of more data objects (i.e., virtual objects) may not eventually provide better throughput. A similar observation appeared in [RIE79].

We will now consider the consistent concurrency control based on synchronization, i.e., S class consurrency control mechanisms. As with locking, we have four methods of propagation and deletion of timestamped requests to access data objects. Such requests are quite similar to locks in the following sense. They do function as locks for any transaction with a more recent timestamp, i.e., any such transaction cannot access the data object which has a pending (i.e., not executed and not deleted) access request placed by the transaction with a less recent timestamp. The timestamped access requests, as well as locks, must be propagated to data objects or sites. However, once they are delivered via some comunication protocol, then they can be granted, in a case of strong synchronization (i.e., SS subclass), only if all preceding access requests were granted and deleted. On the contrary, the lock can be set any time the data object to be locked is not already locked. Similarly, in a case of weak synchronization, i.e., WS subclass, the timestamped access requests can be either granted immediately or after some delay. But in both cases, then either all requests with less recent timestamps must be rejected or they are accepted only after the executed transaction with the more recent timestamp has been rolled back. The timestamped access requests can be deleted in two ways--either immediately after the access was granted and performed, or they can be deleted after the executing transaction is terminated. This is a very important difference from the lock release operation because the locks can be released only after the growing phase of two-phase locking is terminated or after the transaction execution is terminated.

Thus, the rule which requires that the timestamped access request is deleted only after it and all preceding conflicting requests are granted and performed, or after some request with the more recent timestamp has been already granted, is equivalent to the rule which requires that the lock can be released only after all locks are set and the access at the locked data object has been performed. The fact that the timestamped access request can be deleted immediately after it has been granted and performed (in the case where we are not concerned with the domino effect during recovery) suggests the intriguing possibility that, in principle, S class of concurrency control mechanisms might provide a higher degree of concurrency and better performance than MES class. Actually, it is the bd case in which both classes of concurrency control mechanisms differ.

For comparison, we show the bd case for locking and timestamps in Figure 2.

As can be seen in Figure 2, the average number of data objects by the same transaction in the two-phase locking is$((1 + c)/2)m[TA]$, and in synchronization it is $m[Tm] = cm[TA]$, where $m[Tm]$ is the average number of data objects to which the transaction can have a simultaneous access. Since $0 <= c < 1$,then $m[Tm] < (1 + c)/2)m[TA]$, i.e., in the bd case, the S class always has a higher degree of concurrency than two-phase locking.

Of course, concurrency control based on synchronization can deliver time stamped access requests either before transaction execution (case a), i.e., they are delivered to all virtual objects, or they

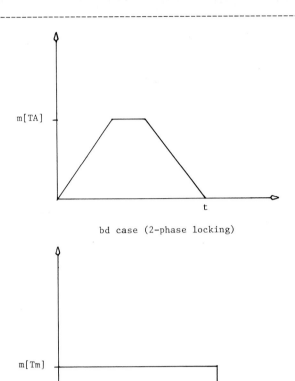

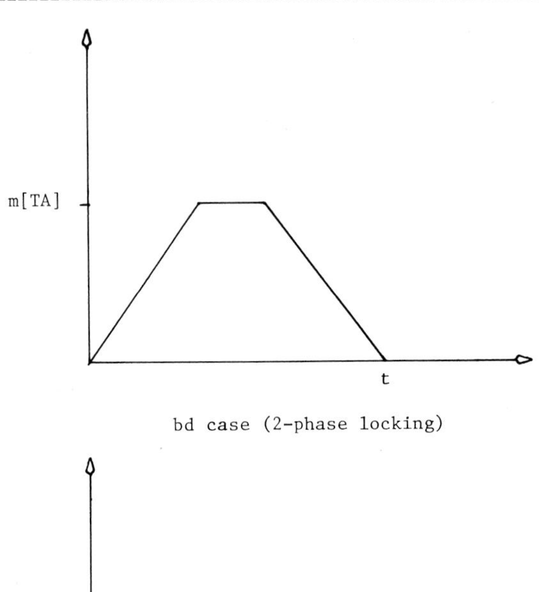

bd case (2-phase locking)

m[Tm]

t

bd case (time stamps)

FIGURE 2

can be delivered on demand during transaction execution (case b), i.e., they are delivered to the actual data objects only. As mentioned before, the time stamped access requests can be deleted either at the end of the transaction (case c) or immediately after the access request is granted and executed (case d). Thus, neglecting potential transaction rejections and/or rollbacks, cases ac, bc, and bd result in the same number of blocked objects per T in both concurrency control classes, i.e.,

$$m[T_{ac_{MES}}] = m[T_{ac_S}] = m[TV]$$

$$m[T_{bc_{MES}}] = m[T_{bc_S}] = (k/4)(3 + c)m[TV] \text{ where } k < 1 \text{ and } c < 1$$

$$m[T_{ad_{MES}}] = m[T_{ad_S}] = ((1 + c)/2)m[TV]$$

However,

$$m[T_{bd_{MES}}] = (k/2)(1 + c)m[TV] > m[T_{bd_S}] = kcm[TV] = m[Tm]$$

To summarize, in the case of requesting access to actual objects during the transaction execution (case bd), the concurrency control based on synchronization gives higher degree of concurrency than two-phase locking. Of course, the reason is that in such a case any transaction running under concurrency control based on synchronization either holds the same number of objects m[TA], but each only for time ct (vs. ((1 + c)/2)t in concurrency control based on two-phase locking), or each transaction holds the average number of m[Tm] = cm[TA] data objects during t (vs. ((1 + c)/2)m[TA] data objects in concurrency control using two-phase locking.)

However, one has to realize that the potential decrease in throughput (or the degree of concurrency) due to locking of a larger average number of data objects has to be compared to the following two inseparable effects in concurrency control based on synchronization:

(a) Average number of data objects held by the transaction during its execution;

(b) Enforcement of time stamp order execution of transactions, which prevents the S class of concurrency mechanisms to achieve the degree of concurrency indicated by the previous analysis; (exactly because of the absence of this requirement, the MEO class of concurrency control mechanisms [BAD79b] can achieve such a high degree of concurrent execution.)

One conclusion that can be drawn is as follows. Any concurrency control method based on synchronization, which can enforce the timestamp order of transaction execution in such a way that the decrease of system throughput due to such enforcement is less than the decrease of concurrency due to locking the average number of (((1 + c)/2)m[TA] - m[Tm]) = ((1 - c)/2)m[TA] data objects, might provide better throughput.

The same conclusion applies to any concurrency control which does not use locking or timestamp execution ordering but still can enforce serially reproducible transaction executions, i.e., class MEO of concurrency control mechanisms. Such concurrency control mechanism, described in [BAD79b] avoids disadvantages of both presently known methods, i.e., having a larger average number of objects locked during t and requiring timestamp order of transaction execution.

5. CONCLUSION

In this paper we have attempted to identify and describe the issues associated with concurrency control for distributed databases. We have also attempted to classify the concurrency control mechanisms into three classes. Finally, we have analyzed and compared the degree of concurrency provided by all three concurrency control mechanism classes.

REFERENCES

[ALS76]
Alsberg, P. et al., "Multi-copy Resiliency Techniques," Center for Advanced Computation, Report CA 6202, University of Illinois, Urbana-Champaign, May 1976.

[BAD78]
Badal, D.Z. and Popek, G.J., "A Proposal for Distributed Concurrency Control for Partially Replicated Distributed Databases," Proc. of the Third Berkeley Conference on Distributed Data Management and Computer Networks, Aug. 1978.

[BAD79]
Badal, D.Z. and Popek, G., "Cost and Performance Analysis of Semantic Integrity Validation Methods,' Proc. of the ACM SIGMOD 79 Int. Conf. on Management of Data, Boston, May 1979.

[BAD79a]
Badal, D.Z., "Concurrency Control and Semantic Integrity Enforcement in Distributed Databases," Infotech State of the Art Report on Distributed Databases, Infotech 1979.

[BAD79b]
Badal, D.Z., "Correctness of Concurrency Control and Implications in Distributed Databases," Proc. of COMPSAC79, Chicago, Nov. 1979.

[BAD79c]
Badal, D.Z., "On Efficient Monitoring of Database Assertions in Distributed Database Systems," Proc. of the Fourth Berkeley Conf. on Distributed Data Management and Computer Networks, Aug. 1979.

[BAD80]
Badal, D.Z., "Comparative Analysis of Concurrency Control Mechanisms for Distributed Databases," (in preparation, Computer Corp. of America Tech. Report).

[BER77]
Bernstein, P., et al., "The Concurrency Control Mechanism for SDD-1," Tech. Report CCA-77-09, Computer Corp. of America, December 1977.

[BER78]
Bernstein, P., et al., "The Concurrency Control Mechanism of SDD-1: A System for Distributed Databases," IEEE Trans. on Software Engineering, Vol. SE-4, No. 3, May 1978.

[BER79]
Bernstein, P., et al., "Formal Aspects of Serializability in Database Concurrency Control," IEEE Trans. on Software Engineering, Vol. SE-5, No. 5, May 1979.

[ELL77]
Ellis, C., "A Robust Algorithm for Updating Duplicate Databases," Proc. of the 2nd Berkeley Conf. on Distributed Data Management and Networks, May 1977.

[ESW76]
Eswaran, K.P., et al., "The Notions of Consistency and Predicate Locks in a Database System," CACM, Vol. 19, No. 11, Nov. 1976.

[ESW77]
Eswaran, K., et al., "Functional Specification of a Subsystem for Data Base Integrity," IBM Research Report RJ 1601, June 1977.

[GRA78]
Gray, J., "Notes on Database Operating Systems," IBM Research Report RJ 2188, Feb. 1978.

[GOL77]
Goldman, B., "Deadlock Detection in Computer Networks," MIT/LCS/TR-185, Sept. 77.

[HAM78]
Hammer, M. and Sarin, S., "Efficient Monitoring of Database Assertions," Proc. of ACM SIGMOD 78 Int. Conf. on Management of Data, June 1978.

[HER79]
Herman, D., et al., "An Algorithm for Maintaining the Consistency of Multiple Copies," ibid. KAN79.

[KAN79]
Kaneko, A., et al., "Logical Clock Synchronization Method for Duplicated Database Control," Proc. of the 1st Int. Conf. on Distributed Computing Systems, Huntsville, Oct. 1979.

[KEL73]
Keller, R.M., "Parallel Program Schemata and Maximal Parallelism," JACM, 3, July 1973, and JACM, 20, Oct. 1973.

[KUN79]
Kung, H.T. and Robinson, J.T., "On Optimistic Methods for Concurrency Control," Proc. of VLDB Conf., Rio de Janeiro, Oct. 1979.

[LAM76]
Lamport, L., "Time, Clocks and the Ordering of Events in a Distributed System," Mass. Computer Associates, Inc., Tech. Report CA-7603-29, Mar. 1976.

[LAM77]
Lampson, B., et. al., "Crash Recovery in a Distributed Data Storage System," (to appear in CACM), Xerox PARC, 1977.

[LEL78]
LeLann, G., "Algorithms for Distributed Data-Sharing Systems Which Use Tickets," ibid. BAD78.

[LIN79]
Lin, W.K., "Concurrency Control in a Multiple Copy Distributed Database System," ibid. BAD79c.

[MEN77]
Menasce, D., Popek, J.G., and Muntz, R., "A Locking Protocol for Resource Coordination in Distributed Databases," (to appear in ACM Trans. on Database Systems), UCLA, Computer Science Dept., UCLA-ENG-7808, Oct. 1977.

[MEN78]
Menasce, D. and Muntz, R., "Locking and Deadlock Detection in Distributed Databases," ibid. BAD78.

[MIN78]
Minoura, T. "Maximally Concurrent Transaction Processing," ibid. BAD78.

[MOL79]
Garcia-Molina, H., "Performance of Update Algorithms for Replicated Data in a Distributed Database," Ph.D. dissertation, Dept. of Comp. Sci., Stanford Univ., June 1979.

[PAP77]
Papadimitriou, C.M, et al., "Computational Problems Related to Database Concurrency Control," Proc. of Conf. on Theoretical Computer Science, Univ. of Waterloo, 1977.

[PAP79]
Papadimitriou, C.M>, "Serializability of Concurrent Database Updates," MIT/LCS/TR-210, March 1979.

[REE78]
Reed, D.P., "Naming and Synchronizatin in Decentralized Computer Systems," Tech. Report MIT/LCS/TR-205, Sept. 1978.

[RIE79]
Ries, D.R., "The Effects of Concurrency Control on Database Management System Performance," Ph.D. dissertation, Comp. Sci. Dept., Univ. of California, Berkeley, April 1979.

[ROS78]
Rosenkrantz, D.J., et al., "System Level Concurrency Control for Distributed Database Systems," ACM TOD, 3,2, June 1978.

[STO75]
Stonebraker, M., "Implementation of Integrity Constraints and Views by Query Modification," Electronics Res. Lab. Report ERL-M514, Univ. of California, Berkeley, March 1975.

[STO77]
Stonebraker, M., "A Distributed Version of INGRES," Proc. of the 2nd Berkeley Conf. on Distributed Data Management and Computer Networks, May 1977.

[STO78]
Stonebraker, M., "Concurrency Control of Multiple Copies of Data in Distributed INGRES," ibid. BAD78.

[THO76]
Thomas, R., "A Solution to the Update Problem for Multiple Copy Data Bases which Use Distributed Control," BBN Report 3340, July 1976.

[THO78]
Thomas, R., "A Solution to the Concurrency Control Problem for Multiple Copy Databases," COMPCON, Feb. 1978.

DISTRIBUTED DATA BASES
C. Delobel and W. Litwin (eds.)
North-Holland Publishing Company

SYNCHRONIZATION OF CONCURRENT UPDATES IN REDUNDANT DISTRIBUTED DATABASES

Milan Milenković

Energoinvest-IRIS
Institute for Computer and Information Systems
Stup, Sarajevo
Yugoslavia

A new decentralized solution to the concurrent update synchronization problem encountered in redundant distributed databases is presented. It guarantees internal and mutual consistency of all database copies, and completion of all submitted transactions in finite time. A new concept of reservation of database entities required for an execution of a transaction is introduced. This strategy prevents deadlocks among conflicting transactions, while not constraining parallelism among the disjoint ones. Efficiency of the solution is improved by global reservation of only write sets of the updating transactions.

INTRODUCTION AND PROBLEM STATEMENT

The spectrum of data distribution in multisite database systems can range from totally distributed (no redundancy) to completely redundant (identical copies of the same database replicated at all sites). The actual degree of redundancy in a particular system is a design parameter that is usually determined as a tradeoff of several considerations: availability, reliability and accessibility that call for higher degrees of redundancy, vs. the costs of storage and maintenance that tend to favor lower degrees of data redundancy. These considerations have been discussed elsewhere (5,6,16,19,22,24). In this paper we address the problem of concurrent update synchronization in distributed databases with higher degrees of data redundancy.

Given that internode communication in distributed systems is usually slow compared to the speed of intranode access, it seems desirable to replicate the database, or its subsets that exhibit high query-to-update ratio and are frequently used by several nodes. This tends to reduce the average query response time and internode communication burden, at the expense of more complicated updates, which in general involve all copies of the replicated data.

In distributed databases there is a possibility that several nodes may attempt to perform concurrent updates that are operating on overlapping data. When redundant data stored at different nodes are involved, consistency conflicts among the concurrent transactions may not be readily detected. Note that replication of data is just an implementation technique for enhancing certain characteristics of the system, and that all those different physical copies conceptually represent a single logical copy. Therefore, all redundant copies must remain mutually consistent, that is, identical or converging to the same state in the presence of updating activity.

This obviously calls for synchronization of the concurrent updates to prevent them from compromising consistency of the database. One approach is to centralize this function and delegate a single node to serve as an update controller for the entire system. With this scheme each update request is subject to approval of the centralized controller. The central node, in turn, has complete information about all intended updates and is thus in the position to reject concurrent conflicting requests in order to preserve consistency of the database. However, centralization of any function undermines some of the fundamental rationales of the redundant distributed database approach, most notably system's availability and reliability.

On the other hand, it is nontrivial to synchronize updates in the distributed fashion. Most of the problems stem from the fact that it is costly for any node to assess the global state of such systems, due to their properties listed below.

1. Absence of common memory.

2. Presence of finite, but variable and relatively long, internode communication delays.

3. Existence of multiple loci of updating activity; any node may attempt an update at any time.

More formally, the problem can be stated as follows:

Given - an arbitrary distributed database whose portions are replicated at various nodes in a distributed computer system,
Devise - an efficient decentralized algorithm for update synchronization that preserves consistency of the database.

In order to be acceptable, a solution must be able to guarantee the following:

a. Internal consistency of the database stored at each node.

b. Mutual consistency of all copies of the database.

c. Completion of any update in finite time, provided the total request rate is within the system's service capacity. Note that this implies absence of deadlocks and critical blocking.

Several solutions to the fully redundant case of the stated problem, that offer some or all of the above guarantees, have appeared in the literature (2,4,5,6,13, 16,24,25). We will briefly outline the basic concepts on which those solutions are based, in order to highlight some of the properties of the solution presented in this paper. This discussion is necessarily limited to very general and fairly crude statements, and is not ment to evaluate the existing solutions. More detailed analyses of some of them may be found in (8,18,22).

The redundant database synchronization problem has been approached in three ways.

1. Global locking (5,6,16). In principle, a site acting on behalf of a transaction communicates with all others to inform them about the intended update and to determine whether or not they have some concurrent updates in progress. In most global locking solutions this process results in driving all sites into synchronization in order to perform the same update. This means that only one of potentially several conflicting updates may be performed at a time, and that the others must be rejected with the option of later retry.

2. Time stamping (2,24,25). The basic idea behind this approach is to associate a separate time stamp with each individually modifiable item of the database. The time stamp reflects the time of the last update performed on the related item. It serves the purpose of ordering the updates applied to a copy of the database so as to preserve consistency. The two solutions that use this approach differ significantly in their methods of ordering the updates, and an interested reader is referred to the original papers.

3. Ticketing (4,13), also called "hopping permit" in (4). An update permit is circ-

ulated among the database sites connected in a virtual ring. Only the site that has the permit, or the "tickets" issued by it, is allowed to update the database. Consistency conflicts are thus avoided by performing the updates on a one-at-a-time basis.

Naturally, each of these schemes has some inherent advantages and drawbacks. The problem with global locking is that some updates must be rejected after they have already incurred the expense of intersite synchronization. The main disadvantage of time stamps is their requirement for additional storage necessary for the time stamps themselves - in some cases this might approximate the size of the database proper. Finally, ticketing reduces the potential parallelism in the system by serializing all updates irrespective of their mutual relationships, i.e. whether they are conflicting or not.

The solution proposed in this paper is based on the concept of reservation of the database entities needed for an execution of a transaction. This technique alleviates many shortcomings of the past approaches while retaining their principal advantages. The idea of reservations is based on the observation that virtually all existing solutions rely on internal locking at an individual site level to maintain internal consistency. Since the overhead of internal locking seems to be inevitable at present, the intention is to modify the locking mechanism in order to make it suitable and relatively efficient in the distributed redundant database environment. To that end, each transaction is assigned a unique time stamp upon its activation. Time stamps are used to serialize execution of conflicting updates throughout the system and thus avoid rejection of concurrent update requests. However, time stamps are maintained only during the lifetime of an incarnation of a transaction and are not stored in the database. The ordering (serialization) affects only concurrent transactions whose data sets overlap, while the parallelism among disjoint transactions is virtually unconstrained.

The solution consists of two protocols (P and O) that are intended to suit the different needs of various types of transactions. Protocol P requires transactions to preclaim their resource requirements, whereas protocol O does not. However, protocol O cannot offer the guarantee of the protocol P that each activated transaction will be run to completion, and will not be subject to restarting.

Finally, the solution offers all required guarantees; it preserves internal and mutual consistency of all database copies and completes all submitted transactions in finite time.

The remainder of this paper is organized as follows. The next section contains working definitions of some frequently used terms, and states the underlying assumptions. The principal results of the paper are to be found in the subsequent section which describes and demonstrates the correctness of protocol P, and then explains protocol O. The remaining sections of the paper contain comparison of the algorithms, analysis of their costs, and a description of an extension of the protocol P that enables it to function in partially redundant distributed databases. A brief summary concludes the paper.

ENVIRONMENT: DEFINITIONS, MODELS, ASSUMPTIONS

In order to avoid ambiguity, several working definitions of the frequently used terms are presented in this section. They are followed by the brief exposition of a model of reservations, and the statement of assumptions that concludes the section.

A database consists of a set of named resources called <u>entities</u> (7).

A set of assertations about the individual entities and their relations is usually denoted as consistency constraint (7).

A transaction is a collection of actions on the database involving the primitives: read, compute and write. We assume that each transaction, when executed alone, preserves consistency.

Each updating transaction, T, reads and writes some database entities. We define a read set of a transaction, RS(T), as a set of entities read by T, and a write set, WS(T), as a set of entities written (modified) by T. In the remainder of this paper we will assume that an entity may be shared by several concurrent readers, but that only one writer may access it at any time. This is implicit in the description of all protocols.

Two transactions are said to be concurrent if one of them is initiated before completion of the other.

Two concurrent transactions are said to conflict if they have at least one entity in common and both transactions require it to be locked/reserved in the exclusive mode. For example, concurrent transactions T1 and T2 are conflicting if

$$RS(T1) \cap WS(T2) \neq \emptyset, \text{ or}$$

$$WS(T1) \cap WS(T2) \neq \emptyset, \text{ or}$$

$$WS(T1) \cap RS(T2) \neq \emptyset,$$

but not if the only nonempty intersection among their data sets is

$$RS(T1) \cap RS(T2) \neq \emptyset.$$

Estimated vs. actual data sets. Entities required for an execution of a transaction may be either estimated in advance (preclaimed), or actually determined during the execution itself. Estimated data sets tend to be larger because, in general, they must include all entities that could possibly be touched by the transaction. However, the advance knowledge of the resources that will be used by a transaction is useful in designing deadlock avoidance and prevention schemes.

During a particular execution, a transaction may use only a small subset of the estimated entities. In those cases it is much more efficient to use and lock only the entities that are actually used. We refer to the collection of such entities as the actual read and write set of the transaction, in order to distinguish them from the estimated ones. They depend on the state of the database encountered during a particular execution, and can be determined only at the run time. Locking of such entities is necessarily incremental, as the transaction reads some segments of the database in order to determine which ones to use (and lock) next. Incremental acquisition of locks can lead to deadlocks that must be detected and rectified. This generally entails rollback of some of the involved transactions and costly undoing of their effects on the database.

In summary, estimation of read and write sets of a transaction simplifies synchronization of the concurrent updates, but may reduce parallelism in the system. On the other hand, the use of actual read and write sets might improve concurrency at the expense of the occasional need for rollbacks. The solution proposed in this paper uses both methods in order to achieve greater flexibility.

Reservations. The concept of reservations, as used in this paper, is based on the following model. A reservation list is associated with every individually reservable entity of the database used by at least one of the active transactions. The reservation list contains an entry for each of the transactions that intends to use the related entity. An entry consists of the transaction's name, time stamp, and of the intended mode of usage: read or write. A transaction is expected to issue reservation requests for all database entities that it intends to use. The use of reservation lists for maintenance of internal consistency of individual copies of the database is described in (15). This paper focuses on the maintenance of mutual consistency of the redundant copies of the database.

A transaction must reserve all of its entities and meet some global synchronization requirements before it is allowed to actually access the reserved database entities. Reservations are used to detect resource contentions and resolve them before the execution of the affected transactions.

We now outline the underlying assumptions of the proposed solution.

Single site access. It is assumed that all entities required by a transaction may be found at a single database site. This requirement is met when the entire database is replicated at several nodes. It is also met in some distributed database systems with partial redundancy.

Time stamps. Each transaction is assigned a time stamp by the database site where it enters the system. Time stamps are assumed to be unique and nondecreasing. Generation of time stamps and their properties are discussed in (12,24,25).

Message sequencing. All messages sent from one site to another are assumed to be delivered, after some finite but variable delay, in the same order as they were sent. No assumption about the relative ordering of the messages sent from two sites to a third one is made. Although not an inherent property of all communication networks, message sequencing can be accomplished by communication protocols. It has been implemented in some existing networks, such as ARPA and DECnet. This assumption is not fundamental to the proposed solution, but it helps to eliminate numerous distracting implementation details.

System's availability. All sites and communication channels are assumed to be available during the message exchange required by the algorithm. Both synchronization protocols described in this paper require regular message exchange between the database sites in the course of update processing. In this way various node and link failures are readily detected. Several methods for handling malfunctions in the redundant distributed database systems, a few of which are applicable to our protocols, are described elsewhere (1,5,16,18,22,23,24,25).

A SOLUTION TO THE FULLY REDUNDANT CASE

In this section we present a solution to the concurrent update synchronization problem encountered in fully redundant distributed databases, and in a subset of the partially redundant database systems that satisfy the single site access assumption. Our solution consists of the protocols P and O that are described in two separate sections after a brief overview. This section is concluded by a presentation of a refinment of the algorithm.

Overview

The solution proposed in this section actually consists of the two protocols, P and O, that use different methods for synchronization of the concurrent updating transactions. Protocol P (for pessimistic) requires synchronization prior to execution of a transaction, whereas under protocol O (for optimistic) the transaction is first tentatively executed, and the protocol subsequently checks whether the tentative update can be made permanent or must be rejected due to consistency conflicts. The protocols are designed to be compatible with each other so that they may be used in the same system concurrently and thus increase its flexibility.

Protocol P works by ensuring that all conflicting updates are applied in exactly the same order to all copies of the database. Ordering is performed according to the time stamps of the transactions.

Each transaction is required to preclaim its resource requirements, i.e. its read and write sets. An execution site, Si, announces T´s update by relaying the names of the entities to be modified and their time stamp to all other database sites. Each site records all outstanding resource requirements in its reservation lists that are maintained in the time stamp order.

When all sites acknowledge its reservation broadcast, site Si is confident that its reservation lists are up-to-date as of the time stamp of T. Transaction T is executed when all older updates that affect its read and write sets are reflected in Si´s copy of the database.

Following the execution of T, Si propagates its updates to all other sites. Reservations set on behalf of T are subsequently removed.

Protocol P

When a transaction T is submitted for execution to the database controller residing at a site Si, the following set of rules constitutes protocol P.

1. (Time stamping) Si assigns a unique time stamp, TS(T), derived from Si´s clock and unique identifier, to the transaction T.

2. (Internal reservation) Si reserves entities from T´s read set, RS(T), and write set, WS(T), internally. If any of those entities is already reserved, T´s request is entered in the associated reservation list according to its time stamp: after all older reservation requests (whose time stamps are smaller than TS(T)), and in front of the younger ones.

3. (Global Reservation) Si broadcasts a reservation message on behalf of T. The reservation message has the following format:
   Reserve; sender´s ID: Si,
   time stamp: TS(T),
   identity of the entities to be reserved: WS(T).
   All reservation broadcasts sent by a site must be ordered according to the time stamps of the transactions themselves, i.e. they must contain increasing, although not necessarily consequtive time stamps.

4. (Acknowledgments) Each site, upon receipt of the reservation broadcast, reserves entities contained in WS(T) in its respective copy of the database according to rule 2. When this process is completed, an acknowledgment is returned to the site Si.
   Acknowledgment; responder´s ID,
   transaction: T.

5. (Execution) Transaction T is executed, using Si´s copy of the database, when the following conditions are met.
   a. An acknowledgment of the reservation broadcast is received from each database site, and
   b. T´s reservations become the oldest in Si´s reservation lists associated with the entities contained in RS(T) and WS(T).

6. (Update broadcast) Si applies updates of T (WS(T)) to its copy of the database, removes internal reservations made on behalf of T, and broadcasts an update message to all other sites.
   Update; values of the entities to be updated: WS(T).

7. (Completion) Upon receipt of the update message, each site applies the specified updates to its copy of the entities contained in WS(T), as soon as the reservations set on behalf of T become the oldest in the related reservation lists. Each such reservation is subsequently removed.

Note that the format of messages, as shown, includes only the information relevant for the description of the algorithm. Implementation related details, such as time stamps of messages, sender´s and receiver´s identity, sequencing, etc., are omitted for clarity.

In order to illustrate the functioning and some properties of the protocol P, we present an example of its operation in Figure 1.

Three database sites: Si, Sj, and Sk, together with their interconnections, comprise the hypothetical system under observation. For simplicity, we assume that intersite communication channels are bidirectional and incur fixed delays: 1M between Sj and Sk, and 2M on all other connections, where M is a unit of time.

We assume that at time M1 sites Si and Sk initiate transactions T1 and T2, respectively, and that T1 is older, that is TS(T1) $<$ TS(T2). Transactions are assumed to use the following database entities:

read sets:	T1: (x,y)	T2: (x)
write sets:	(y)	(y).

Transactions T1 and T2 are conflicting, because

$$RS(T1) \cap WS(T2) \neq \emptyset, \text{ and } WS(T1) \cap WS(T2) \neq \emptyset.$$

In order to shorten the example, it is assumed that each site receives a message, processes it, and sends an optional response in a time negligible in comparison to intersite message communication delays (M). In Figure 1 reservation lists for all database entities of interest are shown, together with the messages sent and received by each individual site.

At time M1, Si and Sk reserve read and write sets of their transactions internally (rule 1, protocol P). Reservations are denoted by names of their parent transactions(T1 and T2).

Due to the distributed nature of the system, in this phase of the protocol P, a site does not know whether some older reservations of the related entities have been put in effect elsewhere in the system. If so, such reservations should be honored prior to execution of the transaction under consideration. To find this out, Si and Sk observe rule 2 and broadcast reservation messages, R(T1) and R(T2), for the entities contained in their transactions´ write sets. Reservation broadcasts also serve the purpose of informing other sites about the intended updates that are in progress. For example, at time M2, site Sj is informed about Sk´s intention to update entity y, and it records reservation of y on behalf of T2 (T2 at Sj, Figure 1, time M2). Sj then sends an acknowledgment, A(T2), to Sk. Note that entity x is not reserved by Sj because it is only read by T2, and therefore was not included in R(T2) broadcast.

At time M3, Si receives and processes R(T2), and sites Sj and Sk receive and acknowledge the reservation broadcast R(T1). Since T1 is older and the two transactions are conflicting, reservations set on behalf of T1 are queued ahead of those requested by T2. To that end, multiple entry reservation lists at Sj and Sk are reordered according to the time stamps of the respective entries. This illustrates the essential difference between the reservations and the simple locks. Reservations are known to be passive until globally confirmed (not used to access the related entities) and in that state they may be moved around without adverse effects.

At the moment M5, Si receives acknowledgments of its reservation broadcast, R(T1), from both Sj and Sk. Site Si executes T1 because all conditions of rule 5 are met (acknowledgments received, and reservations oldest). Si subsequently broadcasts an update message, U(T1), that contains the updated value of the entity y, and removes its internal reservations set on behalf of T1. This is the state shown in Figure 1 at M5. Note that at this time Sk also receives the last acknowledgment of its broadcast R(T2), but cannot execute T2 because its reservations are not the oldest at Sk.

Time	Si				Sj				Sk			
	x	y	Sent	Rcvd	x	y	Sent	Rcvd	x	y	Sent	Rcvd
M1	T1	T1	R(T1)						T2	T2	R(T2)	
M2	T1	T1				T2	A(T2)	R(T2)	T2	T2		
M3	T1	T1 T2	A(T2)	R(T2)		T1 T2	A(T1)	R(T1)	T2	T1 T2	A(T1)	R(T1) A(T2)
M4	T1	T1 T2				T1 T2			T2	T1 T2		
M5		T2	U(T1)	A(T1) A(T1)		T1 T2			T2	T1 T2		A(T2)
M6		T2				T1 T2			T2	T1 T2		
M7		T2				T2		U(T1)			U(T2)	U(T1)
M8		T2						U(T2)				
M9				U(T2)								

Figure 1. An example of protocol P

At M7 both Sj and Sk receive U(T1), apply the update and remove the related reservations. Sk can now complete T2, since all conditions of the rule 5 are met by T2. Subsequently Sk broadcasts U(T2). By M9 this message is received and processed by all other sites, as shown in Figure 1.

This example illustrates an essential feature of the protocol P which is due to the reservation scheme that it uses. Namely, the database sites are not driven into synchronization in order to execute an update, rather they synchronize only the order of application of updates originated by conflicting transactions. The obvious advantage is that there is no need to reject concurrent updates involved in consistency conflicts. In fact, each site is allowed to accept all the transaction load it can handle, because the existence of some transactions in progress does not prevent it from initiating the new ones, irrespective of whether they overlap or not. It should also be noted that protocol P does not require permanent storage of time stamps; a time stamp ceases to exist with the completion of the transaction that it was associated with. These two characteristics, together with the relatively low delay and communication overhead (only write sets of updating transactions are globally communicated and reserved) account for the efficiency of protocol P.

The remainder of this subsection consists of the proofs of corectness of the protocol P. Intuitively, the algorithm works because all conflicting updates are applied in the same order to all copies of the database. Time stamp ordering of transactions assures mutual consistency of all copies of the database, as well as the absence of deadlocks. Completion in finite time is a result of the fact that a transaction may wait only for the transactions that are older than it. A more formal proof is given below.

Claim 1: Protocol P preserves internal consistency of each individual copy of the database.

Proof: Reservations, as used by protocol P ensure exclusivity of access by allowing at most one of the transactions conflicting over an entity to be in the execution phase (rule 5b). Transactions that use reservations are well formed, i.e. they reserve, use, and release resources in separate, non overlapping steps (rules 2 and 6). These two conditions were shown to be sufficient for maintenance of consistency of multiaccess databases (7).

In order to prove that protocol P preserves mutual consistency among the redundant copies of the database, we need the following lemmas.

Lemma 1: Each update performed by a transaction T under protocol P is based on the consistent state of the database, as of the time stamp of T.

Proof: The proof consists of showing that T cannot be executed until all older updates on all entities contained in RS(T) and WS(T) are applied to the database copy used by T. We do this by contradiction.

Assume that it is possible that an update U with the time stamp older than TS(T) is not applied to the copy of the database used by T before execution of T. Internal reservation scheme of the protocol P (rules 2 and 5) ensures that U cannot exist at T´s initiating site. Therefore, U would have to be initiated elsewher in the system. Update U also has to be concurrent with T, since it is assumed not to be completed. From the rule 4 of protocol P it follows that update U must be confirmed by every site, including T´s, in order to be applied to any copy of the database. But in order to be confirmed, U´s reservations must be recorded by T´s site (rule 4). Since TS(U) < TS(T), i.e. U is older, reservations set by T´s site on behalf of U must be queued ahead of those made by T for all entities common to U and T (rule 2). T cannot execute and apply its updates before U´s reservations are used, that is, updates applied to the database copy held at T´s site (rules 5 and 7). Hence, by contradiction, all updates on the entities used by T that are older than TS(T) must be applied to the database copy read by T prior to execution of T.

Lemma 1 augments Claim 1 by stating that an updating transaction observes not just a consistent state of a database copy, but the consistent state of the database as of TS(T). The scope of Lemma 1 is the whole system, not the individual database sites that are the sole concern of Claim 1. Lemma 2, which follows, concernes itself with an arbitrary entity of the database, not just the ones belonging to updating transactions.

Lemma 2: All updates of an entity performed under protocol P are applied in the same order (the time stamp order) to all copies of the database.

Proof: Given Lemma 1, we need only prove that updates of an entity E stored at an arbitrary site S, that does not belong to any pending updating transaction initiated by S, are also performed in the order of their time stamps. We do this by contradiction.

The statement of Lemma 2 is obviously true in the trivial cases of no updates, or when a single update intention on E is active in the system, because no ordering is required under such circumstances.

Suppose that two concurrent transactions, T1 and T2, that intend to update entity E are in progress at two different database sites. Assume that S is not one of those sites and that T1 is older than T2. We want to show that protocol P guarantees that a copy of the entity E residing at the site S will be updated in the T1-T2 order. Since T1 and T2 are overlapping at least over the entity E, T2 cannot apply its update of E to any copy of the database until it sees T1's update of E (Lemma 1). In order for T1 to be executed, it must be confirmed by all sites, including S. Therefore, S must have at least a record of T1's reservations by the time it receives an update message from T2. Rule 7 of protocol P ensures that T2's update of E will not be applied by S until T1's reservation, which is older, is removed, i.e. T1's update is applied. Therefore, by contradiction, it follows that updates of an entity under protocol P are applied in the order of their time stamps to all copies of the database.

Lemma 2 shows why the variability of internode communication delays does not affect correctness of the protocol P.

Claim 2: Protocol P preserves mutual consistency of all redundant copies of the database.

Proof: The proof consists of showing that all copies would become identical, should the updates cease.

From lemmas 1 and 2 it follows that all updates of an arbitrary entity E are executed in the order of their time stamps. If E is ever updated, when the update activity ceases it will have the value of its update with the most recent (youngest) time stamp in all copies of the database. Given uniqueness of the time stamps, all copies converge to the same state and this proves Claim 2.

Claim 3: Assuming a finite number of transactions in progress at any time, and the ability of the system to handle the load presented to it, protocol P guarantees completion in finite time to each transaction run under it.

Proof: The proof is by induction on the number of active transactions. Claim 3 holds if a single transaction is active in the system (n=1), because it does not have to wait for completion of any other transaction. Assume that Claim 3 holds when n transactions are active in the system. We then have to prove that the (n+1)-st transaction completes in finite time. By induction hypothesis, n older transactions that the (n+1)-st may have to wait for, will be completed in finite time. The (n+1)-st transaction then becomes the oldest in the system, does not have to wait since it is not affected by younger transactions, and thus completes in finite time itself.

Protocol 0

Protocol 0 aims at improving efficiency for certain transactions by using their actual read and write sets. After time stamping, each transaction is executed using the copy of the database at the initiating site, Si. All updates are tentatively recorder by the site Si. Execution is required in order to determine the actual data sets of a transaction. Si then engages in communication with other sites in order to determine whether an older transaction executed elsewhere in the system obsoletes the work of T. This happens when read set of T, and/or write set of T were modified by an older transaction, but not updates in the copy of the database used by T. Based on the information gathered from other sites, Si decides whether to accept or reject the tentative updates of T. Si then announces its decision to the rest of the system.

When a transaction is submitted to a database site Si, the following set of rules constitutes protocol 0.

1. (Time stamping) Si assigns a unique time stamp to T, TS(T).

2. (Execution) Si begins execution of T and locks each entity required by T. If an

entity requested by T is not available, T is blocked and its request is entered in the associated lock/reservation list according to TS(T). If a younger transaction initiated by Si owns the entity, the ownership is revoked and the said transaction is restarted. Restarting of a transaction consists of discarding of its tentative updates and releasing of its locks.
When all internal locks are granted to T, execution of T is completed and its updates are tentatively recorded (not in the database proper) by Si.

3. (Tentative update) Si broadcasts a tentative update message on behalf of T. This message contains the values of the entities modified by T and its time stamp, TS(T). All update broadcasts sent by a site must follow the time stamp ordering of the related transactions.

4. (Acknowledgments and rejections) Each recepient of the tentative update broadcast records reservations for the entities contained in WS(T) in its lock/reservation lists according to the time stamp of T. If a younger internal transaction owns some of the specified entities, it is restarted. If an update broadcast has already been sent on behalf of the restarted transaction, a reject message is sent to all other sites. This message will cause the reservations and the tentative updates of the restarted transaction to be discarded by all other sites as well. Following this process, each site acknowledges the receipt of broadcast to Si.

5. (Update broadcast) If T is still active when all acknowledgments are received, Si makes the updates of T permanent. That is, Si applies to its copy of the database the values contained in WS(T) and broadcasts a make permanent message.

6. (Completion) Each recepient of the make permanent broadcast makes the updates contained in WS(T) permanent in its copy of the database, as soon as the related reservations become the oldest in its lock/reservation lists. Such reservations are subsequently removed.

Under protocol O, the entities required by a transaction are locked at its initating site and reserved at all others. The difference is that locks do not have to be globally confirmed and, when granted, the related entities may be accessed and tentatively modified by the parent transaction. In this way the actual, not estimated, read and write sets of the transactions running under protocol O are determined. For reasons of compatibility with the protocol P, all transactions initiated at a database site are announced in the order of their time stamps. This is the motivation for the locking rule 2, that calls for preemption of younger transactions by the older ones. As a side effect, deadlocks among blocked transactions are not possible. Note that time stamp ordering of update broadcasts (rule 3) is maintained for all transactions initiated by a database site. In addition to compatibility with the protocol P, this ensures that all conflicts among the internal concurrent transactions will be detected and taken care of internally.

Intersite communication rules (3,4,5,6) ensure that T's updates can be made permanent only when it becomes certain that they cannot become obsoleted by an older transaction initiated elsewhere in the system. Tentative updates of a transaction are discarded when found obsolete, before being seen by any other transaction.

Correctness of the protocol O can be established by arguments similar to those used for protocol P, but they are not presented here for the sake of brevity. Informally, internal consistency is preserved by local locking, and mutual consistency by rejections of obsolete updates.

It should be noted, however, that protocol O cannot guarantee that transactions run under it will be completed in finite time. The reason is that some transactions may be restarted. In general, a restarted transaction cannot be allowed to retain its original time stamp, because that could violate the time stamp ordering of broadcasts that is required by protocol P. The number of restarts of a transaction is not bounded, consequently completion of such transactions in finite time is uncertain. A simple remedy for this problem is to keep track of the number of restarts for each unsuccessful transaction. When that number exceeds a predefined limit, the affected transaction may be run under protocol P and thus completed in finite time.

As described, both protocols are concerned only with updating transactions. Read only transactions may be executed in one of the following ways.

1. Entities required by a read only transaction are locked internally (in shareable mode) at the initiating site, and the local database copy is read when all locks are granted.

In this way the transaction is guaranteed to see a consistent state of the database, but not necessarily as of its time stamp.

2. Read only transaction is regarded as a null update transaction (empty write set) and run under protocol P or 0, as appropriate.

A read only transaction executed in this way is guaranteed to observe the consistent state of the database as of its time stamp, but at the expense of the delay and overhead of intersite communication.

A Refinement

In this section we describe some modifications that may improve performance of both algorithms when operating in moderately to heavily loaded systems. Performance is increased by reducing delay and the number of internode messages for some updates. In order to motivate this improvement, let us recapitulate the purpose of reservation broadcasts and their acknowledgments in the protocol P.

A reservation broadcast, R(T), serves twofold purpose: (1) it informs its recepients about the intended update, and (2) it prompts them to send an acknowledgment to the broadcasting site. Therefore, upon receipt of all acknowledgments, the broadcaster is confident that its intended update is known to and recorded by all other sites, and that it has received all reservation messages sent on behalf of transactions older than T. The latter is due to the assumed sequencing of internode messages and the time stamp ordering of reservation broadcasts.

When the transaction processing load of the system increases, a lot of messages are exchanged among the nodes of the system. Consequently, a site Si waiting for acknowledgments of its reservation broadcast R(T), may receive several foreign reservation broadcasts that are younger than T. Note that these broadcasts partially fulfill the purpose of acknowledgments, by assuring Si that it cannot be surprised by a message older than the time stamp of its pending transaction T. Hence, transaction T may be safely executed by its initiating site as soon as it receives a message younger than T from every other site. Furthermore, all sites that have sent a younger reservation broadcast prior to receipt of R(T) need not acknowledge it at all.

However, when an update is sent out before the complete acknowledgment of the related reservation broadcast, sequencing anomalies may occur in the form of improper ordering of external and conflicting updates by some nodes. This situation may be prevented with the following modification of the basic algorithm.

Each site maintains a list of time stamps of the most recent reservation broadcast received from every other site. Whenever an update broadcast is sent on behalf of incompletely acknowledged transaction, a current copy of this list is included. Each recepient of such update message postpones the actual updating until receipt of all messages referenced in the list. In normal operation this delaying will rarely be necessary.

This scheme works because a site does not apply an update to its copy of the database until it has at least a record of all older updates. Rule 7 of the protocol P ensures that all older conflicting updates are processed as well.

The extent to which this strategy improves performance of the presented algorithms depends on the probability of receiving younger messages before the acknowledgments from other nodes. In extreme cases, some reservation broadcasts may be eliminated alltogether and the updates may be sent without explicite synchronization. More often, however, the number of acknowledgments and the transaction processing delay will be reduced. The benefits of this modification may be increased and extended to the lightly loaded systems, by inclusion of the following rules in the implementation of the algorithms.

r1. When a node is heavily loaded, or is in the process of preparing a reservation broadcast, it may replace acknowledgments of the foreign reservation messages by its own younger reservation broadcasts. Of course, it is advisable to set a limit on how long can an acknowledgment be delayed in anticipation of a younger reservation broadacst.

r2. A lightly loaded node occasionally broadcasts a "no load, here is my current time stamp" message, which can be used in lieu of acknowledgments by other busy nodes.

Application of these ideas to the protocol O is fairly straightforward.

COSTS OF THE PROTOCOLS P AND O

The costs incurred by these protocols may be attributed to their computational and storage requirements, volume of traffic, and the delay in processing transactions. Contribution of the former two factors is both minor and hard to quantify, and in this section we focus on the volume of traffic and the delay.

For the protocol P operating in the system with n redundant copies of the database, the maximum number of messages per update is:

Point to point:		Broadcast:
n - 1	reservation broadcast	1
n - 1	acknowledgments	n - 1
n - 1	update broadcast	1
3n - 3	messages/transaction	n + 1

With the refinement described in the previous section, some acknowledgments and even the reservation broadcast itself may be unnecessary for certain transactions. Thus, the actual number of messages per update varies, depending on the load of the system, between

$$n - 1, \text{ and } 3n - 3 \qquad (1, \text{ and } n + 1 \text{ with broadcast}).$$

The message count for the protocol O depends on the statistics of rejections of transactions. In the worst case, the number is:

$$(r + 1)(3n - 3) \qquad ((r + 1)(n + 1) \text{ with broadcast})$$

where r is the maximum number of rejections per accepted transaction. In the best case (no rejections), a refined version of the protocol O requires the same number of messages as the equivalent version of the protocol P.

Protocol O requires approximately the same number of messages as protocol P only when the expected number of conflicts is very small, i. e. $r \ll 1$.

From the detailing of messages it follows that the delay per accepted transaction is bounded by

1Mmax, and 3Mmax

where Mmax is a maximum end-to-end message propagation delay. This delay is measured from the inception of transaction until its updates are processed by all database sites. However, each database site "sees" a transaction and holds its reservations during at most 2Mmax. This is due to the fact that the initiating site completes a transaction by sending the final update broadcast, and does not have to wait for it to be received by the adressees. Likewise, all other sites become aware of the transaction one message delay later than the initiating site.

Note that, in absence of synchronization, at least n - 1 messages (1 if broadcast is available) and a delay of 1Mmax are required to propagate an update to all copies of the database. Thus, these numbers should be subtracted from the ones presented earlier, in order to obtain a measure of the overhead incurred by the proposed protocols.

The final remark of this section is that the number of messages is a rather crude measure of the volume of traffic that a protocol imposes on a system. The length of individual messages varies widely for published algorithms, and the one presented here is among the most efficient in that respect. The reason is that only write sets of updating transactions are communicated globally.

COMPARISON OF PROTOCOLS P AND O

Protocol P guarantees acceptance and completion in finite time to all transactions run under it. As shown in the previous section, it requires a comparable number of intersite messages and incurs the same communication delay as protocol O for accepted transactions. However, the degree of parallelism may be lower and the volume of traffic (length of individual messages) higher for protocol P as compared to protocol O. The main reason for this difference is that protocol P operates with estimated read and write sets of its transactions, while protocol O uses the actual read and write sets. The importance of this difference is clearly application dependent.

However, protocol O does not guarantee acceptance to its transactions and thus has some additional overhead for those that are rejected. It also imposes higher storage requirement on the system, because all sites are supposed to keep the tentative updates until their fate is resolved. Still, protocol O appears to have greater potential for efficiency in the systems that have low probability of conflicts among the transactions originated by different sites.

In summary, protocol P should be used for transactions that are long and/or expensive to run, in order to avoid costly restarts. Protocol O, on the other hand, should be used for transactions that are known to have low probability of conflicts, or for which preclaiming of resources is inefficient.

PARTIALLY REDUNDANT CASE - A SKETCH

Protocols P and O were presented assuming virtually completely redundant database enviromment. We now relax this assumption and describe a modified version of the protocol P that operates in partially redundant databases.

Let us assume that a transaction, T, may be submitted for execution to any database site, Si, capable of determining identities of the database sites that maintain entities contained in the read and write sets of T. If some of those entities are stored redundantly, site Si is free to choose a "suitable" copy to be used by T. We will refer to the database sites that maintain entities required by the transaction T as the data sites of T, and to their subset that actually executes T, as a set of the chosen data sites. Following is a brief description of the modified protocol P.

Site Si assigns a time stamp to T, TS(T). Site Si then announces transaction T to the rest of the system via a reservation broadcast. This broadcast contains the time stamp of T and a list of entities contained in its read and write sets. Its purpose is twofold: (1) to cause system-wide reservation of the data sets of T, and (2) to prompt other sites to bring the data sites of T up-to-date as of the time stamp of T.

Updating of a site is accomplished by sending it a message younger than the time stamp of T. This message may be a result of execution of a younger transaction, or, in case of passivity, an acknowledgment. For synchronization purposes, each site must keep track of the most recent time stamp received from every other site.

Upon receiving a message younger than the TS(T) from all other sites, chosen data sites are aware of all updating activity initiated prior to the TS(T). When all older updates that are conflicting with T are processed, the chosen data sites execute transaction T in cooperation.

Following the completion of T, its updates are propagated to all redundant copies of the affected entities. Time stamp ordering of the conflicting updates is observed by all database sites. Reservations set on behalf of T are subsequently removed.

This strategy works because conflicting updates are applied in the same order to all redundant copies of the database. Consistency of the database is preserved because each transaction sees the values of its entities as of its time stamp in both redundant and nonredundant portions of the database. Deadlocks, infinite waiting, and critical blocking are eliminated due to the time stamp ordering of conflicting transactions.

The maximum number of internode messages required by the algorithm, exclusive of the transaction processing itself, is

Point to point:		Broadcast:
n - 1	reservation broadcast	1
d(n - 1)	acknowledgments	n - 1
(d + 1)(n - 1)	total messages	n

where d is the number of data sites. If no acknowledgments are necessary, i.e. the required messages are sent in the course of execution of younger transactions, the respective numbers are reduced to

n - 1, and 1.

The synchronization delay is 2Mmax, where Mmax is a maximum end-to-end message propafation delay.

In the systems where the number of data sites per transaction, d, is large, the number of messages may be reduced at the expense of increased delay by returning the acknowledgments to the initiating site, which in turn updates the data sites.

SUMMARY

We have presented a new solution to the concurrent update synchronization problem in redundant distributed databases that guarantees internal and mutual consistency of all database copies, and completion of transactions in finite time. It combines many advantages of the known solutions to this problem in a relatively efficient manner. The concept of reservations introduced herein does not incur storage overhead beyond the lock/reservation lists that are required for maintenance of internal consistency even in single site database systems, and are in some form present in virtually all solutions published to date. Storage of time stamps is not required, the number and length of internode messages are relatively small, and the basic protocol (P) does not require rejections of transaction run under it. Total synchronization of the database controllers is not required, instead all sites are allowed to process their workloads at their own speeds, provided that conflicting updates are ordered according to their time stamps. Consequently, the incurred synchronization delay affects primarily the response time of individual transactions, and much less the system's throughput. Parallelism among the concurrent transactions that are disjoint is virtually unconstrained.

An alternative protocol (O), that has greater potential for efficiency but cannot guarantee immediate acceptance to all transactions is also presented. The two protocols are designed for compatibility in order to enable a system to run them in parallel and thus increase its flexibility.

A modified version of the protocol P that operates in partially redundant databases is also presented. It requires relatively small number of messages, and incurs small synchronization delay, while offering all guarantees of the basic protocol P.

ACKNOWLEDGMENTS

The author is indebted to Harold S. Stone for his helpful criticisms and continuous encouragement and support during the research reported here. Numerous discussions with Richard Peebles have shaped many of the ideas to their present form. Thanks are also due to Digital Equipment Corporation for providing exposure to a stimulating working enviroment.

REFERENCES

(1) Badal, Z., Popek, G., A proposal for distributed concurrency control for partially redundant distributed data base systems, Third Berkeley Workshop on Distributed Data Management and Computer Networks, Berkeley, 1978, 273-285.

(2) Bernstein, P., et al., The concurrency control mechanism of SDD-1: a system for distributed databases (The fully redundant case), IEEE TSE, SE-4, 3, May 1978, 154-168.

(3) Chamberlin, D., et al., A dedlock-free scheme for resource locking in a database enviroment, IFIP Congress, Stockholm, 1974, 320-323.

(4) Chin-Hwa Lee, et al., Distributed control schemes for multiple-copied file accsess in a network environment, IEEE COMPSAC, Chicago, 1977, 722-728.

(5) Ellis, C., A robust algorithm for updating duplicate databases, Second Berkeley Workshop, Berkeley, 1977, 146-158.

(6) Ellis, C., Consistency and corectness of duplicate database systems, Sixth ACM Symposium on Operating System Principles, Purdue, 1977, 67-84.

(7) Eswaran, K., et al., The notions of consistency and predicate locks in a database system, CACM, 19, 11, Nov. 1976, 624-633.

(8) Garcia-Molina, H., Performance comparison of two update algorithms for distributed databases, Third Berkeley Workshop, Berkeley, 1978, 108-119.

(9) Gray, J., et al. Granularity of locks and degrees of consistency in a shared database, IFIP Working Conference on Modeling in DBMS, Amsterdam, 1976, 365-394.

(10) Enslow, P., What is a "distributed" data processing system, Computer, 11, 1, Jan. 1978, 13-24.

(11) Lampson, B., Sturgis, H., Crash recovery in a distributed data storage system, unpublished paper, Xerox Research Center, Palo Alto, 1976.

(12) Lamport, L., Time, clocks, and the ordering of events in a distributed system, CACM, 21, 7, July 1978, 558-565.

(13) Le Lann, G., Algorithms for distributed data-sharing which use tickets, Third Berkeley Workshop, Berkeley, 1978, 259-272.
(14) Metcalfe, R., Boggs, D., Ethernet: distributed packet switching for local computer networks, CACM, 19, 7, July 1976, 395-404.
(15) Milenković, M., Update synchronization in multiaccess database systems, Ph.D. Thesis, ECE Dept., Univ. of Massachusetts, Amherst, May 1979.
(16) Mullary, A., The distributed control of multiple copies of data, IBM TR, RC 5782, Yorktown Heights, 1975.
(17) Munz, R., Krenz, G., Concurrency in database systems - a simulation study, ACM SIGMOD, 1977
(18) Peebles, R., Concurrent access control in a distributed transaction processing system, Brown Univ. Workshop on Distributed Processing, Providence, 1977.
(19) Peebles, R., Manning, E., System architecture for distributed data management, Computer, 11, 1, Jan. 1978, 40-46.
(20) Ries, D., Stonebreaker, M., Effects of locking granularity in a database management system, ACM TODS, 2, 3, Sep. 1977, 233-246.
(21) Rosenkranz, D., et al., System level concurrency control for distributed database systems, ACM TODS, 3, 2, June 1978, 178-198.
(22) Rothnie, J., Goodman, N., A survey of research and development in distributed database management, Second Conference on Very Large Databases, Tokyo, 1977, 48-62.
(23) Stonebraker, M., Concurrency control and consistency of multiple copies of data in distributed Ingres, Third Berkeley Workshop, Berkeley, 1978, 253-258.
(24) Thomas, R., A majority consensus approach to concurrency control for multiple copy databases, BBN TR 3733, Cambridge, Mass., 1976.
(25) Thomas, R., A solution to the concurrency control problem for multiple copy databases, COMPCON Spring 1978, San Francisco, 56-62.

DISTRIBUTED DATA BASES
C. Delobel and W. Litwin (eds.)
North-Holland Publishing Company

POLYPHEME : AN EXPERIENCE IN DISTRIBUTED DATABASE SYSTEM DESIGN AND IMPLEMENTATION+

M. ADIBA*, J.M. ANDRADE*, P. DECITRE**, F. FERNANDEZ*, NGUYEN GIA TOAN*

* IMAG, B.P. 53X, 38041 GRENOBLE Cedex (France)
** Centre Scientifique CII-HB, B.P. 53X, 38041 GRENOBLE Cedex (France)

Developed at the Grenoble University (France) in collaboration with the CII-HB Scientific Center, the POLYPHEME project addresses the problems of designing and implementing a Distributed Database Management System (hereforth refered to a D-DBMS) on a general computer network.

This paper describes a D-DBMS prototype which has been implemented on the CYCLADES network. The main characteristics of this prototype are : Data Distribution, Request Decomposition, Distributed Executive, D-DBMS Architecture.

1. INTRODUCTION TO POLYPHEME

At the beginning of the POLYPHEME project, one of the basic hypothesis was to make existing and heterogeneous databases cooperate over a general computer network [ADE77].

This bottom-up approach to distributed databases led to some theoretical work on data modelling in heterogeneous environment and relational database distribution [ADI78, ADI78a].

Furthermore, specific problems of distributed database manipulation were studied, among which : decomposition and optimization of user's requests [ADC78, CAL78, NGU78, NGU79], distributed executive design and implementation [ADE77, EUZ79], D-DBMS architecture design [ACE78].

Finally an implementation of a D-DBMS prototype has been done in the context of the French CYCLADES network, using the URANUS relational system [NGU77].

The realization of a completely heterogeneous D-DBMS with all necessary features for real exploitation was out the scope of POLYPHEME but besides its limitations the prototype which has been implemented illustrates interesting aspects in the distributed database field : distribution of relational data, request decomposition, algorithms transportation and distributed execution mechanisms.

For these reasons this prototype can be considered as a synthesis of all the work which has been done in POLYPHEME.

In this paper, we describe the main features of the POLYPHEME D-DBMS, starting in section 2 with the description of data distribution. In section 3, we consider the manipulation of the distributed database given an algebraic relational language. In addition, two different decomposition algorithms, which have been implemented, are presented. The first one is used in the prototype.

+This work was partially supported by the IRIA-SIRIUS project under contracts N° 77-076 and N° 78-008.

In section 4, we describe in more details the architecture of the D-DBMS which is conceptually considered as a network of (abstract) relational machines implemented at two different levels : namely, the local level for managing a given set of relations stored on one computer and the global level for dealing with distributed relations.

Finally we give some concluding remarks and indicate what areas are still being studied as the continuation of POLYPHEME.

2. DISTRIBUTED RELATIONAL DATABASE

2.1. Local and Global relations

A Distributed Relational Database (DRD) consists of a collection of relations each of them being stored at an unique site or spread over several ones in a computer network.

Each distributed relation may be fragmented either in an horizontal or a vertical manner, according to some distribution criteria.

We assume that each fragment is considered in itself as a relation. All the fragments constitute for the DRD the basic relations, while the DRD user is concerned only by derived relations or views [AST76].

We shall refer to a relation as LOCAL if it is stored entirely at one site (Local Relations : LR) and GLOBAL if fragments of it are stored in different sites (Global Relations : GR). It should be noted that these definitions are independent of the design process for building the DRD, i.e. a bottom-up approach starting with local relations and defining global ones [ADI78], or a top-down approach first defining the GR and then spliting them into fragments [ROG77].

Both approaches lead to a DRD where only local relations are physically stored on each computer.

2.2. Specification of the distribution criteria

Several distribution criteria have been studied with respect to the problem of propagating manipulation operators - get, delete, insert, update tuples - from GRs to the corresponding LRs.

We summarize these criteria as follows :

a) HORIZONTAL PARTITION is achieved by defining a GR, for example G, as the union of several LRs, L1, L2, ..., Lp. Each Li, in turn can be considered as a restriction of G.
For example, let us consider three relations SUP1, SUP2, SUP3 respectively stored at three different sites S1, S2, S3, and describing some suppliers with their number (SNO), their name (SNAME), and their town (TOWN).

The global relation SUPPLIER can be defined as the UNION of the following three relations :

SUP1 : TOWN = 'Paris'
SUP2 : TOWN = 'New-York'
SUP3 : TOWN = 'London'

where ':' denotes the restriction operator.

To obtain the GR SUPPLIER, it is necessary to obtain from S1, S2 and S3 the three local relations, to merge them, and to give the result to the user.

The restriction denotes the partitioning of SUPPLIER relation and this information can be used in order to switch some global update operation to the appropriate local databases. For instance when the user wants to insert the new supplier : <S55, 'SMITH', 'New-York'>, this insertion takes place at S2. However to insure that the distributed database is consistent, it is necessary to check if the new key value (here S55) does not exist in any of the local relations [ADA79].

When the value of the attribute used in the distribution criteria is updated, it is necessary for the system to insure the migration of the corresponding tuples.

For instance, changing the town value of <S55, 'SMITH', 'New-York'> from 'New-York' to 'London' implies movement of the tuple from S2 to S3.
When the restriction does not define disjunctive sets of tuples, it may introduce some redundancy in the distributed database.
Consider, for instance, a GR named EMPLOYEE whose attributes are ENO, ENAME, SALARY, with the corresponding LRs :

E1 on S1 with SALARY ≤ 2000
E2 on S2 with 1500 ≤ SALARY ≤ 2500
E3 on S3 with SALARY > 2000.

However these cases can be handled automatically because for each global operation, the D-DBMS is able to determine what are the local operations to be performed [ADI78].

b) VERTICAL PARTITION is achieved by defining a GR named G as the (generalized) join of several LRs : L1,L2,...,Lq. We consider that this partitioning is possible if, and only if, all the Li have the same key domain.

Consider, for instance, two LRs defined as follows : PART1 on site S1, describing some parts with the part-number (PNO) - which is the key attribute -, part-name (PNAME) and part-color (COLOR) :

PART1 (PNO, PNAME, COLOR) on S1

and PART2 on site S2 describing the price (PRICE) of each part :

PART2 (PNO, PRICE) on S2.

Then the global relation PART can be defined as :

PART = PART1 * PART2

where '*' denotes the join operator (here on PNO).

For the sake of generality we have in fact to consider not only the usual intersection-join (or natural join) but also the union-join (or outer-join) which may introduce some undefined values. This union-join operator is particularly useful in a bottom-up approach, where existing parts in S1 may not exist in S2 or vice-versa.

In order to get the entire GR it is necessary to perform the join over the network, choosing to move from one site to another the smallest relations. When it is necessary to insert a tuple, in PART, this new tuple is split into several pieces (here two) each of them being inserted into the correct LR. When the D-DBMS does this, it must insure that each local insertion takes place correctly before assuming that the global operation is completed.

The deletion of a given tuple is performed in a similar manner.

To support the distribution criteria just described, it is necessary to implement a complete and distributed view mechanism. This has not been done in the POLYPHEME prototype. However the problems dealing with the semantic of update operations in a distributed environment are still being investigated as a continuation of POLYPHEME and will be discussed in other publications [ADA79].

In the POLYPHEME D-DBMS prototype, each relation is defined as a local relation indicating the site where it is stored :

```
DEFINE RELATION SUP1 ON SITE S1
       SNO CHAR(3)
       SNAME CHAR(15)
       TOWN CHAR(20).
```

At the global level of the DRD, each LR is a GR. This means that once the distributed database is created the end-user is no longer concerned with data distribution.

3. DISTRIBUTED DATABASE MANIPULATION

We describe in this section the query execution facility as implemented in the POLYPHEME prototype. Concerning the user-level interface, we give only a general overview of the data definition and manipulation facilities (§ 3.1). We then focuse on the query decomposition feature and the distributed execution of subrequests (§ 3.2). At last, undergoing studies and future directions of research are sketched, as planned for the development of our work (§ 3.3).

3.1. Data manipulation interface

Interactive query execution and parametrized transaction handling facilities are supported by the global POLYPHEME relational machines [ADI78]. On-line data definition, retrieval and modification are allowed, as part of the relational interface.

Attribute-based primary-key relation definitions are supported with distribution specification at the sole relation-level. No fragmentation definition is allowed up to now, nor horizontal partitioning definition. In fact, it can be shown that view and global relation definition and implementation are similar for our purpose to preanalyzed transaction handling.

Relational algebra operators are available at the user-level [CODD72], and queries are termed by combination of operands - e.g. basic relations - and operators (JOIN,SELECT,PROJECT,...) in a non-procedural way. Interpretation is made on a binary tree structure [CHA75], pipe-lining tuple results during local sub-trees evaluation (Fig. 3.1).

Partial results are gathered into local temporary relations prior to any movement to other processing locations.

Choosing which sites should participate in the query evaluation process is computed according the following criteria (see Fig. 3.2) :

- operand locations, e.g. basic relations or partial results,
- operand volumes,
- (dynamically-updated) threshold value comparisons, considering next transfer decision possibilities [NGU78].

No attribute selectivity is maintained, such as proposed elsewhere [WON77], [YAO79], [EPS78], nor estimation on partial results cardinalities to tackle with data-movement strategies. The ADD proposal is very similar in that sense to ours [MAH79], since query decomposition is made upon calculation of temporary relations which contain intermediate results. This policy is described in the next paragraph.

Example :

```
at Site 1 : EMP1 (NAME, ADDRESS, AGE, SALARY, JOB, PROJ)
at Site 2 : EMP2 (NAME, ADDRESS, AGE, SALARY, JOB, PROJ)
at Site 3 : PROJECT (E-NAME, P-NAME, BUDGET, DEPT)
GLOBAL VIEW : UNION (SELECT (EMP1, PROJ = 'NASA' & JOB = 'Programmer'),
                     (SELECT (EMP2, PROJ = 'NASA' & JOB = 'analyst')) ;
            ≡ UNION (T1,T2) ≡ T3
Q0 := PROJECT (SELECT (GLOBAL-VIEW, SALARY > 10000), NAME, JOB)
```

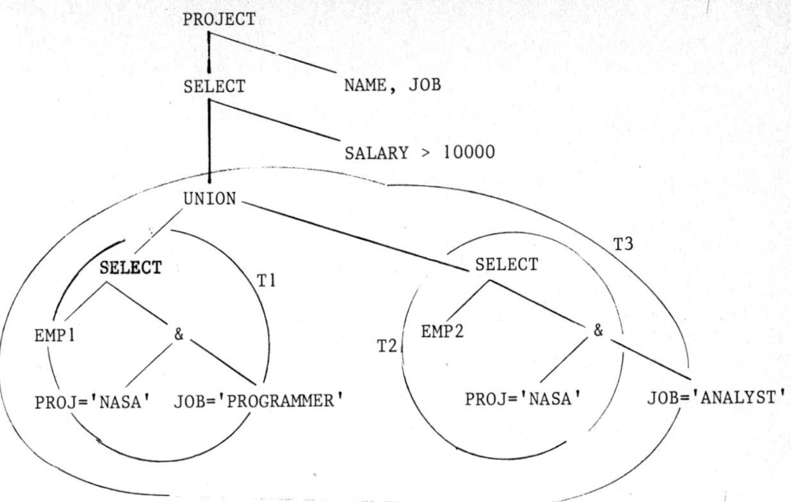

Fig. 3.1

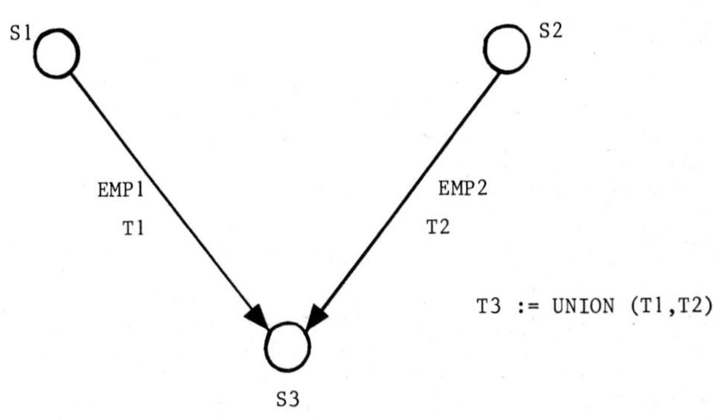

Fig. 3.2

3.2. Query decomposition

We can illustrate the query management process as shown below (Fig. 3.3). A relational algebra source request (A) is typed by some database user at his terminal. Syntactic analysis is made together with pre-interpretation into a usual arborescent structure (B), where nodes represent relational operators or basic operands.

In a second step, localization is performed, using (relation) distribution information given by global machine catalogues (C). This is used to characterize maximum single-site sub-trees, provided :

- all unary operators (Projection, Selection, ...) are executed on the operand's site,
- all n-ary operators (Join, Union, ...) are executed on the same site as their operands, whenever identical.

This is the first phase in query decomposition (D).

Their upon, sub-trees are replaced in the global machine query-tree by temporary relations, intended to receive partial results, Sub-trees themselves are sent to the sites concerned, as for T1 and T2 in Fig. 3.2.

At this point in time, an adaptive decision process is executed to handle further execution. Subsequent results availability and cardinality allow a dynamic transfer control facility (C,D,E) as explained below.

Our policy attempts to avoid selectivities of attributes and intermediate results volume estimations owing to the fact that such information needs very precise analytical knowledge of database content [DEM78] and stable application or transaction profile. Though related work seems very sound and effective, at least some transaction-definition aided-design feature is needed at database design time, and quite useful for highly updating applications.

In previous proposals [YAO79, WON77, EPS78] static decomposition is made prior to any data processing, using estimated results volume to handle data-transfer decisions. Synchronization of partial requests is thus achieved in a one-phase centralized process, by which all execution locations are known in advance, simplifying data-links establishment between all sites involved.

3.3. Optimization

On the other hand, still centralized, but dynamically tuned, is the decomposition feature as experimented in the POLYPHEME project. Distributed execution of queries is achieved using an interacting three-fold control structure, called DOPAGE [FER79], involving :

- operand and operator localization,
- transfer decision process,
- local execution facilities.

Whenever results are available, volume comparison is made with some current threshold value. Transfers are decided considering its results, and thus yield execution locations for further operations. Execution proceeds on the sites concerned, where new partial results will lead to subsequent comparisons with updated threshold values, and so on.

Since DOPAGE does not keep record of statistical data, the decisions concerning localization and nodes transfer are taken with the help of a function which we will hereafter call "threshold Transfer function" (or simply threshold). It gives an idea of the behaviour of the query at any given moment based on the "effective" knowledge of the results already obtained and therefore, it allows or holds the transfer of an operand to its brother-operand location [NGU79, NGU80, MAH79].

We plan two ways for handling the threshold technique :

- just one threshold (single threshold) which value only depends on the volume of the results of terminated nodes ;
- dedicating one threshold to each site (multiple threshold) whose values depend on the single thresholds, but also on hardware characteristics of the machine (machine cycle, failure probability, etc) and exploitation parameters of each site (throughput, etc).

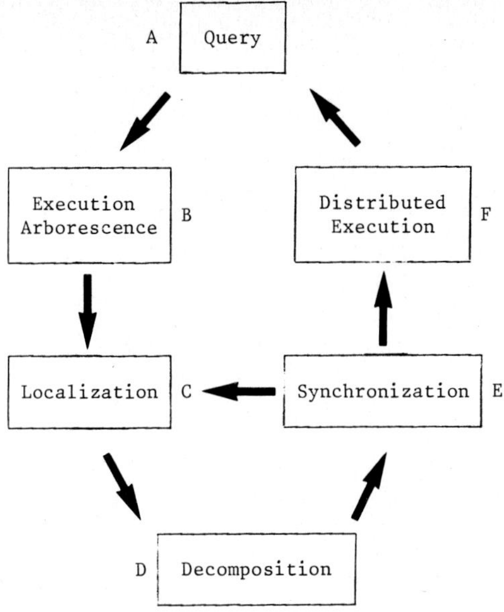

Fig. 3.3 - Query management process

The system exerts an "adaptable control" in so far as the threshold can be parametrized through the variables used (characteristics and type of threshold) [BEL65].

Threshold updating algorithm is today statically defined, and experimental results are described in [FER79], for different evolution functions, such as :

- last N transfers volume average,
- fixed basic operands average,
- logarithmic value of cumulated transfers,
- etc.

As far as research has been driven, this tunable transfer policy seems very interesting for queries involving many geographically spreaded relations.

It seems moreover that parametrizable implementations of DRD [MOH79], need to fit with real-size applications, adaptation of information retrieval strategies, by means of specific application and/or transaction-devoted algorithms. The DOPAGE algorithm is a way to reach an adaptive, thus efficient, execution facility for a general DRD system.

DOPAGE takes a binary tree which has been produced by a syntactical query analyzer and gives in result the sub-trees which are sent gradually towards their execution sites. In addition orders of associated relation (*) transfers are given.

A node can be found in one of the following states : Non-Localised, Localised, or Terminated. At first, the node-operators are in the state NL and the leaves (basic relations) in the state T [FER79].

(*) We only refer to the relations in the sense of local relations, see [ADI78].

Taking a single threshold, the localization rules are the following :

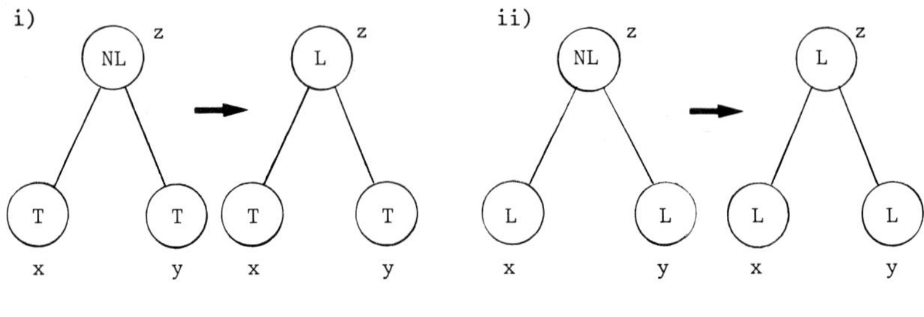

SITE(x) = SITE(y)

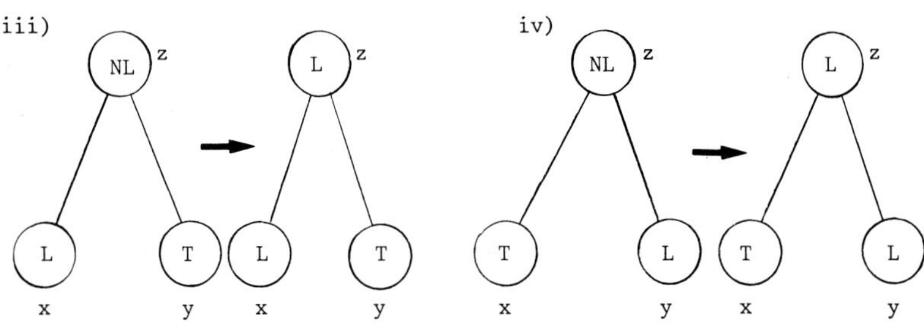

SIZE(y) ≤ THRESHOLD
<u>or</u> SITE(x) = SITE(y)

SIZE(x) ≤ THRESHOLD
<u>or</u> SITE(x) = SITE(y)

A node becomes terminated when the end of the execution of the sub-tree of which it is a root, is communicated to the site (or sites) containing the initial query tree.

Let the following tree, having C as initial site :

<u>Notation</u> :

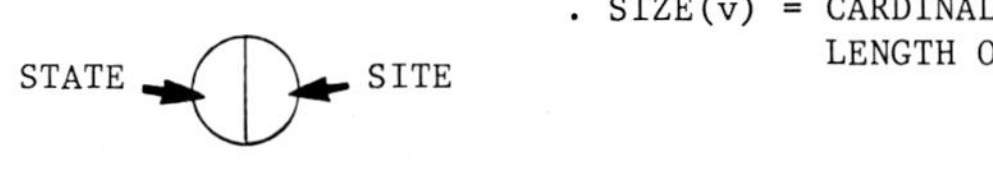

. SIZE(v) = CARDINALITY OF v * LENGTH OF THE TUPLE

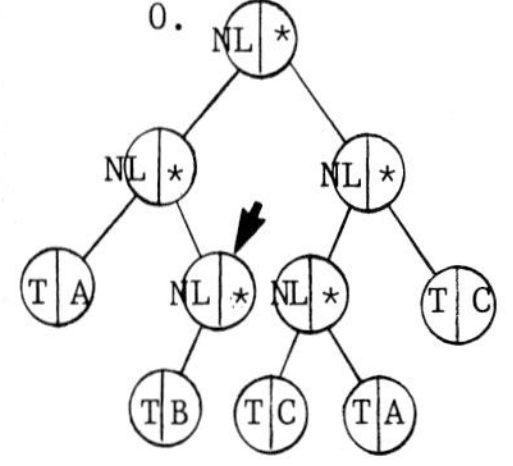

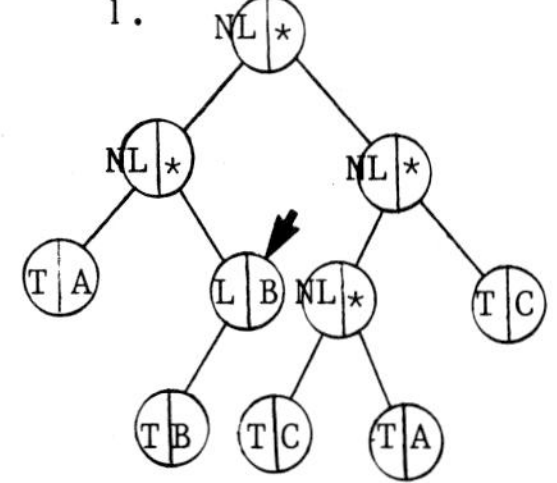

. The sub-tree indicated by the arrow is not maximal

2.

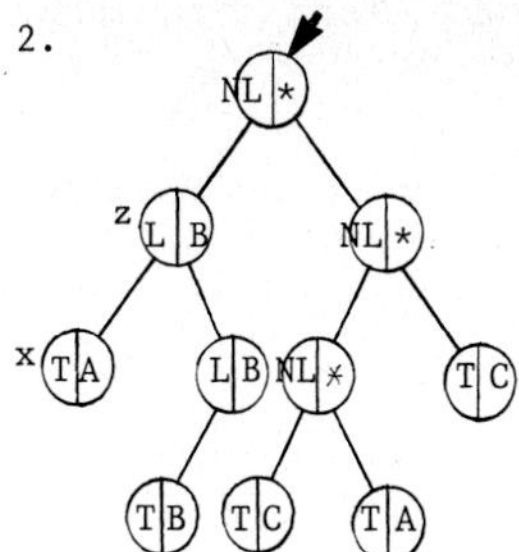

. Suppose that SIZE(x) ≤ THRESHOLD

. The node x is sent to site B.

3.

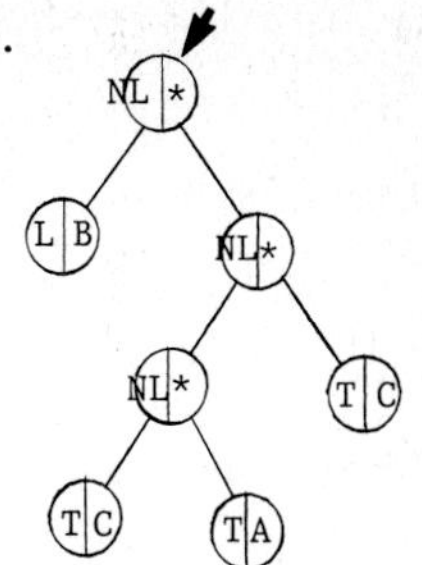

. The sub-tree whose root is z is sent to site B.

4.

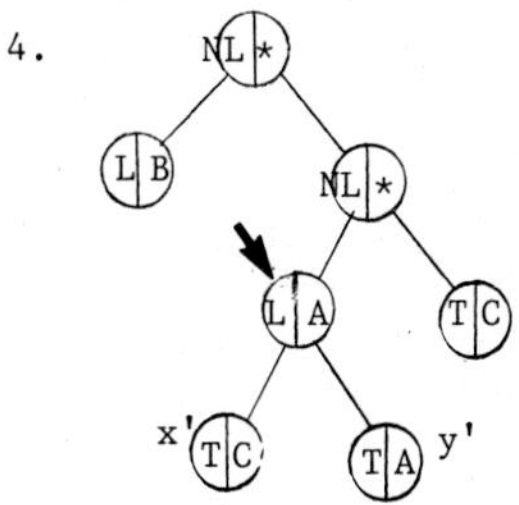

. Suppose that SIZE(x') ≤ SIZE(y').

5.

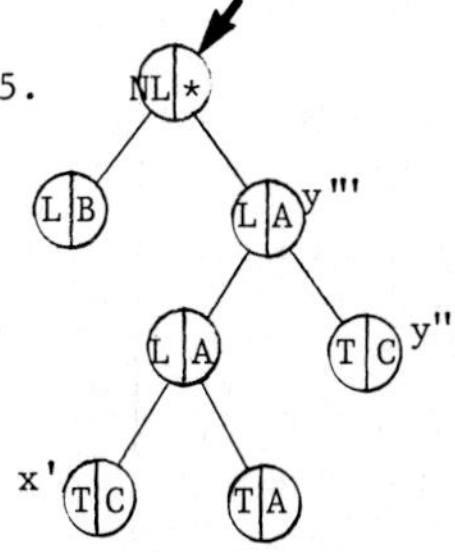

. Suppose SIZE(y") ≤ THRESHOLD

. Node transfer x' and y" towards site A.

6.

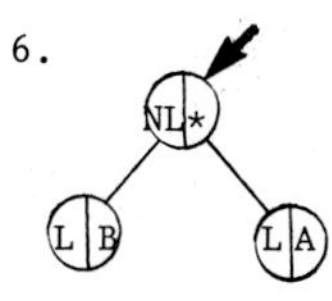

. The sub-tree whose root is y''' is sent to site A.

At this level, DOPAGE finishes its first execution loop. It will be reactivated at the termination of one of the two remaining nodes. Finally, the query-answer will be sent to site C.

However, up to now, no effective distributed decision process has been implemented in any currently designed project, other than cooperation of local processing facilities, through data transfer synchronization [WON77, EPS78, MAH79].

3.4. Distributed decomposition, future trends

As far as system-level engineering is concerned, recent studies on distributed computing systems allow significant improvements in DDB design.

Related undergoing research on query decomposition is described in this section, as extension of the previously described work.

Query management in distributed computing system can be described [LAN78] as a three-step execution scheme, involving :

- predicate evaluation, i.e. question-answering data characterization,
- data-item allocation, needed in multi-user environment,
- information updating.

Much attention has been paid on data allocation policies in concurrent update environments [THO77, ELL77, SEG77, ROS78], and predicate evaluation algorithms through query decomposition [CHU79, YAO79, EPS78, WON77, NGU78, MAH79].

Mainly centralized algorithms have been designed and implemented.

Our most recent work was dedicated to distributed decomposition of queries in a distributed DB system.

In such a case, we assume that all local DB systems support equal-rights DB processors, none of which, in the decomposition process, holds any particular privilege - neither the query receiving one.

It has been shown that in such systems, concurrent distributed data-allocation can be solved by pending requests sequencing on local processors, using a virtual ring and token synchronization mechanism [LAN78].

Such a feature is actually extended to query decomposition on a local micro-processor network, as a tool for transaction aided-design [NGU79].

It uses the previous dynamic decomposition scheme along with its threshold transfer function. All data-movement decisions are broadcasted amongst query-processing participating-sites, and synchronized via token reception at each location. Using an identical synchronization mechanism for query decomposition and concurrent users data-claims is expected to lay the basis for a unified and simple query management feature for DDB.

Besides, specific studies are driven on the threshold updating function (TUF), to experiment an adaptive decision algorithm, using dynamic programming techniques [BEL65]. This is intended for implementation of an efficient decomposition strategy, based on an optimal transfer decisions policy, following a recurrent multistage decision process.

For instance, if the criterion function to minimize is :

$$f(u_o) = \sum_{1}^{n} u_i$$

where u_i is current threshold value at step i of the decomposition process, t_i the ith transfer decision volume, and if the TUF is :

$$u_n = a.u_{n-1} + b.t_{n-1}$$

The following transfer decision t_n will be chosen according to :

$$f_n(u_{n-1}) = \min_{t} [au_{n-1} + bt + f_{n-1} (au_{n-1} + bt)]$$

$$f_1(u_o) = \min_{t_o} [au_o + bt_o].$$

Further details are given in [NGU80].

4. ARCHITECTURE OF THE D-DBMS PROTOTYPE

4.1. Functional overview

The POLYPHEME prototype is designed as a network of abstract relational machines [ACE78].

Each Relational Machine (or RM) is based upon three major components :

1) a NAME space composed with the description of relations and attributes,
2) an OBJECT space composed with the instances of the relations described in the name space,
3) a MAPPING mechanism which realizes the correspondence between object and name spaces.

Each RM provides its user with a data definition and manipulation language based on the relational algebra as presented in section 3.

Basically and according to the implementation described here, there are two kinds of RM :

- LOCAL MACHINE (LM) in which the three components just described are implemented on the same (real) computer. In POLYPHEME this kind of machine is built upon each cooperating database in order to make their behaviour homogeneous.
- GLOBAL MACHINE (GM) in which the name space is implemented on one computer while the object space may be distributed over several computers, each containing a local machine. The mapping mechanism, which determines the location of the relation instances have been partially described in the previous section and will be described in more details.

Through a GM, a POLYPHEME user can define and manipulate a distributed database as shown in figure 4.1.

This distributed database is defined as a set of relations : a relation is the unit of distribution and is stored on one site (see section 2). When a user wants to manipulate relations he does not have to know their location.

The prototype does not support the global view notion, but distributed relations can be formed, i.e. two relations can be logically considered as two fragments of the same relation. These 'virtual' relations are in the user's mind but they can also be obtained using transactions.

The user submits to a global machine elementary requests (query, update) or a sequence of requests constituting a transaction. The system analyzes each request, transforms it into an internal tree structure on which the decomposition algorithm, described in the previous section, is performed.

The result of the decomposition is a tree where each node (relation, operator) is assigned to a given site. It is possible then to determine some subtrees which concern only one local machine.

The implementation of the GM and LMs lies upon three basic software components which are described in the following subsections (see figure 4.1).

4.2. Database Management (URANUS)

The implementation of the POLYPHEME prototype uses a relational system called URANUS [NGU77].

This system can be used independently as a relational system or can provide a

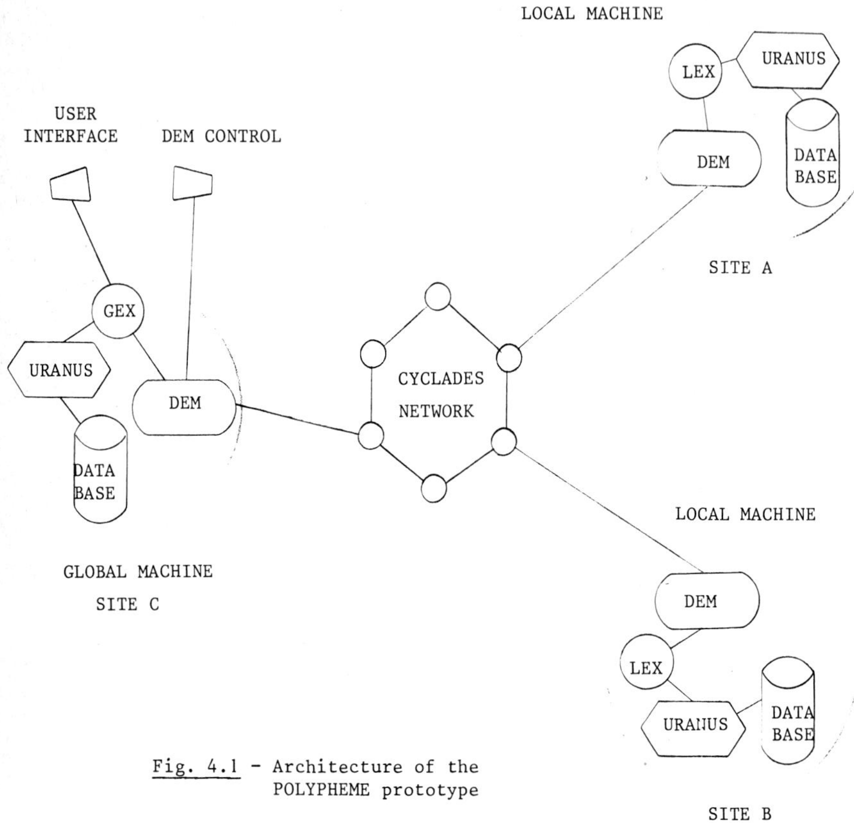

Fig. 4.1 - Architecture of the POLYPHEME prototype

relational interface for an existing network database implemented on the SOCRATE DBMS.

As a relational system, URANUS provides the following basic functions :

- data definition and manipulation language (algebraic oriented),
- transaction management : a transaction is a sequence of elementary requests considered as a whole,
- analysis and parsing of transactions. Each elementary request is transformed into an internal tree form,
- tree interpretation.

URANUS has two basic components, namely the parser which transforms the relational request into a tree, and an interpreter to interpret this tree.

In the previous section, we have described how the parser was modified to take into account distributed relations and to decompose requests.

The URANUS interpreter was incorporated into the prototype and acts as a database server executing data requests submitted either by a GM or a LM.

4.3. Distributed Execution Monitor (DEM)

A special software component has been developped in order to implement, using PL/1, distributed applications.

This component, the Distributed Execution Monitor (DEM), provides the GM and LMs with basic communication and synchronization facilities [AND78, DEA79].

One DEM is implemented on each computer involved in the D-DBMS and offers primitives for asynchronous remote procedure activations (one procedure activation must be considered as the execution initiation of the procedure and not as a procedural call). Between two distant DEM logical connections can be established. Once an activation primitive is invoked the DEM transforms it into messages which are sent, through the CYCLADES network, to the corresponding DEM which, in turn, transforms these messages into procedure activations. The DEM enforces the sequencing and the flow control of messages over each logical connection. A procedure is considered as an atomic unit and the principal services of DEM are the following :

a) open a logical connection
b) close a logical connection
c) activate a procedure on a given site using a previously established connection (when procedure A on site S1 activates B on site S2, A can continue its execution in parallel with B).

Additional services have been defined to control the different remote procedure activations. These services are :

d) acknowledgement of a logical connection opening
e) acknowledgement of the activation of a procedure
f) warning (the user) on logical connection failures (if any).

4.4. Global and Local Execution Monitors (GEX and LEX)

The communication between global and local machines are defined by a special protocol : the POLYPHEME Procedure Activation Protocol or PPAP, which sees local and global processes as a collection of activable procedures.

This PPAP is based upon the DEM services (see 4.3) which insure the synchronization between procedures using remote activations through logical connections between global and local machines. Parallel logical connections can be supported between two machines.

Furthermore the PPAP defines which procedures should be activated and the conventions for parameters passing (values and types), to achieve the following functions :

- logical connection use
- subtrees transmission form
- tuples transmission form
- error handling.

Local and Global processes are implemented respectively by the Global and Local Execution Monitors (GEX and LEX).

The GEX which implements the Global to Local PPAP provides the following functions :

- it handles the dialogue with the POLYPHEME user ;
- it activates URANUS to obtain localized trees from user requests ;
- it determines subtrees for each machine ;
- it extracts and sends each subtree to the concerned local machine. It should be noted, here, that an algorithm is transmited over the network. Subtrees can be sent in any order and interpreted in parallel by the local processors ;
- it receives and stores tuples in response from each subtree evaluation. When all the subtrees have been evaluated, the Global Machine can elaborate the final result for the user.

The Local Execution Monitor, LEX, implements the Local to Global PPAP (or the Local to Local PPAP in the case of a dynamic optimization algorithm).

The main functions of each LEX are the following :
- receive subtrees, reformat them for submission to the URANUS interpreter,
- activate the URANUS interpreter and control the execution,
- take each resulting relation and send the tuples to the relational machine waiting for them.

5. CONCLUDING REMARKS

We have described here the main features of a D-DBMS prototype which has been implemented on the CYCLADES network for the POLYPHEME project.

This description has provided only an overview and we recommend to the interested reader other publications on POLYPHEME (see references).

The prototype is, of course, rather limited : no multi-user mechanism, no recovery procedures, no view support, but it illustrates some important features in distributed databases : data distribution, request decomposition, algorithm transportation, distributed execution.

It should be noted also that this prototype is one of the first D-DBMS implemented in Europe.

Several thesis, articles, research reports have been published since the beginning of POLYPHEME, and some studies are still going on, for instance :
distributed database integrity [AND80], concurrency control, optimal data allocation [PAI79], query optimization [FER79], parallel data processing [EUZ79] and transaction management [NGU80].

Finally the experience gained with POLYPHEME can be a starting point for further research and development in the design and implementation of a general purpose D-DBMS.

ACKNOWLEDGEMENTS

The authors take pleasure to acknowledge the contributions of all the persons working in the POLYPHEME project : Edouard ANDRE, Gilles BOGO, Jean-Yves CALECA, Claude DELOBEL, Christian EUZET, In-Sup PAIK, Andrée STIERS.

Example :

Relations are distributed on three sites :

site 1 (the global site) : PARTDESC (PNO, WEIGHT, COLOR)
site 2 : EMP (ENO, ENAME, SALARY, DNO)
site 3 : DPT (DNO, TOWN)
PART (PNO, DNO).

GLOBAL MACHINE

1) User's Query : Find names of employees whose salary are > 2000 working in the departments located in PARIS and making PART P5.
That is : JOIN (PROJECT (SELECT (EMP, salary > 2000), ENO, ENAME, DNO),
JOIN (SELECT (DPT, TOWN = 'PARIS'),
SELECT (PART, PNO = 5), DNO = DNO), DNO = DNO).

2) Query Decomposition :

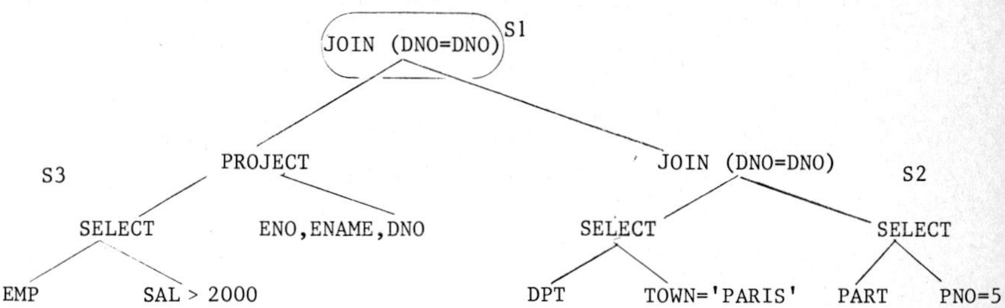

3) Localization :

First each leave in the tree is localized (i.e. the relations EMP, DPT and PART), then the tree is parsed to localize the algebraic operators and determine the subtrees which can be totally interpreted on a single local machine. In this case, we have three monomachine subtrees (see 2)).

4) Transportation :

The monomachine subtrees are sent to the corresponding local machines, using the global to local PPAP protocol.

LOCAL MACHINES

5) Subtree receipt : the local machine receives the sub-trees and reformats them into an URANUS interpretable form.

6) Subtree interpretation : the subtree is interpreted by the URANUS system. The result is a relation.

7) Relation transportation : the resulting relation is transmitted to the global site using the local to global PPAP protocol.

The GLOBAL MACHINE

8) Relation gathering : the subtree resulting-relations are gathered and the remaining tree (if any) is interpreted. The reply is given to the user.

Fig. 4.2 - An execution scenario

REFERENCES

[ACE78] M. ADIBA, J.Y. CALECA, C. EUZET
"A distributed database system using logical relational machines".
VLDB Conference, Berlin, Sept. 1978.

[ADA79] M. ADIBA, J.M. ANDRADE
"Semantic update consistency in a distributed database".
Laboratoire IMAG, Grenoble (Report in progress).

[ADE77] M. ADIBA, C. DELOBEL
"The cooperation problem between different database management systems".
IFIP TC2 Working Conference, Nice, Jan. 1977.

[ADI78] M. ADIBA
"Un modèle relationnel et une architecture pour les systèmes de bases de données réparties. Application au projet Polyphème".
Thèse d'Etat, Grenoble University, Sept. 1978.

[ADI78a] M. ADIBA
"Modelling approach for distributed databases".
ICMOD-ECI Conference, Venise, Italy, Oct. 1978.

[ADC78] M. ADIBA, J.Y. CALECA
"Modèle relationnel de données réparties. Problème de décomposition".
Conférence sur les modèles relationnels. I.P.P. Paris, March 1978.

[AND78] E. ANDRE, P. DECITRE
"On providing distributed application programmers with control over synchronization".
Computer Network Protocol Symposium, Liège, Belgium, Feb. 1978.

[AND80] J.M. ANDRADE
"L'intégrité et le traitement des opérations de mise à jour dans un système de bases de données réparties. Projet Polyphème".
Thèse de Docteur-Ingénieur (to be presented).

[AST76] ASTRAHAN et all
"System R. Relational approach to database management".
ACM TODS Vol.1, #2, June 1976.

[BEL65] R. BELMAN, R. KALABA
"Dynamic programming and Modern control theory".
Academic Press 1965.

[CAL78] J.Y. CALECA
"L'expression et la décomposition de transactions dans un système de bases de données réparties".
Thèse de 3ème Cycle, Grenoble, Sept. 1978.

[CHA75] P. CHANG, J.M. SMITH
"Optimizing the performance of a relational algebra data-base interface".
CACM, Oct. 1975.

[CHU79] W.W. CHU, P. HURLEY
"A model for optimal query processing for distributed databases".
Compcon 79, San Francisco, Feb. 1979.

[CODD72] E.F. CODD
"A relational model for large shared data banks".
CACM, June 1970.

[DEA79] P. DECITRE, E. ANDRE
"Projet POLYPHEME : the DEM distributed execution monitor" (not published).

[DEM78] R. DEMOLOMBE
"A general semantic method for efficiently evaluating AND operators in relational DBMS".
Sept. 1978.

[ELL77] C.A. ELLIS
"Consistency and correctness of duplicate database systems".
Proceedings of Sixth ACM Symposium on Operating Systems Principles.
Nov. 1977, pp. 67-84.

[EPS78] EPSTEIN et al
"Distributed query processing in a relational data base system".
UCB-ERL, April 1978.

[EUZ79] C. EUZET
"Interprétation de graphes pour l'enchaînement de requêtes dans un système de gestion de bases de données réparties".
Thèse de 3ème Cycle, Université de Grenoble, Sept. 1979.

[FER79] F. FERNANDEZ
"Etude d'algorithmes d'optimisation de requêtes dans les SGBD répartis. Mise en oeuvre de l'optimiseur DOPAGE".
Rapport DEA, IMAG, Grenoble, Sept. 1979.

[LAN78] G. LE LANN
"Algorithms for distributed data sharing systems which use tickets".
3rd Berkeley Workshop on Dist. Data Mgt., Aug. 1978.

[MAH79] MAHMOUD, RIORDON, TOTH
"Distributed database partitioning and query processing".
IFIP-TC2 Working Conference, Venice, June 1979.

[MOH79] C. MOHAN
"Distributed database management : Progress, Problems, some proposals and future directions".
WP7802, University of Texas, Austin, May 1979.

[NGU77] NGUYEN GIA TOAN
"URANUS, une approche relationnelle à la coopération de bases de données".
Thèse Docteur 3ème Cycle, Université de Grenoble, Dec. 1977.

[NGU78] NGUYEN GIA TOAN
"L'adaptabilité des bases de données par les moyens relationnels".
Congrès AFCET-Informatique 78, Gif s/Yvette, Nov. 1978.

[NGU79] NGUYEN GIA TOAN
"A unified method for query decomposition and shared information updating in distributed systems".
1st International Conference on Distributed Computing Systems, Huntsville, Alabama, Oct. 1979.

[NGU80] NGUYEN GIA TOAN
"Adaptive dynamic query decomposition for distributed database systems".
(to appear).

[PAI79] In-Sup PAIK, C. DELOBEL
"A strategy for optimizing the distributed query processing".
1st International Conference on Distributed Computing Systems, Huntsville, Alabama, Oct. 1979.

[ROG77] J. ROTHNIE, N. GOODMAN
"An overview of the preliminary design of SDD-1, a system for distributed data bases".
2th Berkeley Workshop on Distributed Data Management and Computer Networks, May 1977.

[ROS78] D.J. ROSENKRANTZ, R.E. STEARNS, P.M. LEWIS
"System level concurrency control for distributed database systems".
ACM Transactions on Database Systems, Vol.3 N°2, June 1978.

[SEG77] J. SEGUIN, G. SERGEANT, P. WILMS
"Cohérence et gestion d'objets dupliqués dans les systèmes distribués".
R.R. n° 77, CICG-ENSIMAG, Mai 1977.

[THO77] R.H. THOMAS
"A majority consensus approach to concurrency control for multiple copy data bases".
Bolt Beranek and Newman Inc., Report 3733, Dec. 1977.

[WON77] E. WONG
"Retrieving dispersed data from SDD-1 : a system for distributed databases".
Computer Corporation of America, CCA-77-03, March 1977.

[YAO79] S.B. YAO, A.R. HEVNER
"Query processing in distributed database systems".
IEEE Trans. on Software Engineering, May 1979.

DISTRIBUTED DATA BASES
C. Delobel and W. Litwin (eds.)
North-Holland Publishing Company

POLYPHEME project : The DEM distributed execution monitor.

Authors : Paul Decitre, Edouard André.

CII-Honeywell-Bull Research center (Grenoble).
C/o IMAG BP53 38041 GRENOBLE CEDEX FRANCE

Abstract:
This paper presents a distributed execution monitor intended for the Distributed Data Base Management System (D-DBMS) POLYPHEME. This monitor allows application programs distributed amongst a set of IRIS80 to cooperate through the CYCLADES network. The first part presents the requirements for a distributed executive in POLYPHEME and external design constraints. The second part describes the programmatic interface illustrated by a brief example. In the third part the internal design is described along with implementation choices.

The POLYPHEME project was partially suported by IRIA-SIRIUS contracts and is the result of a joint effort of CII-Honeywell-Bull research center and University of Grenoble.

Presentation of POLYPHEME.

The POLYPHEME project is a joint project between the CII-Honeywell-Bull research center and the University of Grenoble. It is partially sponsored by SIRIUS (an IRIA pilot project). The main purpose of this research is to test a cooperative approach to D-DBMS. Since the very begining of the joint work we chose to realise a prototype using the CYCLADES network and its host systems in order to demonstrate the feasability of a number of propositions in D-DBMS and distributed execution. We wish to prove that such systems are realitically implementable in short to medium scale of time.

The cooperative approach provides a manager (called global data base manager) with a means of describing the cooperation between existing data bases (refered to as local data bases). Local databases are controlled by autonomous and possibly dissimilar DBMS. A user (called global user) can see the data bases as a single one. He can issue requests to the global data base.

Roughly the transformations applied to a user request include analysis and decomposition followed by localisation and optimisation. All these operations transform the user request in an "execution plan" composed of localized operators and relations (fig 1). The description of the Distributed Data Base prototype which generates these plans is made in /ADI79/. We will describe the techniques used to carry on these execution plans on a set of dispersed computers. The description is limited to the techniques chosen in the prototypes currently in their test phase at Grenoble. A public demonstration of these prototypes is scheduled before the end of 1979.

Distributed executive requirements in POLYPHEME.

The POLYPHEME decomposer transforms a user request into an "execution plan". This execution plan may be represented by a tree where the root is the final result (a relation), the nodes are relational algebra operators and the leaves are relations or parameters. Each node or leave is localized i.e. there is a site name associated with each of them. The partitionning of a tree in a set of mono-site localized subtrees is already made by the decomposer-optimizer /NGU79/.

The purpose of this section is to characterize the synchronisation mechanisms needed to execute these trees.

Query/reply

The first need is to send a query to a remote site, start a remote program to interpret this query and receive replies. In the operating system terminology we identify:

a) The remote activation of a process which takes dynamically into account a querry.

b) A communication means between existing processes as provided by the message control layer found in Open System Architecture /ISO79/.

3) A structured data transport protocol to ensure encoding and decoding of a D.B. query and replies.

Parallel processing

The second need is to execute parts of a query in parallel. This parallelism allows overlapping between queries evaluation, queries and reply transportation and global computation. This is an important way to shorten the global response time.

Error control.

The third need is to detect remote site breakdown and network failure in order to activate save and recovery algorithms. (These algorithms are not implemented in the current prototype).

Concurrency control.

Concurrent access, as failure, may break the consistency of a distributed data base. There is a need of distributed synchronisation to ensure mutual exclusion or serializability /SDD78/. No solution is proposed to this difficult problem in our prototype. Studies on serialisability are under way and propositions will be soon materialized in a distributed transactional system prototype.

Chosen techniques.

Here we describe the choices made in the project without any comparison with other propositions.

A distributed interpreter.

On the global site a global interpreter works on the execution plan (represented by a tree, see fig 1.) It sends subtrees to local interpreters, gathers the replies and executes the global operators as soon as their operands are received. This technique allows an algorithm to be transported from a global to a local site since operators are ordered in a subtree. An equivalant approach may be to transform the subtree in an algorithm (a sequence of operators as JOIN SELECT PROJECT) and to send it to the remote site for execution (or compilation and execution). Algorithm transport is an important optimizing factor in distributed data bases. It permits to send selection criteria to the site where they can be locally applied, reducing so the amount of transfer of unnecessary data.

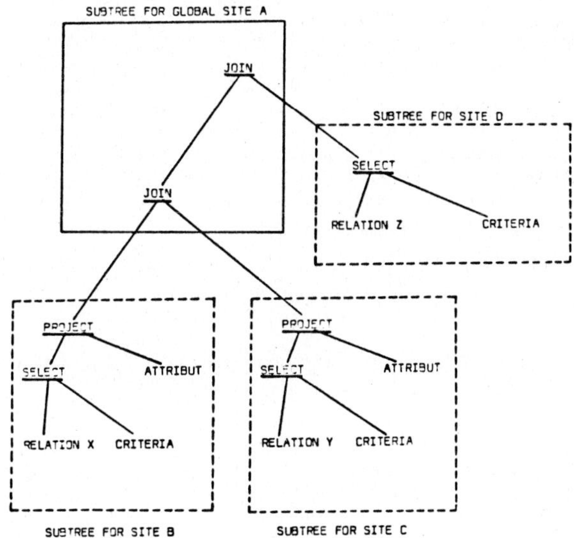

fig 1 : Execution plan represented by a tree.

The distributed interpreter allows parallel activities of each local interpreter. Thus we can imagine three kinds of optimization : the overlap of interpreter execution times themselves, the overlap of data transmission times, the overlap of data transmission times and interpreter execution time by the use of pipelining technique.

System architecture.

The architecture of the distributed executive in the prototype is mainly dictated by external constraints. For availability reasons the prototype had to be built on a set of IRIS80 connected through the CYCLADES or TRANSPAC network. Thus the SIRIS8 operating system running on IRIS80 computers was imposed as well as the programmatic interface to the CYCLADES transport station and the transport protocol. This interface has been available since the begining of the project.

A second external constraint was the programming language. PL1 was the only language which combined all the following properties:

- Availability

- High level with structured data and associated input/output.

- Interfaces to access the external D.B.M.S software (SOCRATE, URANUS,...).

- Debuging aids.

Obviously, a layer was missing between the distributed interpreter (written in PL1) and the transport station level. We chose to build DEM (Distributed Execution Monitor), a layer which permits to write distributed applications in PL1 (cf figure 2). We chose functionnalities as simple as possible to lessen the prototype development delay, but powerful enough to take into account the needs expressed in the previous section. The general idea was to provide distributed application programmers with a basic tool for the development of sophisticated distributed software, and to use the results of these first experiments to decide which mechanisms should be incorporated in a distributed O.S. /HOA78/, /BRH78/, /SOR79/, /IGO78/. Thus, complicated problems such as mutual exclusion, deadlock detection, or management of time-stamps are under DEM user's responsability. But as a conterpart we provide him with a first avalaibale tool to later solve these problems in a high level programming language.

Distributed program description.

In this section we describe the programmatic interface of DEM and a little example of use.

Distributed program structure.

A distributed program is a set of local programs, each of them runs on its own computer (site). A local program is a set of PL1 procedures running under the control of a monitor. The communication between local programs is made through "remote activation" of procedures : when a local program A wishes to send something to local program B it requests the monitor to issue a procedure call, possibly with input parameters, on the remote site B. Thus procedures execute the treatment associated with an inter-site communication event.

Local program structure.

Local program procedures are PL1 external procedures. The local monitor calls a procedure such that mutual exclusion is ensured in that procedure up to the END or RETURN instruction; there are no concurrent access problems between procedures of a local program.

The execution of a procedure is termed an "action", being either a "normal action" or "local action". A normal action is a procedure execution following a remote activation, a local action is a procedure executed for the purpose of asynchronous acknowledgement (error detection, acknowledgement of remote activation).

Communication between dispersed local programs.

Communication between local programs is via remote activation of

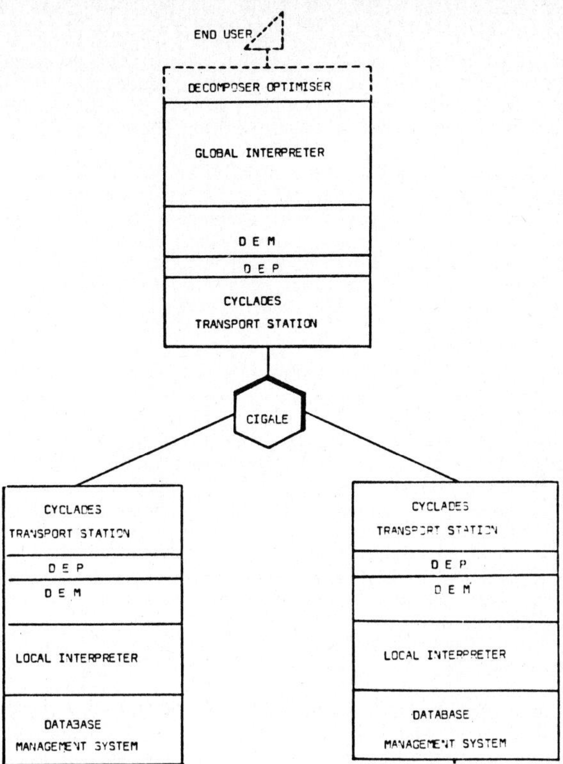

Fig 2 : Distributed execution prototype architecture

procedures. It is an asynchronous remote procedure "call" (a FORK in parallel computing). An action requests its local monitor to activate a remote procedure by the primitive command INIT. DEM will start the corresponding normal action on the remote site. To allow the ordering of several actions on a site and the flow control of remote activations we define an "interaction". All remote activation is made on an interaction.

An interaction is a duplex controlled flow of remote activations opened between two sites.

- A duplex flow (which is the coupling, with a single name, of two simplex flows of activations from A to B and from B to A) brings together a question and its replies.

- The flow is controlled because activations on an interaction do not outrun each other (an interaction keeps the order of INIT), and because each local monitor controls the size of the queue of remote activations waiting on an interaction.

User primitive commands.

The program communicates its requests to the monitor by the execution of primitive commands which are calls to a monitor procedure. The effective parameters of the procedure are the parameters of the primitive. There are five user primitive commands used for communication between local programs.

- OITR : Interaction openning. The user furnishes his name and the name of the remote site. This opening is asymetric, the user remote program being not warned. It is the remote monitor which responds to the opening. The remote program will be informed by the first normal action executed on this interaction. OITR command being asynchronous, the user program is informed of the end of opening phase by a local action running an acknowledgement procedure; its name is given in the OITR command (cf Acknowledgement procedure).

- CITR : Interaction closing. User gives the reference of the interaction to be closed. CITR is a synchronous primitive command.

- INIT : Remote activation of a procedure on an interaction. User gives the name of the remote procedure, input parameters and references. This is an asynchronous primitive which introduces the name of acknowledgement procedure. Input parameters are given in an array of character strings.

- SURVEY : Requests DEM to look after an interaction. DEM will warn the user program of the disapearance of the remote site, of a network breakdown, or a remote closing. This command is asynchronous. It introduces the name of an acknowledgement procedure.

Acknowledgement procedures.

A local action runs the instructions of an acknowledgement procedure. This is the mean used by the monitor to give an asynchronous account of events introduced by asynchronous primitives commands. The name of acknowledgement procedure is given as parameter of the asynchronous primitive command. there are two kinds of acknowledgement procedures introduced in the OITR command:

- ACKOITR : end of interaction opening. This local action gives the completion code of an opening, the monitor's reference of the opened interaction, and it allows the use of this interaction.

- SURV : interaction closing, or error detection. This local action informs the program of closing. There are two main reasons for closing: a remote user command CITR or a network failure.

The third kind of acknowledgement procedure is introduced in the INIT primitive command.

ACKINIT : remote activation acknowledgement. This local action is started after the END (or RETURN) primitive command is issued on the remote site. This is an "end to end" control of the execution of remote procedures.

Example.

We give as example a simplified version of the POLYPHEME distributed interpreter skeleton. To shorten the program we leave aside error recovery and multi-user handling. Besides, we specialize the interpreter to a unique global tree! Nevertheless, this example gives an idea of DEM user's programming facilites and of the interpreter functions.

On the global site A runs the global part of the distributed interpreter. It has to send three subtrees to local interpreters on site B,C,D, then to receive tuple by tuple the three resulting relations from site B,C,D. As soon as a resulting relation is completely received, it evaluates the interpretable part of the global tree.

On the three sites B,C,D runs an occurence of the local interpreter. On reception of a remote request (subtree) it interprets the tree and computes the resulting relation. Then it sends tuple by tuple, preserving the order, the result back to the requester and finaly signals the end of the resulting relation.

On site A, DEM gives the control to the INITIAL procedure where the user starts the application by opening three interactions.

```
INITIAL : PROC;
  CALL OITR(SITEB,REF1,'ACKO','SURVO');open an interaction with site B
  CALL OITR(SITEC,REF2,'ACKO','SURVO');          "                  C
  CALL OITR(SITED,REF3,'ACKO','SURVO');          "                  D
END INITIAL;
```

INITIAL opens one interaction with each site B,C,D introducing SURVO as the procedure to be called on network or site failure and the procedure ACKO as the procedure to be called on each opening completion.

```
ACKO : PROC(ITR,REF,CODE);
/*REF  is the user reference of the opened interaction, ITR is the
DEM reference of this interaction, Code is the completion code.
ACKO  will  be  run  three  times :  once  for  each  interaction
opening.*/
IF CODE = OK THEN DO;
  CALL INIT(ITR,REF,'LOCAL_INTERP',SUBTREE(REF),'ACKINIT');
END;
ELSE DO; error control not taken in account here END;
END ACKO;
```

ACKO, for each interaction opened, requests DEM to activate the LOCAL_INTERP procedure with SUBTREE(REF) as parameter. SUBTREE(REF) is the representation of the subtree to be interpreted on the remote site with which the interaction of reference REF has been opened.

ACKINIT is the name of a local procedure to be executed by DEM at the completion of the remote procedure LOCAL_INTERP.

On sites B,C,D we find :

```
LOCAL_INTERP : PROC(ITR,REF,TREE);
  RESULT=L_INTERP(TREE);
  CALL INIT (ITR,REF,'TUPLE_RECEPT',RESULT(1,*),'ACK_TUPLE');
  IND=1;
END LOCAL_INTERP;
```

TREE is the input parameter containing the subtree received. The interpretation of this subtree is done by the L_INTERP function which returns the resulting relation in the RESULT array of tuples. The first tuple is sent to the calling site (identified through ITR) by the activation of the remote procedure TUPLE_RECEPT.

On site A we find :

```
TUPLE_RECEPT : PROC(ITR,REF,TUPLE);

/* Receive one tuple as result of a subtree remote interpretation
and store it in a temporary relation for further use when all the
leaves of a global operator will be received*/
  CALL STORE (REF,TUPLE);
END TUPLE_RECEPT;
```

At the end of TUPLE_RECEPT execution the control returns to DEM (END statement) which sends an acknowledgement to the calling site (B or C or D). Thus the user acknowledgement procedure ACKTUPLE will be called.
On the site B,C,D we find :

```
ACK_TUPLE : PROC(ITR,REF,CODE);
/*on each end of TUPLE_RECEPT send the next tuple of the relation
stored in the RESULT array. The current tuple to be sent is
indexed by the external variable IND*/
  IF CODE=OK THEN DO;
    IF RESULT(IND,1) NOT = '' THEN DO;
    /* one more time*/
      CALL INIT(ITR,REF,'TUPLE_RECEPT',RESULT(1,*),'ACK_TUPLE');
    END; ELSE DO; on end of resulting relation
      CALL INIT (ITR,REF,'END_OF_REL',DUMMY,'RETURN');
      /*The end of relation is passed to the calling site
      by activation of the remote procedure END_OF_REL*/
    END;
  ELSE DO;
  error control not treated here
  END;
END ACK_TUPLE;
```

The flow control is achieved by the remote activation of TUPLE_RECEPT procedure with ACKTUPLE as acknowledgement procedure. We can improve the efficiency of the flow by anticipation. Two or three extra INIT of TUPLE_RECEPT may be issued in the LOCAL_INTERP procedure. This anticipation allows the overlap between transmission times and execution times. On the end of relation the procedure END_OF_REL is called on the site A.

On the site A we find :

```
END_OF_REL : PROC (ITR,REF,DUMMY);
/* Reception of end of relation. Closing of the corresponding
interaction and calling of the global interpreter to evaluate the
evaluable part of the global tree*/
  CALL CITR(ITR,0);
  CALL G_INTERP(REF);
END END_OF_REL;
```

The procedure G_INTERP evaluates the final result and delivers it to the user. SURVO and ACKINIT are error detection procedures not developed here.

Implementation considerations.

Network architecture model.

We tried to follow ISO early recomendations /ISO79/ for open systems

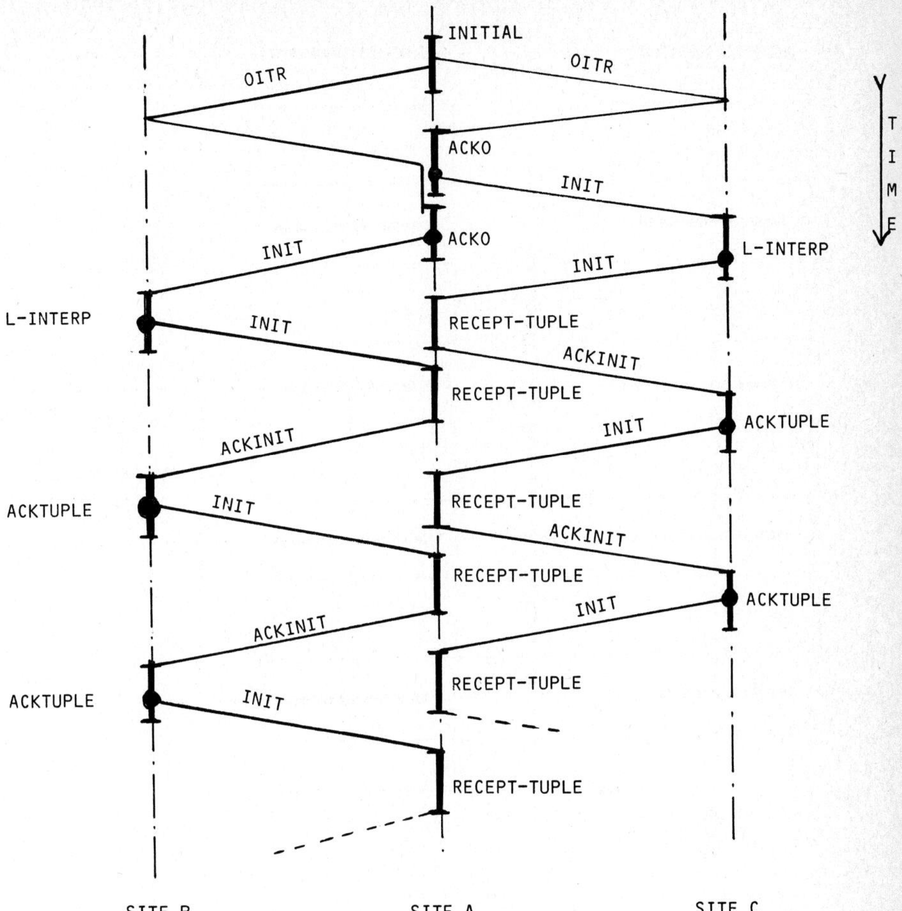

Fig 3 : An execution plan and its partitionning in subtrees.

architecture based on a layered structure. Each layer is constituted of entities which communicate through services of the lower layer. The cooperation between these entities provides entities of the upper layer with services which are available through the interface of the layer. The protocol of the layer is the set of conventions which rules the dialog between entities of this layer.

From hardware connection, which constitutes the lowest level, the network architecture defines more and more logical (structured) levels of interface. The project presented here is designed over available layers up to message management .

Over these existing layers we have defined a distributed execution layer. The previous sections have introduced the distributed execution monitor interface (DEM). The cooperation of these monitors to build the distributed execution service is ruled by a distributed execution protocol (DEP).

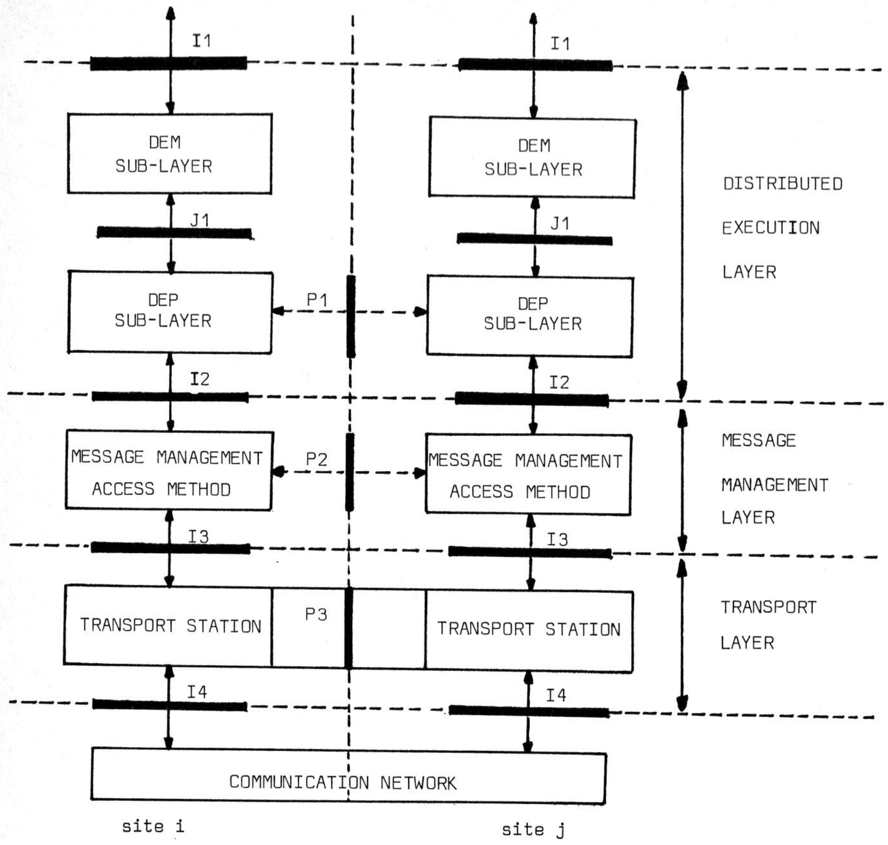

P1 : Distributed execution protocol

P2 : Message Management protocols (connection and dialog protocols)

P3 : Transport protocol

I1 : Distributed execution interface

J1 : DEP interface

I2 : Message management interface

I3 : Transport interface

I4 : Packet switching network interface

Figure 4. Architecture for Distributed Execution.

An other implementation choice is the packaging of the different interfaces. Since we decided to use the same high level language for distributed execution as for data base access, we were practically required to use PL1.

Intermediate protocol interface.

The definition of a level-n protocol in a layered architecture includes two parts:

a-The description of level-n entities and level-n functions. Level-n functions can be defined as level-n commands which can be issued by level-n entities to other level-n entities.

b-The description of the mapping (interpretation) between level-n entities and functions (or commands) onto level(n-1) entities and functions.

In an experimental environment, it is useful to associate one software module to one logical function. The implementation of distributed execution layer shows two sub-layers connected through an internal interface. The DEP sub-layer implements over message management the DEP elementary functions, while the DEM sub-layer implements the DEM primitives over DEP interface. In fact a DEM function can require several DEP functions while some DEP functions are not visible at DEM interface. We took effective advantage of having defined DEP mapping on message management separately for allowing rough design (character encoding for readibility and test), reserving further optimisation without logical modification. Figure 5 shows the software structure.

Though not experimented, we thought that it could be interesting to design different DEM interface (packaged in different language or of different synchronisation type), provided that it still respects DEP access rules which reflect the protocol.

Message management interface.

Message management throughout packet switching network is a standard access method under SIRIS 8 operating system. This message management offers primitives for establishing logical connections (message groups) between a pair of correspondants. Each correspondant is known to the system by a mailbox name. The message management services allow to send and receive messages over properly established connections. Error and flow control is available on every path. This interface is built over a complete set of layers permitting various network configurations. The here described distributed execution system was experimented on the CYCLADES datagram network.

Synchronisation organisation.

Since we intended to demonstrate that asynchronism can be clearly handled in high level languages if an appropriate structure of programming is provided, we applied this principle to our own implementation. The structure of DEM/DEP implementation look like the structure we recomend for user application defined over DEM.

The implementation of an asynchronous interface where answers can be delayed is generally based on synchronisation primitives, implying that the corresponding concepts are incorporated in the programming language. We have explained in /AND78/ our approach using procedure activation as synchronisation basic concept, which allow to use the algorithmic power of high level languages for the expression of elaborated synchronisation conditions. Each layer is implemented by two sets of procedures:

a-A set of procedures corresponds to the primitives of the interface (downward procedures). These procedures are called by upper layer and make calls to lower level downward procedures.

b-A set of procedures corresponding to the interpretation of notifications issued by the lower level (upward procedures). These procedures are called by lower level upward procedures. The names of upward procedures can be fixed by convention and thus be part of the interface definition. But the names can also be introduced as parameters in downward procedures calls. The DEM and Message management procedure find as parameters the names of procedures to be called when a result or a consequence of the execution of the invoked function occurs.

This design appears to be a kind of generalisation of the ON-CONDITION PL1 concept, not seen as an exception mechanism but as the basic tool for synchronisation specification.

In DEM/DEP layer it was decided that code was not preemptible. This avoided going deep into hidden PL1 procedure context and permitted to keep free from supporting special delivery of PL1 compiler. Thus at DEM/DEP level there is only one process shared by all different users. This feature is compatible with our claim that our intention was to investigate parallelism between sites leaving each site taking his optimisation from the number of users.

To keep the network efficient (maximum anticipation on all pathes), a second process is dedicated to message management events handling. Message management contigency routines, called by the system, feed a unique queue on a hign priority level and can preempt DEM/DEP process execution.

Figure 5 illustrates the synchronisation structure of the implementation.

Performances.

All the distributed execution monitor is written in PL1 exept for PL1 interface to message management. This decision should be desastrous for performances in real time operation. We would say here that this model has been designed for logical feasibility demonstration, provided that with sufficent resources the answers can be delivered within reasonable delay. The language must be chosen according with the level of complexity to be expressed. It is not common, unfortunately, that even in new languages we find both high level synchronisation facilities and high level data base access.

Conclusion.

A result of the POLYPHEME project was certainly to show the need for distributed execution facilities as well as for Data Base request decomposition processing. We proposed and experimented a solution compatible with those levels of languages required in Data Base access. The synchronisation requirements were matched with a basic mechanism proving powerful, when associated with the algorithmic possibiblities available in high level languages. The choice of PL1 was dictated by rather external constraints. We think that future high level languages for distributed applications implementation should offer both high level synchronisation features and general data base access primitives.

The monitor presented here shows that distributed applications need not wait for a general purpose distributed operating system to be implemented.

To validate these assumptions it has been decided to start a new research project focused on distributed transactional systems which seem to be a realistic and marketable approach to distributed data base management systems.

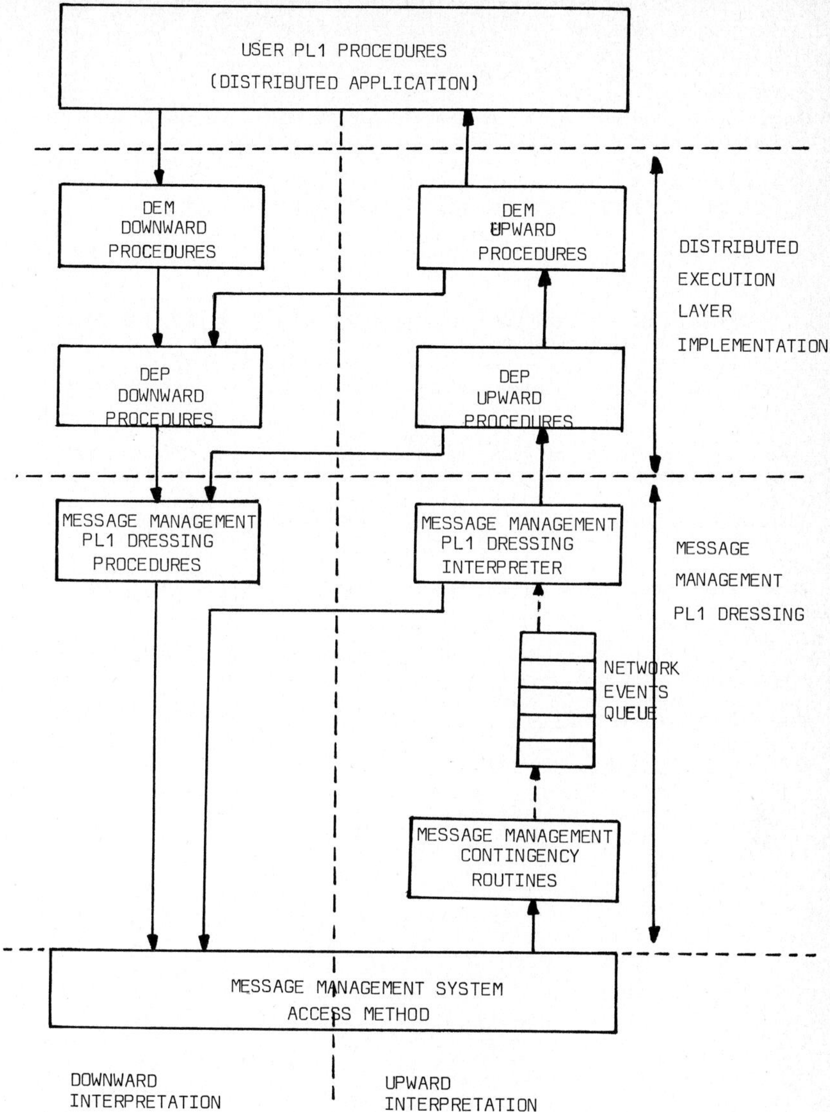

Figure 5. Synchronisation organisation.

The existence of end to end flow control on upper layer make the DEP queue remain limited, provided that respect is taken of anticipation limit. This constraint is watched by DEM interface which drops every request overruning current allowed anticipation.

/ADI79/ ADIBA M., ANDRADE J.M., DECITRE P., FERNANDEZ F., NGUYEN GIA TOAN :"POLYPHEME an experience in distributed data base design and implementation". (proposed to Versailles congress)

/AND78/ ANDRE E., DECITRE P. :"On providing distributed application programmers with control over synchronization". Proc Computer network protocol symposium Liege February 78.

/DAN78/ DANG NG. X., MARTINS J.G., SERGEANT G., WILMS P. "Specifications de definition de SIGSIGOR". Research report 1978 ENSIMAG GRENOBLE.

/FEL79/ FELDMAN J.A. :"High level programming for distributed computer". Comm. ACM 22-6 June 79.

/BRH78/ HANSEN B. :"Distributed processes: a concurrent programming concept. Comm. ACM 21-11 (november 78).

/HOA78/ HOARE C.A.R. :"Communicating sequential processes". Comm. ACM 21-8 August 78.

/ISO79/ "Reference model of Open System Architecture" ISO/TC97/SC16 N117. Version 3 as November 1978

/NGU80/ NGUYEN GIA TOAN :"Adaptative dynamic query decomposition for distributed databse systems". (to appear).

/SDD78/ SDD1 group :Technical reports. Computer corporation of America (Cambridge Mass.).

/SOR79/ J.L.CHEVAL et al. Un projet de systeme distribue: SORTILEGE. RR 150. Universite de Grenoble. January 1979.

/STO79/ M.STONEBRAKER Concurrency control and consistency of multiple copies of data in distributed INGRES. IEEE Transactions on software engineering. vol SE 5 no 3. May 1979.

DISTRIBUTED DATA BASES
C. Delobel and W. Litwin (eds.)
North-Holland Publishing Company

A MULTI-QUERY APPROACH TO DISTRIBUTED PROCESSING IN A RELATIONAL DISTRIBUTED DATA BASE MANAGEMENT SYSTEM

Wojciech Cellary[1]
Daniel Meyer[2]

University of Nancy I
Department of Applied Mathematics
Nancy , FRANCE

A new approach to the optimization of query processing in distributed data base systems is proposed. The optimization concerns a multi-query environment and the mean response time of queries as a system performance measure instead of the single-query environment and the execution time of a query criterion, considered up to date. Two optimization elements are taken into account, namely transmission delays and workload. An heuristic method is outlined to optimize query processing at three complementary levels : decomposition tree structures, localization of nonlocalized operations and query scheduling

1. INTRODUCTION

In this paper we will consider a general approach to the optimization of query processing strategies in Distributed Data Base Management Systems /DDBMS/, using the mean response time of queries as an optimality criterion, since in any data management system the response time obtained is the principal element in the evaluation of system efficiency.

As is known, a distributed system is composed of several nodes interconnected by a transport network. DDBMS, designed for the management of query processing, utilizes local Data Base Management Systems /DBMS/ implemented on different nodes. Every query submitted by a user to DDBMS has first to be decomposed into subqueries executable by the different local DBMS holding the relevant data; then subqueries have to be transmitted to the respective DBMS to be executed. Starting from the results of the subqueries DDBMS performs the set of logical operations /e.g., AND, OR, etc.../ expressed in the query. The result of these operations constitutes the final response returned to the user.

In the distributed environment mentioned above, the execution of a query involves data transmissions which take significant time in comparison with the subquery and logical operation execution time. However, on the other hand, the distribution of the system makes possible the parallel processing of subqueries and logical operations, which is profitable from the point of view of the response time obtained. These two parameters, transmission delay and parallel execution, influence the strategy of query processing.

We can distniguish two kinds of query processing strategies. The first kind are centralized strategies which consist, first, in grouping together, for a given query, all the partial results of subqueries at the node of decomposition and then, in executing all logical operations together. As may be seen from the most recent research, this solution is not the best one in many practical cases because of poor parallelism in the system. The second kind of query processing strategies are distributed strategies, which take advantage of the high parallelism in the system. Because of their advantageous properties, distributed solutions are currently being examined intensively [4,8,11,12].

However, in solutions proposed to date, the optimization concerns only the reduction of the total transmission time. From the point of view of optimization techniques we can once more distinguish two general approaches: static and dynamic. Static solutions use, as the basis of optimization, statistical information concerning the data stored in the system and accessed by queries [12,15] Having this information, all the transmissions necessary for the execution of a given query can be evaluated in advance and thus a strategy of query processing, tending to minimize the response time, can be entirely determined before beginning its processing. On the contrary, in dynamic solutions no information allowing query behavior to be predicted is assumed [4,8,9,10,11]. The evaluation of the execution and transmission times is made step by step during query processing and is used dynamically for determining the strategy.

However, a common feature of all strategies developped to date both static and dynamic ones, is that they consider the optimization of the processing of one query, as if DDBMS was a single - user system.

In this paper, we would like to present the principles of a multi-query approach. We assume that DDBMS is able to receive and to process simultaneously many single and multi-node queries . In our approach we do not look for the optimal processing of each query separately; on the contrary, we look for the optimal processing of the set of queries which are in the system at a given moment.

In the next section we specify the assumptions made. In Section 3 we define the purpose of our multi-query approach, namely the minimization of the mean response time in the system. Section 4 contains the definition of the elements of optimization which we take into consideration: transmission time, external and internal workload in DDBMS. In Section 5 we propose a model of distributed processing. Using this model, we outline, in Section 6 , a heuristic method of optimization of query processing, tending to minimize the mean response time in the system. Section 7 contains some comments on dynamic workload evaluation and Section 8 - conclusions.

2. ASSUMPTIONS

In order to specify the framework of our study, we present the assumptions made.

Assumption 1 : The architecture of DDBMS is the same as that defined within the framework of project SIRIUS [6,7]; so it is a very general one. Every node is simultaneously an access point of DDBMS /reception of queries, decomposition, final response/, storage point/local data base and DBMS/ and processing point /operators/.

Assumption 2 : DDBMS is a relational system [3]. Every processing point holds all the relational operators defined by Codd/JOIN, UNION, INTERSECT, PROJECT, SELECT, etc.../ [3,13]. We admit non-relational DBMS.

Assumption 3 : We are looking for a dynamic solution. DDBMS has no information allowing, at the moment of query decomposition, the volume of data for transmission to be predicted, and thus, a processing strategy to be chosen.

Assumption 4 : Every access point is able, using a mechanism on which we make no assumption [1,4,5,12,14], to decompose each query into a binary relational tree. A tree is composed of a set of localized subqueries submitted for execution to DBMS and of a set of non--localized relational operations which have to be executed by processing points of DDBMS. A single - node query is decomposed into one subquery entirely localized. The structure of the tree established at the moment of decomposition may be changed during execution; the proposed structure is an executable one but not in every case the optimal one.

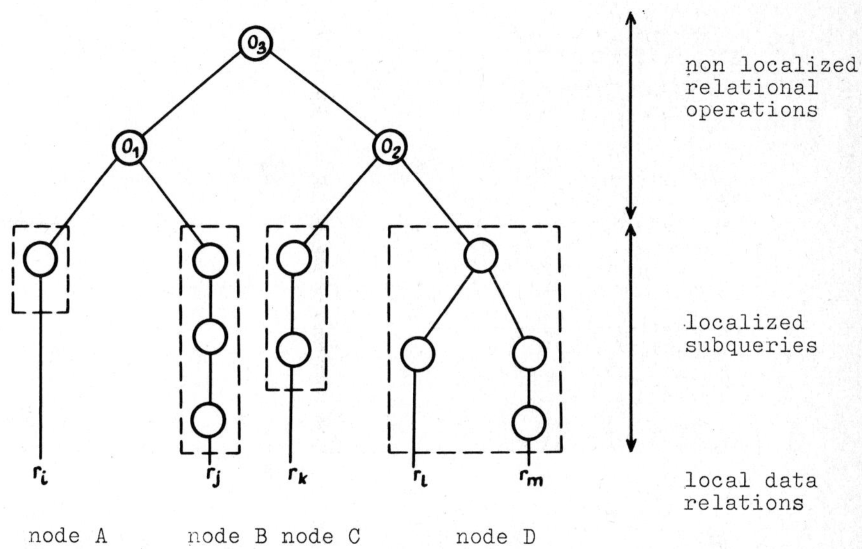

Figure 1
An example of a decomposition tree for a multi-node query

Assumption 5 : For every binary relational tree, we apply the optimization rules proposed by CHANG and SMITH [13] which consist in "pushing down" toward the bottom of a tree unary operators, in any case where it is possible.

Assumption 6 : DDBMS uses a packet switching network for data exchanges. The notion of distance between nodes does not intervene, and the system has no knowledge about routing strategy through the network.

3. OBJECTIVE : MINIMIZATION OF MEAN RESPONSE TIME

As was mentioned above the solutions proposed to date concern the single-query environment. As a result, they consist in minimizing the query execution time T_E. Generally, this time consists of the local execution times of subqueries and relational operations, and of the transmission times. As can be seen in Fig.2, during the calculation of the query execution time, it is necessary to take into account the parallelism of local executions and transmissions.

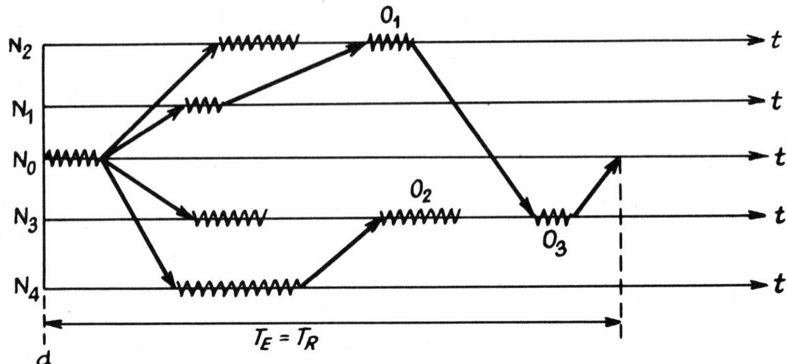

d : time of decomposition
↗ : time of data transmission between two nodes
/\/\/\ : local execution time

Figure 2
Query execution time in a single-query environment for the binary tree represented in Fig.1.

Let us note that from the user point of view it is necessary to minimize the query response time T_R, i.e. the time elapsed between the arrival of a query in the DDBMS and the moment of final response, since this time is observed by the user. Of course, in the single-query environment the execution time and the response time of a query are identical.

In fact, DDBMS is a multi - user system able to process many queries similtaneously. However, the simultaneity of the processing of many relational trees may introduce some waits at the level of local executions of relational operations in the case where a node is involved in many trees. As a result in the multiquery environment, generally, the response time of a query is composed of the execution time and waiting time : $T_R = T_E + T_W$. Waiting time T_W has to be seen as the total time of waits, which , however, because of the parallelism in the system is not necessarily the sum of all elementary waits arising during tree processing.

As a consequence, the separate minimization of the execution time of each tree is generally insufficient for the total optimization of system performance, because of interferences between executions of different trees. For this reason, we propose an approach consisting in the optimization of a global strategy applied to the set of queries, which permits the minimization of the mean response time of the system.

We have assumed that the arrival of queries in the system is random, which raises some difficulties in the calculation of mean response time at a given moment. However, the minimization of the mean response time is equivalent to the maximization of the number of queries entirely completed in a time unit. At any moment of time, the optimal strategy of query processing has to be the one which allows, during each consequtive time unit, the maximum number of queries to be completed.

4. ELEMENTS OF THE OPTIMIZATION PROBLEM

During the minimization of the mean response time, two fundamental elements will be taken into account, namely transmission time and workload.

4.1 Transmission time

As results from Assumption 6, the evaluation of the transmission time depends on the volume of transmitted data, i.e. of the cardinality of the relation received as a result of the execution of a relational operator.

The only parameter of the transport network, which is generally known, is the mean transport time of a message unit /i.e. packet/ between two arbitrary nodes. Thus in first approximation, we can consider the transmission time of a message to be proportional to the number of message units contained in the message. As a result, for our study, we can replace the comparison of the transmission times of two messages by the comparison of their respective numbers of message units. In next sections, we will see the way in which transmission time intervenes as an element of optimization.

4.2. Workload

In many multiprogramming computer systems, the processing capacity is shared in time by different jobs. This sharing influences the job /in our case - query/ execution time obtained : the greater the workload, the longer job execution time. In order to take into account the element of workload in our approach, we distinguish the internal workload and the external workload of DDBMS.

4.2.1. External workload of DDBMS

The different computers which compose DDBMS can be simultaneously used for other applications than executions of DDBMS queries. These "other applications" involve a global external workload of DDBMS, which is irregularly distributed and which is the sum of local workloads. As can be seen, on any node of DDBMS the local external workload influences the execution time of the operations composing queries.

Summarizing, we assume that the duration of the execution of a relational operation depends on :
- the type of the operation /JOIN, UNION, etc.../,
- the cardinality of the data relation/s/ treated by the operation,
- the local external workload on the processing node.

The differences between local external workloads should be taken into account for the localization of non-localized operations of queries. In this meaning, external workload is an element of optimization.

Let us note that external workload can vary not only in space- from node to node - but also in time. In particular cases, on a node and at any time moment, it can be equal to zero.

4.2.2. Internal workload of DDBMS

At any time moment there is a set of queries in the system, and consequently a set of subqueries and relational operations are ready for execution. As was mentioned in Section 3, a node can execute one operation at a time which generally results in the introduction of some waits in the execution of operations. The quantity of work, at a time moment, resulting from the subqueries and relational operations submitted for execution is defined as the internal workload of DDBMS. Global and local internal workloads have exactly the same meaning as the respective external workloads. The internal workload evolves dynamically as queries arrive. The inequality of local int. workloads depends essentially on the quantitative distribution of stored data among the nodes and on the frequency of data accesses formulated in queries. For example, if 90% of data is stored in local data base A, and 10% only in data base B, then it is very likely that the local internal workload of A will be greater than the local internal workload of B. Moreover, there will be probably many more queries concerning only node A than node B.

5. A MODEL OF DISTRIBUTED PROCESSING

In this section we introduce a model which permits the reduction of the problem of distribute processing to a problem of optimization. This model expresses the architectural elements of DDBMS and the mechanism of distributed processing in new terminology specially adapted to optimization problems.

5.1. Distributed processors and queues

Hereafter, DDBMS will be considered as the set of distributed single processors each of them having an associated queue of processes. Generally, processes represent the quantity of processor time required to execute subqueries and the relational operations corresponding to them.

At a moment t, the state of the DDBMS can be represented as in Fig.3.

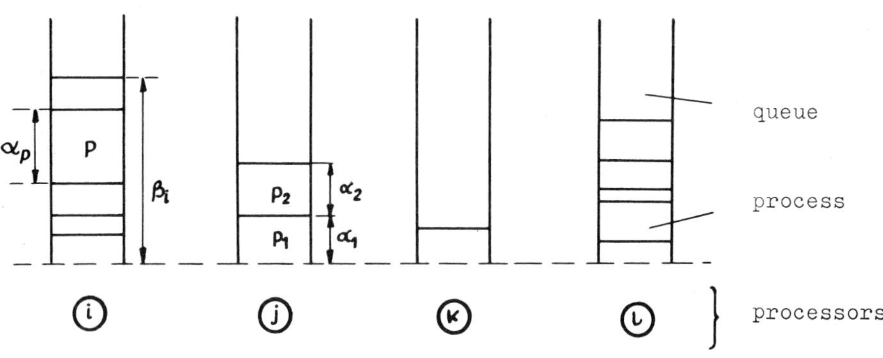

Figure 3
State of DDBMS at moment t

5.2. Distributed processes

As was mentioned, a process corresponds either to a relational operational operation or a subquery. In fact, it can also corresponds to several successive relational operations of the same binary tree if they are executed on the same node /e.g. , an operation JOIN followed by an operation SELECT or PROJECT/. On the other hand, a process can correspond to the whole set of operations composing a subquery. Of course, a single - node query is represented by one process.

In Fig.3 a process p is represented by length α_p in a queue. In accordance with the process definition, α_p represents the quantity of work to be performed, which is measured in required processor time. As was mentioned in Section 4.2.1. this time is influenced by the local external workload, i.e. for a given process p its length α_p increases when the local external workload increases.

At any time, local internal workload is defined as the sum of process lengths. In Fig.3, β_i represents the internal workload of node i. Let us note that in a queue only processes of DDBMS are represented and all other external jobs of the node modify only the respective lengths α and β . In other words, the local external workload is indirectly expressed in the notion and representation of the internal workload.

Let us now consider the relative position of two processors in the same queue. If the schedule on node j presented in Fig.3 is not modified, the execution of process p_1 will precede that of p_2. Moreover, if the execution of p_1 starts at t, then p_2 has to wait during α_1, the duration of the execution of p_1. Let us note that the relative position of a process in a schedule allows its completion time to be evaluated.

5.3. Binary tree of processes

Hereafter we will consider the progressive execution of the binary tree of processes corresponding to the relational binary tree. For example in Fig.1, there are seven processes:
- four localized processes corresponding to the subqueries, and,
- three non-localized processes, each of them corresponding to a relational operation.

The necessary transmissions of data and the "relations" between operations of the same tree, involve precedence relations between processes existing in the queues at a given time moment.

We distinguish four types of processes:
- <u>Receiver</u> : a process which can be executed if the reception of data transmitted by other processes /two at most/ is completed.
- <u>Sender</u> : a process which, at the end of its execution, has to transmit its results to a receiver on another node.
- <u>Non-sender</u> : A process whose results are held for a receiver on the node of its execution.
- <u>Terminal</u> : A process which is not followed by other processes; the results of a terminal constitute the final response to a query and can be sent to the user.

5.4 Binary sub-tree of processes

In this section, we introduce the notion of the binary sub-tree of processes. Every sub-tree is composed either
- of a receiver, a sender and a non -sender , or

- of a receiver and two different senders.

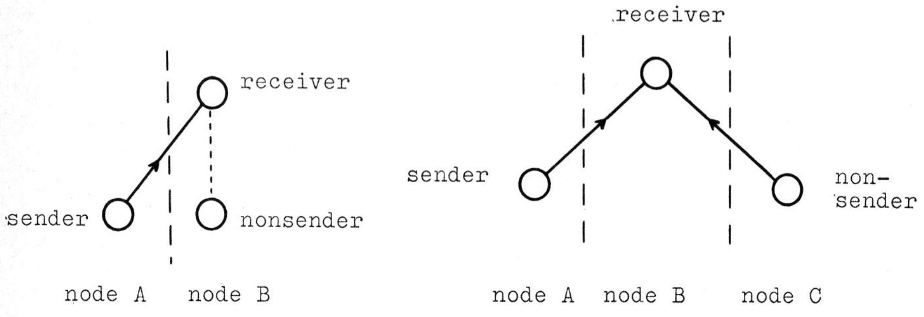

Figure 4
Types of binary sub-trees of processes

5.5. Processing a binary tree of processes

The problem of the processing of a tree can be reduced to the problem of progressive bottom up processing of many sub-trees, using all the possibilities of parallel processing of processes. For example, the tree presented in Fig.5 can be considered as being composed of three sub-trees : (P_1,P_2,P_3) , (P_4,P_5,P_6) , (P_3,P_6,P_7) .

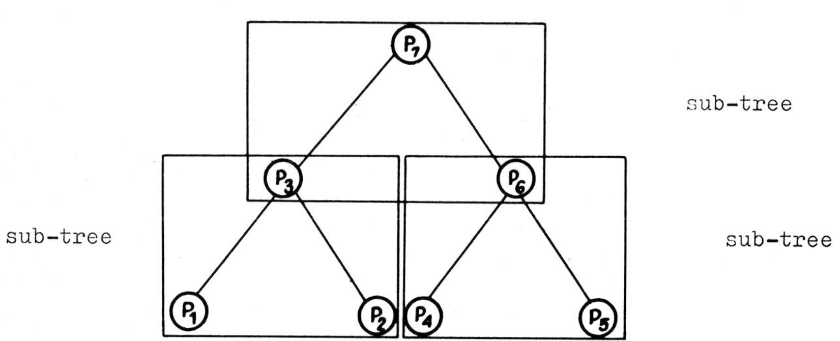

Figure 5
Adjacent sub-trees of a tree of processes

Let us note that if a process belongs to more than one sub-tree, it necessarily changes its type during processing. For example, in Fig.5 process P_3 belongs to sub-tree (P_1,P_2,P_3) where it is a receiver; then, at the processing of sub-tree (P_3,P_6,P_7) , it becomes either a sender or a non-sender.

5.6 Example of tree processing

In Fig.6 we show the way in which the tree presented in Fig.1 can be processed according to our model, we have arbitrarily localized processes P_3, P_6, P_7 on nodes B,C,D respectively. Fig.6 in particular shows the place and duration $\gamma_1, \gamma_2, \gamma_3$ of transmissions, and also the influence of the internal workload on the response time obtained for the query. In this example, we do not assume any particular type of relational operations.

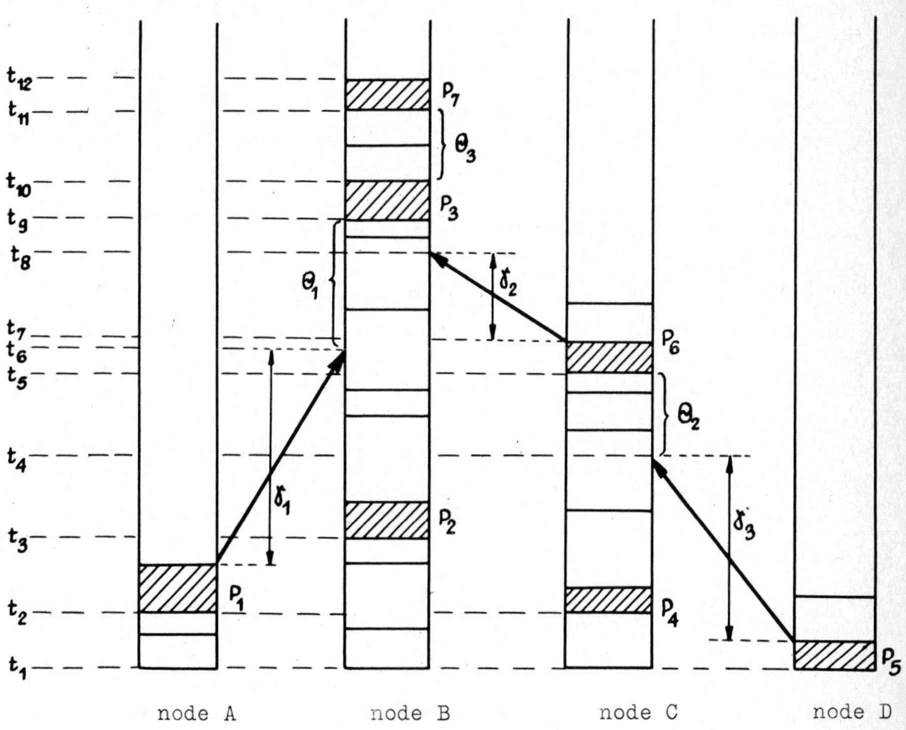

Figure 6

Evolution of the processing of a tree

1/ Sub-tree (P_1, P_2, P_3)
- t_2 : execution of sender P_1
- t_3 : execution of non-sender P_2,
- t_6 : completion of the transmission of P_1 results,
- t_9 : execution of receiver P_3.

2/ Sub-tree (P_4, P_5, P_6)
- t_1 : execution of sender P_5,
- t_2 : execution of non-sender P_4,
- t_4 : completion of the transmission of P_5 results,
- t_5 : execution of receiver P_6.

3/ Sub-tree (P_3, P_6, P_7)
- t_5 : execution of sender P_6,

t_8 : completion of the transmission of P_6 results,
t_9 : execution of non-sender P_3,
t_{11}: execution of terminal / receiver P_7,
t_{12}: completion of the execution of terminal P_7 and, as the result, whole tree.

6. HEURISTIC METHOD OF OPTIMIZATION

6.1. Principles

In this section we are looking for a method of optimization of query processing tending to minimize the mean response time of DDBMS. We consider two essential elements of optimization: transmission time and workload /see Section 4/. We are only looking for a heuristic method because of the dynamic evolution of system states and because of the impossibility of the instantaneous and precise evaluation of the optimization elements in the distributed enviroment. This method does not provide a theoretical evaluation of mean response time, but it is designed for direct control of the processing of each binary tree of processes in order to bring mean response time /even without its calculation/ near to the optimal value.

We distinguish three complementary levels of optimization in accordance with the model defined and presented in Section 5.:

- Optimization of tree structure : at the different levels of the binary tree of processes, we look for the optimal construction of sub-trees /Section 6.2/
- Optimization of sub-tree processing : for every sub-tree, we choose the optimal node for receiver execution ; of course, by determining the directions of data transmissions /Section 6.3/.
- Optimization of process scheduling : at every moment we look for the optimal schedule of processes in queues associated with nodes /Section 6.4/.

6.2 Optimization of tree structure

6.2.1. Choice of tree structure

As was shown in Section 5.5 the processing of a tree is performed bottom up including all possibilities of the parallel processing of sub-trees. This notion of parallelism defines levels of tree processing /e.g. levels (P_1,P_2,P_3) and (P_4,P_5,P_6) in Fig.5. Some cases of sub-queries and relational operation configurations admit different tree structures in the sense of there being many alternatives for sub-tree construction. Thus, the choice of a tree structure can be made from the optimality criterion point of view. Let us consider as an example the data base "PERSONS" distributed in the following way

T.ID*	CHILDREN	T.ID	PROFESSIONS	T.ID	CARS	T.ID	HOUSES
node A		node B		node C		node D	

Let us consider following query: "T.ID of all persons who have more

---

* t-uple identifier

than two children and whose profession is "engineer" and who have a car of type "Renault". As shown in Fig.7, three different tree structures are possible for this query.

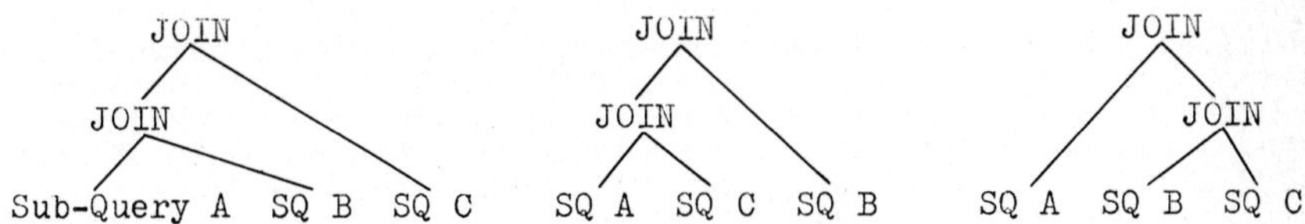

Figure 7
Structures of a tree composed of three subqueries.

In the same way, if we add a fourth condition, concerning the number of houses, to the former query, we will obtain three possible structures.

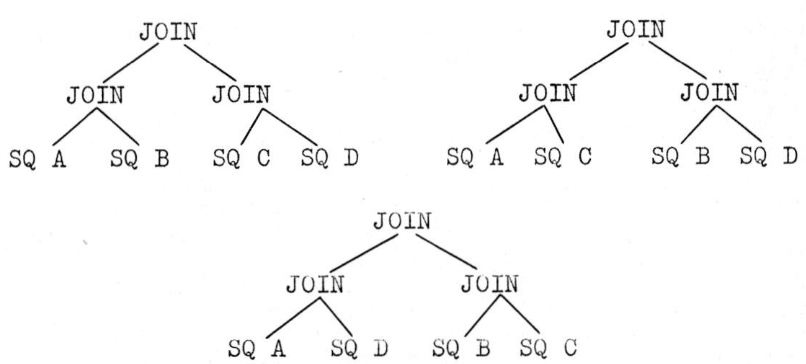

Figure 8
Structures of a tree composed of four subqueries

Let us note that these different structures are only admissible because of identical relational operators JOIN and identical domains of operations T.ID = T.ID .

6.2.2 Optimal sub-tree construction

During the processing of a tree, first, we have to identify all possible structure choices. In other words, at each level of tree processing, we have to associate processes, two by two, in order to construct the sub-trees. The principle element of optimization taken into account is the difference between local internal workloads in queues concerned with a given tree.

Let us now consider the tree presented in Fig.5; let us assume that there exist the possibilities of different constructions of both sub--trees at the lower level, i.e. that relational operations corresponding to processes P_3 and P_6 are identical, and are processed on the same domains. In our method we compare length β /see Fig.3/ of the appropriate queues concerned with the tree in order to estimate the moment of completion of each process P_1, P_2, P_4 and P_5. Then we associate processes two by two in such a way as to bring the expected moments of receiver execution P_3 and P_6 as close to each other as possible. In this manner we try to limit possible waits at higher levels in the tree. Let us note that the structure of a tree is defined dynamically during its processing.

6.2.3 Proposition

A solution can consist in the classification of nodes concerned with a given choice /for example, nodes A,B,C,D in Fig.6/ in the increasing order of their internal workloads. Then, the obtained sequence of nodes can be divided into two subsequences, one composed of weakly loaded nodes and the other of heavily loaded nodes. We propose to associate nodes, two by two, taking the first node of the first subsequence, then the third and so on.

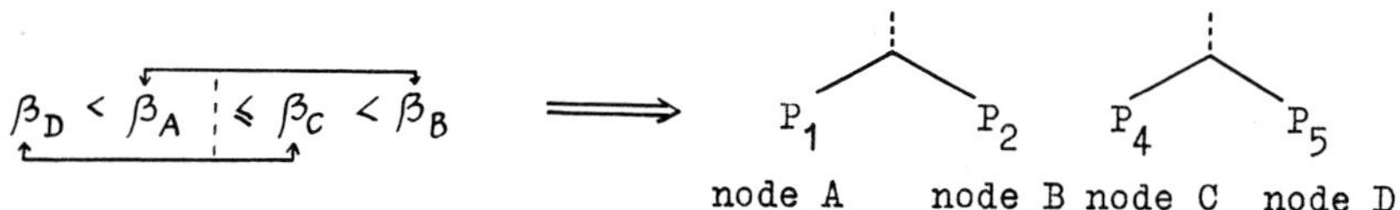

In this manner we hope to reduce gaps between the execution of receivers of the same tree processing level.

6.3 Optimization of sub-tree processing

Three processes constituting a sub-tree are given. Two of them - those ones from the lower level -have just been completed. We have to determine the localization of the receiver, and as a result, the directions of necessary transmissions , and concequently, the types of completed processes on the lower level; they may be sender and non-sender , or two senders. As can be seen in Fig.6, for sub-tree (P_1,P_2,P_3) we have chosen B as the node for P_3 execution and we have decided that P_1 is a sender /transmission time equal to γ_1/ and P_2 is a non-sender. The choice made introduce a waiting time equal to γ_1 . However a question arises: taking into account the volumes of data resulting from the execution of processes and respective local workloads in the system , is this choice the best one?

6.3.1 Trade-off between local workload and transmission time

In our method, we look for the optimal processing of a sub-tree taking into account two parameters : time of data transmission between the processes composing a sub-tree and the local workloads of different nodes.

Let us note that if the minimization of mean response time is considered as the system performance measure, minimal transmission time is not a sufficient condition to guarantee the optimality of the solution. Let us show in an example in which way local workloads and transmission times influence mean response time. Let us consider the processing of sub-tree (P_1,P_2,P_3) on two nodes A and B, P_3 being a receiver. The real problem of receiver P_3 localization arises in the case when:

- there is a significant difference between local workloads of nodes A and B /A highly loaded in comparison with B/, and
- volume of data for transmission from node A to node B is much greater than that for transmission from B to A.

We have two possible solutions.

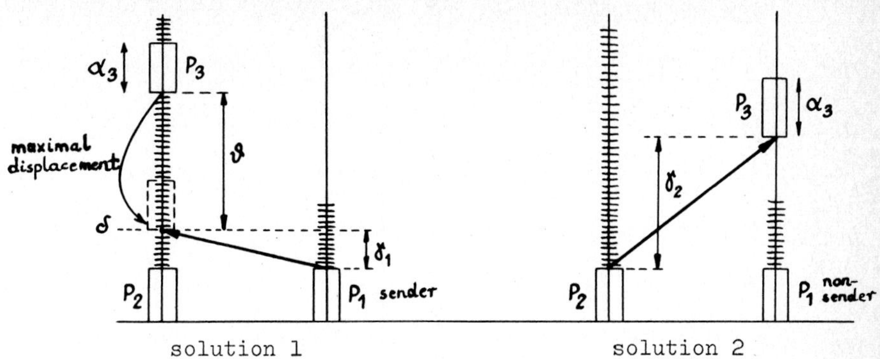

Figure 9
Receiver localization according to
- minimum transmission time /solution 1/
- minimum local internal workload /solution 2/

Solution 1: Receiver localization according to minimum transmission. Transmission is made from node B to node A; process P_1 is decided to be the sender. Receiver P_3 can be executed on node A after moment δ which corresponds to the end of transmission; however, queue A is highly loaded. Now, two cases are possible:

- because of the high workload on node A, waiting time θ is imposed on receiver P_3; this time is damaging for sub-tree (P_1,P_2,P_3).
- process P_3 can be displaced in order to be executed at moment δ ; if such displacement is permitted /cf. 6.4/, sub-tree (P_1, P_2,P_3) is rapidly processed but the execution time α_3 of P_3 damages the mean response time /cf.6.4.2/ in introducing a wait time α_3 affecting all the processes which are following P_3 in the queue.

Solution 2 : Receiver localization according to minimum local workload.

Process P_2 is decided to be the sender; transmission time γ_2 is long compared to time γ_1 /solution 1/. However, the execution time α_3 of P_3 does not influence other tree executions and does not introduce any wait time.

Now, it is necessary to make a decision : which one of the two above solutions should be applied ? To this end, the relative importance of the difference in local workloads and the difference between transmission times has to be examined. However a difficult problem which must be solved is that of recent and periodical knowledge of transmission times on distributed nodes. We examine this problem in the next section.

6.3.2 As asynchronic approach to data exchange during tree processing

In accordance with Assumption 3 before the processing of a sub-tree we have no information allowing volumes of data to be predicted. As a result we assume that decisions concerning receiver localization are made dynamically, during sub-tree processing, at the moment when the necessary information is available.
Moreover we do not require any synchronization between two or more

nodes in order to evaluate and compare volumes of data for transmitting.
Examining sub-tree processing from the point of view of decisions concerning receiver localization, we can distinguish two situations presented in Fig.10. As previously process P_3 is receiver of sub-tree (P_1,P_2,P_3) .

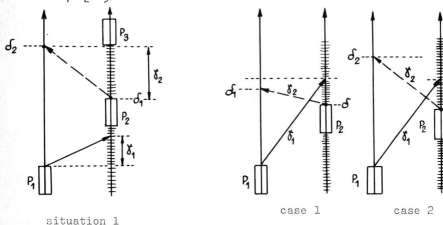

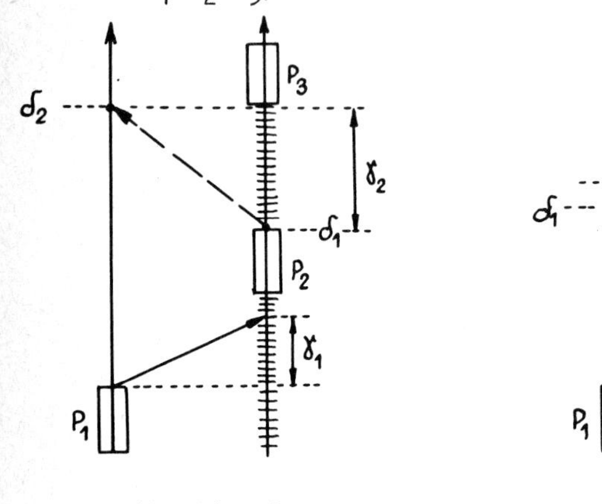

Figure 10
Data exchange and process execution

Situation 1: The completion of P_1 data transmission precedes P_2 execution. This situation arises when workload inequality significantly delays the execution of one process (P_2) in comparison with the other (P_1) . P_1, at the end of its execution, becomes sender and transmits data towards P_2. When data transmission is completed, P_2 is not yet executed.
The decision of P_3 localization is made at δ_1 /the end of P_2 execution/, since at this moment there is enough information about local workloads and transmission times. The workload of node B is known precisely; information about the workload on node A can be systematically provided to node B /and vice versa/ either by a special mechanism of message switshing or by information added to each data message /of course, some delay cannot be avoided/; and the time of P_2 data transmission from B to A can be calculated as a function of data volume which is known since P_2 is completed. Thus, the localization of P_3 on B /without the second data transmission but with possible great delay resulting from high local workload/ or on A /repeated data transmission but execution without delay/ can be decided upon. This decision is made on the basis of the comparison of the contribution to mean response time in the cases of P_3 localization on B or A. /cf.6.3.1/.

Situation 2 : The completion of P_2 execution precedes the completion of P_1 data transmission. In this situation, the decision about P_3 localization can be made in the same way as in Situation I at the moment of P_2 completion (δ) if we assume only that the volume of P_1 data transmission is indicated at the head of the message. In the case of localization of P_3 on A, the remaining part of P_1 data transmission can be deleted. Let us note that generally it can happen that the completion of P_2 data transmission precedes at of P_1 /case 1/.

6.3.3 Choice of a third node for receiver execution

In Sections 6.3.1 and 6.3.2 we have supposed that a sub-tree is always processed on two nodes and, besides the receiver, it is composed of a sender and a non-sender. In fact, in some cases it can be profitable to use a third node for the receiver; then two senders compose the sub-tree.
Let us suppose /Fig.11/ that processes P_1 and P_2 have to be executed on nodes A and B respectively; these two nodes are highly loaded while the workload of another node C is equal to zero. Let us consider the advantages and disadvantages of three possible localization of P_3. We assume that transmission time γ_1, is longer than γ_2.

Situation 1 : Localization of P_3 on A.
This choice corresponds to the minimal transmission time γ_2 for sub-tree (P_1,P_2,P_3) but the execution of P_3 will be significantly delayed because of the workload on A, or, if displaced, it introduces delays for many other queries.

Situation 2 : Localization of P_3 on B.
In this situation, transmission time γ_1, for sub-tree (P_1,P_2,P_3) is maximal and the local workload on B is not negligible but less than that on A. The choice between A and B is made as proposed in Section 6.3.1.

Situation 3 : Localization of P_3 on C.
In this situation, two transmissions have to be made. P_3 execution will immediately follow the longer transmission γ_1, since the local workload of C is equal to zero. Thus, from the point of view of transmission durations, Situations 3 corresponds to Situations 2, but in this case no waits are introduced either for P_3 or for other processes in queue C. It seems to be clear that Situation 3 is better that Situation 2. However, it can still be compared with Situation 1. The higher the workload on A and the smaller the inequality between transmission times, the more beneficial is Situation 3.

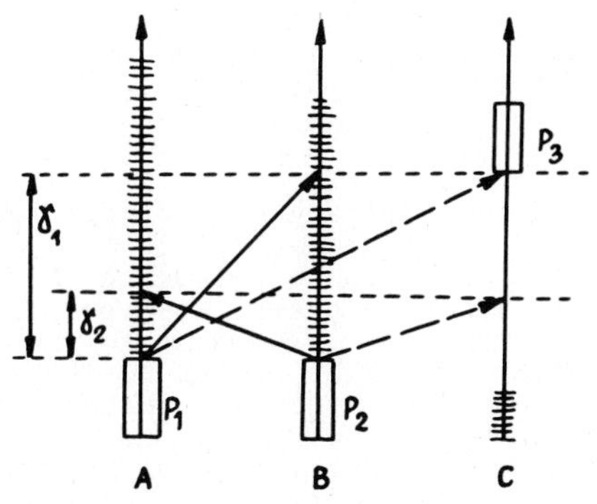

Figure 11
Receiver execution on a third node

6.4. Optimization of process scheduling

In Section 6.3 we mentioned the possibility of process displacements in queues. In this section, we will show that modification of process schedules can improve mean response time. Thus, we allow the order of process execution to be different from the arrival order.

6.4.1 Possibilities of process displacement

We will consider the influence of displacement of processes of different types on the response time obtained.

a/ Displacement of a receiver
Delay in the execution of a terminal receiver will cause an increase in the response time of a query. On the contrary, any advance of terminal receiver execution improves response time by reducing the waiting time θ which follows the moment δ of the completion of data transmission. Of course, the displacement of a receiver is constrained simultaneously by the completion of data transmission from a sender /or senders/ and the completion of non-sender execution /see Cases 1 and 2 in Fig.12/.

b/ Displacement of a sender
The displacement of a sender results in modifying one of two constraints put on the beginning of receiver execution, namely the moment δ of transmission completion. Let us note that in Case 2 presented in Fig.12, the displacement of the sender up to moment ε has no influence on the response time of the query.

c/ Displacement of a non-sender
As in the preceeding case, the displacement of a non-sender may /but not necessarily/ modify constraint δ of receiver execution. For exemple, in Case 1, presented in Fig.12, non-sender displacement up to moment δ will have no influence on the response time of the query.

d/ Displacement of a terminal
From the point of view of the response time of a query, it is always profitable to advance terminal execution since its completion is equivalent to the total completion of the query processing. In the case when the terminal is the single process of a single - node query, there are no constraints put on its displacement. On the contrary in the case of multi - node queries, all the constraints concerning receivers have to be respected.

6.4.2. Influence of process displacement on mean response time

In the previous section, we have discussed the influence of process displacement on the response time of a query. However, in a multi - query environment, the advancement of a process belonging to a query results in delaying other processes belonging to other queries. The possibility of process displacement introduce the problem of competition among processes. Thus, in any case of process displacement, it is necessary, to consider its total influence on the response times of all queries concerned, or in other words, to consider the contribution of process displacement to mean response time. In this way, one may tradeoff the response time improvement in some queries against the deterioration in others. Let us now consider an example /Fig.13/ of such a mutual displacement of sender P_{1j} belonging to query j and non-sender P_2; belonging to query i. As can be seen from Fig.13 and the calculations presented below, this displacement is profitable from the mean response time point of view since the response time of query j decreases while the response time of query i does not change.

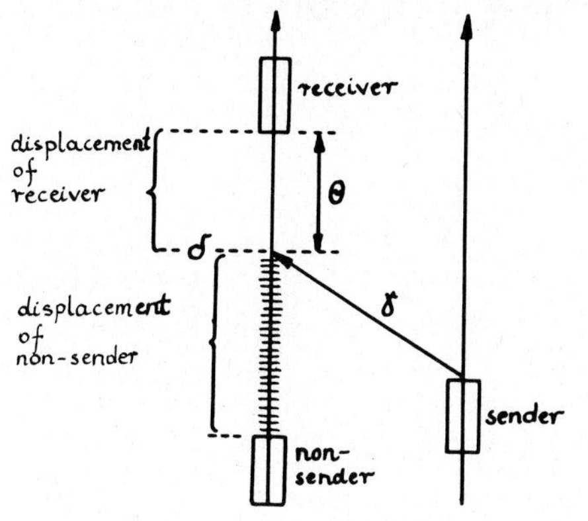

case 1
Transmission completed after non-sender execution

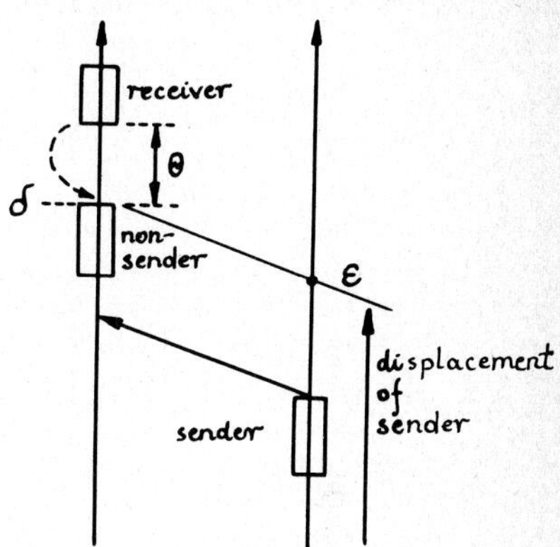

case 2
Transmission completed before non-sender execution

Figure 12
Process displacement possibilities

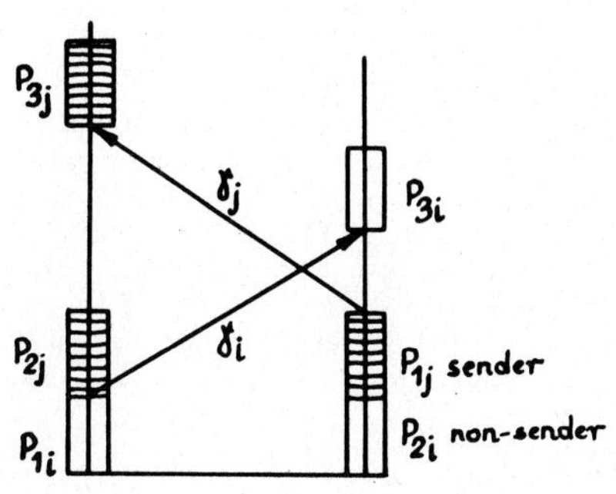

case 1

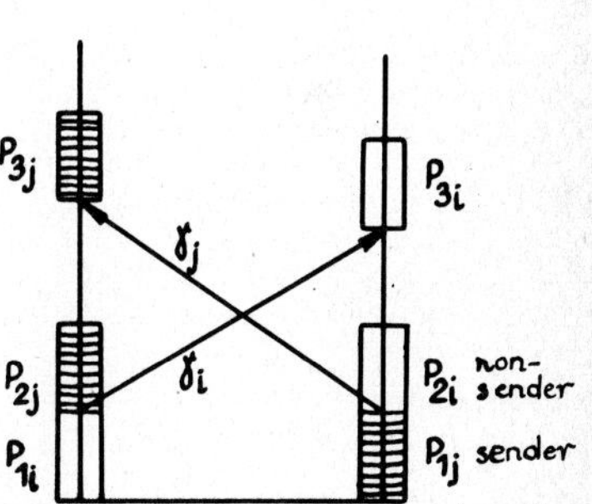

case 2

query i (P_{1i}, P_{2i}, P_{3i})
query j (P_{1j}, P_{2j}, P_{3j})

Figure 13
Process scheduling in the case of two sub-trees

Let us calculate the mean response time MRT for both cases:

$$MRT = 1/2\left[RT_i + RT_j \right]$$

RT : response time
$T(P_i)$: execution time of process P_i

case 1 : $MRT_1 = 1/2\left[\left(T(P_{1i}) + \gamma_i + T(P_{3i})\right) + \left(T(P_{2i}) + T(P_{1j}) + \gamma_j + T(P_{3j})\right)\right]$

case 1 : $MRT_2 = 1/2\left[\left(T(P_{1i}) + \gamma_i + T(P_{3i})\right) + \left(T(P_{1j}) + \gamma_j + T(P_{3j})\right)\right]$

thus, the difference

$$MRT_1 - MRT_2 = 1/2\ T(P_{2i}) > 0$$

As can be seen, the second schedule is better, since its mean response time is less than the mean response time of the first schedule.

With some simplifying assumptions, we have developed in [2] the notion of distributed process scheduling.

6.4.3 Scheduling in accordance with process execution times

In the previous section, we have shown that the mean response time can be improved by process scheduling in accordance with process types : it was profitable to execute sender P_{1j} before non-sender P_{2i} and not vice versa.

However another reason can also be taken unto account in process scheduling, namely the execution times of processes. In accordance with the well known general rules of scheduling , to minimize mean response time, processes have to be ordered in ascending order of their execution times. Let us consider as an example two processes P_1 and P_2 with execution times α_1 and α_2 respectively:

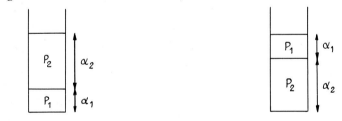

$$MRT_1 = \frac{RT_1 + RT_2}{2} = \frac{\alpha_1 + (\alpha_1 + \alpha_2)}{2} \qquad MRT_2 = \frac{RT_1 + RT_2}{2} = \frac{\alpha_2 + (\alpha_1 + \alpha_2)}{2}$$

$$MRT_1 - MRT_2 = 1/2\ (\alpha_1 - \alpha_2)$$

Since $\alpha_1 < \alpha_2$ then, $MRT_1 < MRT_2$; we conclude that the first schedule is better than the second one.

In accordance with the general rule mentioned above, we will always try to advance short processes, however, taking into account all constraints

6.4.4 Example of process scheduling

In the following example, we show a way in which process types and process execution times can be simultaneously taken into account in scheduling policy. However, let us note that the comparison of some processes is very difficult , so more than one schedule could be valid. Five queries are given: R_a, R_b, R_c, R_d, R_e. As shown in Fig.14, we propose the following schedule.

- three terminal processes P_e, P_c and P_b are scheduled as the first ones in ascending order of their execution times. Thus, the three corresponding queries can be completed quickly;
- moment δ_a corresponds to the completion of data transmission for process P_a. Since it cannot be executed earlier it is scheduled as the last one;
- the order of P_a and P_d is chosen arbitrarily; there is no information concerning the respective receivers and thus this choice cannot be justifies.

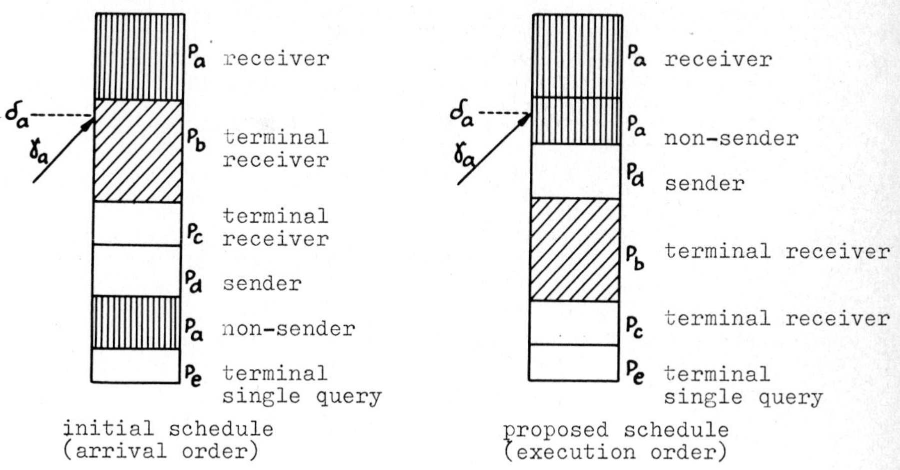

Figure 14
Example of process scheduling

7. WORKLOAD EVALUATION

In this section we would like to make some comments on dynamic workload evaluation in the system. Of course, it is unreasonable for processors to inform all others of queue length changes every time they occur. However, we suppose that the queue length will not vary very rapidly, because of the fixed distribution of data. Thus, we propose to distinguish some levels of queue length and to distribute only information about changes in queue length levels on a given processor. This will result in keeping communication within reasonable limits and should be enough for query processing optimization. Of course, studies are necessary on the interdependenc of the precision of the queue length level determination and the benefits of query processing optimization.

8. CONCLUSIONS

The natural aim of obtaining as great system efficiency as possible results in the need for system performance optimization. We are concerned with system performance optimization in distributed systems which, from a very general point of view are designed for the purpose of establishing direct and close connections among many different groups of users, like the different services of an enterprise, or different commercial agencies, etc. On the other hand, from the economic point of view the implementation and maintenance of such systems is profitable only when high utilization is ensured, that is, when it is shared by many users. The notion of "distribution" is closely connected with the notion of "sharing" in the meaning of simultaneous use.

This multi-use nature of a distributed system must be taken into account in the optimization procedure. For this reason, we propose a multi-query approach to the optimization of query processing in relational DDBMS. The originality of this approach consists in:
- the use of mean response time as a system performance measure,
- taking into account simultaneously workload and transmission times as optimization elements,
- introducing a model definition allowing problems of distributed processing to be expressed,
- the decomposition of the general optimization problem to three complementary levels:
  - . choice of the optimal tree structure for a query,
  - . localization of non-localized operations , and
  - . process scheduling.

The heuristic method of distributed processing optimization presented in this paper is based on all principles listed above. However, we are conscious that this method does not provide a definitive solution and that its further development is necessary.

Moreover, some problems were not considered in this paper, for example distributed process management, and the specific constraints on query processing imposed by updates.

8. REFERENCES

1 CALECA,J.Y.: L'expression et la décomposition de transactions dans un système de bases de données réparties; These, Universite de Grenoble, sept.78.

2 CELLARY,W., MEYER,D ; A simple model od request scheduling in distributed data base systems ; Report FICHI-069, I.R.I.A. /Project SIRIUS/, sept.79.

3 CODD, E.F.; A relational model od data for large shared data banks ; Comm. ACM 13, no 6, june 70.

4 EPSTEIN,P., STONEBRAKER,M., WONG,E.: Distributed query processing in a relational data base system ; University of California, Berkeley 94720, april 78.

5 GOMEZ,R., JACROT,M.; Résolution de questions sur une base de données repartie ; Report 77007 I.R.I.A. /project SIRIUS/, june 78

6 LE BIHAN,J.: Les fonctions d'un S.G.B.D.R. Premiere ebauche de definition Raport SCH.I.021 I.R.I.A. /project SIRIUS/ sept.77.

7 LITWIN,W.: Distributed data bases: a way of thinking about ; IRIA/IGDB Seminar on Distributed Data Sharing Systems, Aix-en-Provence /France/, may 79

8 NGUYEN,G.T.: Optimization de réquetes relationnelles sur des bases de donnees reparties ; Report 78008 I.R.I.A. /project SIRIUS/, sept.78.

9 NGUYEN,G.T.: Interpretation asynchrone de réquetes relationnelles sur des bases de données reparties; Lab. d'Informatique,

Univ. de Grenoble 38 041 Grenoble, jan.79
10 NGUYEN,G.T.: A unified method for query decomposition and shared information updating in distributed systems ; Lab. d'Informatique, Univ. de Grenoble, 38041 Grenoble, apr.79.
11 PAIK,I.S., DELOBEL,C.: A strategy for optimizing the distributed query processing; Lab. d'Informatique, Univ. de Grenoble, 38 041 Grenoble, apr.79.
12 ROTHNIE,J.B., GOODMAN,N., et al ; A Distributed Database Management System for Command and Control Applications ; Report CCA-78-03, jan.78
13 SMITH, J.M., CHANG,P.Y-T.; Optimizing the Performance of a Relational Algebra Database Interface; Comm. ACM 18, no 10, oct.75
14 STONEBRAKER,M., NEUHOLD, E.: A distributed data base version of INGRES ; Univ. of California, Berkeley 94720, 1976
15 YAO,B., HEVNER : Query processing on a distributed data base ; Proc. Third Berkeley Workshop on Distributed Data Management, aug.78.

Footnotes

1. On leave from the Technical University of Poznan, Poznan, Poland.
2. On leave from I.R.I.A. (Project SIRIUS).
   The researches were partially sponsered by I.R.I.A. under contract No. 97loo.

DISTRIBUTED DATA BASES
C. Delobel and W. Litwin (eds.)
North-Holland Publishing Company

Data Distribution Criteria and Query Processing Strategy in a small distributed environment

C. CARLESI - E. RICCIARDI - C. THANOS
Istituto di Elaborazione dell'Informazione
Via S. Maria, 46, PISA - Italy

C. PETACCHI
CNUCE
Via S. Maria, 36, PISA - Italy

Abstract

This paper describes the data distribution criteria and the query processing strategy which have been adopted in a distributed data base management system running on a network of mini-computers. This system is now being implemented at the Istituto di Elaborazione dell'Informazione of the Italian National Research Council, in Pisa.

1. Introduction

A relational distributed data base system, running on a network of mini-computers, is being designed and implemented at the Istituto di Elaborazione della Informazione (I.E.I.) - Pisa, Italy.
The system will be initially supported by a network of three mini-computers:

PDP-11 series 70
PDP-11 series 34
PDP-11 series 40.

The RSX-11M operating system runs on each of these mini-computers. The communication facility is DECNET, a package supplied by the Digital Equipment Corporation. The three mini-computers are located at different Institutes in Pisa. The network is, therefore, homogeneous.
The same system operates on each node of the network. The basic elements of the system architecture are:

- User Interface
- Distribution Module
- Message Handler
- Centralised Relational Data Base Management System (DETAREL)
- Communication facility (DECNET) (Fig. 1).

The User Interface handles the user/system interaction.
The Distribution Module makes the geographical data distribution transparent to the user.
The Message Handler functions as an interface between the Distribution Module and the Communication System.

DETAREL is a centralised data base management system based on the relational data model and running on a mini-computer. It has a non-procedural data manipulation language which uses a decision table support. This language can be used as a self-contained language or incorporated into the FORTRAN programming language (2), (4), (5), (6).
DECNET creates a communication mechanism between objects residing on different nodes of the network. This mechanism allows logical communication channels to be defined so that I/O devices, programs and files can exchange information.
This paper will discuss in detail the data distribution criteria and the query processing strategies.

2. Data Distribution Criteria

The data base is organised according to the relational data model and thus consists of a set of relations. The relations can be divided into:

- local relations
- distributed relations.

Local relations are relations created on one node and accessible only from this node.
Distributed relations are relations which are partitioned into a number of parts and geographically located on the nodes throughout the network. Distributed relations are partitioned horizontally using a distribution predicate. This predicate is a restriction imposed on an attribute of the relation so that a tuple sub-set of the relation can be identified univocally, e.g. in Fig. 2 the relation, Book, is divided according to the predicate: LIBRARY = "constant".
The tuples which satisfy the predicate LIBRARY = "IEI" are located on node 1, those which satisfy the predicate LIBRARY = "SNS" are located on node 2, those which satisfy the predicate LIBRARY = "ISI" are located on node 3, and those satisfying the predicate LIBRARY = "INFN" are located on node 4.
The relation is thus divided into a number of parts, called fragments, which do not have any tuples in common and therefore if they are reassembled the original relation will be reproduced without any redundancy.
The distribution predicate is a simple restriction, i.e. a boolean expression of the form:

<attribute name><rel-op><constant>

where <rel-op> is =,=,>,< e.t.c.

The attribute on which a distribution predicate is defined is called the distribution attribute. Only privileged users are permitted to make update operations on values of this attribute as they can result in the transfer of a tuple from one node to another. It is clear that, in this way, the distribution of a fragment to a node is dependent on its semantics.
A relation can be divided into:

- primary fragments
- secondary fragments.

Primary fragments are the distinct and non-overlapping (not even slightly) parts into which a relation is divided, according to the distribution predicate, e.g., in Fig. 2 the relation BOOK has been divided into 4 primary fragments. All the operations provided by the data manipulation language can be processed on these fragments.
The secondary fragments provide the meccanism to describe relation partitions which exist at other nodes and can be either:

- replicated fragments
- virtual fragments.

Replicated fragments are copies of the primary fragments and can be accessed locally on remote nodes only for read type operations. For update, delete and insert operations the replicated fragment provokes automatic access to its corresponding primary fragment.
The virtual fragment does not actually contain data but is used to access automatically to the primary fragments.
Fig. 3 shows a possible distribution for the relation BOOK. The straight line rectangles represent the primary fragments; the dashed line rectangles represent the replicated fragments; the dotted line rectangles represent the virtual fragments.
A fundamental choice has been to allow the user to access from a node only those data which have been defined on that node as primary, replicated or virtual fragments, i.e. if a fragment has not been defined on a node then it can not be accessed from that node.
In Fig. 3, fragments F1 and F3 cannot be accessed from node 2; fragments F1 and F4 cannot be accessed from node 3; fragment F2 cannot be accessed from node 4; however, the whole relation can be accessed from node 1.

2.1 Data Base Creation on a Node

A data base is created on a node using a data definition language. The syntax of this language is given in Appendix A.
The creation of a distribuited relation on a node implies the creation of the primary and secondary fragments which can be accessed from that node.
The creation of a primary fragment implies the definition of the nodes where replicated or virtual fragments of the primary fragment can be located. Before creating a replicated fragment, authorisation must be requested from the node where the primary fragment is located. The deletion of a primary fragment implies the deletion of all its replicated or virtual fragments. The deletion of a replicated or virtual fragment, however, has no consequences.
As an example, the creation of the relation BOOK on node 1 is shown in Fig. 3.

```
CREATE  RELATION  BOOK
     ATTRIBUTES: 5
                 CODE, CHARACTER, 6, KEY
                 TITLE, CHARACTER, 60
                 AUTHOR, CHARACTER, 20, INDEXED
                 SUBJECT, CHARACTER, 15, INDEXED
                 LIBRARY, CHARACTER, 10, DA

     PRIMARY FRAGMENT
```

```
          DISTRIBUTION PREDICATE: LIBRARY = "IEI"
          REPLICATED AT <NODE 4>
     REPLICATED FRAGMENT
          DISTRIBUTION PREDICATE: LIBRARY = "SNS", NODE 2
     REPLICATED FRAGMENT
          DISTRIBUTION PREDICATE: LIBRARY = "ISI", NODE 3
     VIRTUAL FRAGMENT
          DISTRIBUTION PREDICATE: LIBRARY = "INFN", NODE 4
END RELATION BOOKS
```

2.2 Comments

The approach adopted for the data distribution has some interesting aspects. The data base can be partitioned and replicated using the virtual and replicated fragments. The relations containing these fragments can be "overlapping" or "non-overlapping" depending on whether a given secondary fragment can or cannot contain a copy of its primary fragment. The above example represents a partitioned, replicated and overlapping relation.

It should be noted that our approach does not offer a centralised or decentralised global description of the data. In fact it is not essential to have all the information on the distribution of the relations on the network in order to specify and create a data base on a particular node. In the example given in Fig. 3, the different nodes need only know the location of the primary fragments which interest them. For example, if node 2 intends to keep a copy of the primary fragment F4, the authorisation necessary must be specified in the schema of node 4; node 2 must then authorise nodes 1 and 3 to keep a copy of fragment F2. However, node 2 is in no way aware of the primary fragments F1 and F3, or of the fact that node 1 contains a virtual fragment of the primary fragment F4. Although this strategy lacks the coordination and cooperation offered by a global schema, it does offer a great flexibility in the distribution, partition and replication of the relation on the network as the architecture is determined at the node level. With this approach, it is the responsibility of the data base administrator, at the individual nodes which desire to share data, to agree upon its logical structure and distribution. This is an additional advantage as the restructuring and the redistribution of a relation interests only those nodes directly involved.

3. Query Processing Strategy

3.1 Data Manipulation Language

The DETAREL DML can be used as a self-contained language or incorporated into the FORTRAN programming language, (2), (4), (5).

The operations permitted are the retrieval or update, deletion of information already existing in the data base or the insert of new information.

A decision table is basically divided into four quadrants (Fig. 4). The upper left quadrant contains all the conditions being examined for a particular problem.

The upper right quadrant contains the condition entries. These can be either Y (true), N (false) or a blank (irrelevant condition). A column of condition entries is called a rule.

The lower left quadrant contains the list of DML actions to be executed once the conditions are verified.

The lower right quadrant contains the action entries; these specify the commands to be executed for the corresponding rule. The conditions make it possible to determine, using the entries given in the rules, the actions which should be executed.
A rule is satisfied once the conditions which it contains have been satisfied.
The commands which correspond to the action entries are executed for each rule when it has been satisfied. These actions are executed in a given order when this has been specified by the entries.

3.2 Decomposition of a Query

All queries involving more than one relation are decomposed into sub-queries which involve single relations.
In the examples given below a data base is used which consists of the following relations:

BOOK (CODE, TITLE, AUTHOR, SUBJECT, LIBRARY)
LOAN (CODE, NAME, ADDRESS, TELEPHONE, INSTITUTE)

Example: Find the addresses of everyone who has borrowed books with the subject "Computer Sciences" and the author "Smith". (Fig. 5)

Find the addresses of everyone who has borrowed books with the subject "Computer Sciences" or "Physics" from the IEI library. (Fig. 6)

3.3 Query Processing on one Relation

The qualifying part of a query which involves a single relation can have the following forms:

A	C1∧C2∧...
A1	C1∧⌉C2∧...
B	C1∨C2∨...
B1	C1∨⌉C2...
C	(C1∧C2∧..)∨(Ci∧Ci+1∧..)∨...
C1	(C1∧⌉C2∧..)∨(Ci∧Ci+1∧..)∨...
D	(C1∨C2∨..)∧(Ci∨Ci+1∨..)∧...
D1	(C1∨⌉C2∨..)∧(Ci∨Ci+1∨..)∧...

where Ci is a restriction imposed on an attribute of the relation.
Usually two cases can be distinguished:

a) the distribution predicate is included in the conditions forming the qualifying part of the query;
b) the distribution predicate is not included in the conditions forming the qualifying part of the query.

Let us examine the different forms of the qualifying part of a query with respect to the two cases given above:

Aa) In this case (the distribution predicate is included in the Ci's) the Distribution Module must choose one of the following alternatives:

1) process the query on the local primary fragment;

2) process the query on the local replicated fragment, if the query is read only;
3) send the query to a node with a primary fragment referenced by a local virtual fragment (or a replicated fragment when the query is not read only);

Ab) In this case the Distribution Module must process the query on the local primary fragment (and on the local replicated fragments for read only operations); and simultaneously
- send the query to all the nodes with a primary fragment referenced by a local virtual fragment (and/or a replicated fragment when the operation is not read only).
In Figs. 7 and 8, two examples are given representing cases Aa and Ab, respectively. (The predicate LIBRARY = "constant" is taken as the distribution predicate).

A1a) This case only differs from Aa when the distribution predicate is negated. (See Fig. 9).

In this case, the Distribution Module must:
- process the query on the local primary fragment (and on the local replicated fragments for read only operations) as long as the predicate LIBRARY = IEI is not satisfied in the local node;
- send the query to all the nodes which contain the primary fragment referenced by the local virtual fragment (and/or by the replicated fragments when the operations are not read only) except for the node where the distribution predicate, LIBRARY = IEI, is satisfied.

A1b) This case is the same as Ab.

Ba) In this case, the query

Q WHERE C1∨C2∨...∨Ci-1∨Ci ...

where Ci is the distibution predicate, is decomposed into two queries:

Q WHERE C1∨C2∨...∨Ci-1∨Ci∨...
Q WHERE C1∨C2∨...∨Ci-1∨Ci+1∨...

The first query is processed on the node which contains a primary fragment (satisfying the distribution predicate Ci) referenced by the local virtual/replicated fragment or, alternatively, (for read only operations) this query is processed on the local node if this contains a replicated fragment of a primary fragment satisfying the distribution predicate.
The second query is processed on all the nodes (apart from nodes where the first query was processed) which contain a primary fragment referenced by the local virtual fragment (and/or a replicated fragment for not read only operations).
Figs. 10 and 11 give an example of how the two are produced from the original query.

Bb) This case is the same as Ab.

B1a) This case is only different from Ba if the distribution predicate is negated; two queries are again produced:

Q WHERE C1∨C2∨..∨Ci-1∨ Ci∨Ci+1 ...
Q WHERE C1∨C2∨..∨Ci-1∨Ci+1

The first query is processed on all the nodes which contain a primary fragment (which does not satisfy the distribution predicate) referenced by the local virtual fragment (and/or replicated fragments for not read only operations).
The second query is processed on the node which contains a primary fragment (satisfying the distribution predicate) referenced by a local virtual/replicated fragment.
It can be seen that this case is symetrically the same as Ba.

B1b) This case is the same as Bb.

Ca) In this case, the original query

Q WHERE
(C1∧C2)∨(C3∧C4)∨...∨(Ci-1∧Ci)∨(Ci+1∧Ci+2)∨...

(where Ci is the distribution predicate) is decomposed into the following queries:

Q WHERE
(C1∧C2)∨(C3∧C4)∨...∨(Ci-1∧Ci)∨(Ci+1∧Ci+2)∨...
Q WHERE (C1∧C2)∨(C3∧C4)∨...∨(Ci+1∧Ci+2)∨...

The first of these two queries is sent to a node which contains a primary fragment (satisfying the distribution predicate) referenced by the local virtual/replicated fragment.
The second query is sent to nodes (with the exception of the above node) which have a primary fragment referenced by a local virtual/replicated fragment.

Example: Find the titles of Books with Author "Smith" and Subject "Computer Science" or with Subject "Mathematics" and which can be found in the IEI library.

The two queries produced are shown in Figs. 12 and 13.

Cb) This case is the same as Bb.

C1a) This case only differs from Ca if the distribution predicate is negated. However, the query processing strategy is symetrically the same as Ca.

c1b) This case is the same as Cb.

D) When the query is:

Q WHERE (C1∨C2)∧(C3∨C4)∧...

it is preferable to transform it into the equivalent expression:

Q WHERE (∧)∨(∧)∨ ...

this case is the same as C, described above.
Example: Find the titles of books with Subject "Computer Science" or "Mathematics" and which or can be found in the

IEI library or have as Author "Smith" (fig. 14).
In this case, the expression

$(Ci \vee C2) \wedge (C3 \vee C4)$

is transformed into its equivalent

$((C1 \vee C2) \wedge C3) \vee ((C1 \vee C2) \wedge C4)$

and processed as described for C above.

4. Conclusions

This paper has described the data distribution criteria and the query processing strategy which have been adopted in a distributed data base management system running on a network of mini-computers. This system is now being implemented at the Istituto di Elaborazione dell'Informazione of the Italian National Research Council, in Pisa.
The data distribution criteria adopted offer both simplicity and flexibility in the distribution, partitioning and replication of the relations. The query processing strategy does not take into consideration questions of costs and transmission delays.
The objective of our project was to create an experimental distributed environment in which a number of alternatives could be tried and tested. For this reason we have implemented a modular system so that, in the future, it will be possible to alter or substitute the modules, as required.

Appendix A

Data Definition Language

```
CREATE USER <user-code><data-base-name>
DELETE USER <user-code>
ASSIGN RELATION <relation-name><data-base-name>
                <user-code><access-mode>

CREATE DATA BASE <data-base-name>
DELETE DATA BASE <data-base-name>

CREATE RELATION <relation-name>
       ATTRIBUTES:<attribute number> <attribute name>,
                  <attribute type>,<attribute length>,
                <key> <indexed> <da> <da> <indexed>

       PRIMARY FRAGMENT:
       DISTRIBUTION PREDICATE:<value>
       REPLICATED AT <node i>
       VIEWED AT <node i>

       REPLICATED FRAGMENT
       DISTRIBUTION PREDICATE:<value><node i>

       VIRTUAL FRAGMENT
       DISTRIBUTION PREDICATE:<value><node i>

       END RELATION
       DELETE RELATION <relation name><data base name>
       <PRIMARY FRAGMENT>
       <REPLICATED FRAGMENT>
       DISTRIBUTION PREDICATE:<value>
       <VIRTUAL FRAGMENT>
       DISTRIBUTION PREDICATE:<value>
       END RELATION <relation name>

CREATE LOCAL RELATION <relation name>
DELETE LOCAL RELATION <relation name>
```

BIBLIOGRAPHY

1. Baldisseri, c.; Ceri, s.; Schreiber, f.a. "Basi di Dati Distribuite", Rapporto Interno n. 79-2 Istituto di Elettronica ed Elettrotecnica del Politecnico Milano, Italy, January 1979.
2. Carlesi, c.; Fraccalini, O.; Thanos, c. "DETAREL: a Generalized Minicomputer Relational Data Base Management System", Proceedings - Mini and Microcomputers and their Applications. Symposium, Zurich, Switzerland, June 7-9, 1977.
3. Epstein, R.; Stonebraker, M.; Wong, E. "Distributed Query Processing in a Relational Data Base System", Mem. n. UCB-ERL M78-18 Berkeley, University of California, April 17, 1978.
4. Fraccalini, O.; Thanos, C. "DETAREL: Un Linguaggio Relazionale per Utenti non Programmatori", Nota Interna B76-9 Istituto di Elaborazione dell'Informazione del C.N.R., Pisa, Italy, March 1976.
5. Fraccalini, O.; Thanos, C. "Il Prototipo di un Interprete per il Linguaggio DETAREL", Nota Interna B76-6. Istituto di Elaborazione dell'Informazione del C.N.R., Pisa, Italy, July 1976.
6. Carlesi, C.; Ricciardi, E.; Petacchi, C.; Thanos, C.; Tucci, S. Distributed Data Bases on a Network of Minicomputers, Proceedings - Mini and Microcomputers and their Applications, Symposium, Zurich, Switzerland, May 28-31 1979.
7. Neuhold, E,; Stonebraker, M. "A Distributed Data Base Version of INGRES" 1977 Berkeley Workshop on Distributed Data Management and Computer Networks, Lawrence Berkeley Laboratory, May 1977.

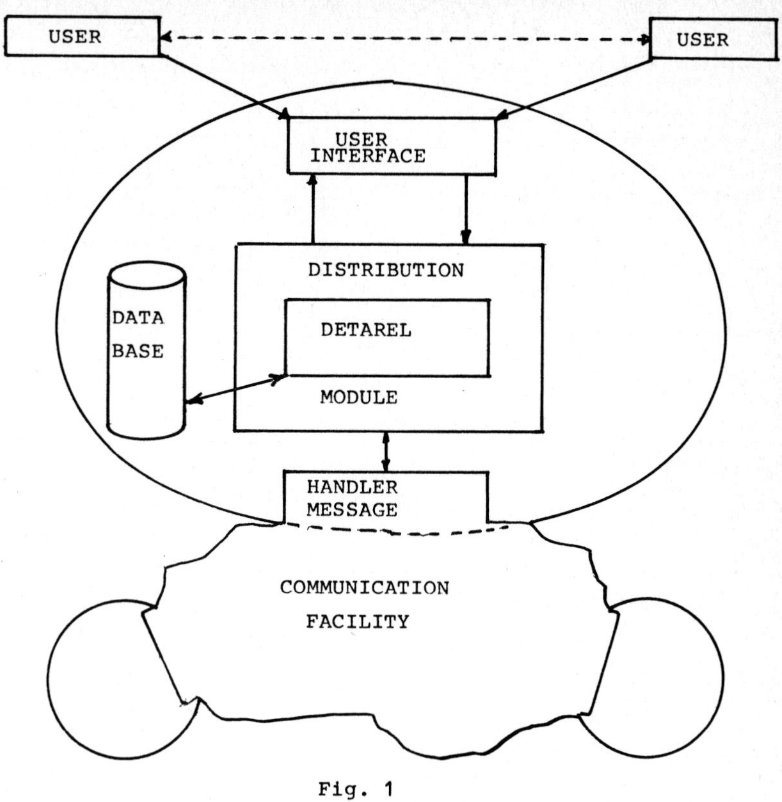

Fig. 1

BOOK	CODE	TITLE	AUTHOR	SUBJECT	LIBRARY	
					I.E.I. I.E.I.	NODE 1
					S.N.S. S.N.S.	NODE 2
					I.S.I. I.S.I.	NODE 3
					I.N.F.N. I.N.F.N.	NODE 4

Fig. 2

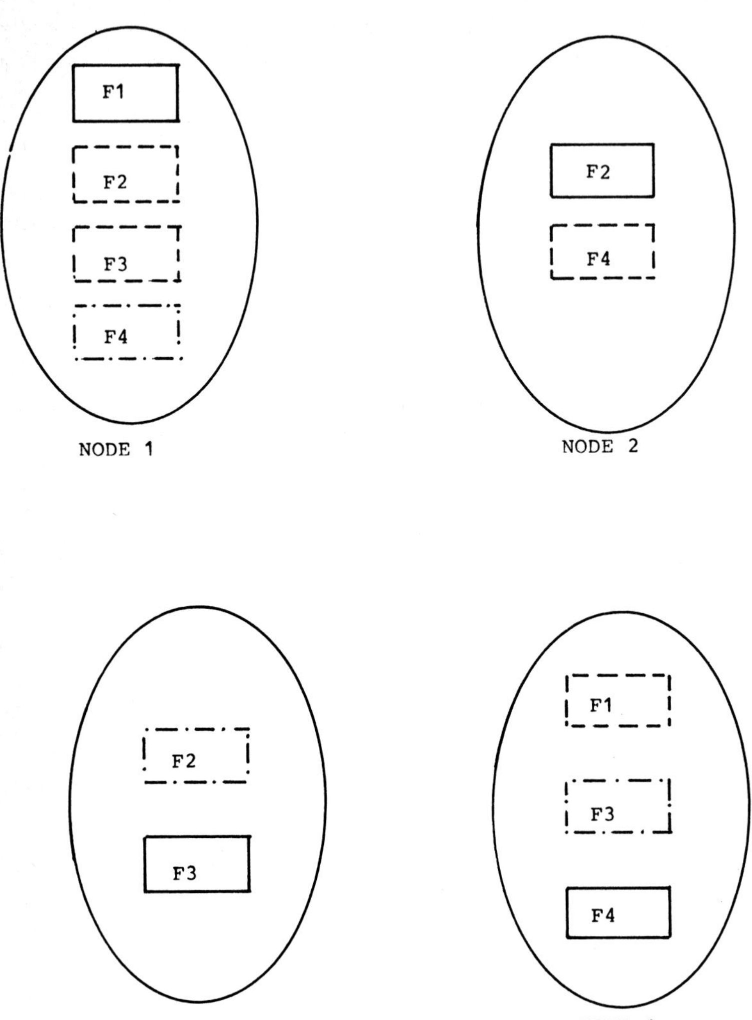

Fig. 3

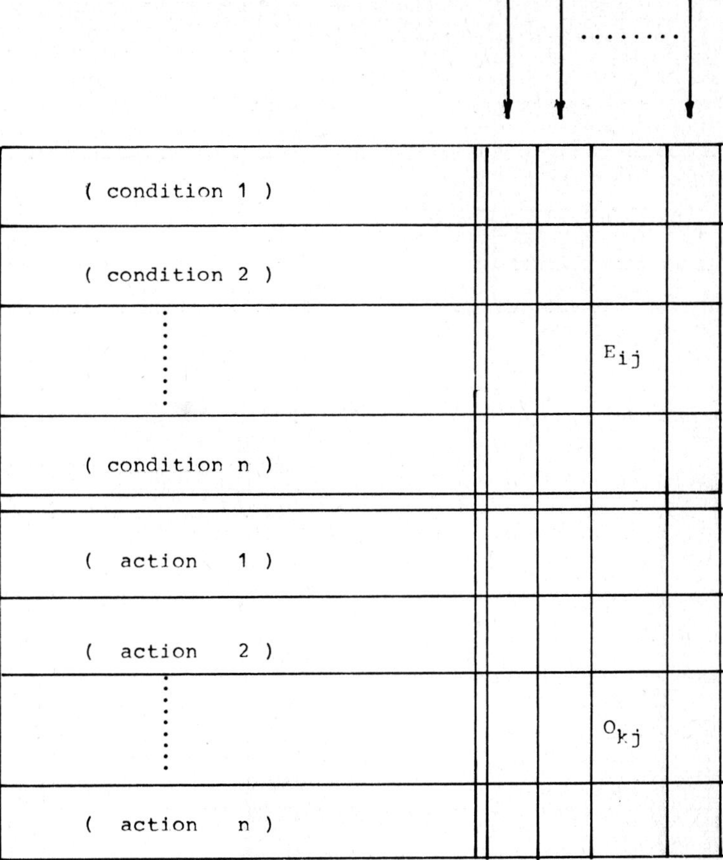
R U L E S
(condition 1)
(condition 2)
E_{ij}
(condition n)
(action 1)
(action 2)
O_{kj}
(action n)

Fig. 4

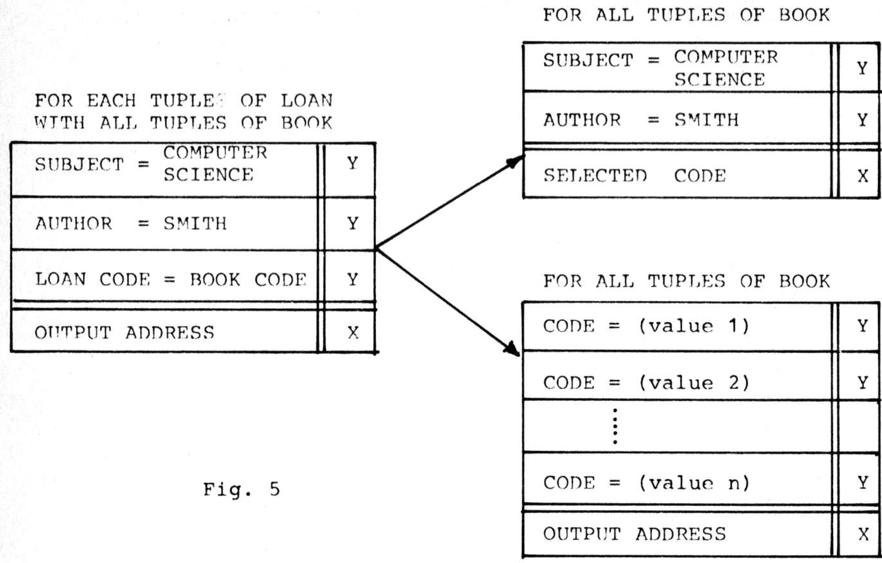
FOR EACH TUPLE OF LOAN
WITH ALL TUPLES OF BOOK
SUBJECT = COMPUTER SCIENCE Y
AUTHOR = SMITH Y
LOAN CODE = BOOK CODE Y
OUTPUT ADDRESS X
FOR ALL TUPLES OF BOOK
SUBJECT = COMPUTER SCIENCE Y
AUTHOR = SMITH Y
SELECTED CODE X
FOR ALL TUPLES OF BOOK
CODE = (value 1) Y
CODE = (value 2) Y
CODE = (value n) Y
OUTPUT ADDRESS X

Fig. 5

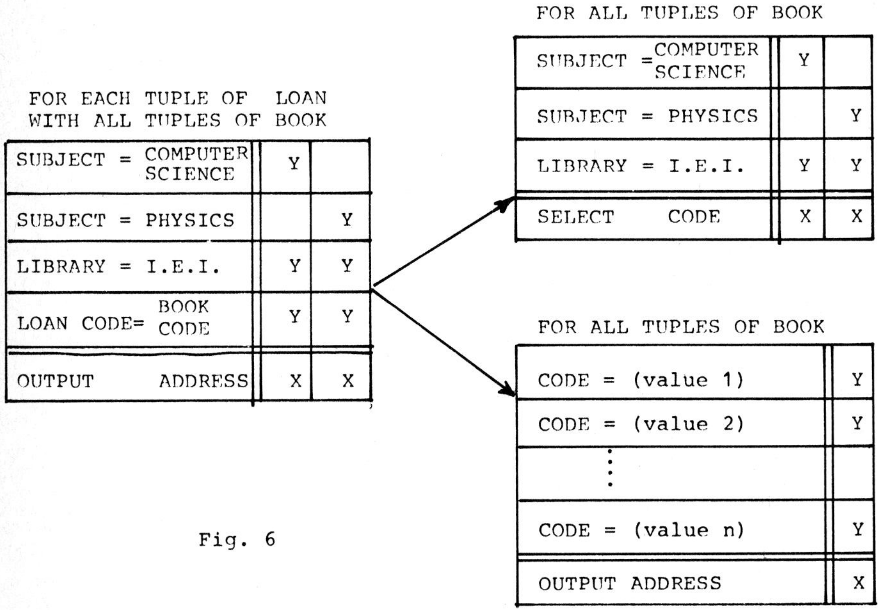
FOR EACH TUPLE OF LOAN
WITH ALL TUPLES OF BOOK
SUBJECT = COMPUTER SCIENCE Y
SUBJECT = PHYSICS Y
LIBRARY = I.E.I. Y Y
LOAN CODE= BOOK CODE Y Y
OUTPUT ADDRESS X X
FOR ALL TUPLES OF BOOK
SUBJECT = COMPUTER SCIENCE Y
SUBJECT = PHYSICS Y
LIBRARY = I.E.I. Y Y
SELECT CODE X X
FOR ALL TUPLES OF BOOK
CODE = (value 1) Y
CODE = (value 2) Y
CODE = (value n) Y
OUTPUT ADDRESS X

Fig. 6

FOR ALL TUPLES OF BOOK

SUBJECT = COMPUTER SCIENCE	Y
LIBRARY = I.E.I.	Y
OUTPUT NAME	X

Fig. 7

FOR ALL TUPLES OF BOOK

SUBJECT = COMPUTER SCIENCE	Y
AUTHOR = SMITH	Y
OUTPUT NAME	X

Fig. 8

FOR ALL TUPLES OF BOOK

SUBJECT = COMPUTER SCIENCE	Y
LIBRARY = I.E.I.	N
OUTPUT NAME	X

Fig. 9

FOR ALL TUPLES OF BOOK

SUBJECT = COMPUTER SCIENCE	Y	
SUBJECT = MATHS		Y
LIBRARY = I.E.I.	Y	
OUTPUT TITLE	X	X

Fig. 10

FOR ALL TUPLES OF BOOK

SUBJECT = MATHS	Y
OUTPUT TITLE	X

Fig. 11

FOR ALL TUPLES OF BOOK

SUBJECT = COMPUTER SCIENCE	Y	
SUBJECT = MATHS		Y
AUTHOR = SMITH	Y	
LIBRARY = I.E.I.		Y
OUTPUT TITLE	X	X

Fig. 12

FOR ALL TUPLES OF BOOK

SUBJECT = COMPUTER SCIENCE	Y
AUTHOR = SMITH	Y
OUTPUT TITLE	X

Fig. 13

FOR ALL TUPLES OF BOOK

SUBJECT = COMPUTER SCIENCE	Y		Y	
SUBJECT = MATHEMATICS		Y		Y
LIBRARY = I.E.I.	Y	Y		
AUTHOR = SMITH			Y	Y
OUTPUT TITLE	X	X	X	X

Fig. 14

DISTRIBUTED DATA BASES
C. Delobel and W. Litwin (eds.)
North-Holland Publishing Company

SIRIUS-DELTA : UN PROTOTYPE DE SYSTEME DE GESTION DE BASES DE DONNEES REPARTIES

J. LE BIHAN, C. ESCULIER, G. LE LANN, L. TREILLE

IRIA/SIRIUS

SIRIUS-DELTA, entrepris dans le cadre du projet pilote SIRIUS de l'IRIA (Institut de Recherche d'Informatique et d'Automatique) a pour objectif la définition et la réalisation d'un Système de Gestion de Bases de Données Réparties (SGBDR) sur un réseau local de mini-ordinateurs. SIRIUS-DELTA offre à l'utilisateur les outils permettant de décrire et manipuler, comme un seul ensemble logique, des données situées sur plusieurs ordinateurs. Il gère des types variés de répartition et de réplication de données, permet l'accès concurrentiel à la base et en maintient l'intégrité en cas de panne d'un ou plusieurs composants.

L'architecture de SIRIUS-DELTA est une architecture en couches correspondant à 4 niveaux fonctionnels :
- fonction de gestion classique de base de données (interprétation de requêtes, accès aux données locales)
- fonction de gestion de données spécifique au contexte réparti (décomposition de requêtes en fonction de la localisation)
- fonction de contrôle réparti (cohérence et résilience de la base)
- fonction d'exécution répartie (activation de processus répartis, transfert de données).

Les solutions retenues pour ces niveaux fonctionnels sont dérivées des études réalisées durant la première phase du projet SIRIUS. Leur intégration dans le cadre de SIRIUS-DELTA permettra de les valider et de fournir le support pour des applications réparties, notamment des applications de bureautique.

INTRODUCTION

L'évolution de l'informatique vers les systèmes répartis est la conséquence des développements technologiques en cours. De nouveaux moyens apparaissent sur le marché : matériels informatiques à la fois compacts, puissants et bon marché, systèmes de transmission de données plus performants et plus économiques qui, associés aux précédents, permettent de répartir les traitements et les données. Potentiellement, on peut en espérer des systèmes plus performants, plus fiables, plus souples et mieux adaptés aux besoins car cette évolution correspond à un besoin des utilisateurs. Les contraintes,imposées par les moyens informatiques disponibles dans les années 60 à 70, ont conduit à centraliser au maximum l'information alors que, par essence, elle est répartie. Les systèmes répartis offrent donc les possibilités d'une meilleure adéquation de l'outil informatique aux besoins des utilisateurs, aussi bien dans les applications administratives que dans les applications industrielles.

Les techniques,développées dans les projets ARPA ou CYCLADES et par la suite proposées par les constructeurs (IBM, UNIVAC, CII/HB ...), permettent d'assurer la communication de l'information dans les systèmes répartis. Mais elles n'apportent aucune solution aux problèmes du traitement, du stockage, du partage et de l'échange de cette information dans ce nouvel environnement. Les techniques, classiquement utilisées dans les systèmes centralisés pour résoudre ces problèmes, sont inutilisables. Une simple adaptation ne suffit pas. Il faut les repenser en fonction des contraintes spécifiques des systèmes répartis.

Depuis 1975, des recherches ont été entreprises dans ce domaine aux Etats-Unis [SDDI78], [STON77] comme en Europe [NEUH77], [HOLL78]. Le projet SIRIUS [LEBI79], que nous décrirons brièvement au paragraphe 1 de ce papier, coordonne les études réalisées en France sur ce sujet.

C'est dans le cadre de SIRIUS qu'à été entrepris la réalisation du système de gestion de bases de données réparties SIRIUS-DELTA dont l'objectif est d'intégrer les résultats obtenus durant la première phase du projet par les prototypes IGOR [DANG78], FRERES [BOSC78], POLYPHEME [POLY79]. Après avoir décrit les fonctionnalités (paragraphe 2) et l'architecture (paragraphe 3) du système SIRIUS-DELTA, nous détaillerons chaque niveau fonctionnel du système : SILOE (paragraphe 4) qui traite des fonctions de gestion de données réparties, SCORE (paragraphe 5) qui assure le contrôle réparti (cohérence et résilience) de la base de données, SER (paragraphe 6), chargé de gérer l'exécution des processus sur plusieurs processeurs physiques. Nous terminerons en indiquant le contexte de réalisation de ce système expérimental (paragraphe 7).

1. LE PROJET SIRIUS

Le projet SIRIUS-DELTA s'inscrit dans le cadre plus large du projet pilote SIRIUS, lancé en juin 1976 par l'Institut de Recherche d'Informatique et d'Automatique (IRIA). Comme les autres projets pilotes, SIRIUS se caractérise par :

- des actions à objectifs définis, dont le coûts et délais sont évalués au préalable
- une participation nationale associant, dans les mêmes équipes: chercheurs, constructeurs, SSCI, utilisateurs
- des contacts internationaux importants et une diffusion massive de connaissances
- une répartition et un suivi de travail assurés par une équipe de coordination.

Dans ce cadre, SIRIUS vise à définir et expérimenter les méthodes et les techniques permettant la conception, la réalisation et l'exploitation de systèmes de "Bases de données réparties", objectif qui touche des domaines aussi divers que :

- les systèmes de processus industriels dans lesquels des processeurs (ordinateurs) spécialisés coopèrent à la réalisation d'une tâche globale
- les systèmes embarqués qui requièrent un haut niveau de fiabilité
- les systèmes multi-processeurs qui se partagent des données, avec ou sans le secours d'une mémoire commune
- les systèmes de bureautique qui permettent la production, la manipulation, le stockage, l'échange d'informations à l'intérieur comme à l'extérieur des entreprises
- les systèmes de gestion pour les applications administratives et industrielles (personnel, production, stocks, réservation, comptes bancaires ...)
- les systèmes d'information du type documentaire (référencesbibliographiques) ou du type informatif (données économiques, annuaires, cours de la bourse ...).

Tous ces systèmes présentent, en commun, des problèmes techniques identiques, à savoir l'échange, le partage, le maintien de la cohérence et de l'intégrité des données réparties sur plusieurs ordinateurs (ou processeurs) interconnectés. Ces problèmes ont, de plus, la caractéristique d'être très interdépendants.

SIRIUS s'est donc donné pour objectif d'apporter, par une approche globale, des solutions à ces problèmes en définissant et en réalisant des systèmes expérimentaux qui aillent jusqu'à démontrer la faisabilité des techniques proposées et leur "intégrabilité". SIRIUS s'est aussi donné pour objectif de réaliser le transfert des résultats du projet vers l'industrie. SIRIUS s'est enfin donné pour objectif de développer, sur le plan national, une compétence théorique et pratique sur ce thème.

Toutefois, la diversité des domaines touchés, risquant de créer une dispersion trop importante des études, celles-ci ont été centrées, dans une première étape, sur les systèmes de gestion et les systèmes d'information répartis. Et pour caractériser l'ensemble des mécanismes généraux, nécessaires à la gestion des données réparties dans de tels systèmes, on a adopté le terme de Système de Gestion de Base de Données Réparties (SGBDR).

La démarche

En 1976, lors du lancement du projet, le domaine des Bases de Données Réparties était entièrement nouveau pour les industriels et il n'avait été abordé que de manière très partielle par quelques chercheurs.

Au démarrage du projet SIRIUS, il a donc fallu, avant toute chose, entreprendre un travail de fond important pour créer un noyau de compétence et assurer des bases théoriques solides sans lesquelles aucune retombée industrielle sérieuse n'était envisageable. Ce travail de fond a été assuré, essentiellement, par les équipes de recherche participant au projet. Il se concrétise, dans une première phase, par le développement de prototypes (IGOR, FRERES, ETOILE, POLYPHEME ...) que l'on peut qualifier de "partiels", en ce sens que chacun d'entre eux aborde un sous-ensemble des problèmes posés par la réalisation des systèmes répartis (et plus particulièrement des SGBDR).

Dans une deuxième phase, les principaux résultats de ces prototypes sont intégrés pour obtenir un SGBDR "complet" (SIRIUS/DELTA) qui assure la description et la manipulation globale de la base de donnée répartie, le contrôle et l'exécution répartie, la survie aux défaillances et la confidentialité.

Des utilisateurs et des industriels participent à ces études et à ces réalisations. Cette collaboration permet d'assurer le transfert des résultats de SIRIUS par leur application dans des domaines tels que les systèmes de gestion, les systèmes documentaires, la bureautique, les nouveaux systèmes informatiques (multi-processeurs, machines base de données). La démarche adoptée dans SIRIUS se caractérise ainsi par 3 types d'actions (recherches, prototypes, application) dont la figure 1 schématise les relations.

2. PRINCIPES GENERAUX ET FONCTIONNALITES

Le projet SIRIUS-DELTA a pour objectif essentiel la réalisation d'un Système de Gestion de Bases de Données Réparties (SGBDR).

Le rôle du SGBDR SIRIUS-DELTA est, du point de vue externe, conceptuellement identique à celui que joue un SGBD centralisé. Ceci induit que :

- il est possible de définir et de manipuler des ensembles de données réparties sur différents ordinateurs comme un seul ensemble logique. Cet ensemble est alors considéré comme une base de données (répartie).

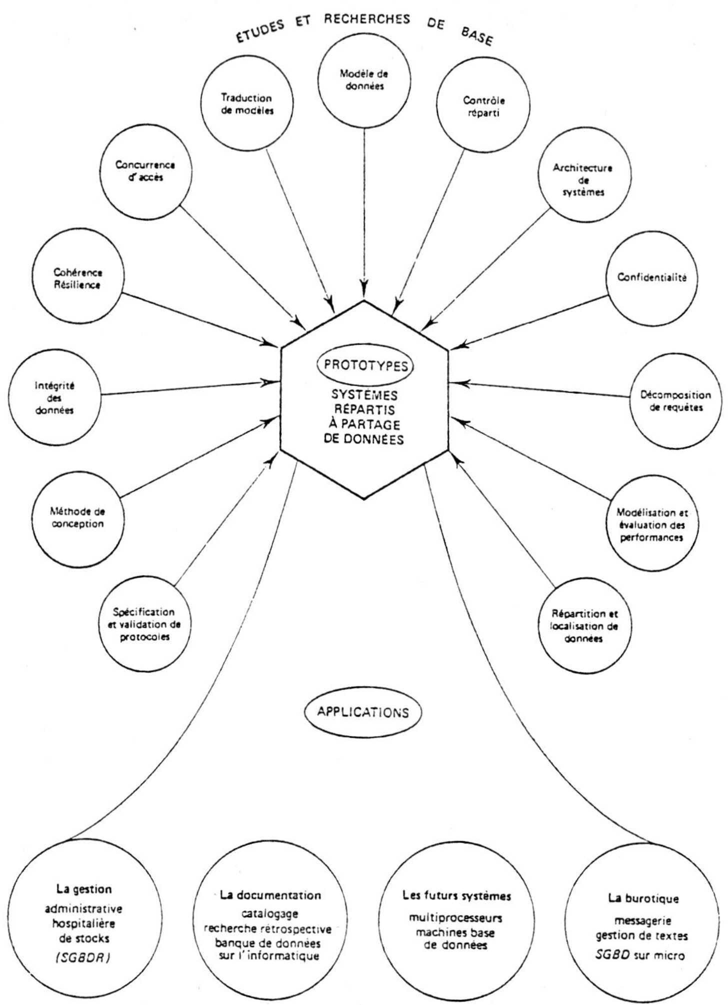

FIGURE 1 - LA DEMARCHE SIRIUS

- la répartition des données doit pouvoir se faire suivant des critères très variés en fonction des besoins de l'application
- l'utilisateur manipule la base de données répartie sans avoir à connaître la localisation des données
- pour des raisons de fiabilité ou de performances, les données peuvent être dupliquées sur plusieurs systèmes. Cette duplication doit être invisible pour l'utilisateur. Le SGBDR doit alors assurer la cohérence des différentes copies lors des mises à jour
- le SGBDR doit également être capable d'assurer la cohérence de la base dans des cas de mises à jour concurrentielles provenant, de manière indépendante , de divers points d'accès au SGBDR. Cette cohérence doit être maintenue en cas de panne de l'un des composants du SGBDR. Il faut donc des procédures de reprises adaptées
- enfin, l'accès à la base de données répartie doit pouvoir être contrôlé. Des dispositifs de protection sont nécessaires pour éviter que les données confidentielles ne soient lues ou modifiées par des personnes non autorisées.

On peut considérer que l'ensemble de ces caractéristiques concourt à rendre l'utilisation des bases de données réparties indépendantes de la manière dont les données sont physiquement gérées. On doit ainsi pouvoir modifier la structure des fichiers, les chemins d'accès, la localisation des données, sans remettre en cause les applications existantes. Cette tendance n'est pas nouvelle car elle est déjà présente dans les SGBD centralisés,mais la répartition lui donne une dimension supplémentaire.

Du point de vue fonctionnel, le SGBDR doit fournir :

- des fonctions de description de la base de données répartie - La base de données répartie doit être écrite au moyen d'un langage de description, ce qui présuppose le choix d'un modèle de données (hiérarchique, réseau, relationnel...). Cette description doit être complétée par des informations permettant de localiser les données dans les bases de données "locales".

- des fonctions de manipulation de la base de données répartie - L'utilisateur doit avoir à sa disposition un (ou plusieurs) langage(s) de manipulation des données de la BDR. Ce langage lui permet d'exprimer ses requêtes au système. Il peut de cette façon interroger, mettre à jour, créer et détruire des données dans la BDR sans avoir à se préoccuper de la localisation physique de ces données (et de leurs différences éventuelles de structure, de format, de type ...), le langage de manipulation constitue donc l'interface d'accès aux données de la BDR.

Les requêtes exprimées par l'utilisateur au moyen de ce langage de manipulation doivent être "évaluées", c'est-à-dire qu'elles sont décomposées (en fonction, notamment, de la localisation des données) en un ensemble de sous-requêtes. Chacune de ces sous-requêtes sera, elle-même, évaluée par l'évaluateur de la machine locale concernée.

Chaque machine locale effectue l'accès aux données locales en fonction des sous-requêtes qu'elles a reçues d'une machine globale et lui fournit, en retour, les données résultantes.

- des fonctions de contrôle - L'environnement des BDR est un environnement où des accès concurrents (notamment en mise à jour) peuvent intervenir de manière aléatoire et où des constituants du système peuvent tomber en panne. Pour maintenir malgré tout la cohérence des BDR, il faut disposer de mécanismes de contrôle réparti adaptés à cet environnement.

- des fonctions d'exécution répartie - Les différentes sous-requêtes, issues de l'évaluation d'une requête globale, doivent être exécutées sur les différentes machines locales concernées. Pour cela, il faut disposer de mécanismes d'exécution répartie permettant d'activer les programmes sur différentes machines, de les synchroniser, de les contrôler (notamment en cas de panne), d'assurer les échanges d'information. Pour cela, la fonction d'exécution répartie s'appuie sur une fonction de transport qui gère la communication de l'information entre les programmes au travers des moyens disponibles (lignes téléphoniques, réseaux locaux ou nationaux, bus...).

Cette architecture de SGBDR, ainsi que les mécanismes nécessaires au bon fonctionnement de ces systèmes, sont "orientés" vers le domaine des systèmes de gestion et des systèmes d'information. Mais la confrontation de ces résultats aux problèmes posés dans d'autres types de systèmes répartis (multiprocesseurs, système de contrôle de processus, bureautique ...) a montré la généralité de certains de ces mécanismes, notamment ceux de contrôle et d'exécution répartie.

3. ARCHITECTURE DE SIRIUS-DELTA

L'architecture de SIRIUS-DELTA doit être considérée de plusieurs points de vue : base de données, fonctionnalités et SGBDR.

3.1. Architecture de la base :

Cette architecture transparait dans les schémas qui décrivent les composants de la BDR. Elle comporte essentiellement deux niveaux : le niveau global, correspondant à la BDR dans son ensemble et le niveau local, correspondant aux BD qui la constituent. [ADIB78], [AFCE76].

3.1.1. Le niveau global de la BDR

C'est à ce niveau que la BDR est considérée comme un tout, comme UNE base.

On y trouve donc le schéma conceptuel de la BDR et tous les schémas externes associés (comme pour une base classique). [ANSI75], [TSIC77]. Dans le schéma interne apparaît la particularité due au fait que la base est répartie : le schéma interne global contient, en effet, la description de la répartition de la base.

3.1.2. Le niveau local de la BDR

Ce niveau contient les constituants fondamentaux de la BDR : les bases dites locales.

C'est dans les bases locales que se trouvent les données, le niveau global jouant un rôle d'utilisateur pour chacune d'elles.

Dans le contexte BDR, le niveau local comprend donc un schéma externe, un schéma conceptuel et un schéma interne par base locale. Si une base locale est également utilisée directement (autrement que via la BDR) le ou les schémas externes correspondant doivent être ajoutés.

3.1.3. Architecture générale de la BDR

L'architecture de la BDR est représentée par la figure 3.a.

Cette architecture est abstraite et ne saurait être transposée à une architecture physique sans précaution. Ainsi, le niveau global peut être pris en charge par un processeur spécifique ou plusieurs, ou encore réparti entre des processeurs qui jouent également un role au niveau local.

Une base locale ne signifie pas non plus nécessairement un processeur en relation biunivoque. En effet, une base locale est associée à chaque couple "processeur, SGBD", ce qui permet d'avoir plusieurs bases locales sur une seule machine physique.

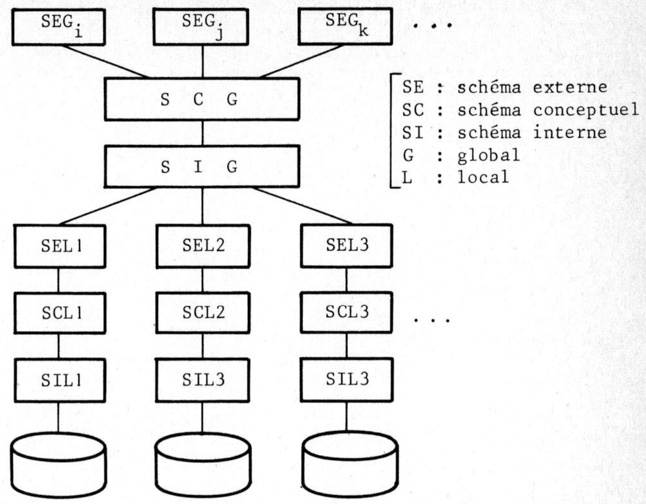

FIGURE 3.a - ARCHITECTURE DE LA BDR DU POINT DE VUE DES SCHEMAS

3.2. Architecture fonctionnelle

Depuis la soumission d'une requête exploitant la BDR jusqu'à la fourniture des résultats à l'utilisateur, un certain nombre de couches fonctionnelles doivent être traversées.

Quatre couches fondamentales apparaissent :

- les fonctions de gestion classique de base de données,
- les fonctions de gestion de données spécifiques au contexte réparti,
- les fonctions de contrôle réparti, en particulier concernant la gestion de la concurrence,
- les fonctions d'exécution répartie et de transport.

Dans SIRIUS-DELTA, le première couche réutilise autant que possible le SGBD existant. Les trois autres couches donnent lieu à trois sous-projets :

- SILOE : localisation et évaluation
- SCORE : cohérence et résilience
- SER : exécution répartie

SIRIUS-DELTA = SILOE + SCORE + SER

3.3. Architecture du SGBDR

Dans le SGBDR SIRIUS-DELTA, on retrouve à la fois l'architecture global-local et les couches fonctionnelles indiquées.

Nous allons proposer un schéma les englobant et indiquer comment une requête "traverse" la structure.

Les trois chapitre suivants précisent ensuite SILOE, SCORE et SER.

3.3.1. Représentation de l'architecture du SGBDR

De manière schématique, SIRIUS/DELTA est structuré comme l'indique la figure 3.b. La partie gauche représente les couches fonctionnelles au niveau global, la partie droite au niveau local.

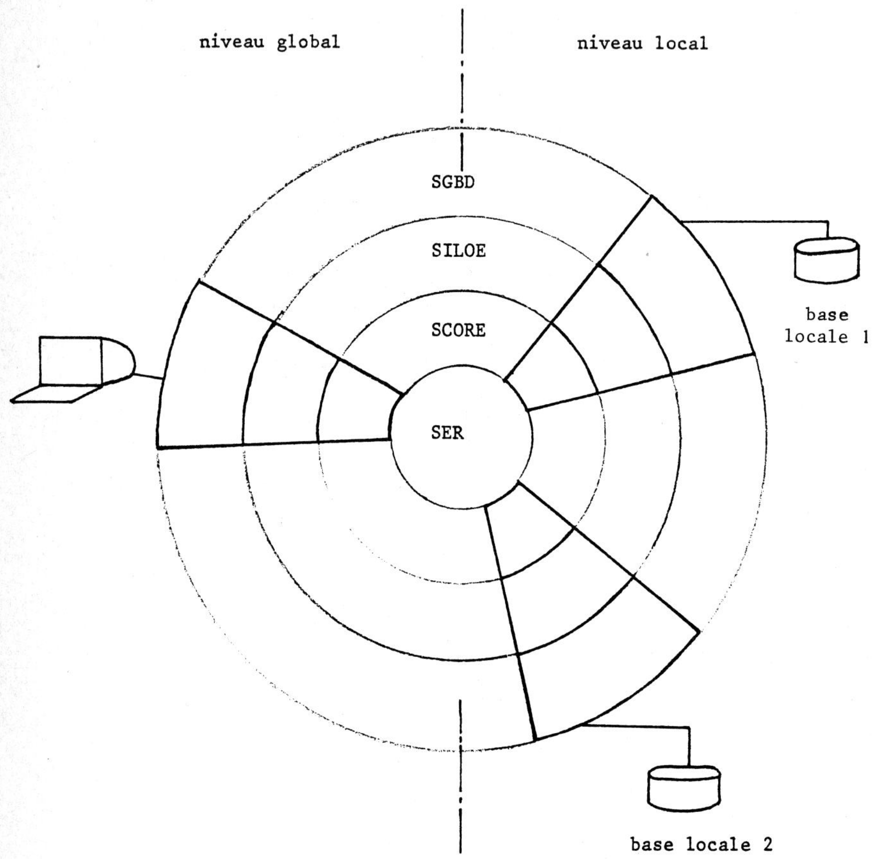

FIGURE 3.b - ARCHITECTURE DU SGBDR SIRIUS-DELTA

3.3.2. Principes de fonctionnement

Pour illustrer ce schéma, nous allons décrire rapidement le traitement d'une transaction par SIRIUS-DELTA.

Soumission (A) : la requête est soumise par l'utilisateur au niveau global, le langage externe du SGBD s'appuyant sur un schéma externe classique. Le filtrage des autorisations d'accès s'opère essentiellement à ce moment.

Analyse syntaxico-sémantique (B) : le SGBD au niveau global, à partir du schéma externe global de l'utilisateur et du schéma conceptuel global, contrôle et analyse la requête. Il la transmet à SILOE-global si OK.

Localisation (C) : SILOE localise les données nécessaires pour le traitement de la requête, en déduit les actions locales à effectuer et les scénarios associés.

Optimisation et production de PEX (D) : Si plusieurs scénarios sont possibles, une évaluation des coûts et performances est faite, conduisant au choix d'un programme d'exécution répartie (PEX) qui devrait être proche d'un optimum.

Identification du PEX (E) : SCORE-global attribue au PEX un identifiant unique.

Activation des actions locales (F) : SER active sur les sites indiqués les actions locales du PEX lorsque les conditions d'activation sont satisfaites.

Contrôle des accès concurrents (G) : SCORE-local assure le contrôle de la concurrence (accès à une même donnée par plusieurs actions locales) : les actions locales compatibles sont exécutées, les autres sont mises en attente selon l'ordre défini par les identifiants de PEX.

Exploitation des bases locales (H) : SILOE-local puis le SGBD gèrent les bases locales, SILOE-local ayant surtout un rôle d'adapteur/traducteur. C'est l'exécution effective des actions locales.

Transports des résultats (I) : SER prend en charge le transport des résultats (intermédiaires ou définitifs) et les synchronisations associées.

Validation des mises à jour (J) : pour une transaction de mise à jour de la BDR, la fin de transaction logique provoque une validation (commitment) par dialogue SCORE global/SCORE local, SILOE local effectuant, via le SGBD, les écritures définitives.

Réponse à l'utilisateur (K) : résultat ou code d'exécution, une réponse de fin d'exécution est fournie à l'utilisateur par le SGBD au niveau global.

La figure 3.c représente le cheminement à travers les couches pour ces phases d'exécution de la transaction.

4. SILOE

SILOE est le sous-système de SIRIUS-DELTA qui assure la localisation des données et l'évaluation répartie des requêtes.

Dans ce paragraphe, nous allons préciser les types de répartition possibles pour une base SIRIUS-DELTA et la description de la répartition, ce qui concerne la localisation, puis nous indiquerons les fonctions de SILOE global et local et son architecture.

4.1. Les types de répartition

La répartition des données d'une BDR peut être extrêmement variée et complexe [SPAC78],[BACH77], [SDD178].

Dans le cadre de SILOE, le problème consiste à définir les types de répartition autorisés et à modéliser la répartition pour la décrire simplement dans le schéma interne global.

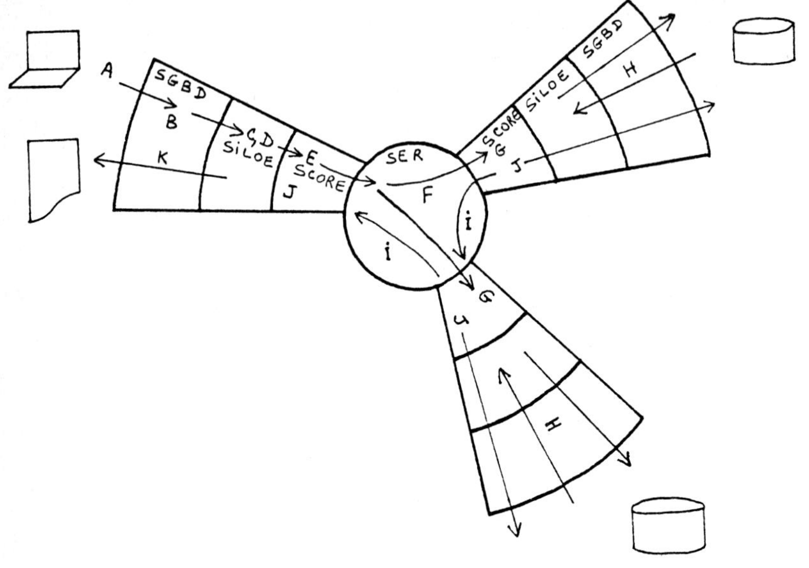

FIGURE 3.c - SCHEMA DE L'EXECUTION D'UNE TRANSACTION

Dans ce qui suit, le modèle relationnel et la représentation par tableaux sont utilisés pour décrire et schématiser les bases de données (globales et locales) [CODD71]. La modélisation et les concepts de répartition proposés s'étendent aisément aux autres modèles de données.

4.1.1. Schématisation de la répartition

Pour représenter schématiquement la répartition d'une base de données, nous proposons un système à trois dimensions, à N+1 plans si il y a N bases locales (voir figure 4.a).

Sur le plan de référence, on figure la base globale par un ensemble de tableaux.

Dans chacun des plans supérieurs, on figure une base locale par des surfaces en correspondance verticale avec les tableaux du plan de référence.

Ainsi, chaque point de l'espace "base globale" correspond à :

- un seul point, donc un seul plan, si la donnée associée est non dupliquée,
- plusieurs points, donc dans plusieurs plans supérieurs, si la donnée existe en plusieurs exemplaires.

Nota : les redondances à l'intérieur d'une base locale ne sont pas prises en considération à ce niveau.

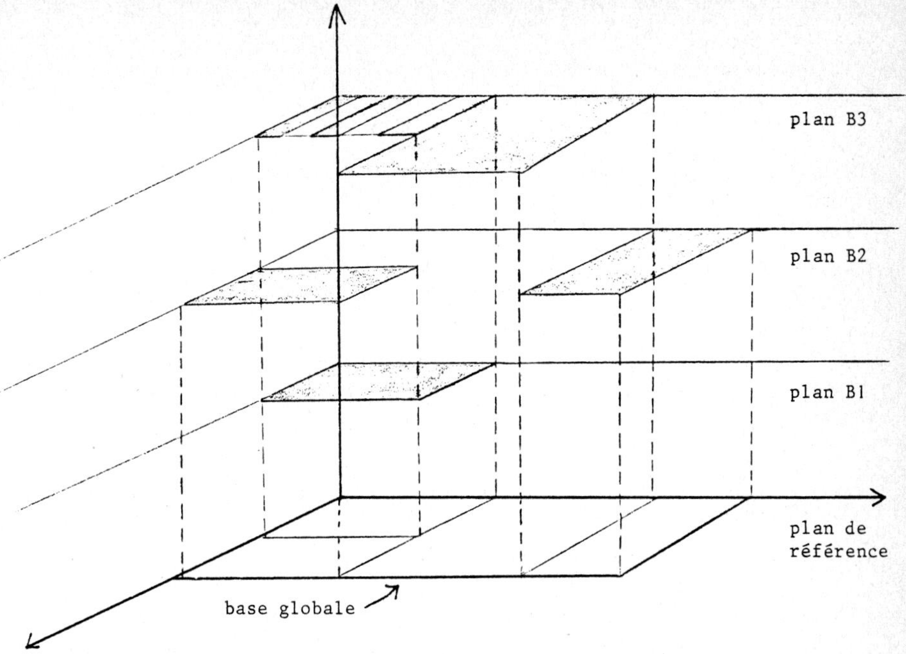

FIGURE 4.a - SCHEMA DE REPARTITION D'UNE BASE

4.1.2. Concepts pour la répartition d'une BDR SIRIUS-DELTA

Partant d'une base globale décrite par un ensemble de relations dans une forme normale appropriée, les concepts fondamentaux permettant d'exprimer la répartition d'une base SIRIUS-DELTA sont :

- ensemble à répartition homogène
- fonction de répartition et
- parcelle.

On appelle ensemble à répartition homogène (ERH) un ensemble dont les éléments sont répartis sans être subdivisés (atomes de répartition).
On appelle fonction de répartition ce qui permet de décider de la localisation d'un atome dans un ensemble à répartition homogène (le terme fonction est pris au sens large).
On appelle parcelle l'ensemble des atomes d'un ensemble à répartition homogène qui se trouvent dans une même base locale.

La définition d'une répartition consiste :

- d'une part à préciser les ensembles à répartition homogène à partir des relations du SCG,
- d'autre part à indiquer la fonction de répartition pour chacun d'eux.

La définition d'un ERH, à partir d'une relation, peut se faire au moyen des opérateurs relationnels classiques qui permettent d'obtenir des sous-relations (découpage vertical/horizontal).

Les fonctions de répartition sont essentiellement de deux types :

- nettes lorsqu'elles indiquent la ou les bases locales effectives,
- floues lorsqu'elles donne la probabilité (]0,1[) de localisation dans les bases locales possibles.

Les fonctions nettes les plus utiles semblent être :

- constante simple

$$F_{ERH} = i \text{ (i=id. Base Locale)}$$

- constante multiple

$$F_{ERH} = \{i,j,k\}$$

- selon attribut(s)

$$F_{ERH}\ (att_1[,att_2 \ldots]) = f$$

  les valeurs d'un ou plusieurs attributs de l'atome déterminant la ou les bases locales.

- indirecte

  la localisation d'un ERH est liée à un autre ERH par exemple sur identité de valeur d'attribut(s) commun(s).

Les fonctions floues s'expriment sous la forme :

$$F_{ERH} = \{(i,p_i)\}\ ,\ p_i \in\ ]0,1[$$

On peut distinguer les répartitions uniformes simples ($p_i = \frac{1}{N}$ si N bases locales), les répartitions non uniformes simples ($\Sigma\ p_i = 1$), avec réplication ($\Sigma\ p_i > 1$) et les répartitions floues selon attribut, par exemple :

- si ville = "PARIS" (BL1, 0.7),(BL2, 0.3)
- si ville = "NICE" (BL1, 0.1),(BL2, 0.8),...

Une répartition telle que celle de FRERES [BOSC78] est formulée par une fonction floue.

4.1.3. Le schéma interne global

Le SIG qui décrit la répartition de la BDR contient essentiellement :

- la définition des ERH à partir des relations du schéma conceptuel global (opérateurs relationnels),
- les fonctions de répartition correspondantes, sous forme de tableau si elles ne sont pas simples.

Le SIG permet à SILOE de localiser les parcelles. Il contient également des informations sur les cardinalités des parcelles, qui sont nécessaires pour optimiser l'évaluation des requêtes.

4.2. Fonctions de SILOE :

4.2.1. SILOE global

SILOE GLOBAL offre deux types de fonctions :

- il assure la gestion du SIG et offre donc à l'administrateur de la BDR les outils de description et de validation de la répartition.

- il assure pour chaque transaction la localisation des données, la production du PEX associé et le contrôle de son exécution.

Nous allons préciser ces fonctions :

- Localisation :

  La localisation se fait en plusieurs étapes qui consiste essentiellement en :

  . définition des ensembles de données conceptuels nécessaires à la transaction (qui peut être faite en bonne partie par le SGBD d'accès)
  . détermination des parcelles possibles qui "couvrent" cet ensemble
  . choix des parcelles optimales selon des critères de coût et temps de réponse ("optimales" d'après la fonction qui les intègre).

  Ce choix est fait à partir d'informations de cardinalité et de sélectivité globales (dans le complément quantitatif au SCG) et locales (dans le SIG) et de configuration (dans un schéma géré par SER).

  SILOE doit en effet tenir compte des caractéristiques des liaisons inter-bases locales et de la situation courante du système (surchage, coupure de ligne,...).

- Production de PEX

  Le choix des parcelles correspond en fait au choix d'un scénario pour exécuter la transaction au moyen d'actions locales (AL). Dans un contexte réparti, les possibilités de parallélisme, tant en exécution qu'en transfert, tiennent une place prépondérante dans ce choix [NGUY79], [CALE78].

  La production de PEX consiste à traduire le scénario dans le langage de commande du SER, à introduire les déclarations de modes d'accès pour l'allocation des objets par SCORE et à formuler les actions locales pour les SILOE locaux.

  Dans le langage de commande du SER, on notera en particulier l'expression de la synchronisation : conditions d'activation, expression de terminaison, ...

  Pour SCORE, SILOE définit les objets utilisés par l'action locale sur la base locale correspondante et pour chacun le mode d'accès. L'objet est l'unité de verrouillage correspondant à un ensemble d'atomes,à un atome ou à une partie d'atome.

- Soumission et contrôle de PEX

  Un dialogue SILOE-SCORE global permet d'identifier la transaction de manière unique dans le système.

  Chacune des actions locales est munie de cet identifiant lorsque le contexte associé est soumis au SER.

  SILOE soumet ainsi tous les contextes d'actions locales (AL) complets du PEX en cours, SER garantissant les conditions d'activation au moyen des variables de synchronisation. Si le PEX n'a pu être soumis totalement, SILOE construit dynamiquement les contextes d'AL d'après les résultats déjà acquis et les soumet au SER au fur et à mesure.

  SER rend compte à SILOE de l'exécution des actions locales en adressant au contrôleur du PEX les codes retour.

Cet ensemble de fonctions ne se déroule pas nécessairement sur un seul processeur. SILOE global peut être lui-même réparti,certaines fonctions se déroulant sur des processeurs distincts.

L'architecture de SILOE global est représentée par la figure 4.b.

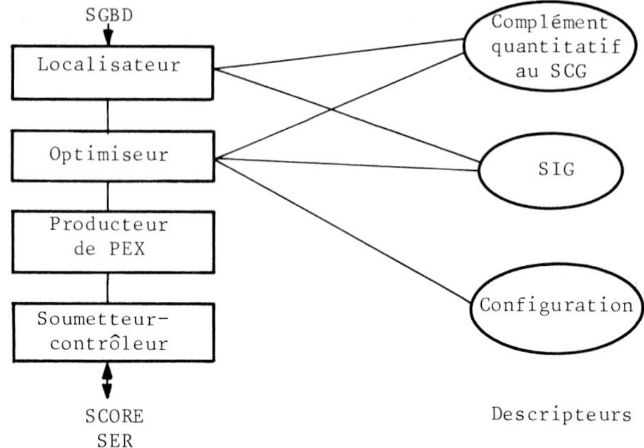

FIGURE 4.b : ARCHITECTURE DE SILOE GLOBAL

Nota : Pour une transaction modifiant la base globale, SILOE prend en charge les contraintes dues à la répartition et génère les actions correspondantes.

4.2.2. SILOE local

Le SGBD associé à chaque base locale n'est pas directement impliqué dans les actions locales. Logiquement, un module interface SILOE global et chaque SGBD local pour adapter les directives au schéma externe associé à la base locale.

La fonction de SILOE local est donc essentiellement de traduire la sous-requête pour le SGBD associé. SILOE local peut également compléter les fonctionnalités offertes par le SGBD local pour offrir une homogénéité de fonctions entre les processeurs.
SILOE local assure en particulier l'écriture différentielle si le SGBD n'offre pas ce service. Les modifications de la base locale ne sont rendues effectives et définitives qu'en fin de transaction dans la phase de validation contrôlée par SCORE.

- Remarque sur la redondance dans une base locale

  Si des données sont dupliquées dans une base locale, tous les problèmes que soulèvent leur gestion (cohérence des mises à jour, utilisation d'une copie lors d'une panne d'un périphérique, etc) sont à la charge du SGBD local.
  Ces redondances n'apparaissent pas au niveau global et sont une particularité de l'organisation interne des bases locales.

5. SCORE

5.1. Introduction

SCORE est le nom donné au niveau d'abstraction (et au logiciel) correspondant au Système de COntrôle REparti assurant la COhérence et la REsilience de la base de données gérée par SIRIUS-DELTA.

La cohérence d'une base de données [ESWA76] peut être détruite pour deux raisons :

1) Interférences entre accès simultanés
2) Défaillances de parties de la base.

SCORE a pour objectif de fournis les mécanismes nécessaires au maintien de cette cohérence. Ces mécanismes sont indépendants de la taille de la base de données, de la complexité des contraintes de cohérence, de la configuration du système-hôte et de sa puissance. Ainsi, SCORE peut être utilisé dans tout système informatique ayant à gérer des structures de données modifiables de manière répartie (voir paragraphe 1).

5.2. Principes généraux

Le modèle suivant permet de décrire les fonctions de SCORE. La base est structurée en objets logiques accessibles individuellement.

SILOE global produit des demandes d'accès aux objets destinées à être traitées par les SILOE locaux. SILOE global passe à SCORE global ces demandes qui sont examinées par les SCORE locaux concernés avant d'être confiées aux SILOE locaux (voir figure 3.c).

On appelle producteurs les processus "SCORE global" et consommateurs les processus "SCORE local". Les caractéristiques de l'environnement considéré sont les suivantes :

- les demandes d'accès aux objets peuvent être générées à tout moment de l'exécution d'une transaction
- l'ordre d'arrivée chez un consommateur des demandes émises par plusieurs producteurs est aléatoire
- l'outil d'interconnexion ainsi que les processeurs physiques accueillant les producteurs et les consommateurs ne sont pas totalement fiables. Cette dernière hypothèse correspond aux hypothèses couramment faites [McQU77,METC76]. Dans ces conditions, les risques encourus sont la destruction de la cohérence de la base de données et l'interblocage entre producteurs.

Plus précisément, les trois objectifs, devant être satisfaits dans tout système de base de données réparti, sont la diffusion coordonnée des demandes, la sérialisation de flots de demandes convergents et la corrélation entre flots de demandes parallèles [LELA79].
L'obtention d'un ordre total [LAMP78] sur l'ensemble des demandes est une condition nécessaire pour atteindre ces objectifs et c'est cette solution qui est utilisée dans SCORE. SCORE vérifie d'autre part que les transactions sont bien formées (lectures en mode partagé et écritures en mode exclusif) et conserve les objets verrouillés jusqu'à la fin de chaque transaction. En conséquence, tout ordonnancement légal de demandes (qui interdit les accès simultanés incompatibles) est aussi un ordonnancement cohérent.

Le problème majeur est donc de définir un mécanisme qui permette de bâtir un ordre total sur l'ensemble des demandes dans un système réparti soumis à des défaillances. Couplés à ce mécanisme, des protocoles de verrouillage/déverrouillage sont utilisés afin de rendre légal (et donc cohérent) tout ordonnancement.

5.3. Le mécanisme du séquenceur circulant

Ce mécanisme fait appel aux trois notions suivantes : anneau virtuel, jeton de contrôle, séquenceur.

5.3.1. Anneau virtuel

Chaque processeur du système possède un nom logique unique et invariant (en particulier les producteurs). Ainsi, l'on peut définir, pour chaque producteur i, un successeur (le producteur présent dans le système dont le nom est le plus petit entier supérieur à i, modulo une certaine valeur). Chaque producteur ne connaît que ses deux voisins sur l'anneau qui est dit "virtuel" car il n'implique aucune topologie physique particulière. Cette organisation logique est également considérée dans [ELLI77]. Des protocoles permettent de maintenir cette configuration en anneau virtuel lorsque se produisent des défaillances, des retraits ou des réintégrations de processeurs ainsi que des extensions de configuration. Ces protocoles utilisent les services offerts par SER.

5.3.2. Jeton de contrôle

Sur l'anneau virtuel circule un message de format particulier appelé le jeton de contrôle. La possession du jeton par un producteur autorise ce dernier à exécuter une opération particulière, appelée "sélection de tickets", qui doit être réalisée en exclusion mutuelle dans le système.

A ce jeton est associé un entier, appelé numéro de cycle, qui est incrémenté à chaque passage par le producteur d'identité x tel que successeur (x) < x. Ce producteur est unique sur l'anneau virtuel. Ce numéro de cycle permet d'une part d'assurer l'unicité du jeton sur l'anneau (ou de chacun des jetons présents sur l'anneau dans le cas de l'algorithme à séquenceurs multiples) et, d'autre part, de détecter la perte d'un jeton à la suite d'une défaillance de processeur et d'en assurer sa régénération [LELA77].

5.3.3. Séquenceur circulant

Le jeton de contrôle contient un objet appelé séquenceur (entier). La primitive "Sélection de ticket" définie sur ce séquenceur fournit la valeur courante du séquenceur et l'incrémente. Tout producteur recevant le jeton de contrôle sélectionne une certaine quantité de tickets (voir plus loin) et passe le jeton à son successeur sur l'anneau. Les tickets servent à estampiller les demandes d'actions émises par les producteurs. Le séquenceur circule donc en permanence sur l'anneau. Bien que le temps de séjour du séquenceur chez chacun des producteurssoit court (deux opérations E/S et quelques additions), il est nécessaire de pouvoir garantir des performances (temps de réponse, par exemple) qui soient indépendantes de contraintes physiques particulières. A cet effet, quatre algorithmes de gestion du séquenceur circulant ont été définis et sont décrits en [LELA78].

5.4. Gestion des actions et des objets - Traitement de l'interblocage

Toute demande d'action peut être émise par un producteur dès l'instant où elle est estampillée. Une demande d'action contient :

- le nom de l'objet concerné (et le nom du consommateur hôte),
- le type d'action,
- le mode d'accès.

Chaque consommateur entretient (virtuellement) une file d'attente par objet, les demandes d'actions étant classées par ordre croissant de tickets. A tout instant s'exécutent "simultanément" sur un objet toutes les actions consécutives (pour l'ordre des tickets) dont les modes d'accès sont compatibles.

Lorsqu'une demande D parvient au consommateur et provoque un conflit, deux cas se présentent :

1) le ticket de D est supérieur au ticket correspondant à la demande en attente d'exécution en tête de la file d'attente. La demande D est mise en attente.

2) le ticket de D est inférieur à certains des tickets correspondant à des actions en cours de traitement. Les actions sont annulées, (sauf si la phase de validation de la transaction correspondante a été initialisée) et replacées en file d'attente (à un rang déterminé d'après leur ticket) et les producteurs demandeurs sont avertis de la réquisition. Ces derniers peuvent décider alors de ré-initialiser éventuellement la transaction correspondante (roll-back) si nécessaire. L'action D est traitée immédiatement.

La réquisition d'objets et la réinitialisation de transactions ne posent pas de problèmes particuliers car les résultats d'actions Ecrire initialisées en cours d'exécution ne modifient pas effectivement la base. Ces résultats sont conservés dans le contexte d'exécution privé de chaque transaction. Ils ne sont inscrits dans la base qu'au moment où la validation finale est demandée ("Commit").

On voit donc que la solution au problème du traitement de l'interblocage utilisée par SCORE est du type évitement sur détection de conflit. Cette solution, basée sur l'examen de tickets, garantit que si deux transactions sont en conflit sur au moins deux objets différents, peut être gérés par des consommateurs différents, le conflit sera résolu de la même manière pour tous les objets concernés. Les ordonnancements qui en résultent ne peuvent donc conduire à des situations d'interblocage. Une approche identique est décrite dans [ROSE78].

Il peut être utile de faire les commentaires suivants. Cette solution ne nécessite aucune gestion de tables représentant (ou tentant de représenter) l'état courant des demandes en cours, ce qui évite d'avoir à traiter les problèmes que posent, par exemple, les techniques basées sur l'emploi de "graphes d'attente".

En contre-partie, il faut décider de la stratégie optimale à suivre dans le cas de réquisition d'objets. Déclencher systématiquement une réinitialisation de la transaction (roll-back) peut être coûteux en termes de cycles UC, mais peut conduire à un meilleur parallélisme. D'autre part, les cycles UC ne constituent pas la ressource la plus chère dans les systèmes actuels ou futurs.

Par contre, ne pas provoquer la libération d'objets détenus par une transaction dont l'une des actions est annulée et mise en attente, peut dégrader les performances en limitant artificiellement le parallélisme. C'est l'effet "escalier".
On notera que, de toute façon, SCORE garantit que toute transaction sera finalement exécutée, le nombre maximum de conflits possibles étant déterminé par la différence entre le ticket de la transaction et les tickets en cours de traitement. Le meilleur choix n'est pas évident.

Nous comptons mettre en oeuvre un programme d'évaluation de performances afin de pouvoir apporter une réponse à cette question.

5.5. Validation finale fiable

Lorsqu'une transaction se termine, SCORE doit rendre effectif l'effet de toutes les actions Ecrire exécutées par la transaction. Les nouvelles valeurs des objets modifiés doivent être écrites dans la base (en les inscrivant sur les supports physiques concernés). Afin de préserver la cohérence de la base, il est nécessaire de garantir que l'ensemble de ces actions exécutées par différents consommateurs constitue une opération atomique, c'est-à-dire que si au moins l'une de ces actions Ecrire est validée, toutes le seront (Commit), l'autre possibilité étant qu'aucune de ces actions n'est validée (transaction tuée).

Bien évidemment, cette propriété doit être vérifiée dans le cas de pannes. SCORE utilise un protocole de validation à deux phases qui permet de survivre à la défaillance du producteur initiateur de la validation. Lorsqu'une telle défaillance se produit, SER le signale à SCORE . Les consommateurs ont alors la possibilité de décider entre-eux s'il faut ou non valider les actions Ecrire et ceci de manière cohérente. Les verrous posés sur les objets sont enlevés. Le protocole de validation a été conçu de telle sorte que les producteurs puissent se comporter comme des systèmes sans mémoire en cas de panne et de reprise.

D'autre part, les tickets sont utilisés pour permettre à un consommateur défaillant qui "rejoint" le système de se synchroniser avec le reste du système et d'obtenir ou de fabriquer un état de la base (ou partie de base) qu'il gère qui soit cohérent avec les autres bases du système.

6. SER

SER est le sous-système de SIRIUS-DELTA qui assure la fonction d'exécution répartie sur l'ensemble des processeurs physiques interconnectés. Nous préciserons tout d'abord les services offerts par SER à SILOE et SCORE, puis nous définirons les concepts de base qui nous permettrons d'exposer les fonctions de SER.

6.1. Objectifs :

Les services que fournit SER sont essentiellement :

- activation de processus à distance,
- enchaînement de processus suivant les modalités d'exécution répartie spécifiées par SILOE dans le PEX,
- transfert d'information entre processus d'un PEX,
- expression sous forme logique et évaluation des conditions d'activation d'un processus, fonctions éventuellement des résultats d'autres processus,
- utilisation à l'intérieur d'un même PEX, des possibilités de parallélisme offertes par la machine multiprocesseur que constitue l'ensemble des processeurs interconnectés,
- détection et signalisation des pannes et des fins d'exécution normales ou anormales des processus. Ce service est essentiel pour le protocole de validation fiable de SCORE.

6.2. Concepts de base

Le fonctionnement de SER est caractérisé par un contrôle d'exécution entièrement réparti qui s'appuie sur trois entités de base : Action Locale (AL), Variable de Synchronisation (VS) et Fichier de Données Temporaires (FDT). Ces trois entités sont utilisées non seulement de manière interne au SER mais également par SILOE pour la formulation du programme d'exécution répartie (PEX) et par SCORE pour les acquisitions de ressources.

6.2.1. Action locale

L'action locale est l'unité logique d'exécution de SILOE. Elle correspond physiquement à l'exécution d'un programme sur un processeur. Ce peut être, par exemple, une requête de consultation sur la base locale ou bien un tri fusion.

Une action locale en cours d'exécution ne réalise aucune opération explicite de synchronisation ou de dialogue avec d'autres AL se déroulant en parallèle. Les seules actions qu'une AL peut avoir sur l'environnement d'autres AL d'un PEX sont la mise à jour de variables de synchronisation et la consommation ou la production de FDT.

6.2.2. Variable de synchronisation

Les variables de synchronisation permettent de gérer les enchaînements d'actions locales. En effet, à toute demande d'action locale, figurant dans un PEX, SILOE peut associer des variables de synchronisation. Pour chaque AL, une condition d'activation, définissant une configuration déterminée des VS associées, permet de fixer le moment de son lancement. De même, une expression de terminaison permet sur fin d'exécution de définir des mises à jour de VS associées à d'autres AL.

On utilisera, par exemple, une variable de synchronisation pour conditionner le lancement d'une AL sur la fin d'une autre. De même, le verrouillage réussi des objets demandés par l'AL entraîne le positionnement par SCORE de la VS associée.

6.2.3. Fichier de données temporaire

SER gère,de manière automatique, une zone de stockage réseau qui est utilisée pour stocker, de manière temporaire, les données d'entrée et de sortie des AL sous forme de fichiers de données temporaires. Les FDT se présentent comme des fichiers séquentiels à articles de taille variable. Ils sont produits sans possibilité de retour en arrière et détruits automatiquement après consommation. SER assure le transfert des FDT de l'AL productrice vers l'AL consommatrice globalement ou en mode pipeline.

6.3. Fonctions du SER

SER constitue par lui-même un système réparti, (i-e) il existe sur chacun des processeurs du réseau un SER local, assurant l'activation et le contrôle des actions locales à ce processeur pour le compte de SILOE.

Un PEX,fourni sur un processeur donné, est composé de commandes demandant l'exécution d'AL sur les différents processeurs. Chaque commande définit le contexte de l'AL en spécifiant les conditions d'activation et les expressions de terminaison ainsi que les FDT qui seront produits ou consommés par l'AL. Le soumetteur de PEX identifie de manière unique et localise, dans chaque commande l'AL, les VS et FDT utilisés.

Un SER local de type "client" assure la prise en compte de chaque commande de création de contexte d'AL et son envoi à un SER local de type "serveur" sur le processeur d'exécution. Une fois le contexte d'exécution mis en place, le SER client n'intervient plus si ce n'est pour des échanges de commandes et d'informations de supervision (indication de panne d'un processeur, compte-rendu de fin d'exécution ou abort). Le contrôle d'exécution est alors décentralisé au niveau des SER serveurs.

L'enchaînement des diverses AL est commandé par l'évaluation des conditions d'activation dont les mises à jour se font de manière totalement répartie, sans référence au processeur initial.

Chaque SER serveur assure pour chaque contexte d'AL :

- la préparation de son lancement, c'est-à-dire l'évaluation de sa condition d'activation,
- le lancement effectif en liaison avec le système d'exploitation local,
- la mise à disposition des données (FDT) nécessaires à l'exécution ,
- le contrôle local de l'exécution ainsi que la prise en compte de la fin normale ou anormale entraînant l'évaluation de l'expression de terminaison et les mises à jour éventuelles de VS distantes,
- la prise en compte des données produites (FDT) et leurs transferts éventuels (données d'entrée d'autres AL).

La structure d'exécution répartie du SER apparaît sur la figure 6.a.

6.4. Remarques générales

SER fait suite et s'inspire de travaux récents dans le domaine des systèmes d'exécution répartie réalisés dans le cadre de SIRIUS, notamment IGOR [SERG78] et MERE [ANDR78]. SER a été conçu dans un esprit de généralité, (i-e) il n'est pas particularisé à une application répartie, en l'occurence SILOE. En effet :

- sur le plan des échanges entre processeurs interconnectés, SER s'appuie sur un service de transport classique (de type niveau 4 de l'Open System Architecture de l'ISO)
- il n'interfère avec les systèmes locaux que par la connaissance d'un catalogue de commandes ou programmes locaux pouvant intervenir dans l'application répartie.

7. CONTEXTE DE REALISATION

La réalisation de SIRIUS-DELTA est effectuée à l'IRIA selon des principes d'implémentation et de validation par étapes, l'objectif final étant un SGBDR général utilisé comme base d'applications démonstratives, notamment dans le domaine bureautique. Nous décrirons tout d'abord les principales étapes, puis nous verrons les aspects matériels et enfin les équipes.

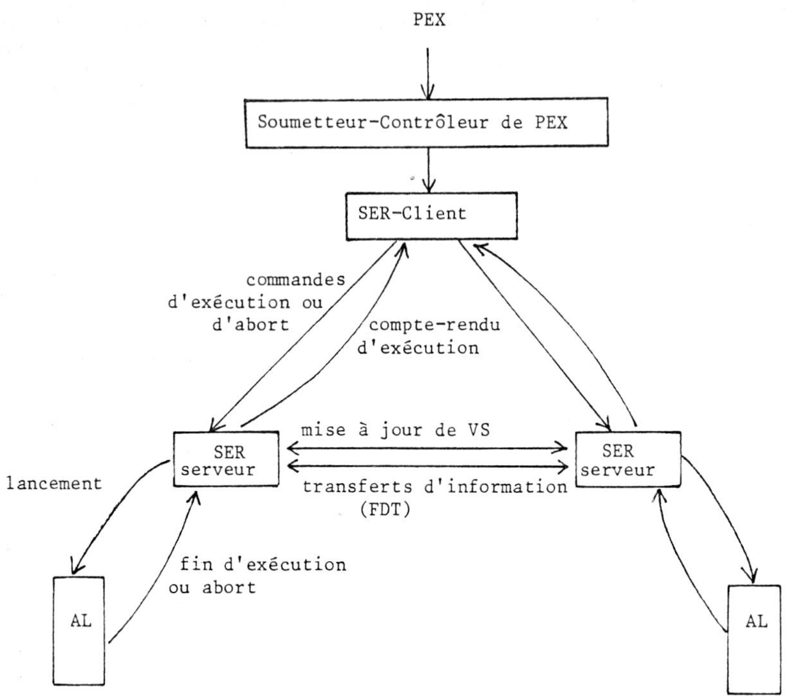

FIGURE 6.a - STRUCTURE D'EXECUTION REPARTIE DU SER

7.1. Phases de développement

SIRIUS-DELTA est articulé selon 5 phases successives :

- étude générale portant sur l'ensemble des problèmes avec pour objectif la définition de l'architecture du SGBDR et de chacun des composants SILOE, SCORE et SER.
- implémentation en consultation simple, permettant à un utilisateur de consulter la BDR dans des cas simples de répartition et un environnement "idéal".
- implémentation en environnement non fiable en consultation complexe dans un contexte multi-utilisateur.
- implémentation des fonctions de mise à jour en environnement non fiable, avec concurrence, donc en intégrant le sous-projet SCORE,
- implémentation en milieu hétérogène tant sur le plan des moyens d'interconnexion que des SGBD (les trois premières étapes étant effectuées sur des systèmes homogènes interconnectés en point-à-point).

La réalisation de SIRIUS-DELTA a débuté en mars 1979, les dates de fin,prévues pour chacune des cinq phases, sont respectivement : septembre 1979, mars 1980, juin 1980, septembre 1980 et janvier 1981.

7.2. Matériels et systèmes

Les premières phases de réalisation sont mises en oeuvre sur un réseau de trois REALITE 2000 d'INTERTECHNIQUE localement interconnectés au moyen de liaisons point-à-point.

Le REALITE 2000 est un mini-ordinateur spécialisé dans la gestion de bases de données. Il est orienté vers une utilisation multi-utilisateurs conversationnelle et basé sur un système d'exploitation microprogrammé à mémoire virtuelle. SIRIUS-DELTA réutilisera largement le logiciel constructeur en conservant, notamment, le langage d'interrogation FRANCAIS.

Par la suite, SIRIUS-DELTA sera ouvert sur des réseaux de communication plus élaborés (réseaux locaux type ETHERNET ou réseau public TRANSPAC). Cela permettra non seulement des évaluations de performances plus réalistes mais également d'aborder l'hétérogénéité avec l'ajout de systèmes autres que les REALITE, notamment, des SGBD en cours de développement sur microprocesseurs au sein du projet SIRIUS.

7.3. Equipes :

SIRIUS-DELTA à l'instar de l'ensemble du projet SIRIUS est issu d'actions communes avec la recherche, les utilisateurs et les industriels de l'informatique.

La conception de SIRIUS-DELTA est effectuée par l'équipe de direction du projet avec l'aide des équipes de recherche SIRIUS.

Pour la réalisation, une équipe d'environ 9 personnes a été mise en place à l'IRIA. Elle est composée d'ingénieurs de l'IRIA et de SSCI, le constructeur INTERTECHNIQUE participant également à l'opération. Dans cette équipe, SILOE est défini et réalisé par G. DANET, C. ESCULIER, A.M. GLORIEUX et B. ROTHENBURGER, SCORE par J. BOUDENANT, G. FERRAN, G. LE LANN, P. ROLIN, S. SEDILLOT et SER par C. LEPENANT, G. SERGEANT et L. TREILLE. SIRIUS-DELTA est réalisé en liaison avec des utilisateurs (SNCF notamment) qui mettront en oeuvre des cas concrets sur le prototype. Par ailleurs, les équipes de recherches utiliseront SIRIUS-DELTA soit pour ajouter de nouvelles fonctionnalités, soit pour expérimenter de nouveaux algorithmes.

CONCLUSION

SIRIUS-DELTA est un système de gestion de bases de données réparties dont les caractéristiques résultent des études et recherches réalisées durant la première phase du projet pilote SIRIUS. C'est un prototype qui démontre la validité et la faisabilité, dans un environnement informatique industriel, de solutions nouvelles propres aux systèmes répartis. Sa mise en oeuvre permettra de mieux connaître le comportement et les performances de ce type de système pour différentes classes d'applications.

REFERENCES

[ADIB78] M. ADIBA, J.C. CHUPIN, R. DEMOLOMBE, G. GARDARIN, J. LE BIHAN : Issues in distributed data base management systems : a technical overview, conference VLDB, Berlin, 1978.

[AFCE76] Groupe AFCET-TTI bases de données réparties : Caractérisation d'un SGBDR, Atelier du Congrès AFCET-TTI, Gif-sur-Yvette, Nov. 1978.

[ANDR78] E. ANDRE, P. DECITRE : On providing distributed applications programmers with control over synchronisation, Computer Networks Protocols Conference, University of Liège, 1978.

[ANSI75] ANSI : ANSI/X3/SPARC study group on data base management systems interim report, FDT, Bulletin of ACM-SIGMOD, vol. 7, n° 2, 1975.

[BACH77] C. BACHMAN : Advances in data base technology proceedings, London, Dec. 1977.

[BOSC78] P. BOSC, A. CHAUFFAUT : Le système FRERES. Contribution à la coopération de bases existantes, interrogation de fichiers sur un réseau de calculateurs hétérogènes, Thèse, Rennes, 1978.

[CALE78] J.Y. CALECA : Projet POLYPHEME. L'expression et la composition de transactions dans un système de bases de données réparties, Thèse, Grenoble, 1978.

[CODD71] E.F. CODD : A relational model of data for large shared data banks, CACM, vol. 13, n° 6, juin 1970.

[ELLI77] C.A. ELLIS : Consistency and correctness of duplicate database systems, Proc. 6th ACM Symp. on Operating System Principles, (Nov. 1977), 67-84.

[ESWA76] K.P. ESWARAN et al. : The notions of consistency and predicate locks in a database system, CACM, vol. 19, n° 11, (Nov. 1976), 624-633.

[HOLL78] E. HOLLER, C. KEIL, H. BREITWIESER : DISCO. Ein datenbankkonzept für kleinrechnernetze auf der basis eines verteilten dateiverwaltungsystems, Karlsruhe, 1978.

[LAMP78] L. LAMPORT : Time, clocks and the ordering of events in a distributed system, CACM, vol. 21, n° 7 (July 1978), 558-565.

[LEBI79] J. LE BIHAN : Le projet SIRIUS. Bulletin de liaison de l'IRIA, Octobre 1979.

[LELA77] G. LE LANN : Introduction à l'analyse des systèmes multiréférentiels, Thèse Doctorat d'Etat, Université de Rennes, (Mai 1977), 202 p., (document SIRIUS CTR.I.004).

[LELA78] G. LE LANN : Algorithms for distributed data-sharing systems which use tickets, Proc. 3rd Berkeley Workshop on Distributed Data Management and computer Networks, (Aug. 1978), 259-272, (document SIRIUS SYN.I.003).

[LELA79] G. LE LANN : Les problèmes de signalisation dans les systèmes informatiques à contrôle réparti, document SIRIUS SYN.I.005, (Mai 1979), 28 p.

[McQU77] J.M. McQUILLAN, D.C. WALDEN : The ARPA network design decisions, Computer Networks, vol. 1, n° 6, (1977), 243-289.

[METC76] R.M. METCALFE, D.R. BOGGS : ETHERNET. Distributed packet-switching for local computer networks, CACM, vol. 19, n° 7, (July 1976), 395-404.

[NEUH77] E.J. NEUHOLD, H. BILLER : POREL. A distributed data base on an inhomogeneous computer network, conference VLDB, Tokyo, 1977.

[NGUY79] NGUYEN GIA TOAN : A dynamic distribution algorithm for relational query interpretation over cooperating data bases, rapport USMG, Grenoble, 1979.

[POLY79] Groupe POLYPHEME : Rapport final du projet POLYPHEME, rapport interne SIRIUS, Nov. 1979.

[ROSE78] D.J. ROSENKRANTZ et al. : System level concurrency control for distributed database systems, ACM TODS, vol. 3, n° 2 (June 1978), 178-198.

[SDD178] Computer Corporation of America : SDD-1 technical reports, Cambridge 1978.

[SERG78] G. SERGEANT et al. : Système d'interprétation généralisé orienté réseau, SIGOR, spécifications de définition, document SIRIUS XEC.I.007, IRIA, Août 1978.

[SPAC78] S. SPACCAPIETRA : Problématique de conception d'un système de gestion de bases de données réparties, Thèse d'Etat (Paris VI), 1978.

[TSIC77] D. TSICHRITZIS, A. KLUG : The ANSI/SPARC DBMS framework-report of the study group on data base management systems, technical note 12, CSRG, Univ. of Toronto, Ontario (Canada), Juillet 1977.

DISTRIBUTED DATA BASES
C. Delobel and W. Litwin (eds.)
North-Holland Publishing Company

CONCEPTS FOR A ROBUST DISTRIBUTED DATA BASE SYSTEM

Bernd Walter

Institut fuer Informatik
University of Stuttgart
Stuttgart
Fed. Rep. of Germany

Concepts which help to implement a robust distributed data base system are presented in this paper. A new process structure helps to maintain system consistency throughout normal and abnormal conditions. The introduction of short-time and long-time failures leads to an extended classification of failures. An adequate set of recovery mechanisms is described.

INTRODUCTION

This paper is based on the author's work in a research group for distributed data base systems (DDBS). The system POREL [18], [19] designed by that group, is a relational DDBS and is currently implemented on top of a computer network with an X.25 interface.

In the following an architecture of a DDBS will be presented, which has been designed according to the aspect of robustness against various classes of failures. Not all of the described mechanisms will be implemented in the POREL system. Note that therefore there may be some differences between this paper and other papers on POREL, e.g. [2].

First of all the overall architecture is described and a transaction processing model is given. After defining the term robustness, an extended classification of failure is introduced. The remainder of the paper contains the description of the various mechanisms needed to provide robustness and a discussion of this proposal.

SYSTEM ARCHITECTURE

The robust mechanisms discussed in this paper are part of a functionally homogeneous DDBS. Functional homogeneity means that all around the network there are local DBMSs with identical sets of data processing and data control functions. The data is stored partially redundant. The user is provided with a SEQUEL-like interface which guarantees network transparency, i.e. the user is not aware of the actual processing sites or even of the distribution of data.

Each local DBMS consists of three types of functional units, compiler, transaction monitor and base machine.

The compiler is composed of two parts. The first part performs all those tasks, which may be regarded as network-independent, e.g. scanning, parsing, generating code etc. The second part performs a network-dependent analysis and modifies the code with regard to distribution and replication of data. The output of the compiler is executable transaction code. It is assumed that a transaction (TA) always represents one user task [6],[23]. All transactions are static in the sense that all processing sites are predetermined at compile-time. In [14] a different approach may be found, which allows to determine processing sites at run time. For more details on our approach see [19].

The transaction monitor (TM) is responsible for the runtime-management of transactions. It coordinates the network-wide processing of all locally initiated multi-site-transactions (a locally initiated transaction, which is to be processed only at the local site, may be regarded as a special case of a multi-site-transaction). This coordination-function includes the requesting of resources as well as the control of commitment and recovery. The TM also controls all local processing of remotely initiated transactions. The lock-manager, which has the exclusive rights to lock and unlock local resources (i.e. the local portion of the data base), is a subcomponent of the TM. A slightly different approach to the architecture of this component may be found in [7].

The base machine (BM) [20] executes subtransactions (subtransactions will be described in one of the following sections). Only a base machine has the right to perform data base accesses (a special log, which is maintained by the TM, is not regarded as part of the database).

Each one of these types of functional units may be implemented by a collection of identical processes, i.e. there may be several base machines, transaction monitors and compilers on each node, running in parallel. Without restricting the generality of our model, in the following discussion we will assume that there are several BMs at each node and several compilers, but only one transaction monitor. The processes are running under direct control of the operating system kernel (a kernel is not a process, but a software extension of the hardware).

After compilation the transaction code is composed of two parts, code for locking the resources and code for the actual data base processing.

The lock code consists of a list of the data units to be locked. Additionally for each data unit it is indicated at which site it is located, using site-identifiers (SID) and whether shared access or exclusive access [6],[9] is requested. The extraction of the lock-requests from the rest of the code to the beginning is possible, since a pre-claiming technique is used in the system (pre-claiming is used to avoid expensive transaction rollback in deadlock situations and to reduce the message overhead of multi-site transactions, pre-claiming allows to use piggyback techniques for sending several lock requests to one site). Predicate locking [6] may be integrated into this approach as well as hierarchical locking [9]. No additional unlock-code is necessary if the TM on the transaction's initiation site does some bookkeeping for recovery reasons anyhow. Note that the code does not predetermine any strategy for exception-handling, e.g. deadlock during the locking-phase.

The processing-code consists of a list of pairs SID/subtransaction (STA) code. The SID identifies the site on which the STA will be processed. The STA code itself is composed of three parts, corresponding to the three phases in the processing of a STA, i.e. code for the input-phase, the execution-phase, and the output-phase. In the input-phase results are received from other STAs or input is provided from the user. During the execution-phase, no messages may be sent or received, only data base processing is done. After the end of the execution-phase results may be sent to other STAs or the user.

Due to the described three-phase-structure, a STA may be regarded as an atomic action [15], [21]. Therefore two rules exist for subtransactions: all processing of a subtransaction must be done at one site and the processing must be three phased, which is important for the recovery mechanisms.

The read and write sets of the various STAs can be modelled as a precedence graph, where the nodes are STAs and the arcs reflect the data flow. As shown for the context of operating systems [4], this graph can be restructured to receive a maximal concurrent system of STAs (the algorithm, described in [4], has to be extended, since in the context of a DDBS the processing site of a STA is of importance; in [4] global and local resources are regarded, in the DDBS environment only global resources, i.e. the data, are of interest). Note that this maximal concurrent representation of a transaction may consist of several unconnected subgraphs.

In the following we will assume that the compiler generates maximal concurrent transaction-code.

The compiler delivers the TA-code to the local transaction monitor (TM). TM generates a unique TA identifier (TAID) [11], composed of a locally generated timestamp and the node identifier. These unique TAIDS define a total ordering [12] of all transactions in the network. This allows the implementation of a rather cheap conflict resolution algorithm [26].

In principle the processing of a transaction is subdivided into a lock-phase, a process-phase and an unlock-phase.

In the lock-phase the TM at the site of origin of the TA sends the lock-requests to those remote TMs, which are responsible for the requested resources and awaits the response. If all locks are granted, TA processing enters the next phase, else some scheduling or conflict solving algorithm has to be applied.

In the process-phase the local TM transmits the STA-code-pieces to those TMs which cooperate in the processing of the transaction. Each of these TMs forwards the STA-code to one of their local BMs. The BMs do the processing of the code in finite time and then return the control to their local TM. The results are collected at the site of origin.

In the unlock-phase, after all TMs cooperating in the processing of the TA have transmitted their end-of-STA messages (commit or abort), all resources locked by the TA are released.

In the section above the system architecture and the principle steps in processing a transaction have been sketched. In the next sections we will describe the architecture and the involved mechanisms in more detail with regard to the aspects of robustness.

ROBUSTNESS

A system is said to be robust against a certain class of failures, if - for a given input - it always produces the same output even though any failure out of that class may occur. Merely the processing time may differ for the various cases. The term robustness has been chosen by the author, because in several discussions it appeared that other terms with a similar meaning (e.g. resiliency, fault tolerance [22]) were often misinterpreted.

According to [14] failures which affect the DDBS fall into the following broad classes:

- Processor and software failures which cause the data base management system at one site to be stopped (without warning) and to be restarted (loss of valatile memory).

- Media failures which make it impossible to retrieve data from the online database.

- Failures in communications between sites of the DDBS.

- Transaction failures caused for instance by violation of integrity constraints.

Many similar classifications have been given elsewhere in the literature, e.g. [13], [10].

Obviously, the time needed to recover from those failures (i.e. the time to detect and classify a failure plus the time needed for recovery) may differ significantly, e.g. from split seconds to several hours or even more. For this reason a further subdivision of each of the given classes of failures is needed. It is suggested to distinguish between short-time-failures and long-time-failures. In the following each of those four classes will be discussed in detail, with regard to the time-aspect.

If a failure of the first class occurs, then in practically the most cases an immediate restart is possible, only sometimes additional maintenance work is necessary. If the system is a centralized one, in both cases all transaction have to wait until the end of the recovery procedure. In a distributed environment this kind of failure means that only some of the transactions and parts of the database are affected. The crash on one site of the network possibly has some side effects to the rest of the system. Some transactions may commit without problems, others may have subtransactions to be processed on the crashed site. There are principally two actions possible concerning the affected transactions. First, these transactions wait until the crashed site has been recovered and all the resources they have locked remain locked during the recovery time. Second, all affected transactions are backed out, all their resources are released, and at the end of the recovery procedure the backed out transactions are restarted. Obviously, in the case of an immediate restart the waiting strategy would be cheaper than the restructuring strategy (restructuring contains backing-out plus some additional work, which will be discussed later). On the other hand, if the recovery procedure takes longer, after some time a point is reached, where resource blocking is more expensive than the restructuring cost (blocking of the resources reduces the system throughput).

Now assume, that a failure of the second class occurs (media failure). Again, the recovery from this kind of failure may be possible in rather short time, e.g. if there is an online-copy of the affected data, or recovery may take up to several hours, e.g. if large files have to be restored from archiv-tape or if the disc-unit must be repaired. And again, two strategies in handling the affected transactions are possible, waiting or backing out (restructuring). Obviously, if an online-copy is available, waiting is a good strategy, else restructuring may be better.

As can be shown easily, the discussion of communication failures would lead to the same results as above, i.e. there are short-time--failures and long-time-failures and it is possible to wait or to restructure.

Only the fourth class of failures cannot be subdivided any more. If integrity constraints are violated, always the whole transaction has to be backed out and no other transactions are affected.

It has been shown that the cost-minimal transaction-handling--strategy depends on the recovery time. The remaining problem is to give an adequate estimate of the costs in advance, or else no meaningful decision is possible.

Assume a simple DDBS, where no replicas exist and where one site is down. The affected multi-site-transactions have to wait for a time-period, which is composed of the time needed to restore the crashed site and to back-out and redo all subtransactions on that site (if there are parallelly processable STAs, then this time-period is slightly reduced, if some STAs of an affected TA can be independently processed). If the time-period is longer than the time needed to backout and redo the STAs of an affected transaction, then backing out is better.

Since in the spare time additional TAs may run, the system-through--put is increased and therefore the costs of restructuring are less than the cost for waiting (note that in a system with replicas restructuring may be more complex). So what is needed is a good estimate of the described time-periods in advance, i.e. estimation of the recovery-time as well as estimation of the restructuring-time.

In the case of media failures good estimations are possible, because each data-unit has a rather fix restorage cost. In the other cases of failures, mechanisms are needed to detect hardware-failures (assuming that long-time-failures will always be hardware--failures). A discussion of such mechanisms is beyond the scope of this paper.

Restructuring time depends on the number of transactions which are affected if a certain site crashes and the time needed to backout/redo each of these transactions.

With the help of statistics on the characteristics of transactions, it should be possible to give estimates of the typical time periods needed to restructure in various cases of failure.

Clearly, further analysis has to be done in this area, but it has been shown that an extended classification of failures and an adequate selection between the strategies waiting and restructuring is a step further to more cost effective robustness mechanisms. In the following chapters we will give robustness mechanisms against short-time-failures and then describe the extensions needed to handle long-time-failures.

ROBUSTNESS MECHANISMS FOR SHORT-TIME-FAILURES

To recover from short-time-failures, a DDBS needs adequate communication protocols, the ability to restart and position processes and facilities to restore the database. In the following such mechanisms will be discussed.

As shown in [25] two protocols are necessary to implement the various types of communication which occur in a DDBS.
A one-phase-protocol is needed for communications of type one--to-one (one source, one destination) and can be implemented using a positive acknowledgement/retransmit technique.
The two-phase-protocol (similar to [13], [5], [10], [14]) is needed for one-to-many-communications (one source, several destinations), where the destinations have to be coordinated.

Assuming that the underlying computer network provides an X.25--interface, each message will be delivered correctly after a finite amount of time and any sequence of messages from the source to one of the destinations will be delivered in the same order as they were sent.

These properties are those of the one-phase-protocol, one message is needed for each occurrence of a one-to-one communication. As shown in [25] the two phase protocol may be implemented on top of the one-phase-protocol.

The two-phase-protocol consists of the coordination-phase (one message to each destination, one information-bearing acknowledgement, i.e. a yes/no vote, from each destination) and the communication phase (if all acknowledgements from the destinations were positive, then one message to each destination plus one non-information-bearing acknowledgement from each of the destinations). Implementing this protocol on top of an X.25-interface requires three explicit messages for each source-destination pair. The information-bearing acknowledgement requires an explicit message, whereas the non-information-bearing acknowledgement is implicitly implemented in internal X.25-levels.

The problem remains that none of the communicators may forget to/from whom it sent/received a message. This point will be discussed in a later section.

Restarting single sites requires the ability to recover subtransactions without affecting subtransactions on other sites. A local process hierarchy will now be described, which realizes such recovery mechanisms.

In the beginning of the restart procedure the operating-system (OS) will be re-installed. To restart the database-system, a kick by the OS is needed, i.e. the OS must have a mechanism which automatically restarts some defined processes after re-installment. Assuming that an OS is composed of a kernel and some system-processes (which are automatically installed, when the kernel is loaded), there should be no problem to install the TM as additional system-process. In the following we will assume that the OS also provides some additional services (supervisor-calls), namely starting and stopping of processes, process control (status information on certain proceses), and interprocess communication supporting the one-phase-protocol.

After the TM has been started by the OS, the TM has to restart the other parts of the database system. To accomplish this task the TM needs information on the status of the local database system before the crash. This information is kept in a so-called transaction-log which is maintained by the TM.

Remember that the TM is concerned with the management of all locally generated transactions (as manager) and with the management of remotely generated sub-transactions (as cohort).

As manager the TM receives the TA-Code from the compiler, does the local locking and requests remote locks. If successful, TM forwards the code of the STAs to the cohorts and to the local base machines. Local base machines have to be controlled (via the operating system) until they commit. After all cohorts and the local base machines - cooperating in the processing of one transaction - have committed, the TM releases all locked resources.

For each of the managed transactions, the TA-log has to contain following information (each entry begins with the TAID):
- TA-Code, which is necessary if a TA has to be restarted, or if single STAs have to be retransmitted to other sites.
- Indication that the lock phase has been ended successful (this may be refined so that every granted lock is indicated).
- Indication that the code of all STAs, which have to be processed remotely, are sent successful to the other sites (maybe refined for single STAs).
- Identifier of the local machines, which are busy for this TA, their mode of operation (DO, UNDO, REDO), and identifier of the processed STAs.
- Indication that the local base machines have committed.
- Indication that all remotely processed STAs have terminated.
- Indication of the global commitment and unlock.
- Indication that the results have been delivered to the requestor (end of TA).

With this information, all transactions can be re-installed, if the end of a phase is not indicated in the log, it will be started all over again (note that the remote TMs must be able to recognize repetition of messages, e.g. lock-requests, STA-code etc. (see also [10], [14]). All local base-machines which have not been committed, will be set into the mode UNDO and afterwards into the mode REDO.

As cohort the TM receives STA-Code from the remote manager and forwards it to a base machine. After the local commitment of the base machine, TA sends a message to the manager and awaits global unlock and commit (abort). For each of these STAs the following entries are to be written into the TA-log (each entry starts with the TAID):
- STA-Code
- Information about the local base machines as above
- Indication that the local BMs have committed and the manager has been informed
- Global commit and unlock (end of STA).

Note that additionally the TM has to log the local lock-table.

Base machines are the only processes having direct access to the data base. To process one STA, one base machine run is needed. Communications occur at the beginning and the end of a run (from/to the TM and other STA processing BMs), each run is finished after a finite amount of time. Due to these properties, a base machine run may be considered as an atomic action. Hence it is possible to implement the three alternative modes of BM-operations without any sideeffects. In the first mode, a STA is executed (DO), in the second mode a STA can be reset, as if it had never been executed (UNDO), and in the third mode a STA is redone (REDO).

UNDO may be implemented using shadow pages [16], [13] or using a pre-image-log [14]. In the environment of a minicomputer the second approach seems to be superior, because less main storage is required. REDO may be implemented using the TA-log described above. The DO/UNDO/REDO principle [10] permits the selective recovery of single STAs (no domino-effect) as well as the selective recovery of single TAs.

Restoring an online data base due to media failure is not a point of discussion in this paper. It is referred to the well known techniques. See for instance [16], [24].

These mechanisms enable the system to recover from all short-time-failures (the non-affected parts of the system have to wait) and allow the on-top-implementation of facilities to handle long-time-failures. The described recovery procedures are mutually non-interfering, i.e. a crash in the TM-restart phase implies just another restart, and a crash in an UNDO-REDO phase just implies another UNDO-REDO. Hence all multiple crashes can be kept under control.

ROBUSTNESS-MECHANISMS FOR LONG-TIME-FAILURES

If the DDBS does not allow the replication of data, then it is a rather easy task to extend the system described above to handle long-time-failures. When a failure occurs, it is decided whether waiting or restructuring is the better reaction. Since restructuring should be done by all sites or by none, it is necessary to coordinate the reactions. This can be done using a two-phase-protocol, where in the first phase a restructuring-request is sent by the site, which detected the failure, to all other sites; in the second phase restructuring is started after all sites have sent an acknowledgement to the restructuring request. Note that failures often will be detected by several sites, therefore some additional synchronization will be necessary (possible solution: if a failure is detected, then send a message to the site with the lowest site-identifier and this site will coordinate restructuring).

If there may be replicas of data, restructuring becomes more complex. To meet its demands a modified primary copy approach is suggested in this chapter. It is well-known that having a primary reduces the synchronization overhead for updating replicated data (see for instance [3], [8], [14]): If an update-TA has to be processed only the primary has to be locked. The updates are then sent to the secondaries before the end of the transaction [23],

[14]. Now, if a primary copy is down, further operations on that data unit are possible after restructuring the DDBS such that one of the secondaries is selected by the new primary. To avoid complex election algorithms, it is suggested to define a linear ordering on the secondaries. If all sites are aware of that ordering and the restructuring-message is sent, they can elect the highest secondary to be the new primary without further message overhead.

A further point to be regarded is the problem of network-partitioning. If a network is partitioned, there may be replicas of data available in one sub-network as well as in another one. Two strategies are possible for handling this case. The first strategy allows to update a data unit only in that subnetwork, which holds the primary copy of this data unit. The second strategy allows the largest subnetwork (it must contain more than half of the original network) to elect new primaries, wherever the original primary is placed, the other subnetworks may not process updates at all. What strategy is used, my be application dependent, but must be fixed before system start.

DISCUSSION

An integrated concept of a robust DDBS has been presented, using well-known techniques as well as new techniques. Among the properties of the proposed methods there are:

- Integration of various locking-strategies is possible, e.g. [6], [9], as well as the use of various locking-granularities.
- Various deadlock-detection algorithms may be used, e.g. [10], [26].
- Linearized or centralized two-phase-protocols [14] are possible.
- Continued operation after network partitioning.
- Maximal concurrent sub-transaction-processing.
- Only distributed algorithms are used.
- Use of hierarchies of replicas minimizes synchronization overhead [3], [8] and allows easy restructuring.
- Process-hierarchies guarantee selective restart and finite runtimes.
- The new classification into short-time-failures and long-time--failures makes it possible to minimize processing costs.

ACKNOWLEDGEMENT

The author is indebted to the members of the POREL Research Group (K. Böhme, U. Fauser, Th. Olnhoff (special thanks), G. Peter, S. Poschik, R. Studer, I. Walter) headed by Prof. E.J. Neuhold. Also special thanks to Mrs. Günthör for typing this script.

REFERENCES

[1] Alsberg, P.A., Day, J., A Principle for Resilient Sharing of Distributed Resources, Proc. 2nd International Conference on Software Engineering, (1977).

[2] Biller, H., Peter, G., Locking Protocols Solving the Redundant Update Problems in Distributed Data Base Management Systems, Proc. IGDD, Aix-en-Provence (May 1979).

[3] Bunch, S.R., Automatic Backup, in: Alsberg, P.A. et al., Preliminary Research Study Report, Technical Report CAC-162, Center for Advanced Computation, University of Illinois at Urbana-Champaign (May 1975).

[4] Coffman, E.J., Denning, P.J., Operating-System Theory (Prentice Hall, Englewood Cliffs, 1973).

[5] Ellis, C.A., A Robust Algorithm for Updating Duplicate Data Bases, Proc. 2nd Berkeley Workshop on Distributed Data Management and Computer Networks (1977).

[6] Eswaran, K.P. et al., On the Notions of Consistency and Predicate Locks in Data Base Systems, CACM 19: 11 (1976).

[7] Fauser, U., Neuhold, E.J., Transaction Processing in the Distributed DBMS POREL, 4th Berkeley Conference on Distributed Data Management and Computer Networks (August 1979).

[8] Grapa, E., Belford, G.G., Techniques for Update Synchronization in Distributed Data Bases, Technical Report, Center for Advanced Computation, University of Illinois at Urbana-Champaign (1977).

[9] Gray, J.N. et al., Granularity of Locks and Degrees of Consistency in a Shared Data Base, Proc. IFIP TC-2 WC on Modelling in Data Base Management Systems (1976).

[10] Gray, J.N., Notes on Data Base Operating Systems, Lecture Notes in Computer Science 60: Operating Systems, an Advanced Course (1978).

[11] Johnson, P.R., Thomas, R.H., The Maintenance of Duplicate Databases, BBN-TENEX Network Working Group, RFC 677 (January 1975).

[12] Lamport, L., Time, Clocks and the Ordering of Events in Distributed Systems, CACM 21:7 (1978).

[13] Lampson, B., Sturgis, H., Crash Recovery in a Distributed Data Base Storage System, Technical Report XEORX PARC (1976).

[14] Lindsay, B.G., Selinger, P.G., Notes on Distributed Databases, Lecture Notes of "Advanced Course on Distributed Data Bases", Sheffield City Polytechnic (July 1979).

[15] Lomet, D.B., Process Structuring, Synchronization and Recovery Using Atomic Actions, Proc. Conf. on Language Design for Reliable Software, SIGPLAN Notices 12:3 (1977).

[16] Lorie, R.A., Physical Integrity in a Large Segmented Database, ACM TODS 2:1 (1977).

[17] Menasce, D.A., Popek, G.J., Muntz, R.R., A Locking Protocol for Resource Coordination in Distributed Databases, Proc. ACM SIGMOD Conf. (1978).

[18] Neuhold, E.J., Biller, H., POREL: A Distributed Data Base on an Inhomogeneous Computer Network, Proc. 3rd VLDB (1977).

[19] POREL-Design Specification (in German), IFI-Berichte 78/4 through 78/13, University of Stuttgart (1978).

[20] Poschik, S., A Portable Relational Interface for the Distributed DBMS POREL, Proc. "Datenbanken in Rechnernetzen mit Kleinrechnern", Karlsruhe (April 1978).

[21] Randell, B., Lee, P.A., Treleaven, P.C., Reliability Issues in Computing System Design, ACM Computing Surveys 10:4 (1978).

[22] Randell, B., Software Fault Tolerance, in: Samet, P.A. (ed.), EURO IFIP 79 (North-Holland, Amsterdam, 1979).

[23] Traiger, I.L. et al., Transactions and Consistency in Distributed Database Systems, IBM Research Report RJ 2555, San José (June 1979).

[24] Verhofstad, J.S.M., Recovery Techniques for Database Systems, ACM Comp. Surveys 10:2 (1978).

[25] Walter, B., Robust Transaction Processing in Distributed Data Base Systems (in German), Proc. German Chapter of the ACM "Datenbanktechnologie", Bad Nauheim (September 1979).

[26] Walter, B., A Distributed Algorithm for Conflict Resolution in Distributed Data Base Systems, Working Paper, University of Stuttgart (June 1979).

DISTRIBUTED DATA BASES
C. Delobel and W. Litwin (eds.)
North-Holland Publishing Company

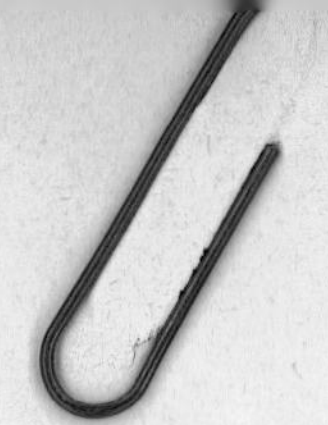

REALIZATION, SYNCHRONIZATION AND RESTART OF UPDATE TRANSACTIONS IN A DISTRIBUTED DATABASE SYSTEM

Rudolf Munz
Technische Universität Berlin
Fachbereich Informatik

Abstract:

Different possibilities for the implementation of update transactions in a distributed database system are considered and evaluated with respect to their synchronization and restart overhead. A simple procedure for preserving consistency of multiple copies is proposed.

1. Description of the environment

A distributed database is stored on several computers of a network which are linked by a communication facility. It is the task of the database system managing these distributed databases to provide a uniform user view of these distributed databases which is not different from a centralized database.

We assume a database which contains records of different types. Records can be thought of being tuples in the relational sense (see Codd /2/). The units of data distribution are subsets of record types. These subsets must be disjoint and for each record there exists a subset to which it belongs. A record type is a special case of a subset. Subsets are defined by the database administrator who assigns a location (node in the network) to each subset. Only complete records and not parts of a record (projections of a tuple) are distributed. An example of a subset definition (see Schweppe /6/ is the following:

```
"STORE SUBSET small_customer OF customer
                             WHERE sales<1000
                             AT LOC department_7"
```

It is possible to create different copies of a subset by assigning different location names to the same subset. The database system must then take care of simultaneously updating these copies, as a record exists only once in the user's view. Reasons for distributing data and keeping copies of records are given by Munz /4/, /5/.

Records are uniquely designated by record keys. The following operations are available for records:

- Addition of a new record: ADD
- Deletion of an existing record: DEL
- Changes of record fields: REPL
- Single record access by the record key: GET
- Access to a set of records: FIND

In the following, different possibilities for the realization and synchronization of ADD, DEL and REPL are investigated.

2. Single record updates by "compare-and-swap"

We assume that the reader is familiar with the problem of synchronizing update transactions in a centralized database environment (see Eswaran et al. /3/).

For update transactions identical to single record updates, a simple and efficient mechanism for a distributed database environment as described above has been proposed by Thomas /7/ (see Bernstein et al. /1/). It is based on time stamping of record updates. This procedure, however, has the disadvantage that inconsistencies (different versions of record copies) are visible for a short period of time. A safer and even simpler scheme for single record updates in a distributed database environment is the following:

Each record contains a version number which is invisible to the user (see figure 1) and which is incremented by one after each update on this record.

version number	user data

Figure 1: Record layout for "compare-and-swap"

If a user wants to update (REPL) or to delete (DEL) a record, he has to access it via GET. The requested record is then delivered together with its version number. If the user calls REPL or DEL after inspecting the record, the database system checks to determine whether the record version on which the user has based its update decision is still valid or not by comparing the version number. If so, the update is performed and the version number is incremented by one. If not, another updater has altered this record in the meantime. In this case, the update decision has been based on an outdated version of this record and may be wrong. This update is therefore rejected and the user has to try it again.

The addition of new records (ADD) causes no problem. They are simply added to the database with a zero version number.

This scheme is simple and cheap, however like the time-stamping mechanism it is a gamble. If update of different users are not likely to collide, it will work satisfactorily. But if users often compete for updating the same record, non-local users, whose access and update is slowed down by the communication facility practically have no chance. It is therefore questionable whether such a scheme is generally useful. Time-stamping and compare-and-swap shift the problem of getting exclusive access to the user.

3. Single record locks

If update transactions are restricted to single record updates, it is a sounder approach to lock the record to be updated. This is usually done by using a lock-list, where type and key of the locked record and the process ID of the user process which holds this lock are entered. If a process requests exclusive access to a record but the request can not be granted, it is placed in a waiting list until the requested record is available. Deadlocks are impossible if processes can only have exclusive access to one record at a time.

If a user process wants to lock a record for which several copies exist, the database system must set locks at all locations where such copies are kept. This setting of locks must not be performed in an arbitrary order. Since two user processes may want to lock the same record simultaneously, the two corresponding database processes may partially succeed (that is, lock several but not all of the record copies) and then wait forever. To avoid this, the locking of copies must proceed in a well-defined order, using for example ascending location addresses. By doing this, deadlocks are avoided during the setting of locks for record copies. However, locking order prevents a broadcast of lock messages.

Locked records are still visible for non-updating users. The database system insures that these readers will either see the old or the new version of an updated record and not a state in-between.

If the updating process issues its update command and afterwards releases the record lock, all record copies are altered and released. Contrary to the setting of locks, the release of the record copies can be done simultaneously or in arbitrary order. After this, the record update is visible to all readers.

There will be a short time delay for the realization of the same update at different locations, that is old and new versions of the same record may coexist during a short period of time. This causes no inconsistencies for a user, since he always sees only one record version (the old or the new one).

4. Update transactions

In general, single record locks are not sufficient in a database environment. One record update will often depend on fields of other records or other record updates. Because of this, database users must have a means of specifying this dependency. A set of dependent updates is called an update transaction (see Eswaran et al. /3/). We will signal the beginning and the end of an update transaction by LOCK (...) and UNLOCK ( ), respectively. Preclaiming is used, that is locks can not be nested. Preclaiming leads to larger locking granularities and thus reduced concurrency, but it avoids deadlocks which are relatively hard to detect and resolve in a distributed environment. It is possible to lock different records, different subsets, and different record types within one LOCK command. Again, these locks will not influence readers, but only lock out other updaters. Readers which want to operate in a level of consistency guaranteeing the reproducability of their read accesses can issue read locks. In the following we will concentrate on write locks. The database system guarantees that all effects of an update transaction are made visible to other database users at once or that, in case of a failure, this update transaction has no effect at all.

This is achieved by establishing a private update file for each updater, thus realizing a deferred update. All updated records are kept in this update file during the update transaction. At the end of an update transaction, they are either made visible in the database or backed out. Backing out an update transaction is simply done by erasing the corresponding update file.

In a distributed database environment, locks are set at locations where copies of the locked record, subset, or record type exist. An update file for this update transaction will also be established at all of these locations. That is, in general, there will be several update files at different locations for one updater. The content of these different update files will not be the same. Each local update file contains only those updates which will effect the subsets stored at this location. The organization of these update files allows the storing and accessing of records of different types within one update file. If a user updates a record, the location of the altered record is determined and it is then entered in the update file(s) of the corresponding location(s). If a record changes its location because of an update, it is marked as deleted in one update file and added as a new record in another update file. For the same reason as explained for single record locks, locking and unlocking must be done in a specific order. However, since several records, subsets, or record types can be locked at the same location, an order for setting locks must also be regarded for different record types, different subsets and different records of the same record type.

When an updater issues a LOCK, in addition to the setting of the required locks, all update files needed are established at the relevant locations. During the update transaction, the updater has a private view of the database, that is, GET and FIND commands must reflect his changes of the database and must therefore inspect his update files for relevant records. If a record is updated, its (new) location is determined and the record is placed in the corresponding update file. At the (successful) end of an update transaction, the UNLOCK is sent to all locations where updatefiles for this update transaction exist. There, all readers are blocked termporarily, the updates contained in the update file are made visible to all other database users, the locks held by this update transaction are removed from the lock list, and the update file is erased. Unlocking can be done in an arbitrary order or in parallel. After this unlocking procedure has been performed successfully at all relevant locations, the update transaction has been completed successfully.

5. The problem of adding a record to a distributed database

The problem is not adding the record, but preserving the uniqueness of the record key. If a record is to be added to the database, the location(s) where this record has to be stored can be determined by evaluating the subset definitions. However, if the subsets of the record type are not characterized by intervals of the record key domain, it is hard to test whether the key of the record to be inserted exists elsewhere at another location. This is necessary, since a record with the same key may already exist in another subset.

To preserve key uniqueness, all locations where subsets of this record type are stored must be checked for the existence of a record with the same key. This is somewhat surprising, since in a centralized database system, the checking of key uniqueness is done almost implicitely by inserting a record (e.g. using B*-trees). Contrary to this, key uniqueness in a distributed database system is considerably harder to achieve. Possible alternatives to eliminate this problem are not convincing:

- to restrict the definition of subsets to contain intervals of the key domain only,
- to do without global key uniqueness and to guarantee only locally unique keys,
- to maintain a global key index at each location, which contains the keys of all records of a record type

The first one is too restrictive. The second one will lead to inconsistencies whose detection will complicate other operations of the database system, for example a direct record access via the record key or a lock request for a particular record. The third alternative is practically impossible because the deletion or addition of a record will cause updates at <u>all</u> locations of the network, not only at the location where subsets of the particular record type are stored. Nevertheless, a global key index makes sense during massive record insertions if it is only established, used and then thrown away.

We decided to guarantee key uniqueness in our distributed database system for these reasons, that is, to test whether there will be a key collision at each record addition. This test can be done simultaneously or in an arbitrary order for all subsets of the record type. However, the situation is similar to the setting of locks, since two updating processes (called "adders") may possibly want to add two different records with the same key at the same time and insert these records after they have detected no key collision. This results in an inconsistency of the database. To avoid such simultaneous actions of two "adders", the intension of adding a record with a particular key must be made known to other "adders" by putting an entry in a reserved-key list. If each "adder" not only checks the local subsets but also the local reserved-key list during its check cycle, not two "adders" can insert two records (of the same type) with the same key. After the successful addition of a record, the "adder" has to remove its entry from the reserved-key list.

This second communication cycle, with all locations where subsets of this record type are stored, can also be done simultaneously or in arbitrary order. If the entries are not removed from the reserved-key list within a certain period of time, a timeout mechanism checks whether the "adder" is still active. If so, the key is kept reserved. Otherwise this reservation is cancelled.

To speed up massive insertions of new records we provide a special command BEGIN_MASS_ADD (record type) which excludes other "adders" from inserting records of this record type and builds up a global index of all keys of this record type. This global key index is kept at the location of the "adder". After this, preserving key uniqueness is as easy as in a centralized database system. If the insertion of records is completed, the global key index is dropped by END_MASS_ADD. For the reasons described above, this global key index is maintained only during the insertion of these records.

If local hardware, software and communication line breakdowns are considered, another penalty must be paid for preserving key uniqueness. If one location where subsets of the record type are stored is down and no copies of these subsets exist elsewhere, no addition of records of this type is possible, as it is impossible to check the unaccessible records for possible key collisions. That is, to perform a single ADD or BEGIN_MASS_ADD all records of the mentioned record type must be accessible. (If one relevant location goes down after a BEGIN_MASS_ADD, it is still possible to add records except for those which are to be stored at this location.) This situation can only be circumvented by some organizational measures. Locally, a record type with the same record structure but a different type name must be defined. Then all records are added to this local record type. When the needed locations are up again, all inputted records can be transferred to the correct record type. As key collisions are possible during this transfer, such a "spooling" mechanism requires supervision at this phase or it will produce a list of errors.

These points show that the uniqueness of record keys is much more difficult providing for in a distributed database system than in a centralized database system. The consequence for the application philosophy of a distributed database system (which preserves key uniqueness) is to define subsets only by intervals of the key domains or to require that record types which are distributed by more complicated subset definitions should consist of relatively stable members. Record types with a relatively high member volatility should not be distributed (except by using intervals of the key domain) but be kept entirely at one location or shifted as a whole from one location to another. A more rigid solution would be to require that all record fields used for the definition of the data distribution should be a part of the record key, that is, to extend the record key by the distribution fields. User experience is needed to evaluate whether these properties of a distributed database system will cause problems in practical applications.

6. Consistency of subset copies

If a subset is involved in an update transaction, all (possibly existing) copies of this subset must be updated simultaneously. One possible way of doing this has been discussed in chapter 3 and 4. There, however, the underlying assumption was that all parts of the network (hardware, software, communication lines) are intact. This will not be true in practice and one goal in designing a distributed database system is to provide at least a partial availibility of the data even if some nodes or communication lines are down. Therefore, restart/recovery measures must be developed which take care of the consistency of subset copies, that is, which guarantee that all copies of a subset have the same update status.

To be more specific, we will discuss our restart/recovery measures by using an illustration of a network configuration. The solutions presented can however be easily generalized. The illustrative configuration is shown in figure 2.

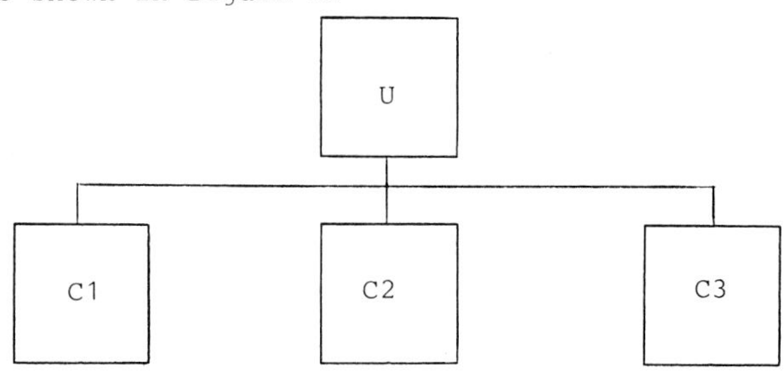

Figure 2: Illustration of a network configuration

The node where an update transaction is performed is designated by U. This update transaction concerns one subset of which copies exist at the nodes C1, C2, and C3.

For this update transaction, four different cases of breakdowns will be distinguished and discussed:

Case 1: Breakdown of U during the setting of its locks at C1, C2 and C3.

Case 2: Breakdown of U after the setting of its locks and during its update transaction.

Case 3: One of the nodes where a copy of the subset exists (that is C1, C2, or C3) is down or unreachable at the time of the update transaction of U.

Case 4: Breakdown of U during its unlocking phase.

6.1 Solution to case 1. The consequence of a breakdown of type 1 is that locks exist at some nodes, say C1 and C2, but not at all nodes, for example, not at C3. Because of the breakdown of U, the locks held by U will never be released. Since all updaters set their locks in the same sequential order, say C1, C2, C3, no update of this subset is possible if the subset copy at C3 is not locked.

To cope with these locks which will never be released and which may therefore cause infinite waiting for other updaters, a timeout mechanism is used. The timeout mechanism checks whether the process holding a lock is still active after a certain deadline is reached. If so, the lock is kept. Otherwise, this and all other locks held by this process are preempted and its update transaction is backed out. Note that this backout only takes place if a timeout is detected and the process holding the locks is no longer active. If it is still active, a new timeout period starts.

6.2 Solution to case 2. Case 2 is not very different from Case 1. The updater has succeeded in setting all locks at C1, C2, and C3. In case of a breakdown during its update transaction, the same timeout mechanism, as explained in 6.1, will release its lock and back out its updates, that is, erase its local update files.

6.3 Solution to case 3. If, for example, C2 is down at the time when U performs an update on the subset stored at C1, C2, and C3, the subset copy at C2 will not reflect this update.

Therefore, when C2 is up again and restarted, it has to check whether this subset has been updated during its downtime. This check can be done by inspecting the subset copy of C1 or C3. Since it would be too slow to check this recordwise, a quicker procedure is explained in 6.4.

For the updater U, the fact that C2 is down at the time of setting the locks for this subset is simply ignored.

It is the task of C2 at restart time, to get the newest state of this subset either from C1 or from C3. Of course, if the only copy of this subset exists at C2 and C2 is down, U can not perform the intended update. On the other hand, if, at the restart time of C2, the nodes C1 and C3 are both down, C2 has no chance of aquiring the latest update state of this subset. In this situation, C2 can only allow accesses to this subset (possibly giving a warning that this might not be the newest state of this subset) but no updates. (Updates are impossible until all three nodes are up again.) Updates under these conditions would lead to serious inconsistencies after C1 and C3 are up again, since then two different versions of the same subset exist, no one can be designated to be the new or the old one.

A similar situation arises, if C2 is still up but unreachable because of a breakdown of communication lines. If communications have become impossible between different nodes where a copy of the same subset exists, no one of these nodes may allow updates for this subsets for the same reasons as described above.

<u>6.4 Solution to case 4.</u> This is the most difficult case and therefore the most interesting. A breakdown of the updater U during its UNLOCK phase may have the consequence that this UNLOCK only reaches C3 and C2 but not C1. Thus, C3 and C2 will make the updates of U visible in their subset copy. At C1, however, the subset copy remains in its old state, since the timeout will release the locks held for this subset and erase the update file of U after a specified time.

A possible existing inconsistency of subset copies is checked at this moment, by allowing C1 to inspect the subset copies at C2 and C3. The check whether the subset copies at C1, C2 and C3 are identical is simplified by assigning a version number to each subset copy which is incremented by one if an update transaction is performed. This simple, but useful measure allows an easy check, whether C1 has missed an update or not: the version numbers of the copies at C1, C2 and C3 are simply be compared.

The difference between two update states can easily be determined and transmitted, if log tapes are used and the version number of each update transaction is written onto the log tape. If no log tapes are used, the whole subset copy must be transmitted. The use of version numbers to designate the update status of a subset copy also facilitates the restart of a downed node, for example the restart of C2 as discussed in 6.3. C2 can easily determine if and how many update transactions it has missed during its downtime by comparing its version number of this subset copy with those of C1 and C2. By telling either C1 or C3 its (possible) old version number, C2 can get the updates it missed from the log tape of the other node.

An important consideration when using version numbers in a distributed database environment is the achieving of a unique enumeration of all update transactions for a subset. This is done by unlocking copies of a subset sequentially in a well-defined order (and not simultaneously or in arbitrary order as would be normally possible). When sequentially unlocking, each updater has to start at the same location to unlock a particular subset. There, a unique version number can be assigned to this subset update. As the number of subset copies is assumed to be small, the sequentiality of this procedure can be tolerated.

Ideal moments to additionally check subset copies consistency is during the sequential locking and unlocking phases. If a subset is locked or unlocked at a location, its current version number is returned. If a copy of this subset is locked or unlocked elsewhere and a different version number is detected, measures to reinstall copy consistency by transforming the older subset copy to the newest state must be taken.

7. Restart and update transactions

Providing for the consistency of copies is only one aspect of the realization of update transactions in a distributed database environment. To explain other aspects of update transactions, figure 2 will be used again, but with another interpretation. The role of U remains unchanged, it is the node where the update transaction is performed. The nodes C1, C2, and C3 are now assumed to keep three different subsets and not three copies of the same subset as in the previous chapters. Now we assume an update transaction where the updater U wants to change all three subsets stored at C1, C2, and C3.

The timeout mechanism will detect and back out all updates at C1, C2, and C3 if the updater U breaks down during the setting of locks or during its update transaction. If, during the update transaction of U, one of the nodes where a relevant subset is stored goes down, U will detect this and back out its update transaction.

Again, the critical case is if U goes down during its emission of UNLOCKS. Thus, some nodes, for example C3, will receive this UNLOCK but others for example C1 and C2 will not. Consequently, the effects of this update transaction will be made visible at C1, but the effects will be backed out by the timeout mechanism at C2 and C3.

This must not happen since an update transaction is either realized completely or not at all. Therefore, each node participating in an update transaction must be told which nodes are involved in the update transaction and receive the identification of the update transaction (location of the updating process, its process ID and its transaction counter). This information is given to C1, C2, and C3 at the time the lock is set and is kept there in the update file of this updating process. If, for example, C1 performs a timeout of lock list entries, it must not simply erase its local update file for this transaction. Instead, C1 has to use the information it received at lock time to query all relevant nodes whether they have received an UNLOCK for this update transaction. If one of them has, C1 will also realize the updates in its update file. If none of them has, C1 will back out this update transaction locally. These measures will lead to the desired effect of an update transaction being realized completely or not at all.

Another possible type of breakdown is, if C2, for example, goes down during the update transaction of U. At restart time of C2, an update file still exists and C2 must get informed about the fate of the corresponding update transaction. If U has detected the breakdown of C2, it will back out this update transaction. In the worst case, U has issued it UNLOCKS but C2 has gone down before it received an UNLOCK. Therefore, the same scheme as described above must be used for restart purposes at C2. C2 must query all nodes which participated in this update transaction whether one of them has received an UNLOCK for this update transaction. If so, the updates are realized at C2, too. If no relevant node has got an UNLOCK, the updates are backed out. There could be difficulties when getting this information from all of the relevant nodes because some of them might be down. In this case, the locks held by this transaction at C2 must be re-established. That is, no updates are allowed which may possibly collide with this transaction until the question whether the updates of this transaction should be realized or backed out is answered.

8. Recovery

Recovery from a loss of secondary storage in a distributed database environment is not very different from the recovery problem in a centralized database system. If secondary storage is lost, an older state of the database system must be established using a tape copy. This older state can then be actualized by processing the log tape or manually if no log tape exists. The possible existence of subset copies in a distributed database environment is advantageous in such a situation, since a subset's newest state can be re-established by transmitting a copy from another node.

Acknowledgements

This work is part of the design process of a distributed database system based on a network of minicomputers. This system is designed and implemented within the VDN project at the Technical University Berlin, sponsored by the Federal Ministry of Research and Technology of Germany (FKZ 081 5011 A).

The author wishes to thank H.-J. Schneider and H. Schweppe for stimulating discussions and helpful comments.

References:

/1/ P.A. Bernstein; D.W. Shipman; J.B. Rothnie: Concurrency Control in SDD-1: A System for Distributed Databases, Part 1: Description, Technical Report CCA-03-79, Computer Corporation of America

/2/ E.F. Codd: A Relational Model of Data for Large Shared Data Banks, CACM 13, No. 6, June 1970

/3/ K.P. Eswaran, J.N. Gray, R.A. Lorie, I.L. Traiger: On the notions of consistency and predicate locks in a database system, CACM Vol.19, No.11, November 1976

/4/ R. Munz: System architectures for managing distributed databases, Proceedings "Datenbanken in Rechnernetzen mit Kleinrechnern", Informatik-Fachberichte 14,Springer-Verlag,1978.

/5/ R. Munz: Gross Architecture of the Distributed Database System VDN, Proc. IFIP TC-2 Working Conference on Database Architecture (G. Bracchi, G.M. Nijssen (eds.)), North-Holland, 1979

/6/ H. Schweppe: On different classes of predicates for distributing data, Proceedings "Datenbanken in Rechnernetzen mit Kleinrechnern", Informatik-Fachberichte 14, Springer-Verlag, 1978

/7/ R.H. Thomas: A Majority Consensus Approach to Concurrency Control, ACM TODS Vol.4, No.2, June 1979

DISTRIBUTED DATA BASES
C. Delobel and W. Litwin (eds.)
North-Holland Publishing Company

ENSURING CONSISTENCY IN A DISTRIBUTED DATABASE SYSTEM BY USE OF DISTRIBUTED SEMAPHORES*

Fred B. Schneider

Computer Science Department
Cornell University
Ithaca, New York 14853
U.S.A.

Solutions to the database consistency problem in distributed databases are developed. It is shown how any solution to the consistency problem for a centralized database system that involves locking can be adapted for use in distributed systems. This is done, constructively, in two steps. First, it is shown how locking can be implemented in terms of semaphores. Then, a semaphore implementation that is suitable for use in distributed systems is developed.

1. INTRODUCTION

A database can be viewed as a collection of entities, each of which has a value. The *state* of the database is defined in terms of the values of these entities. Typically, a database system will have a set of assertions, called *consistency constraints*, associated with it. These assertions characterize the valid states of the database. For example, in an accounting database one would expect to find the constraint "the sum of the debits and credits for each account is 0." If all the consistency constraints are satisfied by a database state D, then the database is said to be in a *consistent state*. This will be denoted C[D].

A user of a database system may view or alter portions of that database by means of transactions. A *transaction* is a sequence of primitive operations on the entities of the database. Some examples of primitive operations are: <read entity e_i>, <write entity e_j>. Execution of a transaction causes a mapping from one database state to another. Transactions are assumed to preserve consistency. Therefore:

$$\text{(I)}: \quad (\forall\, T\text{: T a transaction:} \quad (\forall\, D\text{: D a database state:} \\ ((C[D] \ \underline{\text{and}}\ T(D) = D') \Longrightarrow C[D'])))$$

A set of transactions is processed *serially* if transactions are processed one at a time, the next transaction being initiated only after completion of the previous one. Clearly, if a set of transactions is processed serially, and the database is initially in a consistent state, then the database state will be consistent immediately prior to, and after, each transaction is processed. This follows directly from (I), above. Notice that if a set of transactions is processed concurrently (i.e., not serially) the resultant state of the database may not be consistent. This is because transactions may "interfere" with each other; a transaction may reference some parts of the database as they were before execution of another transaction, and other parts as they were after that execution. The *database consistency problem* is concerned with devising and implementing schemes so that the result of concurrent execution of a set of transactions is the same as could be obtained by some serial execution of those transactions. Solution of this problem is important for the construction of database systems that support the concurrent

*This research was supported in part by NSF grant MCS-76-22360.

execution of a number of transactions. Typically, solutions involve defining restrictions on the execution of a transaction (e.g., "no entity may be locked after any entity has been unlocked"[3]).

In this paper, solutions for the database consistency problem in distributed databases are developed. It is shown how any solution for the consistency problem in centralized databases involving locks can be adapted for use in distributed systems. Distributed semaphores [10], an extension of a synchronization approach proposed by Lamport [4], are used for this purpose.

Section 2 of this paper discusses distributed systems, and some of the problems associated with implementing distributed database systems. Section 3 contains the development of some solutions to the database consistency problem in centralized database systems. These solutions are extended for use in distributed database systems in section 4 and section 5. Section 6 contains a discussion of our results and attempts to put them in perspective.

2. DISTRIBUTED DATABASE SYSTEMS

A <u>distributed system</u> is a system that is made up of more than one processor in which the only way processors can communicate with each other is by means of a communications network. Thus, in a distributed system processors do not directly have access to shared memory. Each of the processors, along with its memory and peripheral devices, is referred to as a <u>site</u>.

A distributed database system can be implemented by storing some subset of the entities that make up the database at each site s. Let e_s denote the set of entities stored at site s, and let E denote the set of all entities that make up the database. Any implementation where

$$E = \bigcup_{s \text{ a site}} e_s$$

is a distributed implementation of the database. There are many ways in which the entities that comprise E may be divided among the various sites. They can be characterized as follows. A distributed database system is <u>fully redundant</u> if every entity is stored at every site; <u>partially redundant</u> if some entities are stored at more than one site; and <u>partitioned</u> if no entity is stored at more than one site. Each organization has its advantages, depending on the nature of the database and its use. Note that in both fully redundant and partially redundant organizations some mechanism must be devised so that all copies of an entity have the same value. This is called the <u>multiple copy consistency problem</u>. We shall require any solution to the database consistency problem to solve the multiple copy consistency problem, as well.

For a number of reasons, the solution of the database consistency problem initially appears to be more difficult for distributed systems than for centralized systems (i.e., systems with shared memory). Solutions have been proposed ([1], [11] for example), but they tend to be difficult to understand and to verify formally. Reasoning about distributed systems is made difficult by the fact that no site can ever know the state of the entire system. The only way for sites to find out state information is by exchanging messages, which involve finite delays (of uncertain lengths). Thus, upon receiving such a message, the receiver can only learn of a past state of the originator of the message.

3. SOLUTION OF THE CONSISTENCY PROBLEM

Consider a database system where $T = \{t_i | 1 \le i \le n\}$ denotes the set of all possible transactions. The operation of the system in an environment in which there is one (and only one) copy of each entity can be modelled as follows.

DB: <u>cobegin</u> $t_1 \mid\mid t_2 \mid\mid \ldots \mid\mid t_n$ <u>coend</u>

where <u>cobegin</u> $S_1 \mid\mid S_2 \mid\mid \ldots \mid\mid S_n$ <u>coend</u> denotes concurrent execution of statements $S_1, S_2, \ldots, S_n$. If execution of each transaction is atomic, then by using the method of Owicki and Gries [6] it can be shown that the results of the execution of DB can be obtained by serial execution of the component transactions. (This exercise is left to the reader--it is tedious and not very enlightening.) This should not be surprising, since each transaction is atomic, and thus any valid execution of DB must involve executing the component transactions in some (unspecified) serial order.

The atomicity of each of the transactions could be ensured in a number of ways; some of which have broader applicability than others. For example, each transaction would appear to be atomic if it contained at most one primitive, and primitive operations referred to one entity and executed as atomic actions. A second approach might require that no two transactions reference the same entity. Both clearly restrict transactions unacceptably. By using a synchronization mechanism, the atomic execution of each transaction can be assured without unreasonable restrictions.

A <u>semaphore</u> [2] is a non-negative integer on which two operations, P and V, are defined. The semantics of these operations are as follows:

{sem=c <u>and</u> c>0} P(sem) {sem=c-1}

{sem=c} V(sem) {sem=c+1}

A single sempahore is used to guarantee the atomic execution of each transaction in the following program.

DB': <u>var</u> sm : <u>semaphore</u> <u>initial</u> (1);

<u>cobegin</u> P(sm); t_1; V(sm) || P(sm); t_2; V(sm);

|| ... || P(sm); t_n; V(sm) <u>coend</u>

Again, it can be easily verified that this is a solution to the database consistency problem. Although the system appears to be concurrent, in fact <u>only</u> serial execution of the transactions will result. However, by using one of the solutions to the database consistency problem that involves only locking, the grain of interleaving can be made much finer. These solutions ensure that transactions appear atomic with respect to each other. (Thus, we are precluding solutions that involve preemption, such as those found in [8].) Typically, these solutions associate a lock bit with each entity in the database and define a protocol that restricts when a transaction may lock and unlock entities. These solutions, therefore, define restrictions on the structure of transactions. Examples of such protocols can be found in [3], [9], and [7].

Solutions that use lock bits can easily be translated into solutions that use semaphores. Associate with each entity e a sempahore sm_e with initial value 1. The primitive operations <lock entity e> and <unlock entity e> are translated to $P(sm_e)$ and $V(sm_e)$, respectively. It should be clear that semaphores used in this manner implement locking.

Consider any set of transactions T that obey the restrictions of some "locking" solution to the database consistency problem. Note that any such solution must require that a transaction lock an entity prior to accessing it. A new set of transactions T' can be formed from those transactions in T, by translating the lock and unlock primitives into P and V operations as outlined above. The resultant system can be modelled by the following program:

DB": <u>var</u> sem_{e1}, sm_{e2}, ... sm_{em} : <u>semaphore</u> <u>initial</u> (1);

<u>cobegin</u> t'_1 || t'_2 || ... || t'_n <u>coend</u>

where the t'_i may contain P and V operations, and are atomic with respect to each other.

Solutions to the database consistency problem obtained in this manner have two drawbacks.

1. Semaphores have been defined in terms of shared memory. Thus, the use of semaphores will preclude the generalization of these solutions to distributed systems.

2. It was assumed that there was one (and only one) copy of each entity. This restricts the use of such solutions in fully or partially redundant database organizations.

These issues are addressed in the next two sections.

4. DISTRIBUTED SEMAPHORES

It is possible to implement semaphores without using shared memory. Semaphores implemented in such a fashion are called <u>distributed semaphores</u> [10]. A distributed semaphore is defined such that for every P operation that is completed by a process, an associated V operation has been performed.

In order to implement distributed semaphores, certain assumptions regarding the communications network are necessary. They are:

<u>Broadcast Assumption</u>: If a site <u>broadcasts</u> a message, that message will be received by every other site.

<u>Message Order</u>: All messages that originate at a given site are received by other sites in the order they were broadcast.

A timestamp ts(m) will be associated with each message m. It is assumed that timestamps are consistent with causality. Thus, if event V_1 can in any way affect V_2, the the timestamp associated with V_1 will be smaller than the one associated with V_2. Lamport has proposed a scheme to generate such timestamps without the use of a central clock or shared memory [4]. In that scheme, each site L has a unique integer name <u>name(L)</u> and a local clock c_L associated with it. Each local clock is updated as follows:

1. L increments c_L between any two successive events at L.

2. If event V is the broadcast of message m by site L, then m contains a timestamp $ts(m) = c_L$. Upon receipt of message m, site L' sets its clock $c_{L'}$ so that $c_{L'} = \max[ts(m), c_{L'}+1]$.

Site names are used to resolve ties between identical timestamps, resulting in a total order of events that is consistent with causality.

For each distributed semaphore ds_i that is to be implemented, a message queue is maintained at each site. This message queue will contain messages--arranged in ascending order by timestamp--received by this site concerning semaphore ds_i.

Furthermore, it is assumed that whenever a message is received at a site, an acknowledgement message is broadcast to all other sites. (Acknowledgement messages are not acknowledged.) A message m is fully acknowledged at site L if an acknowledgement message for m has been received by L from every other site in the system.

Let $V\#(ds_i,x)$ be the number of "V semaphore ds_i" messages with timestamp less than or equal to x that have been received by the invoking site. Define $P\#(ds_i,x)$ similarly for "P semaphore ds_i" messages. The values of these functions can easily be computed from the message queue corresponding to semaphore ds_i at the site. P and V operations on distributed semaphores are then implemented as follows:

$V(ds_i)$: Broadcast message "V semaphore ds_i"

$P(ds_i)$: Broadcast message "P semaphore ds_i" and let tc denote the timestamp on this message. Then, wait until any message m' concerning ds_i is received and fully acknowledged and

$$V\#(ds_i,ts(m'))\geq P\#(ds_i,tc)$$

The derivation and proof of the correctness of this implementation appears in [10].

It is not necessary to store the entire message queue for each semaphore at every site. Instead, the relevant information from the message queue can be encoded in a few integer variables. Due to the message order assumption, after a message m is fully acknowledged at site L, no message m' where $ts(m') < ts(m)$ will be received at L. Furthermore, the implementation of distributed semaphores outlined above requires only $V\#(ds_i,x)$ and $P\#(ds_i,tc)$. Therefore, the information in the initial portion of the message queue--those messages up through the last fully acknowledged message--can be stored in two integer variables: P# and V#. As messages are received, they are put in a bounded message queue. The capacity of that queue need not exceed the number of sites in the system. Whenever a message m" becomes fully acknowledged, the values of P# and V# are updated as follows. For every "P semaphore ds_i" message currently in the bounded message queue with timestamp less than ts(m"), P# is incremented by 1. That message is then deleted from the queue. The same is done for V# and "V semaphore ds_i" messages. As before, in order to perform a P operation, a site broadcasts "P semaphore ds_i." The site then waits until the value of P# when that message is deleted from the bounded message queue is exceeded by the value of V#.

By using distributed semaphores it is therefore possible to implement in a distributed system any solution to the database consistency problem that uses locking. Thus, DB" of section 3, in addition to being a solution to the consistency problem in a centralized environment, will solve that problem in a distributed system, provided the issue of multiple copy entities is resolved.

5. THE MULTIPLE COPY CONSISTENCY PROBLEM

Consider the situation where there are multiple copies of some of the entities in the database, as would be the case in a partially or fully redundant distributed database. In order to satisfy the multiple copy consistency requirement, all copies of each entity must have the same value at the finish of every transaction. Thus, in effect, the set of consistency constraints has been augmented with additional assertions about the equality of all copies of a multiple copy entity.

Transactions preserve consistency, and therefore it may be necessary to alter the implementation of each transaction so that all copies of a multiple copy entity are updated. Note that a transaction need read only one copy of the entity (a local copy will suffice). This is because each entity is locked before it is accessed in a transaction. Consequently, at most one transaction may access a particular entity at any time. Furthermore, each transaction views the database in a consistent state--which now includes a requirement that all copies of an entity be equal. Therefore, at the beginning of the execution of a transaction, all copies of each of the entities referenced by the transaction are identical.

In order to update a multiple copy entity, a transaction broadcasts to all other sites a timestamped message containing the entity and its new value. Each site need save only those messages that deal with entities stored at that site. However, upon receipt of such a message, a site must broadcast an acknowledgement message to all other sites, even if the entity that is the subject of the message is not stored at that site. Note that the updates described by a message may not be applied to the database at site L until that message is fully acknowledged at site L. This is because prior to that time, other messages may be received that describe updates to the same entities, but have smaller timestamps. After that time, no such messages will be received (due to the message order assumption). The fact that update messages and distributed semaphore messages all use the same communications network (where message ordering holds over _all_ messages) ensures that when a transaction executes, the local copy of every entity has its correct value. This is because, prior to accessing an entity, a P operation on a semaphore associated with that entity is performed resulting in the broadcast of a message that must be fully acknowledged for the P to complete. This serves to "flush" all update messages to that site from the communications network.

6. DISCUSSION

Distributed semaphores were originally developed to facilitate the solution of synchronization problems in distributed systems. We conjectured that the difference between a distributed synchronization problem and a centralized concurrent programming problem was merely one of implementation details, which could be ignored if a suitable synchronization mechanism was defined. This conjecture has been validated for the database consistency problem. It was shown how any solution to the database consistency problem that used locking could be adapted for use in distributed database systems.

Every attempt has been made here to make as few assumptions about the implementation environment as possible. Thus, the solutions developed are applicable in a broad range of systems. In general, optimizations require some detailed knowledge of the implementation environment; by making restrictions on the environment--knowing more of its properties--more optimization is possible. For example, if it is known that each site will initiate transactions with high frequency, then acknowledgement messages can be abolished. The acknowledgement by site L' for a message m that originated at site L is the receipt by L of message m' that originated at site L', where ts(m') > ts(m). Similarly, if a stipulation is made about the communications network--that it has "true" broadcast capability (as in Ethernet [5], for example) then to process a transaction in a system with n sites requires only n+2 transmission cycles (delays). This is derived as follows:

1	Broadcast "P" messages
n-1	Acknowledgement messages
1	Update non-local entities
1	Broadcast "V" messages
n+2	

This compares favorable with the bounds obtained in [11].

One of the often mentioned benefits of distributed systems is that they can be designed so that they continue to function despite the failure of one or more sites. The use of a particular synchronization mechanism should not preclude this. In particular, note that in our implementation of distributed semaphores if a site fails, then no subsequent messages will ever be fully acknowledged at any site. However, a more complex implementation of distributed semaphores can be defined that does not have these problems. The interested reader is referred to [10] for a discussion of this mechanism.

ACKNOWLEDGEMENTS

G. Andrews, J. Archer, D. Gries, G. Levin and R. Schlichting read an earlier draft of this paper and furnished helpful comments.

REFERENCES

[1] Bernstein, P.A., D.W. Shipman, J.B. Rothnie, and N. Goodman, The Concurrency Control Mechanism of SDD-1: A System for Distributed Databases, Computer Corp. American, TR CCS-77-09, December 1977.

[2] Dijkstra, E.W., Cooperating sequential processes, F. Genuys (ed.), Programming Languages (Academic Press, New York, 1968).

[3] Eswaran, K.P., J.N. Gray, R.A. Lorie, and I.L. Traiger, The notions of consistency and predicate locks in a database system, CACM 19, 11 (November 1978) 624-633.

[4] Lamport, L., Time, clocks and the ordering of events in a distributed system, CACM 21, 7 (July 1978) 558-565.

[5] Metcalf, R.M., Ethernet: Distributed packet switching for local computer networks, CACM 19, 7 (July 1976) 395-403.

[6] Owicki, S.S. and D. Gries, An axiomatic proof technique for parallel programs I, Acta Informatica 6 (1976) 319-340.

[7] Ries, D.R. and H. Stonebraker, Effects of locking granularity in database management systems, ACM TODS 2, 3 (September 1977) 233-246.

[8] Rosenkrantz, R.E. Stearns, and P.M. Lewis, System level concurrency control for distributed database systems, ACM TODS 3, 2 (June 1978) 178-198.

[9] Silberschatz, A. and Z. Kedem, Consistency in hierachical database systems, to appear in JACM.

[10] Schneider, F.B., Synchronization in a Distributed Environment, Technical Report 79-391, Computer Science Department, Cornell University (September 1979).

[11] Thomas, R.H., A solution to the concurrency control problem for multiple copy data bases, Digest of Papers COMPCON (1978).

DISTRIBUTED DATA BASES
C. Delobel and W. Litwin (eds.)
North-Holland Publishing Company

RECONSTRUCTION OF CONSISTENT GLOBAL STATES IN DISTRIBUTED DATABASES

G. Schlageter
Fernuniversität Hagen
Praktische Informatik
Postfach 940
D-5800 Hagen

P. Dadam
Universität Dortmund
Abteilung Informatik
Postfach 500 500
D-4600 Dortmund 50

The problem of reconstructing an earlier consistent global state of a distributed database is considered. Two classes of solutions are presented, one called loosely synchronized solutions, the other one non-synchronized solutions. In the case of loosely synchronized solutions, a global checkpoint actually exists as a set of local checkpoints; nevertheless, the costs of writing a global checkpoint are comparatively low. A loosely synchronized solution is discussed in detail. In the case of non-synchronized solutions a global checkpoint no longer exists, so a required consistent global state has to be constructed in a more complicated way. The principles of non-synchronized solutions are outlined.

INTRODUCTION AND BASIC NOTIONS

The recovery problem in database systems essentially consists of two parts, namely undoing of non-terminated transactions, called <u>rollback</u>, and <u>reconstruction</u> of a consistent database state from <u>an old version of the database</u> (dump) using after-image logfile information. The rollback problem in distributed databases seems to be easily solved in principle, if appropriate synchronization and commit protocols /CoB, GaJ, Gra/ are applied. The reconstruction problem in distributed databases is much harder in some respects, there are even doubts whether reconstruction can always be done to a consistent global database state /ACD/. Many "obvious" solutions are too uneconomic and inefficient to be applicable in real systems. Though there are some solutions to aspects of the problem /ACD, Gra, Jou, MuS/, the problem has not been investigated in depth so far. In this paper the reconstruction problem is discussed, and possible solutions are presented.

We consider a distributed database to consist of one logical database which is physically distributed over the computers (sites) of a computer network. Each site has its own autonomous database manager responsible for the local part of the database; the database managers communicate one with each other in order to perform "global" transactions which require data on several sites.

To perform a global transaction a <u>subtransaction</u> is executed at each site involved. One of the subtransactions, the <u>primary process</u>, acts as a coordinator for all subtransactions; the other subtransactions are called <u>secondary processes</u>. We assume that, in principle, the two-phase commit protocol /Gra/ is applied to coordinate the subtransactions, so that a global transaction can always be terminated or undone as a whole. A transaction which has not yet committed is called non-terminated. The state which we reach if we roll back all non-terminated transactions at a certain point of time is called the actual consistent state of the database.

To a much larger extent than in centralized systems, the complexity of reconstruction varies in distributed systems according to the failure situation:

Local reconstruction: reconstruction is necessary because of a so-called hard failure (failure in the database itself, e.g. mass storage destruction). The local database manager, say A, has to reconstruct the actual consistent state of its local database. This is done by a dump of the database and by the usual after-image logfile. Non-terminated global transactions which involved A have to be rolled back. The main point about local reconstruction is that reconstruction is restricted to the local database, the only thing other sites may have to do is to roll back non-terminated transactions.

Global reconstruction: reconstruction is necessary because of some failure which requires the global database to be restored to some old consistent state, not the actual one. In this case many sites may be involved in the reconstruction process, where the task is not restricted to undoing non-terminated transactions. The problem is how to reestablish an old consistent state of the distributed database.

Though global reconstruction should be rare in a real system, there certainly must be some support to prevent such situations from resulting in a total catastrophy. As is obvious from centralized systems, there are various reasons for which global reconstruction in a distributed database may be required. For instance, if a logfile is partially destroyed on site A, local reconstruction cannot be done to completion; consequently, other sites have to reestablish older states which correspond to the one reachable at A. Or, logical errors are detected in the database, which cannot be isolated and corrected in a systematic way (data deterioration). This also may result in the necessity to do global reconstruction up to some point of time where the database still was correct.

GLOBAL RECONSTRUCTION - THE PROBLEM

In centralized database systems failures which require reconstruction are resolved by the use of

- dumps
- after-image logfile
- checkpoints.

Checkpoints are marks in the logfile which indicate that at this moment of time the database was in a consistent state (as far as was known at that time). A checkpoint is written when no transaction is active in the system. For ease of expression, we say that a checkpoint contains a transaction T, if T was terminated before the checkpoint was written.

Reconstruction starts from a dump, and writes the after-images to the dump until the specified checkpoint is reached.

In distributed database systems we would like to have the following scenario:

- local dumps
- local after-image logfiles
- global checkpoints.

Global checkpoints are recorded on each logfile. Reconstruction starts from appropriate local dumps, and the after-images are restored up to the specified checkpoint on each site.

The main problem is the production of a global checkpoint, since it has to be recorded as a set of local checkpoints.

To see the synchronization problem to be solved, assume that site A broadcasts 'write checkpoint' to all other sites. Let a global transaction T access data on sites B and C. Due to communication delays the situation of figure 1 may occur: while the checkpoint on C contains T, the checkpoint on B does not contain T, so that the global checkpoint is inconsistent. Simple broadcasting of 'write checkpoint' is not sufficient to get a consistent global checkpoint.

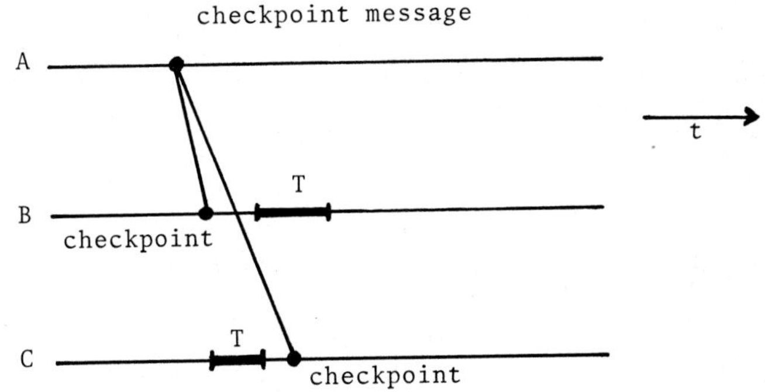

figure 1: example of inconsistent global checkpoint due to a global transaction

A first approach would be the direct extension of centralized checkpoints to the distributed system. This has been proposed in /Jou/. To realize the global checkpoint each site records a local checkpoint in coordination with all other sites. The coordination must be such that all local checkpoints are written in a period of time when no transaction is active. Before writing a local checkpoint, all sites must have reached this state of inactivity. Note that this condition must in general be satisfied even if there are no transmission delays in the system: As shown in figure 2, while site A is already inactive some subtransaction may still be passed to it from site B. Site A can write its checkpoint only after B has reached the inactive state also. This may result in a long interval where no transaction can be started in the whole system. It is obvious that this solution may be very costly because of high communication overhead and large processing delays.

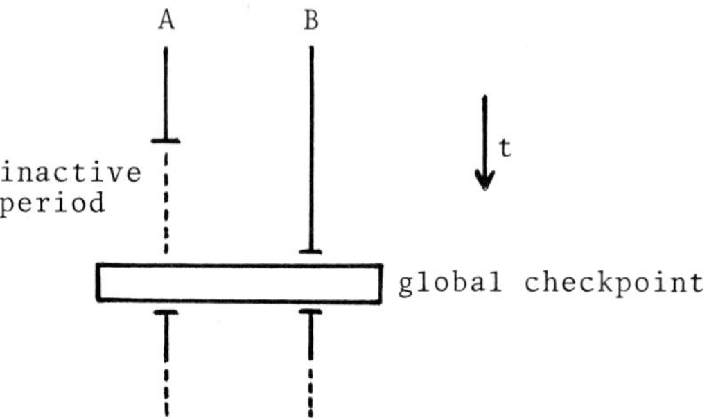

figure 2: Global checkpoint writing

Furthermore, there is a high interdependency of the sites: all sites have to write their checkpoints at the same time, irrespective of their actual activities.

As will be shown in this paper, there are various possibilities of avoiding the "strong" coordination of this centralized approach. A first idea is to retain the notion of a global checkpoint, but to apply less severe synchronization mechanisms to produce the checkpoint. In fact, to have a consistent state of the database, it is not necessary to make all sites write their checkpoints at the same time; it is sufficient to apply synchronization methods which guarantee that the following lemma is satisfied:

<u>Lemma 1:</u>

A global database state C is consistent, if the following holds:

(1) For each transaction T, C contains either all subtransactions or none of them;

(2) if T is contained in C, then each predecessor T' of T is also contained in C. (T' is a predecessor of T if it modified data which T accessed at some later point of time.)

Lemma 1 does not require anything like "simultaneous writing of local checkpoints". As will be seen, it opens a wide range of possibilities to solve the reconstruction problem.

Lemma 1 can be exploited to provide global checkpoints without the above outlined strong coordination of all sites. We call a solution of this type <u>loosely synchronized</u>.

A second idea is to renounce all synchronization with respect to the writing of checkpoints, such that no consistent global checkpoint is available. Reconstruction is based on independent local checkpoints. A consistent global state can be constructed from the local checkpoints and the logfile information, provided that the logfile information is properly chosen. <u>Non-synchronized solutions</u> are an attractive approach, since the overhead during normal operation of the system is minimized. This should be a major design criterion for methods to support global reconstruction, since global reconstruction is supposed to be a rare event. Some results about non-synchronized solutions are presented at the end of the paper.

A LOOSELY SYNCHRONIZED SOLUTION

We start from the following basic assumptions:

1. Only a small portion of all transactions is global (a generally accepted assumption stated often before in discussions about distributed databases).

2. Global checkpoints are produced in large intervals (at least with respect to possible communication delays and transaction execution times).

In the centralized approach outlined in the previous chapter the overhead to synchronize the local checkpoints is only necessary because of the global transactions. Because of assumption 1 situations as in figure 1 should be rare, and thus the synchronization overhead may be too costly. With this in mind, we propose the following:

Loosely synchronized solution

A. Checkpoint writing

The global checkpoints are numbered in ascending order, $C_1, C_2, \ldots, C_i$; consequently all local checkpoints forming a certain global checkpoint C_i have the same sequence number.

1. Initiator: broadcasts 'checkpoint C_i'.
   (The problem of which site should be the initiator, and what should happen if it crashes, is not discussed here again.)

2. Each local database manager:
   - performs local checkpoint C_i as soon as it is possible for it
   - resumes transaction processing after writing the checkpoint.

B. Transaction management for global transactions

1. Primary process at site X starts secondary process at site Y by the message (T,i),

   T = specification of the secondary process,

   i = number of latest checkpoint performed on X.

2. Action at Y after having received (T,i):

```
if actual number of checkpoint at Y = i then start T
   else if actual number of checkpoint <i then
              make T wait until actual number of
              checkpoint = i
        else  reject T.
```

   The rejection of T by site Y results in the rollback of the global transaction T. ■

This procedure guarantees that a set of all checkpoints with the same checkpoint-number represents a consistent global checkpoint.

Proof:

We have to show that lemma 1 is satisfied. For this purpose it is sufficient to show that global transaction T, if executed after c_i and before c_{i+1} at site A, is executed after c_i and before c_{i+1} at each other site also. This is enforced in a simple way by the checkpoint-number included in the start messages for secondary processes:

If the secondary process finds a lower checkpoint-number at its site than the one given by the primary process, then it has to wait, until the correct checkpoint is performed. Thus, a transaction which starts at checkpoint-number i (primary process) is performed at least at checkpoint-number i on each site.

On the other hand, if the secondary process finds a higher checkpoint-number the whole transaction is rolled back. Thus a transaction startet at checkpoint-number i is performed at most at checkpoint-number i on each site.

Hence, a transaction started at checkpoint-number i is either completely performed at checkpoint-number i or is rolled back. ∎

Note also, that deadlock between checkpoint requests and global transactions is not possible: this is easily seen by the fact that the above procedure clearly separates the transactions into those completely run before and those completely run after a global checkpoint. In the same way, indefinite delay for a checkpoint or for a global transaction due to the checkpoint procedure cannot occur, provided that each site starts its checkpoint with a small delay as compared to the checkpoint interval.

The main point about the above procedure is that the performing of checkpoints is not coordinated apart from the 'write checkpoint' message. The sites are relatively free to choose the time of checkpoint writing. The checkpoint is written immediately after the inactive state is reached, and processing of transactions is resumed immediately after the local checkpoint writing. Transaction management guarantees consistency of the global checkpoint by ensuring that all subtransactions of a global transaction run in the same checkpoint interval. There is the risk of transaction rollback, but, as was already indicated, situations requiring rollback will be very rare (only a small portion of transactions is global, etc.); this is especially true, if the following points are satisfied:

- checkpoint messages reach all sites with little delay (broadcasting)

- the subtransactions of a global transaction are started with little delays

- a site does not start global transactions (primary processes) after receiving a checkpoint message and before performing the checkpoint.

In many proposals and designs of distributed database systems preclaiming of resources is applied to prevent global deadlock. In this case the possible rollback in the above procedure actually is no longer a real rollback: because of preclaiming, a transaction only starts processing if it has acquired all resources it will need; we only have to introduce the additional requirement that a resource can only be acquired, if its site has the same 'checkpoint state' as the site of the primary process.

Robustness

Because of the checkpoint-numbers it is no problem to find a consistent global checkpoint at any time provided that all sites are up. Since checkpoints are performed independently, global transactions still can be processed if a site is down unless they require this site.

Obvious but usual problems in networks may arise if the initiator of the global checkpoint goes down after sending some but not all of the checkpoint messages. Global transactions may have to wait in this situation because a local checkpoint is not performed. There are various solutions to this problem. For instance, the site which has a global transaction waiting for a new checkpoint to be done knows that something went wrong, if this transaction waits unduly long and if no checkpoint message arrives. The repair actions to be started in this case are straightforward.

NON-SYNCHRONIZED SOLUTIONS

We only give a rough impression of non-synchronized solutions. A more detailed investigation and implementation proposals are presented in /DaS/.

Non-synchronized solutions are characterized by the fact that local checkpoints are performed in a fully uncoordinated way, i.e. each site performs a checkpoint whenever it is suitable for it. Even the frequency of checkpoints may vary between different sites.

To get a consistent global state it is not sufficient to restore each local database up to a specified checkpoint, since no provision at all is made to prevent inconsistencies between local checkpoints, as e.g. in figure 1. In addition to local checkpoints, after-log and/or before-log information has to be used to construct a consistent global database state.

We say that a global state S contains a local checkpoint c_A, if S contains all transactions contained in c_A.

Consider the following basic reconstruction problem:

> A site A can only recover to a checkpoint c_A.
> The recovery process has to construct a
> consistent global database state which contains c_A.

Whether this problem can be solved depends on the information recorded in the logfiles. It is not difficult to show that the construction of the global state is possible in principle, if detailed logfile information is available, which essentially means that all output-input dependencies between transactions are recognizable from the logfiles. But even in this case, it is not so easy to see, however, whether there exists a feasible, and hopefully efficient method to do the construction. In fact, it is not necessary to have detailed logfile information, which would be a hard requirement from a practical point of view; it is sufficient to know whether a transaction T may have seen data modified by T', provided that these 'potential' dependencies are unambiguous, i.e. either T is potentially dependent on T', or T' on T, but not both. It is not necessary to record read operations to have unambiguous potential dependencies, unambiguity can be guaranteed by exploiting in a very simple way the properties of the two-phase commit protocol, for example. In the following, the basic idea of a non-synchronized solution will be outlined.

We say that T is <u>dependent</u> on T', if T used, or - if detailed information is not available - may have used date modified by T'.

The solution is based on the following observation:

> Given local backup to checkpoint c_A, the global database is in a consistent state, if all global transactions are undone for which A executed subtransactions after c_A. The rollback of a transaction T implies the rollback of each transaction T' dependent of T.

So, the crucial point of any non-synchronized solution is to determine the set of global transactions in which site A was involved after writing c_A; this must be possible though the logfile information of A after c_A is lost. It is sufficient to ensure that one can determine at each site X, X $\neq$ A, which transactions affecting both X and A are not contained in c_A; call this set of transactions TR(X). All transactions T, $T \in \bigcup_{X, X \neq A} TR(X)$, have to be rolled back together with all transactions T' dependent on T.

One can show that only very little overhead is required to enable the determination of TR(X). Basically, the following simple rules are sufficient:

- Each site informs all other sites about the recording of its local checkpoint, the messages are sent immediately before the checkpoint is written.

  The checkpoint message is recorded in the logfile of each receiving site.

- The execution of a secondary process is acknowledged to the primary process; if the execution happened before a checkpoint, then the acknowledgement is sent before the checkpoint message, otherwise after it. The acknowledgements are recorded at the site of the primary process.

If these rules are satisfied, and if the communication system guarantees that the sequence of messages is preserved, then a site X can easily determine the set of global transactions TR(X), after A has signalled a necessary recovery to c_A. The positions of the acknowledgement entries relative to the checkpoint message entry in the logfile of X clearly indicate whether a subtransaction was executed on A after or before c_A.

Because of dependent global transactions, sites may be involved in the recovery process which did not execute a global transaction together with A. The recovery process may spread over the sites of the network in a recursive way. The control of this process is an interesting problem. One solution would be to centralize the determination of the set of transactions to be rolled back, but this is not necessary.

Of course, it is not mandatory to use rollback as the method of recovery; one may as well use dumps and after-image information at the other sites, too.

Non-synchronized solutions are possible and practically feasible. The attractive feature of these solutions is that the normal operation of the distributed database system is not slowed down by the recording of global checkpoints, and that each site is perfectly free of when to write its checkpoints. This advantage has to be paid for in the case of global reconstruction, since the reconstruction process is much more complicated than in the case of global checkpoints. If global reconstruction is sufficiently rare - as it should be -, non-synchronized solutions are certainly an interesting approach. As was indicated already, some detail questions remain to be discussed.

CONCLUSION

It has been shown that reconstruction of a consistent global state can be supported in distributed systems in various ways. The presented solutions do not require strong coordination of all sites in order to perform global checkpoints. Two classes of solutions have been discussed.

The loosely synchronized solution is based on global checkpoints, but avoids the strong synchronization of conventional global checkpoints, and the therefrom resulting disadvantages. The non-synchronized solutions have only been outlined. These solutions do no longer realize global checkpoints. There is no coordination at all as to the performing of local checkpoints, and a consistent global state has to be constructed when required. The feasibility of a construction process has been illustrated informally.

REFERENCES

/ACD/ Adiba, M., et al.: Issues in distributed database management systems: a technical overview. Proc. 4th Int. Conf., VLDB, Berlin, 1978, 89-110

/CoB/ Colliat, G., Bachman, C.: Commitment in a distributed database. Preprints IFIP TC-2 Working Conf. on Data Base Architecture, Venice, June 1979, 100-114

/DaS/ Dadam, P., Schlageter, G.: Recovery in distributed databases based on non-synchronized local checkpoints. Forschungsbericht, Universität Dortmund, Abteilung Informatik, Sept. 1979

/GaJ/ Gardarin, G., Jouve, M.: The execution kernel of a distributed database management system. Preprints IFIP TC-2, Working Conf. on Data Base Architecture, Venice, June 1979, 1-19

/Gra/ Gray, J.: Notes on data base operating systems. In: Operating Systems, Lecture Notes in Computer Science 60, 1978, 393-481

/Jou/ Jouve, M.: Reliability aspects in a distributed data base management system. Proc. AICA '77, DATA BASES, 199-209

/MuS/ Munz, R., Schweppe, H.F.: Concurrency control in the distributed database system VDN, VDN-Report 16/78, Projekt "Distributed Database", Technical University Berlin

DISTRIBUTED DATA BASES
C. Delobel and W. Litwin (eds.)
North-Holland Publishing Company

A CONCURRENCY CONTROL MECHANISM AND CRASH RECOVERY FOR A DISTRIBUTED DATABASE SYSTEM (DLDBS)*

Chuen-Pu Chou and Ming T. Liu

Department of Computer and Information Science
The Ohio State University
Columbus, Ohio 43210
U.S.A.

This paper presents a concurrency control mechanism for the Distributed Loop Database System (DLDBS). The mechanism uses distributed control and is deadlock-free, simple to implement and robust with respect to failures of communication links and hosts. It does not use global locking, does not reject transactions, and has good performance (high throughput and low delay). Arguments for the correctness of the algorithm as well as crash recovery procedures are also presented. Finally, performance analysis of the algorithm in terms of three measures (message traffic, delay, and throughput) is made.

I. INTRODUCTION

Conceived as a means of investigating fundamental problems in distributed processing and local networking, the Distributed Double-Loop Computer Network (DDLCN) is designed as a fault-tolerant distributed system that interconnects midi, mini, and micro computers through careful integration of hardware, software and communications [1]. A prototype of DDLCN, interconnecting eight DEC LSI-11/23 microcomputers and one DECsystem-20 computer system, is currently being implemented under an NSF grant.

The Distributed Double-Loop Computer Network is a local network using a loop topology. It has two communication loops to transmit messages in opposite directions [2, 3]. Each host is connected to the network by a microprocessor-based Loop Interface Unit (LIU), which has its own RAM, ROM, and sufficient computing power to work as a front-end processor for the host [4]. The LIU design is unique in that it incorporates tri-state control logic, thereby enabling the network to become fault-tolerant in instances of link failures by dynamically reconfiguring the logical directions of message flow.

In the design of the Distributed Loop Database System (DLDBS) for DDLCN [5], we have considered two types of nodes. First, there are Loop Request Nodes (LRNs) where users can make their requests to DDB. Second, there are Loop Data Nodes (LDNs) which contain the physical data and the DBMS needed to satisfy the requests. In DDLCN, the DEC-20 computer and four LSI-11/23 microcomputers equipped with enough disk storage will be used as both LDNs and LRNs. The remaining four LSI-11/23 microcomputers will be used as the LRNs only. Thus there are 9 LRNs and 5 LDNs, as depicted in Figure 1. The Inter-Database Control Software (IDCS) in DLDBS is a group of algorithms to solve the problems of distributed concurrency control, distributed crash recovery, etc.

---

*Research reported herein was supported by NSF grants MCS-77-23496 and MCS-79-07767.

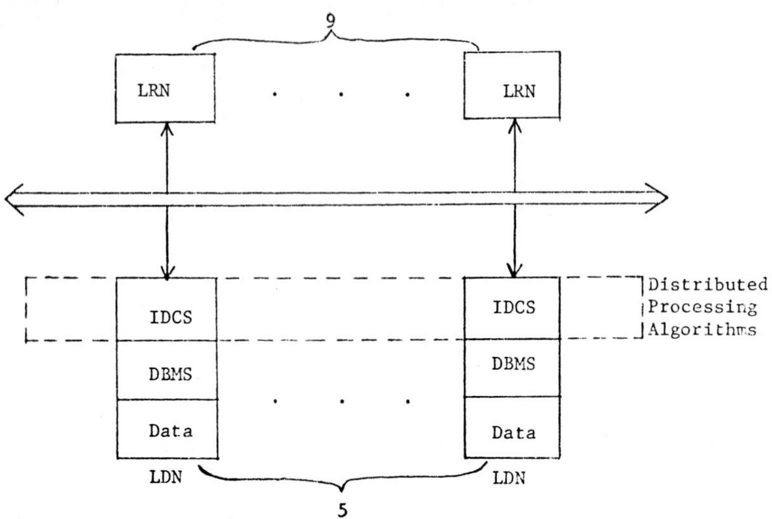

Figure 1

DLDBS Architecture

During the past several years, many solutions to the distributed concurrency control problem have been proposed in the literature [6, 7]. However, most of these algorithms either require high internode communication traffic or use a global locking approach, thereby degrading performance or not having enough robustness to withstand network crashes. For DLDBS, there seems to have two attractive solutions to the concurrency control problem : Thomas' majority consensus algorithm [8] and Ellis' decentralized parallel algorithm [9]. In the majority consensus algorithm, a given update is serially propagated host by host, which is inefficient for use in DDLCN, since DDLCN has multi-destination routing facilities [10]. The complexity of the algorithm and the storage overhead due to timestamps labelled on database data are also reasons for not using this algorithm in our design. The decentralized parallel algorithm is an attractive candidate for a local network that has a fast broadcast facility. However, this algorithm uses a global locking mechanism and is robust only with respect to failures of nodes other than the one controlling the update, since the initiating node has control all the time over the progress of the transaction. Both of these two algorithms also use rejection to resolve transaction conflicts, which may increase communication traffic and processing delay.

This paper is based on an earlier work by the authors [5]. It describes a simple and efficient concurrency control algorithm for DLDBS. The algorithm has characteristics as follows.

1. It uses distributed control.
2. It is robust with respect to both communication system and database site failures.
3. It does not reject transactions due to transaction conflicts.
4. It does not use global locking mechanisms and does not use timestamps to label database data.

5. It prevents deadlocks, so that no separate distributed deadlock detection mechanism is needed.

6. It can automatically execute more transactions issued from a heavily loaded site than from a lightly loaded site.

7. It requires only n messages per update for synchronization (where n is the number of database nodes in the network), and has good throughput and low delay.

8. It is simple and easy to implement.

In this paper, we restrict our discussion to a case called the fully duplicated distributed database, meaning that a complete copy of the entire database is maintained in each site. A consideration of this algorithm for the partially duplicated case has already been worked out and is described in a separate paper [11].

II. OVERVIEW OF THE ALGORITHM

2.1 Preliminary Definitions

Priority : A priority assigned to a transaction is an ordered pair $P = \langle E, N \rangle$, where E is a non-decreasing integer generated by a local counter of an LDN that is incremented each time a transaction arrives. Thus no two transactions emanating from the same LDN have the same number E. N is a preassigned number for each LDN. $P1 = \langle E1, N1 \rangle$ of a transaction is said to have higher priority than $P2 = \langle E2, N2 \rangle$ of another transaction if either (i) $E1 < E2$ or (ii) $E1 = E2$ and $N1 < N2$. Note that E may be reset to zero during system maintenance.

The notions of internal consistency and mutual consistency are described in [8]. The definition of transaction, schedule, serial schedule, schedule equivalence, and conflict that appear in this paper can be found in [14].

2.2 Overview

This subsection presents an informal outline of our concurrency control algorithm. The algorithm is assumed working on top of a communication subsystem which has reliable end-to-end protocols [10]. In normal cases (no site crashes or link failures), the protocols in the communication subsystem can guarantee that (1) a transaction message will eventually be delivered to all destinations and that (2) transaction messages from a node are delivered in the order they were sent.

All nodes which possess a copy of the database are called the Loop Data Nodes (LDNs). The distributed software residing at each LDN to enforce mutual consistency among database copies is called the Consistency Enforcer, which is a component of the Inter-Database Control Software (IDCS). Each local DBMS at an LDN has its own processes to handle local concurrency control when local transactions are executed concurrently. It is assumed that distributed transaction processing is initiated by user processes, each of which is local to one of the LDNs. User processes may be either processes representing some remote on-line users or processes on behalf of application programs [5].

Without loss of generality, it is assumed that when a user tries to access DLDBS by sending a transaction, a user process is created in an LDN. After some integrity checking is done and the transaction is considered valid (consistency at this level is not our interest here), the user process sends this transaction (in case of an update transaction) to IDCS. Then, a network-level concurrency control will be enforced. After the Consistency Enforcer finishes its job, the local DBMS starts to execute the update transactions and local concurrency control will be enforced there. Note that in the case of a retrieval transaction, the user process may pass the transaction directly to its local DBMS.

For convenience of discussion, the progress of an update transaction is divided into three phases. Phase I (the transmitting phase), and phase II (the selecting phase) are handled by the Consistency Enforcer, whereas phase III (the processing phase) is by its local DBMS. Note that the different phases of different transactions or the same phase of different transactions may overlap in the same site.

Phase I : Transmitting Phase. After the Consistency Enforcer of an LDN receives a transaction from a user process, a priority as described in Section 2.1 is assigned to the transaction. The LDN then broadcasts a transaction message to every LDN. As soon as an LDN receives a transaction message, it puts the transaction message in a queue called the Execution Waiting Queue (EWQ). After the broadcast completes, the Consistency Enforcer is ready to accept the next transaction from other user processes. (A broadcast in the algorithm is said to be completed when the sender is informed by the communication subsystem that every destination has received the broadcast message.) Note that in normal cases, a broadcast message in this phase is guaranteed to be delivered to all destinations by the communication subsystem using reliable end-to-end protocols as assumed above.

Phase II : Selecting Phase. Transactions waiting in an EWQ will be selected by the Consistency Enforcer and then dispatched to the local DBMS for processing. Since the "higher than" relation among priorities of different transactions forms a total ordering [15], for preserving mutual consistency, we will enforce that every LDN dispatches transactions in its EWQ according to this total ordering. For this purpose, we always dispatch the transaction which has the highest priority among all transactions which have not yet been dispatched. However, the highest priority transaction in an EWQ may not be the true highest one, since it is possible that the true highest priority transaction is still on its way of transmission. If we defer this selection until there is at least one transaction from every LDN in the EWQ, the highest priority transaction in the EWQ is the true one. The reason is that since transaction priorities from the same node are assigned, sent out and received in decreasing order of priority, an arriving transaction from an LDN will always have a lower priority if the EWQ already has a transaction issued from the same node.

Assertion 1 : If any two transaction messages issued from the same site move into EWQ in decreasing order of priority (increasing value of E), and if the selection rule in A3 (see Section III) is followed, then all transaction messages can be dispatched in a total ordering according to their priorities.
Proof : As discussed above.

Phase III : Processing Phase. After transactions are dispatched to the local DBMS for processing, the concurrency control problem is changed from a distributed environment to a centralized environment. For exploiting concurrency, we like the transaction processing to be executed in an interleaved manner. The problem in this phase is : "Given a set of transactions arriving in a priority order, can we concurrently execute these transactions such that a schedule of transactions is equivalent to a serial schedule of transactions determined by the priority order ?". A simple solution, for example, can be that the local DBMS always locks (using a granularity lock scheme described in [13]) all necessary resources before a transaction is allowed to be executed, and unlock resources after transaction execution is finished. Therefore, non-conflict transactions can be executed in an interleaved manner, and conflicting transactions are executed in a serial manner according to a priority order.

Assertion 2 : If transactions are dispatched to the local DBMS according to their priority order, they can be executed such that a schedule of transactions is equivalent to a serial schedule of transactions determined by the priority order.
Proof : As discussed above.

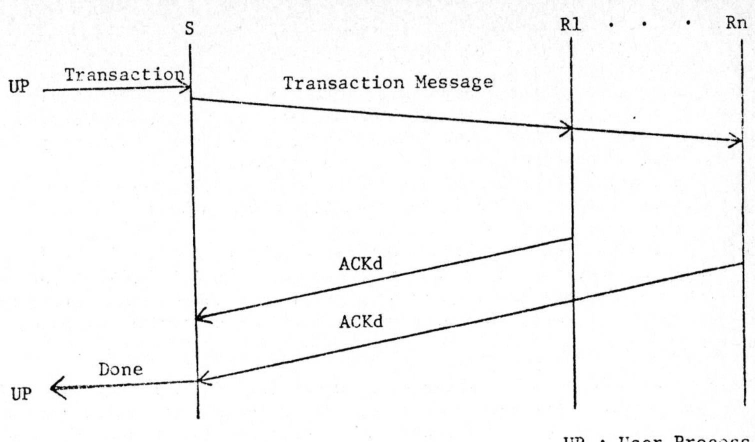

UP : User Process

S : Sender Site

Ri : Receiver Site i

Figure 2

Algorithm Protocols

III. THE ALGORITHM (NORMAL CASE)

The algorithm, in the case that the network communication and processing system are in normal operating condition, is stated formally below (see Figure 2).

Data structure : Each site has an Execution Waiting Queue (EWQ), a digital counter CNT for generating a non-decreasing integer E, a time-out CLOCK, and a flip-flop STATE (STATE = 0 means user processes can send a transaction to IDCS; STATE = 1 is the forbidden state).

Initialization : E <- 0, CLOCK <- 0, STATE <- 0, CLOCK starts ticking.

(A1) When STATE = 0, the Consistency Enforcer of IDCS accepts an update transaction from an user process. If the Consistency Enforcer has not received any transaction from user processes and the value of CLOCK exceeds the time-out period Tw, a dummy transaction is created. Then, STATE <- 1. A priority is assigned to the transaction by the LDN. The priority is an ordered pair P = <E, N>, where E has the value of CNT, after CNT is incremented by one. N is a preassigned number for each LDN. (Because all the values of E are integers generated independently by a local LDN, they may be unsynchronized eventually if the generating speed of E on each node is different. However, all the values of E can be kept within tolerable synchronization by setting a local E equal to the E of an incoming transaction message from another LDN if the incoming E has a value higher than the local one [15].)

(A2) A transaction message (Priority, Transaction) for the transaction is then put into the local EWQ and also broadcasted to all other LDNs. After the broadcast is completed, the local LDN sets STATE <- 0, CLOCK <- 0, and lets CLOCK start ticking . On the receiver side, as soon as it receives a transaction message it saves the transaction message in EWQ.

(A3) A transaction is selected from an Execution Waiting Queue (EWQ) by the Consistency Enforcer for dispatching to the local DBMS if both of the following two conditions are satisfied :

(a) There is at least one transaction from every LDN pending in the Execution Waiting Queue of the LDN. (A transaction is said to be pending if it has been accepted by an LDN, but has not been selected and dispatched for processing. The transaction could be a dummy transaction.)

(b) The transaction selected has the highest priority among all the (real and dummy) transactions pending in the Execution Waiting Queue.

(A4) After a transaction is selected and dispatched to the local DBMS, it will process the transaction in a way to preserve the consistency of the database; that is, transactions are executed in such a way that the schedule of transactions is equivalent to a serial schedule of transactions determined by their priority order.

(A5) As soon as a local DBMS finishes the execution of a transaction, an ACKd is sent to the sender of the transaction. After the sender receives an ACKd from each of the receivers, the sender notifies the completion of the update transaction to the user process.

If the Consistency Enforcer does not receive a transaction request in a time period Tw, a dummy transaction is broadcasted to all other LDNs to prompt processing of transactions. Note that a dummy transaction only contains its priority P, and processing of a dummy transaction actually takes no computing time. Furthermore, if the Consistency Enforcer detects that its local EWQ has no real transaction pending, the dummy transaction generating process can be temporarily suspended until a real transaction enters the EWQ again. This fact is useful when the DLDBS may not receive any transaction request for a time period, and to stop generating dummy transaction in that time period can save time wasted in performing useless work.

Assertion 3 : If the EWQ of a node has no real transaction pending, dummy transaction generation on this node can be stopped until a real transaction enters the EWQ again.

Proof : The generation of dummy transactions is to ensure that a real transaction in a site can be dispatched without being delayed indefinitely due to slow sending of real transactions from some other sites. Let Se be a site whose EWQ contains no pending real transaction. Assume that the site Se continuously sends a dummy transaction (Td) under this circumstance. We like to prove that the dummy transaction Td generated from the site Se is useless for the purpose of dummy transaction generation.

When the site Se has no real transaction pending, there are two cases possible in the network:

(1) There is no real transaction pending at any site. In this case, sending a dummy transaction Td from Se is obviously useless.

(2) There is a real transaction (Tr) pending at some site (St). Since Tr is in St and according to the requirement in the transmitting phase that a transaction message is received by every node, Tr is also in Se eventually. However, because of transmission delay, there are two cases possible.

(a) Tr is on its way of transmission to Se. As soon as Se receives Tr, by the requirement of the algorithm, Se will resume generating dummy transactions which can cause Tr to be dispatched without the need of Td from Se. Therefore, to let Se continuously send a Td during the time interval between the transmission of Tr from St and the arrival of Tr at Se is useless for the purpose of dummy transaction generation.

(b) Tr is already received by Se. Since the local EWQ of Se has no real transaction pending, Tr must have been dispatched already. In this site,

recalling the rule in the selecting phase, Tr can be dispatched only when there are a set of transactions which qualify Tr to be selected. From the requirement in the transmitting phase, this set of transactions also exists on St eventually. Therefore, Tr in the EWQ of St will be dispatched without the need of Td from Se. To continuously send a Td from Se in this case is also useless.
Thus, we conclude that a site keeps on sending a dummy transaction when its EWQ has no real transaction pending is useless for the purpose of dummy transaction generation.
Thus assertion 3 is true.

From above we can see that dummy transactions are seldom generated in a heavily loaded network and the generation of dummy transactions is also suspended during the time period when the DLDBS is not receiving any real transaction requests. These facts imply that the communication cost incurred by the generation of dummy transactions in our algorithm is very low.

IV. ROBUSTNESS OF THE ALGORITHM

4.1 Requirements of Robustness

The preceding section has outlined the operation of the algorithm under a normal condition. However, in practice there are many ways in which abnormal conditions may arise. By an abnormal case, we mean the case of site crashes and communication link failures.

By robustness of the algorithm, we mean that the following three requirements are maintained in an abnormal case.

(R1) The system will continue operating in spite of site crashes and communication link failures.

(R2) A transaction message will eventually be put into the EWQ of either every site or no site.

(R3) If a transaction message is put into an EWQ, it will be dispatched and executed to completion sooner or later; and all transactions are eventually dispatched in a total ordering according to their priorities.

Note that R1 is the basic requirement of robustness, and R2 and R3 are conditions needed for the DLDBS to recover from crashes and failures and to lead correctly to a mutually consistent state.

4.2 Communication Link Failures

Our algorithm requires that each node has a (direct/indirect) path to every other node. Therefore, as long as no site is partitioned from the network, communication link failures do not create any difficulty to the algorithm.

When the network becomes partitioned, the partition which has a majority of nodes in the network still can continue operating and treats the nodes in the other partition the same as crashed sites. Note that only one partition is allowed to operate; otherwise, inconsistency among databases in different partitions may occur. Using the recovery algorithm for site crashes to be described below, the network can return to a consistent state after the partitions are repaired. In DDLCN, network partition is rare due to the tri-state control mechanism built into the interface [3].

4.3 Site Crashes

This subsection will first show how the algorithm can continue operating in the case of one or more site crashes. Then, it shows how the DDB will recover from anomalies and lead to a consistent state when a crashing node has been repaired. Note that the site crash considered here may be a memory loss, which means that transaction information stored in EWQ, the CNT value, and ACKd information will be lost after the crash.

4.3.1 Reliable Broadcast

To satisfy the requirement R2, we need a "reliable broadcast" facility [6], which guarantees that a broadcast message will reach either every destination or none when the sender crashes during the broadcasting. To provide a reliable broadcast facility for the algorithm, we require that every site keeps a Last Transaction Array (LTA). This array consists of the last transaction message (real or dummy) received from each site. Recalling that the broadcast protocol in the algorithm is a "one-message-at-a-time" protocol, the existence of the last transaction message from a site implies that all previous transaction message broadcasts issued from the same site are already complete. Only a broadcast for the last transaction message from a site can be an incomplete broadcast. Therefore, as soon as a site ascertains that another site is unreachable, the last transaction message received from that crashed site is broadcasted to all other active nodes. Duplicated messages thus produced are rejected (The priority of a transaction message is uniquely generated; thus, LTA can be used to reject transaction message duplicates). Let us consider a simple example. Suppose that a node S1 broadcasts a transaction message to nodes S2, S3 and S4. We further suppose that S1 crashes during the broadcasting such that S2 receives the transaction but S3 and S4 do not. After S2, S3 and S4 learn of the crash, they broadcast their last received transaction messages from S1 to each other. Thus the last broadcast message from S1 received by S2 will later be received by S3 and S4. The messages broadcast by S3 and S4 are duplicated messages and thus are rejected.

4.3.2 Recovery Algorithm

Withdrawal of a crashed site. Suppose that a site (Sd) detects a crash happening on a site (Sf) after Sd tried to send a transaction message to Sf, and eventually concludes that Sf is unreachable. The sender site Sd then puts this transaction message as well as all transaction messages whose ACKds from Sf have not yet been received, into a recovery array created for Sf. A recovery array is a buffer storage to buffer all transactions which will later be executed by the crashed site, and may be duplicated to achieve robustness in the case that any active site may crash before Sf recovers. The site Sd also broadcasts the unreachable site's ID to all other sites, and deletes Sf from its local up-list. The up-list keeps the IDs of all active LDNs in the network. Any active site receiving the broadcast from Sd will also buffer its transaction messages whose ACKds from Sf have not yet been received, and update its up-list.

It is possible that Sf is also a sender at the time of its crash. In this case the facility to achieve reliable broadcast as described in the previous subsection is initiated. After every active site receives the last broadcast message from Sf, this transaction message is stored in the recovery array of Sf because this transaction message may not survive in Sf after a memory loss crash.

From now on, broadcast messages are sent to database nodes which are in the up-list and the selection rule in A3 is also changed to consider only the transaction messages from active LDNs. Any transaction messages (real transaction messages only) and ACKds destined for the unreachable node Sf are sent to the active nodes which have a copy of the recovery array for the crash site and are logged into the recovery array.

Reinstatement of a repaired site. Upon its recovery, site Sf broadcasts an <I-am-up> message to all other sites. It also makes a request to a site having a recovery array copy (if that site is not active, contacts another one) to obtain its recovery array, and the current up-list (other site may crash during the crash period of Sf). Any active site which receives the <I-am-up> message will update its up-list and consider that the recovery site Sf has rejoined the network. When recovery site Sf receives the first transaction message from another node, it synchronizes its CNT value and resumes its normal operation in the network.

Reconstruction of EWQ. After site Sf receives a copy of its recovery array, it starts to reconstruct its EWQ. In case of a memory loss crash at site Sf, all transaction messages in the recovery array will be put into EWQ. In case it is not a memory loss crash, only those transaction messages which are in the recovery array but not in EWQ will be added to EWQ. After the EWQ is reconstructed, dispatching of transactions is restarted in site Sf according to the selection rule of the algorithm. Apparently, while the recovery site reconstructs its EWQ and executes those buffered transaction messages, it may receive new transaction messages generated after it rejoins the network. Those newly generated transaction messages can be directly put into EWQ, because the dispatching of transactions is according to the order of their priorities instead of the order of their entry into EWQ. From above, the time delay for a repaired site to resume its role in the network is short, and again the algorithm for reinstatement is simple.

Under a typical operational environment that the system is not overloaded, all transaction messages accumulated in a recovering site will be executed and the operation in the network will return to its normal condition.

Nested Crashes. The last problem not yet addressed is what happens when a recovering site fails while it is in the midst of recovering operation. This problem can be solved as follows. When a buffered transaction message completes its execution, the recovering site sends a special acknowledgement to other sites which have a copy of the recovery array, and then this transaction message is deleted from the recovery array. Should a crash happen before all buffered transaction messages are completed, those transaction messages which have not been completed (still kept in the recovery array) can reenter EWQ in the same fashion as described above and be executed after the site recovers.

V. CORRECTNESS

This section presents arguments to show the correctness of our algorithm. The first subsection shows that the algorithm is robust, and the second shows the algorithm is correct in both normal and abnormal cases.

5.1 Correctness of Robustness

No mechanism yet developed can achieve 100 percent robustness [7]. The degree of robustness that can be attained depends on how much cost we like to pay. An algorithm is said to be robust if the recovery mechanism can satisfy the degree of robustness it claims under the assumptions it specifies.

The degree of robustness for our algorithm is that it can satisfy conditions R1, R2 and R3 of Section 4.1 under multiple site crashes and link failures. The assumption for robustness is that the ACKd information which can be stored in only one memory word as a bit map is stored in a stable storage (one that holds its data throughout system crashes or can easily recover its data after a crash). Another assumption is that a sender and a receiver will not crash so close in time that there is no enough time to do some critical jobs (such as creating a recovery array, etc). The latter assumption is not needed if all critical information (such as transaction messages in an EWQ) is stored in a stable storage.

To show the robustness of our algorithm, let us consider the 7 cases shown in Figure 3. A transaction will be in one of the 7 cases when a crash happens.

A. In case the crash site is a sender.

Case 1 : Crash happened before a transaction is broadcasted. After recovery, all information about the transaction is lost, and the user process must send the

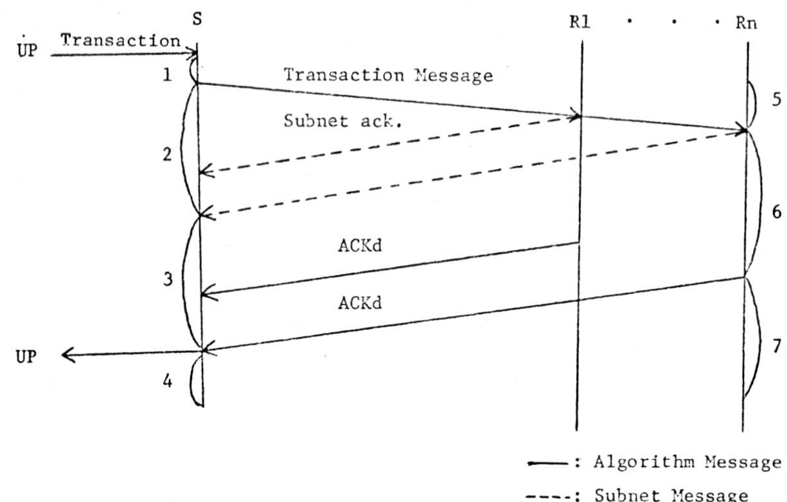

Figure 3

7 cases when a crash happens

transaction again.

Case 2 : Crash happens when a transaction broadcast is going on. The reliable broadcast facility discussed in Section 4.3.1 can ensure that the transaction message will be received by all destinations or none at all.

Case 3 : Crash happened before all ACKds for a transaction are received from the destinations. Since ACKd information is stored in stable storage, those ACKds received before the crash survive, but those ACKds generated during the crash are buffered in a recovery array and will be available to the recovering site.

Case 4 : A transaction processing is completed. A crash will have no effect on it.

B. In case the crash site is a receiver.

Case 5 : Crash happens before a transaction message is received by the crashed receiver. In this case, this unreceived transaction message will be buffered in a recovery array by the sender according to the recovery algorithm and will be received by the crashed receiver after the receiver recovers.

Case 6 : Crash happens during the interval when a transaction message is waiting for dispatching or is under execution. According to the recovery algorithm, all these transaction messages will be put into the recovery array, and will be executed while recovering. To make the transaction execution idempotent (repeatable), all outputs the transaction performs are placed in a temporary file, and will be recorded on a permanent database only after the transaction execution is entirely completed.

Case 7 : A transaction execution is completed on the receiver site. A crash will have no effect on it.

The recovery algorithm shows that the network can continue to operate in the face of site crashes and link failures; thus, R1 is true. Reliable broadcast in case 2 and the discussion in case 5 ensure that a transaction message will exist in the

EWQ of every site or no site. The recovery array in case 6 ensures R2 is true even though some transaction messages which are already in the EWQ may temporarily be lost due to site crashes. Thus R2 is true. According to cases 3, 5 and 6, a transaction generated before a crash (either in transmission, in EWQ, or under execution) will eventually be dispatched according to a priority order and to be executed to completion, although it may be interrupted and delayed by the site crash. According to the recovery algorithm, transactions generated during crashes are buffered in a recovery array; and, by Assertion 1, they can be dispatched according to a priority order during site recovering. Therefore, all transactions, no matter when they are generated (before, during or after crashes), can be dispatched according to their priority order. This is true for an active site as well as for a recovering site. Thus R3 is true.

5.2 Correctness of The Algorithm

In this subsection, we will show that our algorithm can satisfy the following three conditions in both normal and abnormal cases :

(C1) It preserves mutual consistency of the multiple copy database.
(C2) It preserves internal consistency of the database.
(C3) It is deadlock-free.

Instead of directly proving C1, C2 and C3, we will first argue that the algorithm can satisfy three conditions:

(T1) A transaction message will eventually be put into the EWQ of every site or no site.

(T2) All transactions can be executed such that a schedule of these transactions is equivalent to a serial schedule of transactions determined by their priority order.

(T3) The algorithm is deadlock-free.

In a normal case, T1 is true from the above discussion in the transmitting phase. In an abnormal case, T1 is the same as R2; thus, we know T1 is true. In a normal case, steps A1 and A2 of the algorithm ensure that two transaction messages issued from the same site enter the EWQ in decreasing order of priority. From rule A3 and Assertion 1, all transactions can be dispatched according to their priority order; and from Assertion 2, T2 is true in a normal case. R3 also tells us that all transactions can be eventually dispatched according to their priority order and be executed to completion; from Assertion 2, T2 is true also in an abnormal case. Once a transaction is put into EWQ, it will be forced to be dispatched for processing sooner or later by incoming real or dummy transactions. Thus, there is no permanent waiting and T3 is true.

T1 implies that every LDN has the same set of transactions and T2 says that these transactions will be equivalently executed in the same order; thus, mutual consistency among database copies can be preserved. Therefore C1 is true. The serializability implied in T2 ensures internal consistency of database [14]; thus C2 is true. T3 is the same as C3.

VI. PERFORMANCE OF THE ALGORITHM

We will now analyze the performance of this algorithm in terms of three measures : message traffic, delay, and throughput.

(1) Message traffic. It is the number of messages required to accomplish an update transaction. Let us assume that there are n multiple copies of the database. In counting the number of messages transmitted, we do not include the subnet acknowledgement. Consideration of traffic depends on the types of protocols used :

(a) Multi-destination protocol: This is the case in DDLCN [10].

1 to broadcast a transaction message to other sites.

n-1 to transmit ACKd.

(b) Point-to-point protocol: such as the case in ARPANET.

n-1 to send a transaction message to other sites. ACKd to the sender can be piggy-backed on the next transaction message (real or dummy) to the sender.

(2) Delay. There are four distinct time periods for completing a transaction : (a) time taken to broadcast the transaction message; (b) time waiting in EWQ for dispatching; (c) time taken to process the transaction; (d) time taken for transmitting an ACKd from a destination to the sender. The delay time discussed here is the sum of time taken in (a), (b), and (d) ((c) is not included, since it depends on the nature of the transaction and types of the database). Let us assume the time taken to broadcast a message is Tb, the time taken to transmit a single message is Ts (in DDLCN, Tb ≑ Ts), and the average inter-arrival time between two update requests at a node i is Tai. The waiting time of a transaction in an EWQ closely relates to the time-out period Tw (for sending a dummy transaction) and Ta. Note that Tw is a design parameter of the system. In the best case, where Twi = 0 for each node i, the worst delay for any transaction is 2 Tb + Ts (one Tb for (a), one Tb for (b), and one Ts for (d)); the shortest delay for a transaction is Tb + Ts (as soon as the transaction enters the EWQ, it is qualified to be dispatched). In the worst case, where Twi = Tai-Tb, the worst delay for a transaction is Tb + (Twk + Tb) + Ts = Tb + Tak + Ts (one Tb for (a), one Tak for (b), and one Ts for (d)), where Tak >= Tai, for each node i. If Tak is long, we may adjust time-out period Twk such that Twk + Tb is a fraction of Tak.

In the case of Twi = 0 for each node i, if in 2 Tb time units no real transaction is issued from any node, the EWQ of any site will contain no real transaction, and dummy transaction generation is suspended. Because a dummy transaction is generated only when it is necessary and itself is a very short message, it will not increase communication traffic. Therefore, in a local network such as DDLCN which has high communication bandwidth, a choice of Twi = 0 for each node i may be justified.

(3) Throughput. It is defined as the number of transactions executed per time unit. In the best case, when Tai <= Tb for each node i, the throughput of the system is n/Tb transactions per time unit since each node can contribute one real transaction in every Tb time units and, on the average, there are n transactions that can be dispatched in every Tb time units. When Tai >= Tb for some node i, assuming Tak is the longest inter-arrival time, the throughput will be in the range n/Tak <= throughput <= n/Tb. Now, from the nature of the algorithm, we can see an interesting feature. The system can automatically execute more transactions issued from a heavily loaded node than from a lightly loaded node. For example, if Ta1 = 3 Ta2, then every time the system executes one transaction issued from node 1, it also executes 3 transactions issued from node 2.

The performance of this algorithm compares favorably with other techniques such as the majority concensus algorithm [8] which requires, in the best case, n + n/2 + 3 messages per update and (n + n/2 + 3)Ts for delay; and the decentralized parallel algorithm [9] which requires 2n messages per update, 2 Tb + 2 Ts for delay, and has the best throughput of n/(2 Tb + 2 Ts), assuming no transaction rejection would happen.

VII. CONCLUSIONS

We are now in a position to summarize some characteristics of the algorithm.

1. The control of the algorithm is fully distributed. After the transmitting phase completes, the sender does not have control over the progress of the transaction. Each site processes transactions independently according to the rules of the algorithm.

2. The distributed nature explains the robustness of the algorithm. The algorithm is robust with respect to site crashes and link failures.

3. No rejection of transactions occurs. Rejection of a transaction causes resubmission of the transaction at a later time and thus increases inter-node communication traffic and delay.

4. This algorithm does not use a global locking mechanism nor timestamps to label database data.

5. The algorithm is deadlock-free, which is achieved as a side effect of the algorithm, and no separate distributed deadlock detection method is needed.

6. This algorithm can, by its nature, execute more transactions issued from a heavily loaded site; therefore, the system will not be clogged at busy nodes.

7. This algorithm is simple and easy to implement.

This algorithm requires only n messages per update transaction for synchronization, where n is the number of database nodes in the network. It has a good throughput of n/Tb transactions per time unit and the shortest delay of Tb + Ts time units in the best case. We have claimed that this algorithm can preserve mutual consistency and internal consistency in both normal and abnormal cases. The algorithm is easy to implement in a low-cost local computer network like DDLCN.

REFERENCES

[1] Liu, M. T., et al., System Design of the Distributed Double-Loop Computer Network (DDLCN), Proc. First International Conference on Distributed Computing Systems 10 (1979) to appear.

[2] Wolf, J. J. and Liu, M. T., A Distributed Double-Loop Computer Network (DDLCN), Proc. 7th Texas Conf. on Comp. Syst. 11 (1978) 6.19-34.

[3] Wolf, J. J., Liu, M. T., Weide, B. W., and Tsay, D. P., Design of a Distributed Fault-Tolerant Loop Network, Proc. 1979 Intl. Symp. on Fault-Tolerant Comp. 6 (1979) 17-23.

[4] Tsay, D. P. and Liu, M. T., Interface Design for the Distributed Double-Loop Computer Network (DDLCN), Proc. 1979 National Telecommunications Conference 11 (1979) to appear.

[5] Chou, C. P., Liu, M. T., and Pardo, R., Distributed Data Base Design for a Local Computer Network (DDLCN), Proc. First International Symp. on Policy Analysis and Information Systems 6 (1979) to appear.

[6] Rothnie, J. B. and Goodman, N., A Survey of Research and Development in Distributed Database Management, Proc. VLDB 10 (1977) 48-62.

[7] Bernstein, P. A. and Goodman, N., Approaches to Concurrency Control in Distributed Data Base Systems, Proc. National Computer Conference 6 (1979) 813-820.

[8] Thomas, R. H., A Majority Consensus Approach to Concurrency Control for Multiple Copy Databases, ACM Trans. on Database Systems 6 (1979) 180-209.

[9] Ellis, C. A., A Robust Algorithm for Updating Duplicated Databases, Proc. Second Berkeley Workshop on Distributed Data Management and Computer Networks 5 (1977) 146-158.

[10] Pardo, R. and Liu, M. T., Multi-Destination Protocols for Distributed Systems, Proc. 1979 Computer Networking Symposium 12 (1979) to appear.

[11] Chou, C. P. and Liu, M. T., Concurrency Control and Crash Recovery in the Distributed Loop Database Systems (DLDBS), in preparation.

[12] Bernstein, P. A., et al., The Concurrency Control Mechanism of SDD-1 : A System for Distributed Databases (the Fully Redundant Case), IEEE Trans. on Software Engineering 5 (1978) 154-168.

[13] Gray, J., Notes on Data Base Operating Systems, in : Operating Systems : An Advanced Course, Lecture Note on Computer Science 60 (Springer-Verlag, 1978) 393-481.

[14] Eswaren, K. P., Gray, J. N., Lorie, B. A., and Traigen, I. L., The Notions of Consistency and Predicate Locks in a Database System, Communication ACM 11 (1976) 624-633.

[15] Lamport, L., Time, Clocks and Ordering of Events in a Distributed System, CACM 7 (1978) 558-565.

DISTRIBUTED DATA BASES
C. Delobel and W. Litwin (eds.)
North-Holland Publishing Company

PROCESS STRUCTURE ALTERNATIVES TOWARDS A DISTRIBUTED INGRES

R.A.C. Thomas

Vrije Universiteit, Wiskundig Seminarium
De Boelelaan 1081
1007 MC Amsterdam
The Netherlands

A distributed data base management system - DDBMS - can be thought of as a collection of co-operative local DBMS's. We discuss the overall architecture of a DDBMS, designed as a homogeneous Ingres system, in terms of process structure requirements. Finally we show how the homogeneous distributed Ingres system can be simulated on a single Unix machine.

1. INTRODUCTION

One of the gains of a DBMS is the notion of data independence. Now, extending this philosophy, distributed DBMS's should take care of singularities introduced by geographically dispersed data. The most accepted view of a DDBMS is one in which data is stored on distinct computers, each running a local DBMS to manipulate the local partition of the data base. The computers participate in a communication network. The local DBMS's co-operate, giving users on each computer the illusion of one large local data base.

DDBMS's are divided into two categories: heterogeneous and homogeneous DDBMS's [2]. A DDBMS is (fully) homogeneous, if the local DBMS's are all the same and the supporting hardware is too.

We feel that properties of the hardware should not be reflected in the DDBMS terminology, because they affect implementations only. Therefore, we will drop the second condition. In practice, this means, that in homogeneous DDBMS's all local DBMS's run on the same virtual machine.

Normally, distributed data is said to be geographically dispersed over the nodes of a computer network. It is sufficient, though, to define distinct portions of the data base, each portion with its own administrative organization. Whether or not the portions are located on distinct computers is an implementational detail.

The main characteristic of a DDBMS is, that each portion of the data base is controlled by its own local DBMS, whilst the local DBMS's co-operate to control the distributed data base as a whole.

Using these notions, we shall discuss a homogeneous distributed Ingres system in terms of process structure requirements. Ingres is a relational DBMS, developed at the University of California, Berkeley. The design and implementation of a distributed version is under progress at the Free University of Amsterdam. The object of this paper is to focus on the possible process structures of the local Ingres systems.

The features of the original Ingres system are described extensively elsewhere [7], therefore, they are summarized only in the next section. In sections 3 and 4 the network and data model are presented, respectively. Then in section 5, we describe the functional aspects of distributed Ingres and its implications on the Ingres process structure. This paper served as a framework for further study on distributed data base systems. Therefore, related topics as distributed query decomposition, consistency, concurrency control, recovery and data base integrity will be dealt with in subsequent papers. Finally, we show how a homogeneous distributed Ingres system can be simulated on a single machine.

2. LOCAL INGRES PROCESS STRUCTURE

The design considerations of Ingres are well-known [7] and need not be discussed presently. For the sake of understanding, the Ingres process structure is reviewed.

Because of address space limitations (64K bytes), Ingres evolved into a multi-process system. Processes communicate via pipes; the inter-process communication mechanism under Unix [2]. The process structure of Ingres, version 6.2, is shown in figure 1.

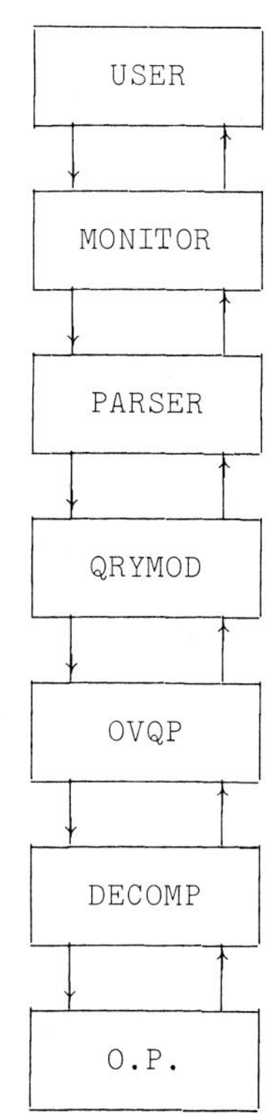

figure 1: Ingres process structure version 6.1

Figure 1 shows the Ingres system while used interactively. The user interacts with the Monitor process, which performs non-data base actions only. It stores the user supplied QUEL (QUEry Language) statements in a query buffer. On user request, this buffer is sent to the Parser, where the QUEL statements are parsed and transformed into query trees. Query trees are modified by QRYMOD, the QueRY MODification process, in order to provide for access control as well as integrity constraints and views [4] [5] [8].

The modified query trees are passed via OVQP to the DECOMPosition process. Here, the decomposition strategy is applied [12], breaking the query into one variable (relation) queries, which are evaluated by the One Variable Query Processor (OVQP). O.P. stands for Overlay Process. Each overlay contains some data base utilities, which can be invoked by DECOMP or by the Parser. Data base utilities include functions as: "create a relation", "destroy a relation", "print a relation", "modify the storage structure of a relation" and "give information on a relation".

Ingres is a single user system. This means that for each user there is a collection of Ingres processes. Furthermore, note that queries are evaluated, one quel statement at a time and that at any moment one process is active only.

3. NETWORK MODEL

As mentioned before, the objective is to design a homogeneous distributed Ingres system. Because Ingres runs under the Unix operating system only, all computers involved have to be Unix machines.

Let all computers be inter-connected by means of communication lines, while all low level communication problems are hidden in a universal network protocol. Assume each computer can address any other machine in the network. Because users may fire queries at all nodes, it seems reasonable to let all nodes be equally powerful in query processing.

Two further assumptions are to be made. Firstly, processes should be enabled to fork processes on remote machines. Forking is the way co-operative processes are created under Unix. Any Ingres request will lead to the invocation of an Ingres system. To deal with a distributed query, i.e. a query over relations located at, at least, two different partitions of the data base, the original Ingres system must invoke Ingres systems on all machines involved in that query. The original Ingres system, i.e. the one servicing the user, is called Master Ingres. Ingres systems invoked by Master Ingres are called Slave Ingres.

Secondly, we assume Ingres systems communicate via pipes in much the same way ordinary processes do. Messages will then be structured like messages within a single Ingres system, using the pipe structure format [9].

The necessary extensions to the Unix operating system are likely to be implemented in Unix version 7, which is to appear shortly [3].

4. DATA MODEL

Ingres is a relational DBMS, so data is stored as relations. In our model a relation is the unit of distribution, meaning that relations are located on one node only. So, no copies are kept. On each site system catalogs are maintained in special system relations.

The information involved has been categorized [6] as follows:

1. relation name
2. parsing information (domain, names formats, etc.)
3. performance information (number of tuples)
4. consistency information (protection, integrity, constraints, and views)

According to distributed query decomposition requirements, as described in a parallel paper [11], we have chosen for 1, 2 and 3 to be present on each machine, while consistency information is kept locally only.

There are two ways to do query decomposition. Either, it can be done by Master Ingres for all the relations used, or it can be done by all active Ingres systems, where each system will modify all references to its local relations.

When the first option is used, all consistency information must be kept up-to-date at all nodes, which will cause considerable network traffic overhead. On the other hand, Slave Ingres can do without the QRYMOD process. We have chosen in favour of the second option to simplify updates of the consistency information.

Normal users will not be aware of the data distribution. Of course, dba's must be. Relations can be local - known at one site only - or they can be distributed - known at more than one site.

Users may create local relations for their own usage. These private relations can be made plublic by the dba by installing the protection information in the local system catalogs. Furthermore, the dba may distribute relations over some or all of the nodes of the network. Then, system catalog information of catagories 1, 2 and 3 of this relation are included in the system catalog of the specified nodes.

5. FUNCTIONAL DESCRIPTION

Let us assume that a computer network has N nodes, names S1 - Sn. A distributed data base has been dispersed over all sites. The data base part on site Si is called DBi. Every DBi consists of both system catalog relations and data relations. The same system catalog relations are present at each DBi, although their contents will differ from site to site. Because of the distribution criterion, each set of data relations is unique.

As an example, let there be three relations: parts, supplier and supply, located in data base partitions DB1, DB2 and DB3 respectively. The relations are defined by:

```
parts (pnum,pname,color,weight,qoh)
supplier (snum,sname,city)
supply (snum,pnum,quan)
```

Assume a user logged on to the system at site S1, invoked Ingres and posed the following query:

> Retrieve the number and names of red parts, supplied by suppliers living in either San Francisco or San Diego, who supply at least one thousand pieces at a time.

In QUEL this query would look like:

```
range of (P,S,Y) is (parts,supplier,supply)
retrieve (P.pnum,P.pname)
where   P.color = "red" and
        (S.city = "San Francisco" or
         S.city = "San Diego") and
        Y.quan >= 1000 and
        P.pnum  = Y.pnum and S.snum = Y.snum
```

Let us see what actions are to be taken by the Ingres system.

Master Ingres will parse the query, thereby checking the names of relations and domains, transforming the query into its internal representation. This is possible, because system catalogs of categories 1 and 2 are kept on each machine.

The first thing to do now is to invoke Slave Ingres systems at nodes listed in the active node table. The active node table is obtained from the relation names used in the query and the system catalogs. It contains the site-numbers and the data base names of the data base partitions {DB1, DB2, DB3} on the given sites {S1, S2, S3}. Master Ingres generates messages for the Unix network handler:

```
invoke "ingres_slave DB2" at site S2
invoke "ingres_slave DB3" at site S3
```

After a Slave Ingres has been started, it sends a ready message to Master Ingres and waits for further input.

After all sites have become active, Master Ingres will send all necessary information to the remote sites. The kind of information, as well as the order in which information is sent to the remote sites, depend upon the decomposition algorithm used to answer the query.

We will distinguish centralized and decentralized distributed query processing. In a centralized distributed decomposition algorithm, the decomposition is controlled by Master Ingres alone. Then, the query will be broken into series of queries, each one local to exactly one site.

The example query, for instance, could lead to:

```
send to S2:

     retrieve into temp1 (S.snum)
     where    S.city = "San Francisco" or
              S.city = "San Diego"
     move temp1 to S1

send to S3:

     retrieve into temp2 (Y.snum,Y.pnum)
     where    Y.quan >= 1000
     move temp2 to S1
```

While Master Ingres waits for the intermediate results, it may or may not process the sub-query:

```
retrieve into temp3 (P.pnum,P.pname)
where    P.color = "red"
```

Then, after all results have reached Master Ingres, the remaining query can be solved locally. This query will read as follows:

```
range of (P,S,Y) is (temp1,temp2,temp3)
retrieve (P.pnum,P.pname)
where    P.pnum = Y.pnum and S.snum = Y.snum
```

On the other hand, when using a decentralized distributed query decomposition algorithm, all Slaves are provided with all, or at least most of, the internal representation of the query, like the query tree and the range table. Now all Ingres systems, the Master and all Slaves, will work co-operatively, sending each other intermediate results based upon some optimalization criteria. This mechanism is described in the parallel paper [11].

The inter-Ingres communication is controlled best by an independent process, say the Distributor. Especially when a decentralized distributed query decomposition algorithm is being used, intermediate results can be sent to Ingres systems, which are busy doing local query processing. The Distributor should run in parallel with the other Ingres processes to empty the network pipe as soon as possible. Therefore, it is not possible to run the Distributor as another overlay process. A natural extension of Ingres is shown in figure 2.

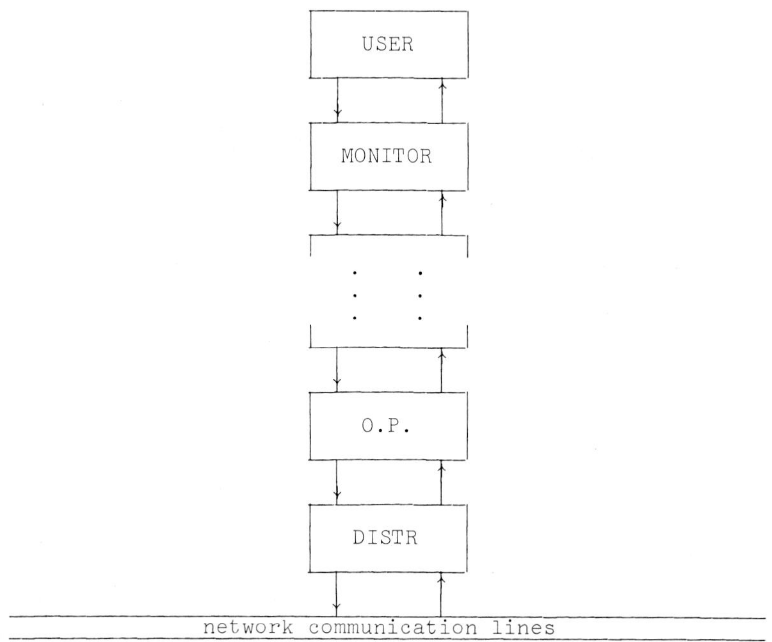

figure 2: Master Ingres

Due to system overhead the pipe mechanism is quite expensive. To improve performance we rearranged the Ingres process structure in order to reduce pipe usage. The following considerations were taken into account.

- OVQP will accept commands of DECOMP only. Nevertheless, OVQP has to pass all QRYMOD messages down to DECOMP and ready messages from DECOMP to QRYMOD. Thus, OVQP is taken out of the lineair structure and it is connected to DECOMP only.

- Some QUEL statements like "retrieve", "append", "delete" and "replace", are translated into query trees. After modification by QRYMOD, the query trees are sent to DECOMP for processing. Therefore, QRYMOD and DECOMP will be connected directly.

- Other QUEL statements like "create" and "destroy", are executed by one of the overlays of the O.P. process. OVQP and DECOMP do not interact, but they have to pass the message down to O.P. anyway. The solution here is to pipe O.P. to QRYMOD. Note, however, that DECOMP does interact with O.P. still. For instance, when temporary relations are to be created. Thus, the DECOMP to O.P. connection should not be altered.

Now, all messages are sent to the addressed processes directly. In that sense, the pipe usage in the new Ingres process structure is optimal. The proposed structure is given in figure 3.

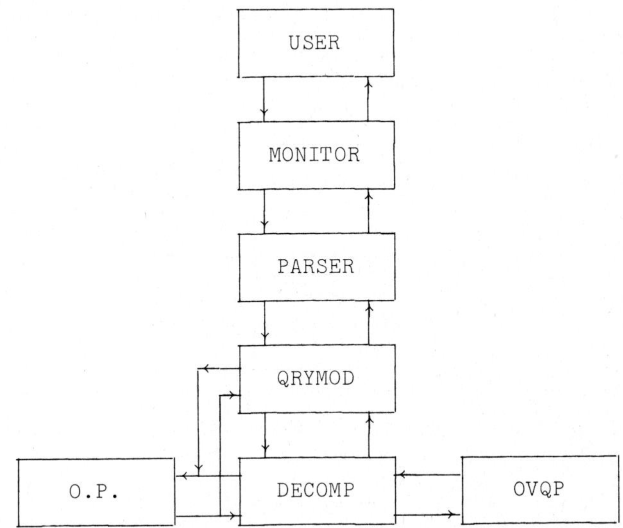

figure 3: Alternative process structure.

Note that the O.P. process is connected to both QRYMOD and DECOMP, using the same pipe. Because one process can be active only at any time, this construction will not cause any harm. O.P. will either work for QRYMOD, or for DECOMP and these processes wait for O.P. to finish, before they communicate with other processes. This new process structure has been implemented at the Free University.

Now, let us see, what distributed Ingres will look like. During query processing by DECOMP, the main task of a Distributor is to manage incoming and outgoing relations. Requests to send relations are given by DECOMP. Incoming relations may arrive at any time, that means, before or after DECOMP has asked for them. Because of these direct conversations, it seems reasonable to pipe the Distributor to DECOMP.

The new configurations of Master and Slave Ingres are given in figures 4 and 5.

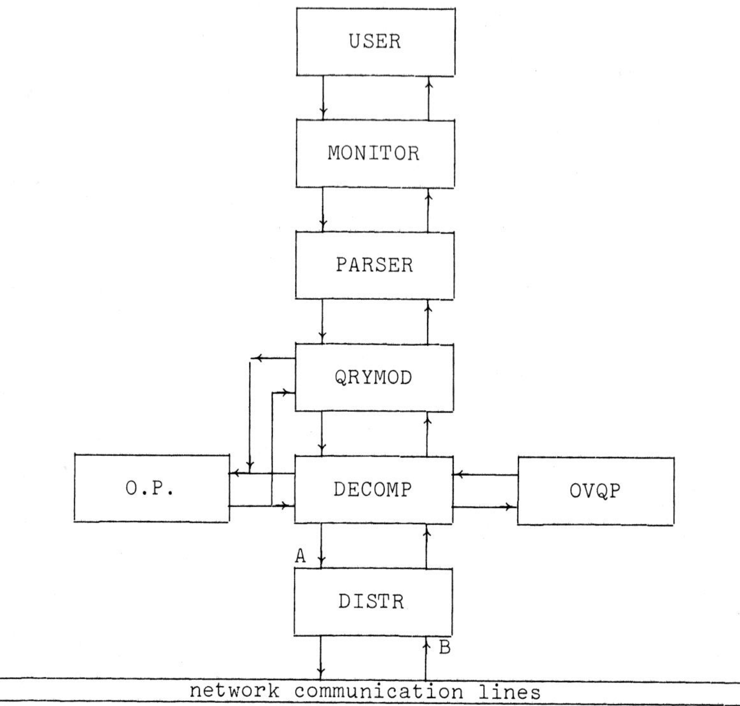

figure 4: Master Ingres

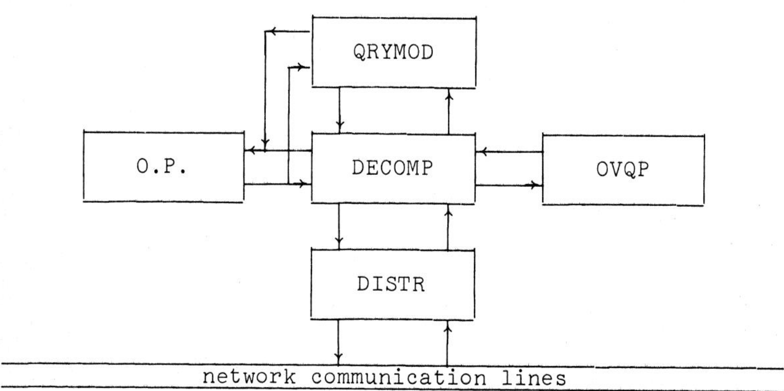

figure 5: Slave Ingres

Yet, the Distributor has got another synchronization problem. After it has passed the query tree to QRYMOD, it can read pipe A to collect the next DECOMP-command. In the mean time relations may be coming in from remote sites. Instead of processing these incoming messages, the Distributor may be blocked, while DECOMP is performing local query processing. However, when the Distributor decides to read pipe B, it might be the case that DECOMP wants to transmit one or more relations, while there is no relation sent by any remote Ingres. Now the Distributor is blocked on pipe B for ever.

To solve this problem, the Distributor should have one read pipe only, shared by the network communication system and by DECOMP.

For the sake of symmetry, QRYMOD and Distributor in Slave Ingres may be connected as indicated in figure 6.

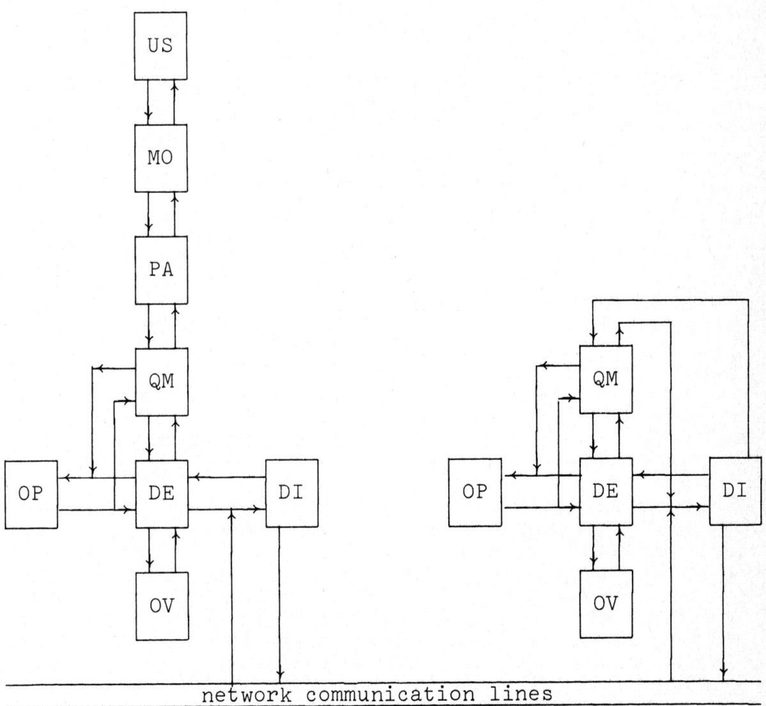

figure 6: Pipe usage in distributed Ingres.

In Slave Ingres QRYMOD receives the query from the Distributor, as if it were accepting input from the Parser in Master Ingres. Thus, when the query is solved, QRYMOD will send a sync message upwards. In Slave Ingres this message is eaten by the Distributor, who will sync to Master Ingres before it dies. Now, the Distributor is the only process, who can tell the difference between Master and Slave Ingres.

Let us summarize the Distributor activities in both Master and Slave Ingres, when a decentralized distributed query decomposition algorithm is used.

Distributor in master mode.

1. Get instructions to fork Slave Ingres systems and all necessary info from DECOMP.

2. Fork Slave Ingres systems.

3. Send processing info and query tree to Slaves.

4. Perform one of the following tasks:
   a. store DECOMP requests for remote relations, or
   b. store incoming relations, or
   c. send local relations to remote sites as indicated by DECOMP, or
   d. store sync messages sent by Slaves, or
   e. store DECOMP sync request.

5. Send sync message to DECOMP, whenever all requested relations have been received, or, when all Slaves have sent a sync message and DECOMP is waiting for it, else go to step 4.

Distributor in slave mode.

1. Read processing info and query tree from Master Ingres.

2. Pass it to QRYMOD.

3. Perform one of the following tasks:
   a. store DECOMP requests for remote relations, or
   b. store incoming relations, or
   c. send local relations to remote sites as indicated by DECOMP, or
   d. send a sync message to Master Ingres after QRYMOD has finished.

4. Send a sync message to DECOMP, whenever all requested relations have been received, else go te step 3.

Note, that synchronization problems introduced by locking and commitment protocols, to ensure data base consistency and to enable recovery, respectively, are not included here.

Furthermore, note that the Distributor has to deal with incoming relations. It would be most efficient, if these relations were included into the system's administration. Therefore, the Distributor has to send commands to the Overlay Process in order to create temporary relations. Because O.P. may be busy, due to a DECOMP request, messages of DECOMP and Distributor may get mixed. To overcome this problem, the Distributor should fork its own O.P.

6. A SIMULATION MODEL

The Unix to Unix communication facility is as yet not in existence at the Free University. Therefore, the computer network had to be simulated on a single machine.

Remember that ultimately, processes on different Unix-machines in a computer network use the pipe mechanism to communicate in the same way as they do when located on the same machine. Thus, the network extensions of the operating system may be reflected by a single Unix process, called the Network Process, or NP for short. NP will be piped to all instantiations of Ingres for one user. See figure 7.

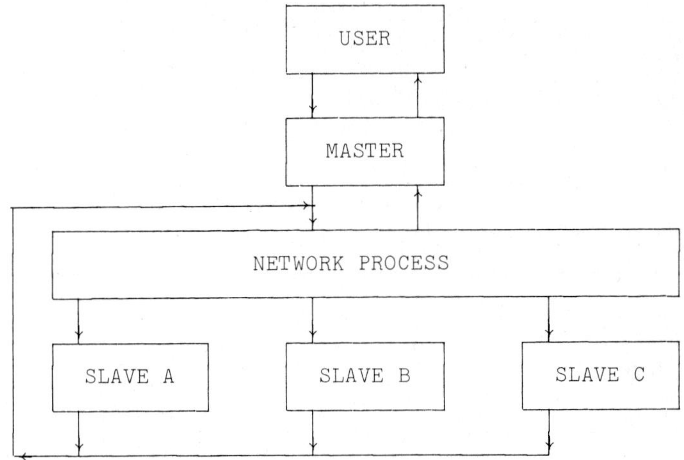

figure 7: Distributed Ingres simulation model.

NP will act as a multiplexer between the Ingres systems. Messages sent to NP, are supplied with a mailing address, i.e. a unique number of the site, where the addressed Ingres system is located.

Using one NP, a thirteen node network can be simulated. The limiting factor is the number of open files per process, whilst pipes are counted as open files. At our installation, on a PDP-11/45, 15 open files are allowed.

On the other hand, Ingres allows for multiple relation queries up to a maximum of ten relations. When more NP's are used any network may be simulated. As an example see figure 8.

Because Ingres is a single user system, several Ingres systems may run simultaneously on the same Unix system.

The main purpose of this model is to test effectiveness, in terms of communication cost and total response time, of the distributed query decomposition algorithm, which is under construction presently [11].

But recovery mechanisms may be tested too. For instance, during normal operation one may kill one of the slave Ingres systems, thereby simulating a site crash.

Note, that according to the given definition the model simulates a homogeneous distributed data base management system. The data bases, which constitute the distributed data base, are stored as local data bases in the datadir directory of the Ingres superuser. Therefore, each local data base should have a unique name. Of course, this requirement will be dropped in a multi-computer environment. But, even then, the ability to use different names for the constituent data bases introduces more flexibility in extending the distributed data base.

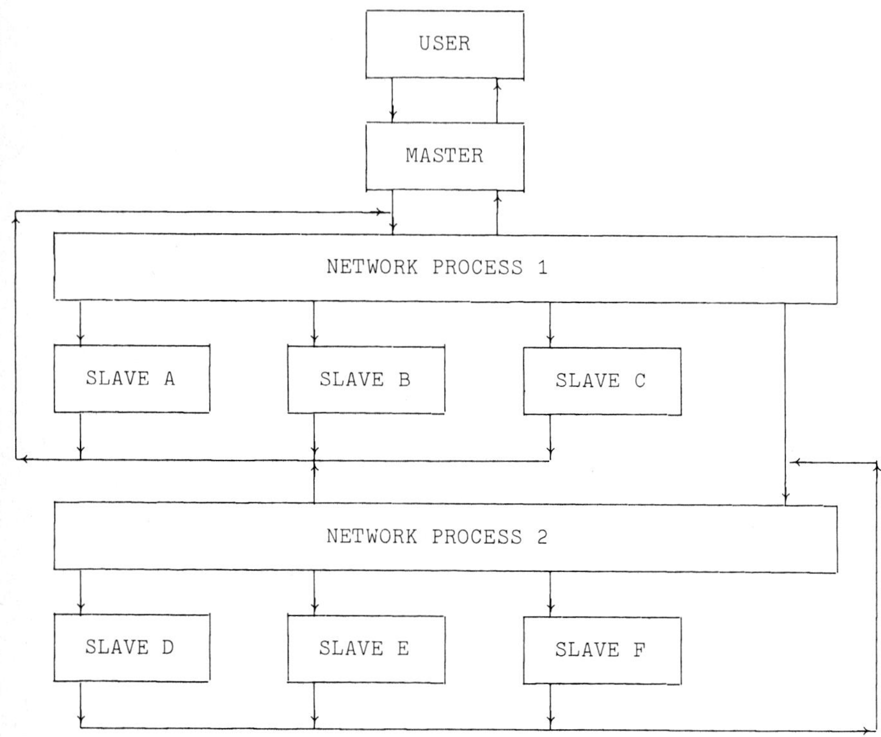

figure 8: An extended network model.

7. REFERENCES

[1] Draffan, I., Distributed Data Base Architecture, Sheffield City Polytechnic, UK (to appear).

[2] Ritchie, D.M. and Thompson, K., The Unix Time-Sharing System, CACM 17 (July 1974) 365-375.

[3] Ritchie, D.M. and Thompson, K., The Unix Time-Sharing System, The Bell System Technical Journal, Vol. 57 No. 6 Part 2 (July-August 1978) 1905-1929.

[4] Stonebraker, M. and Wong, E., Access Control in a Relational Data Base Management System by Query Modification, Proc. 1974 ACM Nat. Conf., San Diego, Calif. (Nov. 1974) 180-187.

[5] Stonebraker, M., Implementation of Integrity Constraints and Views by Query Modification, Proc. 1975 ACM-SIGMOD Conf. on Management of Data, San Jose, Calif. (June 1975).

[6] Stonebraker, M., A Distributed Database Version of Ingres, Proc. of the second Berkeley Workshop on DDM and Computer Networks, Berkeley, Calif. (May 1977).

[7] Stonebraker, M. et al, The Design and Implementation of Ingres, TODS 1 (Sept. 1976) 189-222.

[8] Stonebraker, M. and Rubenstein, P., The Ingres Protection System, Proc. 1976 ACM Nat. Conf., Houston, Tex. (Oct. 1976).

[9] Thomas, R.A.C., A Commentary on Synchronization of the Data Base System Ingres, Dept. of Comp. Sc., Free University, Amsterdam, Report IR-26 (Nov. 1977).

[10] Thomas, R.A.C., A Commentary on Storage Structures and Access Method of the DBS Ingres-5.1., Dept. of Comp. Sc., Free University, Amsterdam, Report IR-32 (April 1978).

[11] Thomas, R.A.C., A Decentralized Query Processing Algorithm for a Distributed Relational Data Base Environment (to appear).

[12] Wong, E. and Youssefi, K., Decomposition - A Strategy for Query Processing, TODS 1 (Sept. 1976) 223-241.

DISTRIBUTED DATA BASES
C. Delobel and W. Litwin (eds.)
North-Holland Publishing Company

DESIGN OF OPTIMAL DISTRIBUTED DATABASE SYSTEMS

J. AKOKA
Associate Professor, Head of the Research Center
Ecole Supérieure des Sciences Economiques et Commerciales
B.P 105
95001 - CERGY
FRANCE

In this paper we present a global model for the design of distributed database systems. The model allows to find the optimal allocations of databases and programs, and to define the optimal routing disciplines for the messages flowing in the network. Our model takes into account the return flow of information and investigates its effects on the optimal location of databases in the network. It considers the case of full-dependency between programs and databases. Finally it investigates to what extent the optimal location of databases is independent from their storage costs. From the solution procedure viewpoint, our algorithm is more general than previous approaches since it can determine the optimal solution even if we introduce additional constraints which are specific to any organization. It is shown that our model and the solution perform better than past models.

INTRODUCTION

In previous works, most of the research focused on the problem of minimizing the operating cost of a distributed database. A great deal of attention has been devoted to the problem of optimal distribution of the files over a network of computer systems.

One of the earliest studies of the file allocation problem was done by Chu (1). He developed a linear-programming model allocating files so that the allocation yields minimum overall operating costs subject to the following constraints : (i) the expected time to access each file is less than a given bound, (ii) the amount of storage needed at each computer does not exceed the available storage capacity. His model includes storage costs, queuing delays, and communication costs. But he assumed that the number of copies of each file in the system is known. In a later paper Chu (2) develped a procedure to determine in advance how many redundant copies of a file are required to achieve a desired level of reliability. Then, he inserted this number into the model, and the basic sheme remains unchanged.

Whitney (3) also formulated a similar model. He applied it to the design of a network topology and to the allocation of file copies. A communication network optimization procedure is developed. He showed that, for certain communication cost functions, the tree topology is less expensive than any non-tree topology. In addition he showed that the system delay is minimized when there are as few independent channels as possible.

Casey (4) developed a procedure for finding a minimal cost solution. Heuristic methods are used in this paper to find "good" solutions. The main difference between his paper and Chu's paper (2) is that the number of copies of files and their locations are treated as variables. He showed that the proportions of update traffic to query traffic generated by the users of a given file in the network could be used to determine an upper bound on the number of copies of the file present in the least cost network. He applied his algorithm to real data for the ARPA network and has thus shown the process feasible for networks of moderate size. He indicated that when update traffic equals query traffic, it is efficient to store all files at a central node.

Recently, Levin and Morgan (5) (6) developed models that allow partial dependencies between files and programs. In another paper (7) they developed a dynamic model for the multi-period case. In this model, the access time request are assumed to be known for the next T periods. However, the assuption that the access request patterns are static over time was relaxed and a dynamic model which considers transition costs was suggested.

In an another paper (8) Levin and Morgan provided a framework for research in optimizing distributed databases. They developed three models related to static file assignment with complete information, dynamic file assignment with complete information, and file assignment with incomplete information.

In a recent study, Chu (9) developed several models to study the performance of file directory systems for operating in the star network and distributed network topologies. He studied the cost-performance tradeoffs of three classes of directory system.

A particular attention should be devoted to Casey's paper (10) dealing with the design of tree networks for distributed data. He formulated a model locating information resources and choosing a topology for a network of distributed data files. In this model, he retains features such as discrete capacity assignment, economy of scale, and distinction between query and update transactions. He developed a heuristic method and formulated an algorithm solving the problem. The algorithm was tested for the special case of tree design. In their paper Mahmoud and Riordon (11) examine simultaneously the problems of file allocation and of link capacity allocation in order to achieve a minimum cost-design subject to constraints of file availability and network delay. The objective function contains two main costs : communication and file storage costs. The set of constraints is : the delay constraints and the file availability constraints.

As we can see most of the past models assume :
(i) Partial-dependency between programs and databases
(ii) No return flow of information
(iii) Independance between databases and their storage costs.

The major contributions of our model are precisely to lift up these restrictive assumption and to propose a more general solution procedure.

This paper is organized as follows : paragraph (II) is devoted to the description of the model and its assumptions. A particular attention is given to the différences existing between this model and Levin-Morgan's model.

In (III) we develop an algorithm which is based on the concept of Branch and Bound procedures. However, we limit a priori the number of nodes representing the subproblems to be solved at each node. Computational results are described for three different cases in paragraph (IV) and some conclusions are drawn and presented in (V).

II - THE GENERALIZED MODEL

II.1 - Assumptions and Modelling Aspects

In this section, we consider a distributed information system. The set of nodes is denoted by K.

At each node of the network, one or several databases may be installed. We do consider traditional files as well as databases where all the data used by a specific node are included, which may be a manufacturing unit of a large geographically dispersed company. The set of databases is denoted by N. The cost that is associated with each database is the storage cost, which is denoted by C_{kd}, the storage cost per unit length of database d at note k. The storage cost can be the same at each node of the computer network when the types of storage devices used to store the database are the same. On the contrary, when the types of storage devices are different, the storage costs can be different. For example, the storage cost of database using tapes can be less expensive than the storage cost of the same database, using disks.

Since we consider a heterogeneous distributed system, we should consider a set of programs devoted to the use of the databases. The set of programs is denoted by P. The cost of storage of program p at note j is denoted by S_{jp}.

There are two communication costs that occur : (a) Q_{ij} represents the communication cost per query unit from i to j ; (b) U_{ij} represents the communication cost per update unit from i to j. It is obvious that Q_{ij} and U_{ij} are dependent upon the distances between nodes i and j. Q_{ij} can be different from U_{ij} since the updates can be done during the night when the communication cost are lower.

Since we are studying a general heterogeneous system, we assume full-dependency between databases and programs. Therefore, in order to process a given transaction both the relevant program and the relevant database must be accessed. A given transaction (query or update) to database d located at node k, from a user located at node i, should be first processed by the relevant program p that may reside at node j. As a consequence, the transaction from note i should be first routed to node j. During its processing by program p, an access request to database d located at node j. Therefore, different assignments of programs will yield different distributions of request rates to the databases. As a consequence, there will be two different communication costs for queries and updates : a communication cost for queries and update from users to programs and a communication cost for queries and updates from programs to databases.

In our model, we explicitly take inot account "the return flow of information". By this, we mean the flow of information that a user in the network gets as a response to its queries. There are two types of return flow of information :

(a) γ_{ij} = estimated ratio of size of response to size of request from a user situated at node i to a program located at node j.

(b) γ'_{jk} = the estimated ratio from a program located at node j to a database situated at node K.

Finally, since we assume dependency between databases and programs, we have to define the concept of expansion factor. Lest us call l_1 the length of the query issued from users to programs, and l_2 the length of the resultant query issued from programs to databases, then $\alpha = (l_2)/(l_1)$ is the expansion factor for the queries. Similarly, β will be the expansion factor for updates.

We do not define an expansion factor for responses back to users since, in general the response given by the databases to programs is the same as the one transmitted by programs to users. Our model will provide us with an optimal distributed database systems if :

(i) an optimal allocation of the databases is obtained. We may have at a specific node one or more databases.

(ii) an optimalallocation of the programs is defined

(iii) an optimalmessage routing discipline is obtained. This includes the routing disciplines for message flowing between users and programs and for messages flowing between programs and databases.

Our problem is to determine these optima allocation at minimum cost.

II.2 - List of the variables

Let us first define the decision and the non-decision variables used in the model.

Non-decision variables

K set of nodes
N set of databases
C_{kd} storage cost of database d at node k
P set of programs
S_{jp} storage cost of program p at node j
γ'_{ij} estimated ratio of size of response to size of query requests from node i to a program located at node j
γ_{jk} estimated ratio of size of response to size of query from requests from program located at node j to database situated at node k
α expansion factor for query message
β expansion factor for update message
λ_{jpd} query traffic to database d processed at node j by program p
μ_{jpd} update traffic to database d processed at node j by program p
Q_{ij} communication cost per query unit from i to j
U_{ij} communication cost per update unit from i to j
Q^d_{ip} query traffic from node i to database d via program p
U^d_{ip} update traffic from node i to database d via program p

Decision-variables

x^d_k = 1 if a copy of database d is allocated to node k
0 otherwise

Z^p_j = 1 if a copy of program p is stored at node j
0 otherwise

X^d_{ijp} = 1 if transactions from node i to database d are routed to node j via program p
0 otherwise

X_{jkpd} = 1 if transactions from node j to database d are routed to node K and are processed by program p
0 otherwise

II.3 - The model

The objective function to be minimized is then :

$$F = \sum_{d,k} C_{kd} X^d_k$$ Storage cost of database (OF1)

$$+ \sum_{j,p} S_{jp} Z^P_j$$ Storage cost of programs (OF2)

$$+ \sum_{i,j,p,d} Q^d_{ip} Q_{ij} X^d_{ijp} (1 + \gamma'_{ij})$$ Communication cost of queries from nodes to programs

$$+ \sum_{i,j,p,d} U^d_{ip} U_{ij} X^d_{ijp}$$ Communication cost of update from nodes to programs

$+ \sum_{j,k,p,d} \alpha\lambda_{jpd} Q_{jk} X_{jkpd} (1 + \gamma_{jk})$ Communication cost of queries from programs to databases. (OF5)

$+ \sum_{j,k,m,d} \beta\mu_{jpd} U_{jk} X_k^d$ Communication cost of updates from programs to databases. (OF6)

Subjet to the following constraints :

- To assure the existence of a feasible solution, there must be at least one copy of each database and program, i.e.,

$$\sum_k X_k^d \geq 1, \quad \forall\, d \in N \qquad \text{(CST1)}$$

$$\sum_j Z_j^p \geq 1, \quad \forall\, p \in P \qquad \text{(CST2)}$$

- To assure that every transaction to every database via every program which is related to it and from every node, will have a defined route

$$\sum_j X_{ijp}^d = 1, \forall\, i \in I=K, p \in P, d \in N \qquad \text{(CST3)}$$

$$\sum_k X_{jkpd} = Z_j^P, \forall\, j \in J=K, d \in N, p \in P \qquad \text{(CST4)}$$

- To assure residency of the appropriate database and programs in accordance with the defined routes :

$$\sum_i X_{ijp}^d > \sigma\, Z_j^p, \forall\, j \in J=K, p \in P, d \in N, \sigma = \text{number of nodes of the network} \qquad \text{(CST5)}$$

$$\sum_i X_{jkpk} > \sigma\, X_k^d \quad \forall\, k \in K, d \in N, p \in P \qquad \text{(CST6)}$$

- To assure that program p can reside only in nodes at which it can be processed.

$Z_j^p = 0 \quad \forall j \notin Ip, p \in P$ where Ip is the set of nodes where program p can be processed. (CST7)

- Binary constraints :

$X_k^d = \{0 \text{ or } 1\}$ for all $k \in K$ and $d \in N$

$Z_j^P = \{0 \text{ or } 1\}$ for all $j \in J=K$ and $p \in P$

$X_{ijp}^d = \{0 \text{ or } 1\}$ for all $i \in I=K$, $j \in J=K$, $p \in P$, $d \in N$ (CST8)

$X_{jkpd} = \{0 \text{ or } 1\}$ for all $j \in J=K$, $k \in K$, $d \in N$, $p \in P$

The model is similar to the Levin-Morgan Model (6), in the sense that like our model, Levin-Morgan's model determines the optimallocations of databases and programs in a computer network, and defines the message routing disciplines.

However, there are some important differences between Levin-Morgan's approach and our approach. The most important differences are :

(1) Our model takes into account the return flow of information. This aspect is modeled in the components (OF3) and (OF5) of our objective function. That is an important aspect that changes the final optimal allocation of databases and programs, as it will be shown in the following pages. Levin-Morgan's models (as well as previous models of distributed database systems) ignored this aspect.

(2) The main contribution of Levin-Morgan's model resides in the fact that it can handle the case of heterogeneous computer networks. In other words, they did not assume independencies between programs and databases. However, only one aspect of this dependency is considered, namely the one stating that in order to access a database, one should first access a program operating on the database. The routing variable used in their model is :

$$X_{jkd} = \begin{cases} 1 & \text{if transactions from node j to database d are routed to node k} \\ 0 & \text{otherwise} \end{cases}$$

As it can be seen, this routing discipline variable does not indicate which program (among all those residing at node j) can process the database d located at node k. This is a serious shorcoming of their model, since it cannot handle the case where a full-dependency between programs and databases exists. In other words, their model ignored the fact that in order to access a specific database, it is necessary to access first only the program <u>strictly related</u> to this particular database. This is a more general case than the one considered by Levin-Morgan's model. To allow us to deal with the case of full-dependency, we defined the following variable :

$$X_{jkpd} = \begin{cases} 1 & \text{if there are transactions from nodej to database d located at node k, and which is processed by program p} \\ 0 & \text{otherwise.} \end{cases}$$

This permits us to define routing disciplines to databases via their related programs. The effects of this routing disciplines are modeled in the components (OF5) and (OF6) of our objective function.

(3) In their formulation, Levin-Morgan state that :

$$\sum_k X_{jkd} \leq 1, \forall j \in J = K, d \in N$$

(In other words, we have to a ssure that every transaction to every file via every program and from every node, will have a predefined route).

This type of constraint has two important shortcomings :

(i) It does not take into account the case of full-dependency between programs and databases.

(ii) It contradicts the definition of x_{jkd} which states that there is a routing discipline between programs and databases only if there exists a program at note j. By taking the sum over k for all nodes j, there always exists a least one routing discipline at every node j, whether or not a program is located there. As a consequence, a contradiction of their definition will always occur. To avoid these two shortcomings, our formulation states that :

$$\sum_k X_{jkpd} = Z_j^p, \forall j \in J = K, p \in P, c \in N$$

By doing so : (i) we assure that every transaction to every database via only the related program p and from every node, will have a predefined route. (ii) A routing discipline exists from node j only if $Z_j^p \neq 0$ (i.e. only if a program exists at node j.)

Another important difference in the approaches taken to solve the model will be described in the next paragraph. But let us first describe the solution procedure.

III - THE SOLUTION PROCEDURE

In order to simplify the notations used, let us call our objective function $\phi(x)$, the constraints $h_\ell(x)$. Therefore, the simplified formulation of our model is :

$$(P)\quad \begin{cases} \min \phi(X) \\ \text{subject to :} \\ h_\ell(X) < 0 & (c\text{-}1) \\ 0 \leq X \leq 1 & (c\text{-}2) \\ X = 0,\ 1 & (c\text{-}3) \end{cases}$$

where the components of vector X are X_k^d, Z_j^p, X_{ijp}^d, X_{jkpd}

We assume that :

(i) $\phi(x)$ is a nonlinear function, continuously differentiable
(ii) constraints (c-1) define a domain which is convex
(iii) constraints (c-2) define a parallelotope (π). (π) is assumed to be bounded.

Let us now describe our algorithm.

Step 1 relaxing the last constraint $(x = 0,1)$, solve the following continuous non linear programming problem :

$$P\ (S)\quad \begin{cases} \min \phi(X) \\ \text{subject to :} \\ h_\ell(x) < 0 \\ 0 \leq x \leq 1 \\ x \text{ continuous} \end{cases}$$

In order to do so, we use the GRG (12) algorithm since Colville (13) found it faster than other nonlinear codes.

At the end of Step 1, we obtain either integer or continuous values for the variables.

a) If all the variables are integer, go to end.
b) if only some variables are integer, go to step 2.

Step 2 The Binary Bounded Branch and Bound Method

This step is based on Abadie's (14) BBB method. Il allows us to determine the integer optimal values of the variables X_{ijp}^d, X_{jkpd} and Z_j^p. To do so, the method solves a set of continuous nonlinear programming problems, corresponding to the nodes of the arborescence. These continuous problems are put in a master list. At iteration 1, the master list contains problem P (S). This problem was already solved in Step 1. At any iteration t, let $\hat{x}$ be the best integer solution obtained so far. We set $\hat{\phi} = \hat{\phi}(\hat{x})$ (or, $\hat{\phi} = +\infty$ if no integer solution was obtained). The general procedure to be used is :

(1) . If the master list is empty, terminate the computations ;
(If $\hat{\phi} < \infty$, then $\hat{x}$ is the optimal solution.
If $\hat{\phi} = +\infty$, then there is no solution to the problem).

. If the master list is not empty, go to (2).

(2) Solve the last problem put in the master list (call it WP)
let X be the solution obtained, with $\phi^* = \phi(x^*)$
. If $\phi^* > \hat{\phi}$, remove WP from the master list and go to (1).
. Otherwise, go to (3).

(3) If all x_j , $j \in E$, are integers, then X is an integer solution better than X.
Let $\hat{X} = X$, and $\hat{\phi} = \phi^*$, remove WP from the master list, and go to (1)
. Otherwise, go to (4).

(4) Choose a non-integer X_β , $\beta \in E$ and consider the following three problems :

(a) the problem derived from WP with $X_\beta = [X_\beta^*]$

(b) the problem derived from WP with $X_\beta = [X_\beta^*] + 1$

where the symbol [ ] means the integer value.

(c) the problem derived from WP with a certain variable

$$X_\alpha = \begin{cases} [X_\alpha] - 1 \\ \text{or} \\ [X_\alpha] + 1 \end{cases}$$

- If both problems (a) and (b) were not already solved, add them to the master list and go to (2).
- If both problems (a) and (b) were already solved, remove WP from the master list add to this list problem (c) and go to (2).
- If only either problem (a) or problem (b) was solved, remove WP from the master list, add to this list problem (c) and the unsolved problem (either problem (a) or problem (b)) and go to (2).

The main differences between this method and the traditional branch and bound methods are the following :

- Steps (1), (2) are the same in both methods. But, traditional branch and bound methods deal with linear problems, whereas our method deals with non linear problems.

- Step (2) of traditional branch and bound methods can be summarized as follows (15) ;

- Choose a non-integer X_β, $\beta \in E$, and add to the master list the following two new problems :

  (a) the problem derived from WP with $X = [X_\beta]$

  (b) the problem derived from WP with $X = [X_\beta] + 1$

As a consequence, the same variable X_β can be chosen at each node of the arborescence, thus, increasing considerably the number of problems stored in the list.
In other words, Step 2 of traditional branch and bound methods leads to an increase of the number of the nodes of the arborescence, thus making it very difficult to solve large-scale integer problems. On the contrary, by using Step 2 of our method we force the variable X_β, once fixed at a given integer value, to keep this value.

in all the nodes of its descendence. As a consequence, we limit a priori the number of nodes (i.e. problems) to be stored in the master list. This number is equal to N, where N is the number of the variables of the problem and not 2^N as in the case of traditional branch and bound methods. Hence, we can solve integer large-scale problems, which is the case of our model.

A more detailed version of this algorithm can be found in (16), (17), (18) and its application to a real-life examples for the design of distributed systems in (19). From the solution procedure viewpoint, there is an important difference between Levin-Morgan's method and our algorithm. In Levin-Morgan's work, databases and programs are separated and a staged minimization approach is tried. The stagging used is the following :

(1)	(2)	(3)
Min databases Location	Min programs location (given databases location)	Min message routing (given databases and programs location)

To solve minimization problem (2), they assume that storage costs for programs are zero. This assumption implies that programs are basically stored everywhere. As a consequence, program locations are chosen a priori by the designer. This contradicts Levin-Morgan's argument that it is necessary to minimize the number of copies of a program due to the problems of maintaining updated versions of a program in a heterogeneous network. In other words, Levin-Morgan solve the problem by avoiding it. This may invalidate their solution in the case of homogeneous computer networks, where the programs are not a priori excluded from some nodes. On the contrary, in our approach we do solve the problem, including its program cost component, without choosing a priori the locations of the programs.

This leads us to a more general conclusion. In most of the cases, the introduction of new additional constraints (such as storage constraints, dependencies between databases, etc.) will lead to a violation of Levin-Morgan's decomposition technique thus making their solution procedure non-applicable ; whereas our solution procedure can handle any type of additional constraints, due to the fact that it is a general mathematical programming algorithm.

IV - COMPUTATIONAL RESULTS

Some of the differences between our distributed database system model and Casey's and Levin-Morgan's models are illustrated using the following example. The data for this example was taken from Casey's five-node example and is given below.

SOURCE \ DESTINATION	$Q_{ij} = U_{ij}$ Cost per Megabyte Shipped 1	2	3	4	5	Q^d_{ip} Query Traffic	U^d_{ip} Update Traffic
1	0	6	12	9	6	24	2
2	6	0	6	12	9	24	3
3	12	6	0	6	12	24	4
4	9	12	6	0	6	24	6
5	6	9	12	6	0	24	8

We make the same assumptions as Levin-Morgan :

- The expansion factors α and β are equal to 1.
- Only one program and one database are considered.
- Both queries and updates must be processed by program p, which allow us to access the database.
- Program p can be processed only at node 2 and node 3.

We will consider three different cases :

First case - No return flow of information an no storage cost of database.

We first assume that there is no return flow of information to queries and that the storage cost of database and program is negligible. This is exactly the case treated by both Casey and Levin-Morgan. Therefore, $C_{kd} = s_{jp} = 0$ and $\gamma'_{ij} = \gamma_{jk} = 0$. Figure 1 summarizes the optimal costs associated with both Casey's and Levin-Morgan's model and our model.

FIGURE 1. COST OF DATABASE ASSIGNMENTS : CASE 1

Location of database copies at node	Program/file Independence Casey	Program/file Dependence Levin / Morgan	Program/file Dependence AKOKA
1	860	1830	1830
2	972	972	972
3	1038	1038	1038
4	915	1896	1896
5	915	2085	2085
12	852	1110	1110
13	774	1260	1260
14	726	1758	1758
15	867	2037	2037
23	856	762	762
24	730	1188	1188
25	735	1179	1179
34	804	1176	1176
35	729	1299	1299
45	753	2013	2013
123	810	912	912
124	762	1386	1386
125	759	1317	1317
134	756	1452	1452
135	753	1497	1497
145	705	1995	1995
234	760	954	954
235	765	999	999
245	717	1425	1425
345	711	1452	1452
1234	792	1176	1176
1235	789	1167	1167
1245	741	1593	1593
1345	735	1713	1713
2345	747	1215	1215
12345	771	1413	1413

The optimal database assignment under Casey's assumptions is obtaines when database copies are stored at nodes 1, 4, 5. The cost associated whith this assignment is 705. However, when the assumption of dependency between databases and program is made, the utilization of Casey's model leads to suboptimal results. The associated cost is 1995. The optimum found by Levin-Morgan is when copies of the database are stored at nodes 2 and 3. This is the same database assignment found by our algorithm.

However, a careful analysis shows that the optimal solutions provided by Levin-Morgan's model and our model are:

Levin-Morgan	Akoka
$x_2^1 = x_3^1 = 1$	$x_2^1 = x_3^1 = 1$
$z_2^1 = z_3^1 = 1$	$z_2^1 = z_3^1 = 1$
$x_{121}^1 = x_{221}^1 = x_{331}^1 = x_{431}^1 = x_{521}^1 = 1$	$x_{121}^1 = x_{221}^1 = x_{331}^1 = x_{431}^1 = x_{521}^1 = 1$
$x_{121} = x_{221} = x_{331} = x_{421} = x_{421} = x_{521} = 1$	$x_{2211} = x_{3311} = 1$
all the remaining variables are equal to zero	all the remaining variables are equal to zero.

In Levin-Morgan's results, the existence of x_{121}, x_{421} and x_{521} contradicts their definition of x_{jkd}. These variables are equal to zero in our results, which conforms to the definition of x_{jkpd}. Notice that the existence of these additional variables did not lead to an increase of the objective function. This is due only to the fact that we have only one program and one database. In the case of multiple programs and multiple databases, an increase of the optimal value of the objective function will occur, thus leading to a suboptimal solution for the Levin Morgan model.

Second Case - Existence of Storage Cost for Database

Let us relax the assumption made in the previous section and consider that there exist a cost related to the storage of the database (but not for program). It is generally considered that, given that the storage cost is the same at each node the optimal assignment of database will be the same as in the previous case. This may be true for small database where the storage cost is negligible. For real life database, the storage cost is important, and therefore can have an effect on the optimal location of databases. Let us show it. For a storage cost C_{kd} of $ 500 a month which is a reasonable estimation for large database) our model gives us the following results (figure 2).

FIGURE 2. Cost of Database Assignment - Case 2
(Storage cost = $ 500)

Location of database copies at node	Akoka's Model	
1	2330	
2	1472	New optimal solution
3	1538	
4	2396	
5	2585	
12	2110	
13	2260	
14	2758	
15	3037	
23	1762	Previous optimal solution
24	2188	
25	2179	
34	2176	
35	2299	
45	3013	
123	1912	
124	2886	
125	2817	
134	2912	
135	2992	
145	3495	
234	2454	
235	2499	
245	2925	
345	2952	
1234	3176	
1235	3167	
1245	3593	
1345	3713	
2345	3215	
12345	3913	

As we can see, the optimal solution obtained without considering the storage cost of databases occurs when the copies of the database are stored at nodes 2 and 3. When we consider explicitly the sotrage cost of database, the new optimal solution is obteined when we store the database only at node 2. This is due to the fact that when we have a high cost of storage of the database (which is the case for large databases), it is preferable to minimize the number of copies of the database to be stored. In this example, if the database is sotred at nodes 2 and 3, the total cost is $ 1762. The storage cost is only $ 1000 (about 57 percent of the total cost) while the communication cost for queries and updates is $ 762 (about 43 percent of the total cost). Therefore, the storage cost is higher than communication cost. This tends to push the storage of database to a solution that minimizes the number of copies . This precisely is the case when we store the database at node 2 only. An important conclusion that can be drawn from this example is that the optimal location of databases are not independent from their storage costs, when this storage cost is not negligible or is the same at every node of the network. Does this conclusion hold when the storage cost is different from one node to the others.

Given the structure of our distributed database systems model, and if we assume that the storage cost of databases is different at each node (this is possible when the copies of the database are stored on different storage devices such as disks or tapes), then it is possible to consider once again that the optima assignment of databases is dependent on their storage cost. To show it, let us use the results obtained in Case 1. Let us consider that is nodes 1, 3, 4 and 5, it is possible to use slow speed disks in order to store the database, while at node 2 we can use high-speed disks. Furthermore, let us consider the storage cost at nodes 1, 3, 4 and 5, equal to $ 100, whereas the storage cost at node 2 is equal to $ 700. Using the model we will obtain the assignment given in Figure 3. As we cans see, the optimal location of the database copies changes. The new optimal solution, equal to $ 1.138 is obtained when the database is stored only at node 3.

Figure 3. Different Storage Costs at the Nodes

Location of database copies at node	Program/File dependence Akoka's model	
1	1930	
2	1672	
3	1138	New optimal solution
4	1996	
5	2185	
12	1910	
13	1460	
14	1958	
15	2237	
23	1562	Previous optimal solution
24	1488	
25	1979	
34	1376	
35	1499	
45	2213	
123	1912	
124	2386	
125	2317	
134	1652	
135	1697	
145	2195	
234	1854	
235	1899	
245	2325	
345	1752	
1234	2176	
1235	2167	
1245	2593	
1345	2113	
2345	2215	
12345	2513	

As a conclusion we can state the following :

1. If the storage cost of database is null or negligible, the optimal locations of database copies are independent from their storage cost. But it is not recommended to sotre the databases at every node of the network. This will increase the cost of updates.

2. If the storage cost of database is not negligible, and if it is different at every node of the network, the optimal location of database copies is not independent from their storage cost. Therefore, it is recommended to minimize the number of copies to be stored in the distributed system.

3. If the storage cost of database is not negligible, and even if it is the same at every node of the network, the optimal location of database copies is not independent from their storage cost. The recommendation described in point 3 still holds.

Another important aspect not considered by Levin-Morgan's model is the effect of the return flow of information on the optimal location of databases. Let us investigage this effect in more detail.

<u>Third Case</u> - <u>Existence of the Return Flow of Information</u>

Let us relax the assumptions made in the previous section and consider that there exist a return flow of information for queries. In our case, we consider that the return flow of information is two times the length of the query. Of course, the model is very general and considers the return flow of information as an input parameter. The value of such parameters is organization (or application) dependent.

A possible way to estimate it is by using some econometric method of estimation using past data.

For the storage cost of database, we consider two different cases :

(a) the first case is when the storage cost of database is negligible
(b) the second case is when the storage cost of database is equal to $ 500 per month.

The results obtained are summarized in Figure 4, and, the following remarks can be made :

Figure 4. Cost of Database Assignments - Case 3

Location of database copies of node	(a) Storage cost Negligible	(b) Storage cost $ 500 per month
1	4854	5354
2	2556	3056
3	2766	3266
4	5064	5564
5	3981	4481
12	2694	3694
13	3042	4042
14	4206	5206
15	5091	6091
23	<u>1770</u>	<u>2770</u>
24	3636	4656
25	2793	3793
34	2922	3922
35	3033	4033
123	1968	3469
124	2970	4470
125	2901	4401
134	3180	4680
135	3318	4818
145	4443	5943
234	1986	3486
235	2007	3507
245	3039	4539
345	3180	4680

Location of database copies at node	(a) Storage cost Negligible	(b) Storage cost $ 500 per month
1234	2184	4184
1235	2205	4205
1245	3177	5177
1345	3456	5456
2345	2223	4223
12345	2421	4421

1. If we compare the results obtained in case 1 and in case 3 - (a), we can see that there is no change in terms of optimal location of the database copies. In both cases, the optimal solution is obtained when the copies of the database are stored in nodes 2 and 3. This can be shown if we recall the formulation of the objective function.

$$\text{Min } F = \sum_{d,k} C_{kd} \; X_k^d \qquad (1)$$

$$+ \sum_{j,p} S_{jp} \; Z_j^P \qquad (2)$$

$$+ \sum_{i,j,p,d} Q_{ip}^d \; Q_{ij} \; X_{ijp}^d \; (1+\gamma'_{ij}) \qquad (3)$$

$$+ \sum_{i,j,p,d} U_{ip}^d \; U_{ij} \; X_{ijp}^{d} \qquad (4)$$

$$+ \sum_{j,k,p,d} \beta\lambda_{jpd} \; Q_{jk} \; X_{jkpd} \; (1+\gamma_{jk}) \qquad (5)$$

$$+ \sum_{j,k,p,d} \beta\mu_{jpd} \; U_{jk} \; X_k^d \qquad (6)$$

Since the storage costs are negligible expressions (1) and (2) are negligible. Besides, the return flow of information does not have any effect on the updating costs.Therefore, expressions (4) and (6) are constant. If we let $(1 + \gamma'_{ij}) = \gamma_1$ and $(1 + \gamma_{jk}) = \gamma_2$ for all i, j, k we can rewrite expressions (3) and (5) in the following manner.

$$\gamma_1 \sum_{i,j,p,d} Q_{ip}^d \; Q_{ij} \; X_{ijp}^d \qquad (3')$$

$$\gamma_2 \sum_{j,k,p,d} \alpha\lambda_{jpd} \; Q_{jk} \; X_{jpd} \qquad (5')$$

Therefore, the role of γ_1 and γ_2 is the same at every node of the network.

Their effect will not change the optimal location of the database as long as the query cost is bigger than the update cost. This can be obtained by minimizing the number of copies of the database to be stored. That was precicely the aim of case 1 (when we considered the return flow of information and the storage cost equal to zero). Therefore, the optimal solution will not change. Notice, however, that the optimal cost will change due to the cost of the return flow of information.

The main conclusion that can be drawn is that the optimal location of database is independent from the return flow of information, given that the total query cost is larger than the total update cost and given that the storage cost of database is negligible.

Would this conclusion be valid if the storage cost is not negligible ? to answer this question, let us compare the results obtained in case 2 and those obtain in case 3-(b). The only differences between both cases is that in the latter we consider the existence of a return flow of information equals two times the length of the queries. The results show that when there is no return flow of information but only a storage cost (equal to $ 500 a mont), the optimal location of the database is at node 2. If we keep the same storage cost and we take into consideration the return flow of information, the optimal solution changes to nodes 2 and 3. This is due to the fact that if the database is stored at a single node, the incremental cost of queries due to the return flow of information is more important than the storage cost. This tends to shift the location of the database from given a single to multiple nodes. As a consequence, we can draw the following conclusion : given the existence of a storage cost for the database, their optimal location is not independent from the return flow of information.

V - CONCLUSION

In summary, we have been able to develop and to apply our model for distributed database systems and show that :

1. Although similar to Levin-Morgan's model, our model is more general since it assumes full-dependency between programs and databases. It is also more accurate than Levin-Morgan's model.

2. We have shown that the existence of storage cost has an effect on the optimal location of databases.

3. For the first time in distributed database models, we have introduced the concept of return flow of information and we have shown that is has some consequences on the optimal location of databases in the network.

4. That our solution procedure is general enough to handle additional constraints. (This is not the case of Levin-Morgan's procedure which can be violated by the introduction of new constraints).

   Besides, a computer code was developed for our algorithm that makes it easier for users designing and evaluating distributed systems. The users need only to enter the data related to their problems without having to deal with any programming aspects. This code, although slower than heuristics, leads to optimal solutions which may be a critical factor in real-life examples. It costs only $ 3 to run each case describes in paragraph (IV). Although it is very difficult to evaluate the cost of running a larger problem, our experience with the algorithm and its computer code allows us to set an upper bound of one minute of CPU time, to run a problem having about 600 variables. This is due to the fact that our algorithm limits a priori the number of nodes to be stored in the computer main memory.

REFERENCES

(1) CHU, W.W., "File Allocation in a Multiple Computer System," IEEE Trans. Computer C-19 (10), 1969, pp. 885-889.

(2) CHU, W.W., "Optimal File Allocation in a Computer Network," in Computer Communication Networks, (eds.) N. Abramson and F. Kuo, Prentice Hall, Englewood Cliffs, N.J., 1973, pp. 82-84.

(3) WHITNEY, W.K.M., "A Study of Optimal Assignment and Communication Network Configuration in Remote-Access Computer Message Processing and Communication Systems," SEC Technical Report no. 48 systems Energy Lab., Dept of Electrical Engineering, University of Michigan, Septembre 1970 (Ph.D. Dissertation).

(4) CASEY, R.G., "Allocation of Copies of a File in an Information Network," AFIPS Conference Proceedings, 40, 1972, pp. 617-625.

(5) LEVIN, K.D., "Organization Distributed Databases in Computer Networks," Ph. D. Dissertation, University of Pennsylvania, 1974.

(6) MORGAN, H.L., K.D. LEVIN, "Optimal Program and Data Locations in Computer Networks," Report 74-10-01, Dept, of decision Science, the Wharton School University of Pennsylvania, 1974.

(7) LEVIN, K.D. and H.L MORGAN, "Dynamic File Assignment in Computer Networks Under Varying Access Request Patterns," Invited paper, ORSA/TIMS Joint National Meeting, Chicago, April 1975.

(8) LEVIN, K.D. and H.L. MORGAN, "Optimizing distributed Databases - A Framework for research," AFIPS Conference Proceedings, 44, 1975.

(9) CHU, W.W., "Performance of File Directory Systems for Databases in Star and distributed Networks," AFIPS, Vol. 45, 1976, pp. 577-587.

(10) CASEY, R.G., "Design of tree networks for Distributed Data," AFIPS Conference Proceedings, 42, 1973, pp. 251-257.

(11) MAHMOUD, S. and J.S. RIORDON, "Optimal Allocation of Ressources in Distributed Information Networks," ACM Transactions on Database Systems, Vol. 1, n° 1, March 1976.

(12) ABADIE, J. GUIGOU J., "Gradient Reduit Generalise," note E.D.F. H.I 069/02 (1969)

(13) COLVILLE, A.R. "A comparative Study of Nonlinear Programming Codes," IBM NYSC Report 320-2949 (1968).

(14) ABADIE J., "Une méthode Arborescente pour les Programmes partiellement discrets," R.I.R.O., 3ème année, Vol. 3, 1969.

(15) AKOKA, J. "Méthodes Arborescentes de Résolution des Programmes Nonlinéaires Totalement ou partiellement discrets", Thèse 3ème cylce, Université de Paris VI, Paris, 1975.

(16) ABADIE, J., H. DAYAN AND J. AKOKA, "Quelques Expériences Numériques sur la Programmation non-linéaire en Nombres entiers," R.A.I.R.O. Recherche Opérationnelle, Vol. 10, n° 10, October 1976.

(17) AKOKA J., "Bounded Branch and Bound Method for Integer Nonlinear Programming Problems," WP 904-77, Sloan School of Management, MIT, January 1977.

(18) AKOKA J,, and DAYAN H., "A Comparative Study of Some Branch and Bound Algorithms in Integer Nonlinear Optimization", Tenth Int. Symposium on Math. Programming, Montreal, Aug. 27-31, 1979.

(19) AKOKA J., "Design issues in Distributed Management Information Systems", Ph. D. Thesis, Sloan School of Management, MIT, 1978.

DISTRIBUTED DATA BASES
C. Delobel and W. Litwin (eds.)
North-Holland Publishing Company

SPECIFICATION AND VALIDATION OF TWO RING-STRUCTURED SYNCHRONIZATION PROTOCOLS FOR DISTRIBUTED DATA SYSTEMS

Serge M. Miranda

CERISS
Université des Sciences Sociales
Place Anatole France
31070 TOULOUSE Cedex
FRANCE

A good deal of attention has been devoted in recent literature to synchronization protocols for distributed data systems. However much work is still to be done in the area of formal specification and validation where only two proposals have been made:

- Ellis proposed a formalism based on L-Systems(ELLI77)-b
- We presented a solution using the appealing concept of abstract data types (algebraic approach) in (POPE79).

The purpose of this article is to show how the latter formalism can be used to provide a uniform formal framework for specification/validation of other synchronization protocols. In this paper, we concentrate on two major algorithms which are ring-structure based: Ellis' and Le Lann's solutions.

In the first section we recall the major features of both protocols in a comparative way after presenting the "mutual-consistency" concept.

In the second section we propose our formalism with a theorem concerning strong mutual consistency of duplicated objects; then we explicit the specification and validation (mutual consistency, serialization) of these two protocols.

INTRODUCTION - THE DATA CONSISTENCY CONCEPT

A data base can be viewed as a collection of <u>entities</u>; values of these entities define a state of the data base. The concept of consistency in Data Base Management Systems (DBMS) is twofold:

- "<u>internal consistency</u>" is associated with integrity constraints defined on data to meet real-world restrictions. When integrity constraints are satisfied after data modification the data base will be said to be internally consistent, or in an internal consistent state (the constraints characterize the valid states of the data base)

- "<u>external consistency</u>" corresponds to the control of concurrent transactions which may conflict when sharing common entities. If no provisions are made, problems such as "lost-update", "phantom entities" may arise and internal consistency may be violated. Locking was the only mechanism used to ensure external consistency in DBMS (even in DBTG with its commercial version DMS1100); locking can be "high-level" (logical level), "low-level" (physical level) (BLAS79) or "med-level" (MIRA 80) (global access path level). However, locking is one of the five necessary conditions for deadlock and a solution must be given to this problem; when taking into consideration distributed DBMS, both types of consistency must be ensured for concurrent transactions which can originate anywhere in the underlying network and handle scattered data. There after I shall use the acronym DDB for distributed data bases.

From the distributed environment characteristics, we infer the need:

- to integrate key factors like PERFORMANCE and ROBUSTNESS in the design of synchronization protocols,

- to develop a FORMALISM which takes into account the distribution and the execution parallelism.

This paper focuses on the latter point.

Internal consistency of a distributed DBMS will be called mutual consistency when involving remote entities; identity is a particular case of an integrity constraint leading to the well studied problem of duplicated entities which must converge to the same state should update activity cease (THOM75)...

Numerous solutions have been proposed to ensure mutual consistency. In this paper we are concerned by two proposals making use of a VIRTUAL RING STRUCTURE either for sequencing (Le Lann) or transmission (Ellis) with their formalization using abstract data types. In the first section we shall only give an extremely brief outline of both protocols. The interested readers are urged to study references quoted below for complete understanding of these algorithms.

COMPARATIVE PRESENTATION OF ELLIS' AND LE LANN'S PROTOCOLS

PRINCIPLE OF LE LANN'S PROTOCOL (LELA76) , (LELA77),(LELA78)-a,(LELA78)-b

One of the key issues in the design of a decentralized-control locking protocol is the allocation of a unique identification number to each transaction; this is basic to any (feasible) deadlock-prevention mechanism. For example in (POPE79) and (ELLI77) a priority system making use of a timestamp, a rejection number,... is considered.

Le Lann proposes an original algorithm based on a virtual sequencing ring of controllers participating in the distributed DBMS. A permit circulates on this ring; it plays the part of an allocator of unique id-numbers (called tickets) for each transaction (INTREQ) which is taken into account by a given site ("internal" transaction to this site).

At the end of this allocation, each ticketed transaction (EXTREQ) is broadcasted to the concerned controllers and the permit is transmitted to the successor in the virtual ring.

Here we only consider the initial version of the algorithm where only one permit circulates on the ring.

A waiting list composed of chronologically-ordered transactions is attached to each entity.

A transaction will be ready for execution for a given entity whenever it appears in front of each list of the duplicated entity (each transaction having a lower ticket number will have been executed for this entity). This state is known to the initiator by the reception of n ACKREQ (with (n+ 1) duplicated entities). In this algorithm, parallelism of non-overlapping transactions is possible. This protocol can be applied to fully - or partially - redundant data bases. However, it would be important to see (in real life) whether this parallelism will not disappear with a heavy load in favour of a serial functioning close to a POLLING system where each site executes its internal transactions in turn.

PRINCIPLE OF ELLIS' PROTOCOL (ELLI77)-a(ELLI77)-b

The virtual ring of transmission and the priority system are used to define a simple synchronization protocol.

For each internal transaction appearing in a controller, there is a revolution initiated (an update message - EXTREQ - is transmitted to the successor in the ring). There are two cases for a receiving controller:

a) if its hasn't initiated a transaction (passive status) it transmits any received message (without any control) to its successor.

b) if it has initiated a transaction (active status) it places any incoming request with lower priority on a waiting list (it is important to note there is not a rejection but suspension); it transmits any higher priority request to its successor.

The processing of a transaction includes two revolutions:

a) the first one corresponds to a global acceptation of the transaction by each concerned controller (the request has been recognized as the one with the highest priority).

b) the second one is associated with the correct modification of each copy (UPDS or UPDW message depending on the existence or not of a local waiting list for lower priority requests). In this protocol we cannot have the possibility of concurrently performing updates that do not conflict; such a drawback is bound to the fact that updates must lock the entire data base (!) However there exist at least two major advantages inferred from the virtual ring of transmission:

(i) each site only has to know the predecessor and the successor in the ring

(ii) the protocol requires verylittle state information. Improvements of Ellis' protocol which avoid the drawbacks mentioned here are proposed in (GARC79).

COMPARATIVE PRESENTATION OF BOTH PROTOCOLS

We chose a certain number of criteria we estimated important for a potential classification of synchronization protocols. The following figures (fig. 1 and 2) give the respective paths of Ellis' (noted "———"), and Le Lann's (noted "----") protocols. Then we explain this representation by criteria.

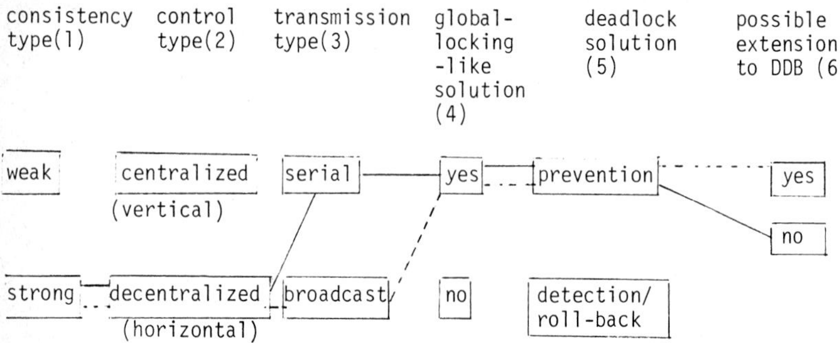

Figure 1 General Features

(1) Mutual consistency can be twofold; we shall refer to "strong" consistency when the most current (consistent) versions are available to any access; and "weak", when the data available for access are consistent but not the most current. Examples of weak-consistent protocols are given in (THOM75) and (WILM79)-b). Both protocols considered here are strong-consistent protocols.

(2) The control will be said to be "centralized" when there exists a privileged controller to which each request is sent (examples of centralized-controlled protocols are given in (MENA77),...) When each controller is functionally homogeneous, the control will be said to be decentralized ;a distinction between "partially" - and "fully" - decentralized control is introduced in (MIRA79).

(3) The transmission type may be bound to the underlying-network configuration; it is not the case for the studied protocols where it is a matter of policy. Ellis chose a serial transmission on the virtual ring while Le Lann considered a broadcasting scheme for the synchronization messages.

(4) Both protocols include a first step of synchronization where exclusive access to the required entities is attained:

- In Le Lann's protocol, this corresponds to the presence of the given request at the top of the waiting list of each duplicated entity.

- In Ellis's protocol, it is associated with the first revolution in the ring. However, in this proposal, the grain of locking is the whole data base; this is not the case in Le Lann's scheme where only manipulated entities are locked. This represents an implicit form of a global locking.

(5) There are two basic ways to deal with deadlock (as in many other life problems): prevention or restoration ("detection/roll-back"). Deadlock-detection synchronization protocols for distributed DBMS were defined in (MENA78), (SEEM79),....

Here both protocols use prevention methods; conflicts between concurrent transactions (which overlap) are avoided by making use of a unique network identifier attached to each transation:

- the "ticket" in Le Lann's scheme, which is allocated when the "permit" passes in the corresponding controller,

- the "priority" in Ellis' solution, which is a couple composed of a transaction number (event count) and a controller number.

This unique identifier induces a network sequencing of each transaction. Serialization is ensured in both protocols as the mutual consistency proof will show. Current developments of Le Lann's protocol consider a detection/roll back mechanism. It is important to note that the original sequencing scheme proposed by Le Lann is a priori independent of the locking methods built on top of it.

(6) Ellis's protocol was primarily defined for duplicated entities; the suspension feature for a lower-priority transaction prevents from extending this protocol in a distributed DBMS: "dynamic locking", "locking domain re-evaluation" need a rejection scheme instead of a suspension one; therefore mutual consistency cannot be achieved with this ring protocol, when considering transactions manipulating remote entities in a distributed DBMS.

Le Lann's sequencing scheme can be used in a distributed DBMS; the fact however, that a waiting list and a directory are attached to each entity, restricts the applicability of this protocol to distributed DBMS defined with a <u>large</u> grain of locking.

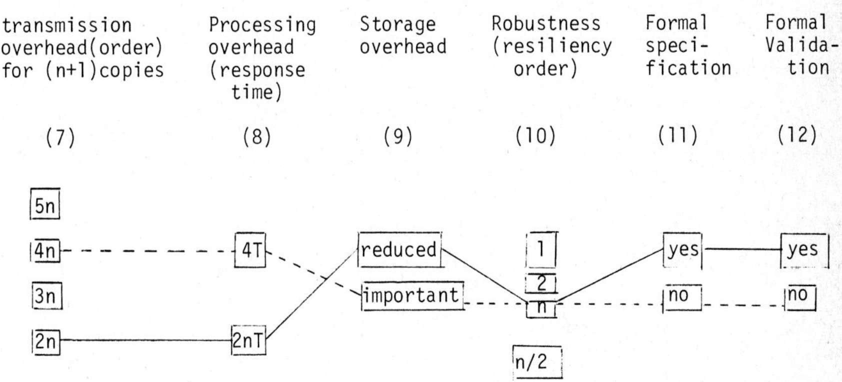

<u>Figure 2</u> Performance and other Considerations

In a synchronization protocol, overhead is threefold:

(7) <u>The transmission overhead</u> for (n+1) duplicated entities is in the order of :

(i) 2n for Ellis' solution:

n (EXTREQ)	1 st revolution
+n (UPDS)	2nd revolution

Note that in this protocol based on serial/looping transmission, each of these messages plays the part of an acknowledgement message. A formal analysis of performances for Ellis' protocol is presented in(GARC79).

(ii) 4n for Le Lann's protocol:

$$n\ (EXTREQ) + n\ (ACKREQ) + n\ (UPD) + n\ (ACKUPD) + \theta n$$

The last two messages correspond to a two-phase commit step and θn to the extra-traffic generated for mutual suspicion (such an overhead is the price paid to make the ring robust); this update step is mandatory when considering robustness or partially-redundant data bases (it is the purpose of the protocol to be general enough to encompass distributed DBMS synchronization.) EXTREQ plays the part of a temporary update request when at the head of the queue and UPD of a permanent update request.

(8) The processing overhead (in terms of T, average network-transmission time) is $4\ T + \theta T$ for Le Lann's solution since there is a broadcasting policy and $2n.T + \theta T$ for Ellis who chose a serial transmission. The response time of Ellis' solution (like THOMAS' one) grows linearly with n. When considering M conflicting requests with higher priority (Ellis) or lower ticket number (Le Lann), θT can be respectively estimated to $2\ n\ T.M$ and $3T.M$.

(9) In Le Lann's solution, the storage overhead is rather important since a transaction waiting list and a repertory are attached to each duplicated entity (especially if the entity grain is fine). If the entity grain is large then parallelism is reduced. In Ellis's solution waiting lists are kept only on the initiating "active" controllers which represents a lower storage overhead; however, in this protocol, there is no possible parallelism among concurrent transactions.

(10) Alsberg in (ALSB76) introduced the concept of "n-host resiliency" as the minimum number of simultaneously-failed hosts in a critical phase which cause service to be disrupted. Typical centralized and ring protocols are respectively 1- and 2- host resilient.

Thomas's solution is for example $\left\lceil \frac{n}{2} \right\rceil$-host resilient (THOM75).

Both protocols do not consider network-partitioning; they are potentially n-host resilient.

Robustness was particularly studied in Le Lann's protocol (ring reconfiguration after a node failure, permit regeneration,...). The fact that a controller has failed is known by mutual suspicion. Some of these solutions can be extended to Ellis' protocol to render it robust.

(11) The only existing formal specifications of synchronization protocols have been made:

- by Ellis and Wilms (WILM79a) with derived forms of Petri-nets (respectively L-Systems and Nutt's networks)

- by Miranda/Popek (POPE79) with abstract data types (algebraic approach).

(12) Formal proofs of correctness are inferred from the specifications by Ellis and Popek/Miranda. A comparison of these formalisms is made in (MIRA79). The purpose of the following sections is to point out the abstract data type approach with its attractiveness as a uniform and rigorous framework for synchronization-protocol specification and validation. The underlying idea of our approach is to introduce a new degree of transparency to the four types of transparency presented in (TRAI79) - location transparency - replication transparency - concurrency transparency - failure transparency: the synchronization-protocol transparency. Whatever the synchronization protocol is, we

point out three basic primitive operators which represent the only knowledge of the inner and outer layers where the synchronization is used. The operator semantics (depending on the protocol) is hidden and can be switched according to the suitability of the chosen protocol.

Because of space limitations, it is not possible to detail:

(i) the algebraic approach of abstract data types (see (MIRA80) for this),

(ii) the formalization of a synchronization protocol (a complementary in-depth treatment can be found in a companion paper (MIRA79))

(iii) the specification/validation of robustness (shown for a given protocol we defined - DLP - in (POPE79))

In the following sections, we present the formalization of Ellis' and Le Lann's protocol using algebraically-specified data types after a rapid introduction to the basic concepts of the chosen formal tool.

ABSTRACT DATA TYPE FORMALISM FOR SYNCHRONIZATION PROTOCOLS

Abstract Data Types (ADT's)

An ADT is a collection of sorts, operators and axioms which may be used to define any data type or structure.

The ADT concept represents the melting pot of several well-known concepts used in programming languages and operating systems: "procedure ", "capability", "hiding", "encapsulation", "type", "immutability", "modularity",....

Object-oriented languages (embodying ADT's) can be categorized in two families:

1. - The first one corresponding to the PROPOSITIONAL approach can be traced from MILNER's work on SIMULATION (MILN71) to HOARE's contribution on DATA CORRECTNESS (HOAR72) which led to the ALPHARD language (WULF76).

2. - The second associated with the ALGEBRAIC approach which stems from research conducted by Burstall (BURS77)-a and other authors in ARTIFICIAL INTELLIGENCE. The OBJ language (GOGU78), (TARD77) is representative of this family.

We chose the algebraic approach which seems more adequate to complex-structure formalization (PAOL77), (LOCK78).

The ADT concept seems appropriate whenever there exists the need to formalize objects with their manipulation operators; this explains the current attention for its applicability to layered-system design (DBMS, computer network.....) (PAOL77),....

Our paper is a contribution to what Tsichritzis (TSIC77) called "the application of ADT in the resolution of a typical DBMS problem".

Algebraic approach (GOGU76) (TARD77) (GUTT78)....

We briefly recall the major features of the algebraic approach for ADT's as presented in (GOGU76).

An ADT can be defined as a MANY-SORTED ALGEBRA which is a family of sorts with operations among them ("Carriers"). The sort specifies the types used in the definition; two basic kinds of sorts are involved in an ADT specification: the sort being defined and any number of sorts assumed previously defined in a similar fashion (i.e. the boolean sort includes the usual constants T and F, and is assumed to have been defined in its own right with the same methodology; other built-in ADT's we may use are INTEGER, QUEUE,....)

Operators of the algebra are indexed by pairs (w,s) where $w \in S$ (sort of the operands) and $s \in S$ (sort of the results) the symbol $\Sigma w,s$ will be used for the set of all operations with index (w,s); Σ is used for the union of all the sets $\Sigma w,s$ and is called the "signature" of the algebra.

A Σ-algebra is therefore determined by a triple $\langle S, \Sigma, \mathcal{E} \rangle$ where:

S is the set of "sorts", $S = \{ s^1, s^2, \ldots\ldots, si, \ldots\ldots sn \}$ denoting the various types of objects which are required for that definition.

Σ is the set of operation, $\Sigma = \{\Sigma_{w,s}\}$, whose operands and results are objects making up the sorts in S (SYNTAX description).

$\mathcal{E}$ is the set of equations which describe the semantics of each $\Sigma_{w,s}$ of Σ ; each algebraic equation (or axiom) defines the results of various combinations of operators applied upon various operands.

Two many-sorted algebras are called Σ-algebras if they have the same signature.

A very important concept is the one of Σ-homomorphism; Definition: given two Σ-algebras A and B, a Σ-homomorphism, $h : A \longrightarrow B$, is a family of functions $\langle hs : As \longrightarrow Bs , s \in S \rangle$ mapping each carrier in A in the corresponding carrier in B while preserving the operations, i.e.

$\forall \sigma \in \Sigma w,s$ the diagram

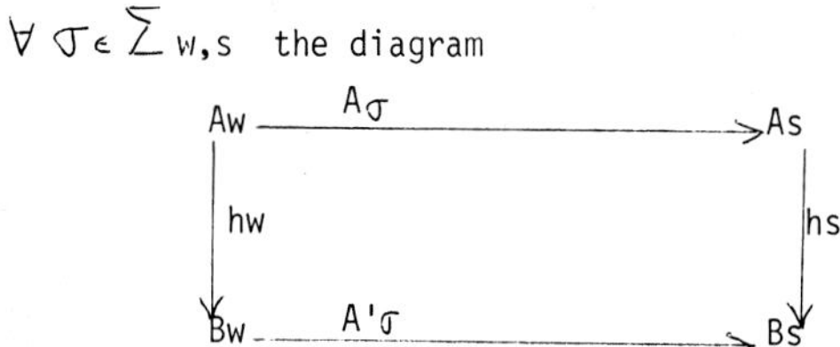

commutes.

We shall use the Σ-homomorphism concept to express:

(i) parallelism among remote operators (Σ-isomorphism)

(ii) layered abstractions between the distributed data base and the underlying transmission facility in one hand; between the distributed data base and the local DBMS in the other hand.

In the next section we shall apply this method to the formalization of both ring-structure protocols.

It is important to note that the ADT definitions of a particular type is not unique; however, it should meet the following goals:

(1) The operators should not be redundant.
(2) The equations must not be contradictory.
(3) The operators and axioms should be as simple as possible.
(4) The equations should be constructed in such a way that they lead forcibly to unique reduction into the canonical representation (the concept of canonical representation is introduced in (MIRA 79) in the context of synchronization-protocol formalization)

(5) We shall use a formalism close to OBJ-0 (TARD77) (GOGU78) (GOGU77) (TARD79)

which represents one of the basic language encompassing algebraically-specified data types; Guttag's system for symbolic execution of ADT's seems to suffer some inadequacies mainly at the syntactic level (TARD79)

OBJ-0

OBJ-0 is an object-oriented language defined by GOGUEN (GOGU76) and implemented by TARDO (TARD78); this language is very close to NPL language, now called HOPE defined in (BURS77)-b . In OBJ-0, an algebra is a 4-tuple:

$\langle$ SORTS, OPS, VARS, SPECS $\rangle$ where

SORTS, OPS, SPECS correspond respectively to S, Σ , $\mathcal{E}$ and VARS includes the definition of the working variables used in the axioms.

The error-operators ("ERROR-OPS") and their semantics ("ERROR-SPECS") may be naturally defined in this language; an extensive discussion of "error algebras" is presented in (GOGU77).

The general syntax of an operator is given by:

$$\underbrace{\text{O P}}_{\text{Operator name}} \quad : \underbrace{\text{S1, S2, ...SN}}_{\text{Operand sorts}} \longrightarrow \underbrace{\text{Sp}}_{\text{result sort}}$$

Operator name (under bars are used for place-holders)

Operand sorts (N : arity of the OP operator)

result sort

Prefix, infix, postfix, distributed-fix declarations are possible in OBJ-0.

Each sort has an equality relation which is built-in with syntax:

$$\_\_\_ := \_\_\_ \quad : \ S, \quad S \longrightarrow S$$

Hidden operators may be declared with the key-word "HIDDEN" placed after the result sort.

We shall often use conditional equations in the algebraic specifications ; a formal theory of conditional equations in ADT's is developed in (THAT76).

In the specifications of a synchronization controller using ADT's, we shall neither use place-holders in OPS nor consider ERROR operators.

SYNCHRONIZATION PROTOCOL FORMALIZATION USING ALGEBRAICALLY-SPECIFIED DATA TYPES

A protocol is best stated via an abstract means which is accurate and representation independent.

Horizontal - control algorithms offer symmetry advantages for specification (thus simplifying the proofs of correctness).

Protocols are said to be message-driven: reception of a synchronization message causes a series of actions (and eventually a message transmission) to be executed.

The current trend in operating systems is to shift synchronization semantics from processes to the shared objects (ANDL78).

Our research belongs to this trend.

We introduce the concept of "shared object state" necessary for encompassing the semantics of the attached manipulation operators in a simple way. A change of state is the result of the execution of an operator bound to the occurrence of an event (here a synchronization-message).

These states enable us to specify the different protocol steps; they allow:

1. The simplification of operator semantics.
2. The simplification of the validation process by encapsulating the functioning of a given controller.
3. The setting of clear re-entry points for the recovery procedure.
4. The expression of parallelism among remote controllers by using homomorphisms among remote states.

We formalize the operators attached to state switching by using the abstract data types.

This approach offers the same advantages as Petri-nets (representation independence.....)with additional ones such as:

- simple rigorous formalism for inferring proofs of correctness,
- robustness integration in a natural way (POPE79)
- semantic framework from which correct implementations can be derived (GUTT78)

A synchronization protocol will be depicted as a set of Σ-homomorphic algebras.

One of the key issues in a distributed-environment is to represent the parallelism among remote operations; we express it in the following way:

- definition of a global abstract data type (SYNCM) associated with the global operations in the originating controller and of coupled abstract data types (SYNCS) associated with the participating controllers.

- definition of a Σ-homomorphism between SYNCM and SYNCS

Such a formalism enables us to prove easily some assertions about both protocols like the mutual-consistency feature (in a fail-safe environment).

Mutual consistency theorem (strong consistency)

Theorem:

Let Fi represent the state of the ith copy available (open and stable) for retrieval/update. We say that a synchronization protocol ensures (strong) mutual consistency if and only if:

(i) there is an homomorphism φ mapping each Fi state while preserving the operations of the protocol, i.e.,

$\forall (i,j)$; the diagram
$i \in (1,n)$
$j \in (1,n)$

$$\begin{array}{ccc} Fi & \xrightarrow{(1)} & F'i \\ \varphi\downarrow & & \downarrow\varphi \\ Fj & \xrightarrow[(1)]{} & F'j \end{array}$$

(2) commutes.

n number of duplicated objects

(1) Successive steps of the protocol

(2) (F'i) is associated with the new version of the ith copy and Fi with the old one.

(ii) Conflicting transactions are SERIALIZED (definition of serialization is given in the next section).

A proof of this theorem is given in (MIRA79)

RING-STRUCTURED PROTOCOL FORMALIZATION

This section is concerned by the algebraic specification and validation of Ellis' and Le Lann's protocols.

For a given session we have two types of controllers; one where the transaction originates and the others which participate in the synchronization process. It is the reason why we introduced two exclusive abstract data types SYNCM and SYNCS to formalize a controller. This distinction is made for the sake of simplicity.

In a decentralized-control environment, a transaction may be initiated in any controller. Therefore we may have several conflicting sessions (several simultaneous SYNCM during a finite time). We introduced three global operations called PREPAREG('), SETG('), UNSETG(') applied to the global virtual object (POPE79); the global (virtual) object consists of each local object semantically tied during a manipulation.

A formal treatment of the 'globality' concept is presented in (Bill79).

PREPAREG (') corresponds to the initialization step (temporary update, security checking, conflict resolution,....) without any object modification

SETG (') corresponds to the modification step of the global object.

UNSETG (') is associated with the commitment step.

Both types of algebras make use of two major ADTS which are defined at an underlying functional level in a similar fashion:

- the message type defined at the transport level of the computer network with basic operators like TRANSMIT, RECEIVE, WAIT,....

- the local object defined at the DBMS level with operators PREPAREL, SETL, UNSETL (we have in mind the extension of this formalism to distributed - DBMS synchronization). The operators are given an explicit form in (MIRA80) at the access path level of a local DBMS using the DIAM framework.

Other ADTs used in the specifications are Transaction, Boolean, Integer, QUEUE,

Definition: two conflicting transactions are said serialized when the global sequences PREPAREG(') - SETG(')-UNSETG(') associated with each transaction do not overlap in the modification phase. Other consistency (transaction atomicity,....) may be derived from this formalism in a natural way (MIRA79).

ELLIS' PROTOCOL FORMALIZATION

The Σ-algebra SYNCM corresponds to a controller which receives an internal request (INT. REQ.) and initiates a synchronization session ("active controller") The Σ-algebra SYNCS corresponds to a controller in the virtual ring which manages a copy, which has not initiated a global transaction and which participates in the synchronization session ("passive controller").

OBJECT	OPERATORS	COMMENTS
Global entity (GE)	PREPAREG (M, GES)	GES: Object state in the ith site;
	SETG (M, GES)	M: message
	UNSETG (M, GES)	P: Priority attached to M
	ID (GES)	ID: Identity operator

Fig. 3: SYNCM Signature

OBJECT	OPERATORS	COMMENTS
Global entity (GE)	PREPAREG' (M, GES) SETG' (M, GES) UNSETG' (M, GES) ID' (GES)	

Fig. 4: SYNCS Signature

A global entity state (GES) is a triple which can take four different values in each controller.

(1) (Fi,-,-); free (available for retrieval/modification).

(2) (A,pi,-);the corresponding controller is active and the internal transaction gets the priority pi

(3) (A,pi,pk);the corresponding controller is active and the current transaction gets priority pk with pk > pi (pi attached to the internal transaction).

(4)(P,pk,-);the corresponding controller is passive and the current transaction gets priority pk.

We do not need, a state representation attached to a local object (difference with (POPE79) or Le Lann's formalization) since the whole data base is blocked when a synchronization session is initiated (the "blocked" status corresponds to a "Passive" or "active" controller).

OBJECTS	OPERATORS	COMMENTS
Message (M)	TRANSMIT((M, P),I)	We indicate the parameters of importance
M ∈{INTREQ, EXTREQ, UPDS, UPDW}	RECEIVE((M,P), (S,I))	(S,I) = parameters of the receiving controller
	WAIT (M,P)	
STATUS (S) S ∈ (free, active, passive)	ID (S)	Identity ID (S) = S
Local entity (LE)	PREPAREL (LE) SETL (LE) UNSETL (LE)	
Transaction T	PROCESS (T)	Modification operator
Priority (P)	DEFINE (P.I)	(P,i) will be noted Pi
QUEUE (Q)	ENQ (T,P),Q)	IN
	DEQ (T,Q)	OUT
	FRONT (Q)	element in front
	EMPTY? (Q)	Q empty ?

Fig. 5 Signature of other involved types

Other operators used in the specifications are those attached to INT and BOOL like: TEST (A,B) = IF A = B THEN TRUE ELSE FALSE
SUP (A,B) = IF A > B THEN TRUE ELSE FALSE

The specifications of Ellis' protocol are presented in Annex 1 using an OBJ-close language.

The definition of specifications is made by considering every message - reception possibility in a given controller. The reception of a given message will entail a series of local actions (state switch,....) and the transmission of output messages (general case). For example, from the specifications of a SYNCM controller, we infer the following informations:

- PREPAREG corresponds to the reception of an INTREQ message when the local state of the controller is "FREE"

- SETG corresponds to the reception of the EXTREQ after one complete revolution in the virtual ring.
- UNSETG corresponds to the reception of the final UPD message (UPDS) after one complete revolution in the virtual ring.

We may note also a close semantics attached to states (A, Pi, Pj) and (P, Pj): the state (A,Pi,Pj) initially plays a role identical to (P,Pj) and then after a completion of the current transaction (having greater priority Pk), this state is identical to (A, Pi,-).

<u>Σ-parallelism</u>

We want to express the Σ-parallelism between two participating controllers namely SYNCM and SYNCS.

In order to do so we introduce the following morphism which defines a correspondance between remote states

$$(F,-) \xrightarrow{\quad\varphi\quad} (F,-)$$ (old and new versions of stable and open states)

$$(A,Pi) \xrightarrow{\quad\varphi\quad} (P,Pi)$$ (unstable states where any new INTREQ is rejected)

<u>NOTES</u>: (i) F stands for "free". A for "active"; P for "passive."
(ii) we only represent significant states in the diagrams.

These paired states, corresponding to an environment without conflicts are said to be SYNCHRONIZATION HOMOGENEOUS.

<u>Assertion 1</u>: In an environment without concurrency conflicts, the protocol ensures mutual consistency.

<u>Proof</u>: The proof is straightforward. We get the following diagram commutations by making use of the Σ-algebras equations:

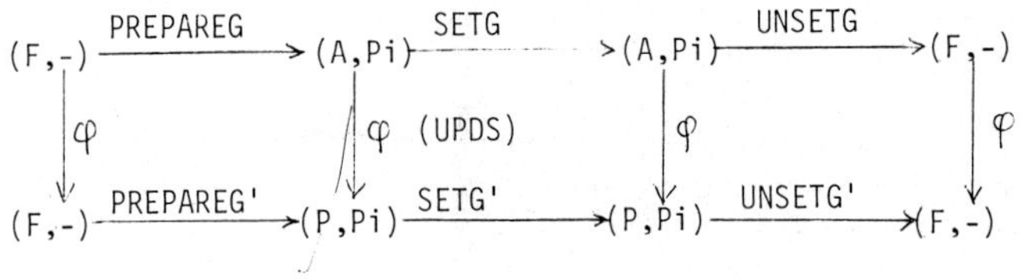

$$\begin{array}{ccccccc}
(F,-) & \xrightarrow{\text{PREPAREG}} & (A,Pi) & \xrightarrow{\text{SETG}} & (A,Pi) & \xrightarrow{\text{UNSETG}} & (F,-) \\
\downarrow \varphi & & \downarrow \varphi \ \text{(UPDS)} & & \downarrow \varphi & & \downarrow \varphi \\
(F,-) & \xrightarrow{\text{PREPAREG}'} & (P,Pi) & \xrightarrow{\text{SETG}'} & (P,Pi) & \xrightarrow{\text{UNSETG}'} & (F,-)
\end{array}$$

The mutual consistency theorem is therefore proved in this simplest case.

<u>Assertion A2</u>: The protocol ensures mutual consistency when there is a <u>FINITE</u> set of concurrent conflicting transactions.

<u>Note</u>: In this protocol an INTREQ can only be taken into account if the local controller state is F.

The proof of this assertion may be reduced to two concurrent transactions Ti and Tj (with Pi $>$ Pj) since there is a total ordering of transactions. It is important to see that the states (A, Pj, Pi) and (P,Pi) are equivalent for the messages of the type (M, Pi) corresponding to the current transactions;

(A, Pj, Pi) is associated with a blocked internal transaction having priority Pj ($Pj < Pi$).

Let us introduce the following morphism φ' characteristic of a conflicting situation:

$$(A,Pi,-) \xrightarrow{\varphi'} (A,Pj,-) \text{ with } Pi > Pj$$

The paired states are said to be SYNCHRONIZATION COMPATIBLE. Let us show that these states are rendered synchronization homogeneous after a certain number of transitions (depicted in Annex 2). From the Σ-parallelism we infer mutual consistency with serialization.

NOTE: The commutation diagrams are constructed from left to right. Initially all states are (Free, -); then synchronization session(s) may be iniated. Each row in the diagram corresponds to the successive transitions performed on a given controller and φ represents the functional correspondence (associated with a synchronization message) between paired states.

Such a diagram is built in an exhaustive way looking at every possible transition (given by the specifications). We may imagine such a progressive construction made by a special program, in an automatic way.

Le Lann's Protocol Formalization

The Σ-algebra SYNCM corresponds to the controller which received the internal request and which broadcasts the request (EXTREQ) to the associated controllers whenever it gets an available ticket number for this request.

The Σ-algebra SYNCS is attached to a controller which reveives an EXTREQ and which will acknowledge it by the ACKREQ as soon as the EXTREQ is at the head of the request waiting list associated with each copy.

A shared entity state (GES) consists of a 3-tuple:

$$\langle CS, RS, ES \rangle$$

where: (i) CS is the controller state which can be "Master" (M) or Slave" (S)
(ii) RS is he request state which can be "EXEC," "NONEXEC" and "OVER"
(iii) OS is the object state which can be F (free), O (occupied) or B (blocked)

The free entity state (in the mutual-consistency theorem) corresponds initially to (-, NON EXEC, F) and after the modification to (-,OVER,F). The signature of SYNCM and SYNCS are identical to the previous ones with the operators PREPAREG('), SETG('), UNSETG(').

The other types and operations not indicated in Figure 6 are identical to the ones presented in Figure 5.

We have a global queue (GQ) associated with the internal requests blocked without tickets, and a transaction queue attached to each entity (Q).

OBJECTS	OPERATORS	COMMENTS
Message (M) M∈{INTREQ, EXTREQ, ACKREQ UPD, ACKUPD, PERMIT, ACKPERMIT}	TRANSMIT (M,i) RECEIVE (M, S, i,j,) WAIT (M)	S ∈ E{CRED, DEB} <i,j : site id.>
Controller state (CS) CS ∈ {M, S}	ID (CS) SWITCH (CS) = $\overline{CS}$	M : Master S : Slave
Request state (RS) RS ∈ {EXEC, NONEXEC, OVER}	ID (RS)	NONEXEC : the transaction is ticketed but not in front of the queue Q EXEC : the transaction is ticketed and in front of the local queue Q OVER : the transaction is completed
Object state OS OS∈{F, O, B}	ID (OS)	

Figure 6 - Other involved types

Σ - parallelism

The morphism φ which defines SYNCHRONIZATION HOMOGENEOUS states is :

$$(-, \text{NONEXEC}, F) \xrightarrow{\varphi} (-\ \text{NONEXEC}, F) \quad \langle \text{idle state} \rangle$$
$$(M, \text{EXEC}, O) \xrightarrow{\varphi} (S, \text{EXEC}, O) \quad \langle \text{EXTREQ message} \rangle$$
$$(M, \text{EXEC}, B) \xrightarrow{\varphi} (S, \text{EXEC}, B) \quad \langle \text{total ACKREQ ; UPD} \rangle$$
$$(-, \text{OVER}, F) \xrightarrow{\varphi} (-, \text{OVER}, F) \quad \langle \text{total ACKUPD} \rangle$$

Assertion A1 : In an environment without concurrency conflicts, the protocol ensures mutual consistency.

Proof : The Σ-equations of SYNCM and SYNCS enable us to write down the following commutations :

$$\begin{array}{ccccccccc} (-,\text{NONEXEC},F) & \xrightarrow{\text{PREPAREG}} & (M,\text{EXEC},O) & \xrightarrow{\text{SETG}} & (M,\text{EXEC},B) & \xrightarrow{\text{UNSETG}} & (-,\text{OVER},F) & \langle \text{master site} \rangle \\ \downarrow\varphi & & \downarrow\varphi & & \downarrow\varphi & & \downarrow\varphi & \\ (-,\text{NONEXEC},F) & \xrightarrow{\text{PREPAREG}} & (S,\text{EXEC},O) & \xrightarrow{\text{SETG}'} & (S,\text{EXEC},B) & \xrightarrow{\text{UNSETG}'} & (-,\text{OVER},F) & \langle \text{any slave site} \rangle \\ (1) & & (2) & & (3) & & (4) & \end{array}$$

We get the Σ-parallelism given in the mutual consistency theorem with F = (- ,NONEXEC,F) and F' = (-, OVER,F).

Assertion 2 : In an environment with a finite set of concurrent conflicting, transactions, the protocol ensures mutual consistency.

We may reduce the proof of this assertion to two transactions Ti and Tj (with TQi <TQj) since we have a total sequencing system among transactions.

In such an environment, we temporarily have two SYNCM algebras associated with the ith and jth controllers; we show in ANNEX 4 that in every case one is suspended until the completion of the other. The proof given in ANNEX 4 is presented in a vizualizable manner since the key point in the verification of the mutual consistency theorem is the existence of Σ-homomorphisms which may be depicted as commutation diagrams.

CONCLUSION

We proposed a uniform and formal specification of two ring-structured protocols. From these specifications we inferred a proof of mutual consistency ensured by both protocols. This proof also shows the SERIALIZATION of conflicting transactions.

This paper focuses on a fail-safe environment ; robustness may be formalized with abstract data types in a similar way as shown for a decentralized-control protocol in (POPE79) (with a formal proof of self-synchronization in case of any failure in the network).

The attraction of our approach based on algebraically-specified data types resides in the potentialities it offers to describe and validate formally the numerous protocols defined in the literature (only a partial list of protocols is given in the references).

Weak-consistent protocols like (THOM75), (WILM79) have been formalized that way in (MIRA80) and a weak-consistent theorem has been given in (MIRA79).

This semantic framework bridges the gap left by contributions to synchronization-protocol design.

However this approach presents the drawback of not including the time variable in the specifications ; therefore such a formalization must be completed by a response time evaluation of each transition.

In a certain way, we may consider Bochmann's "regularity" concept (BOCH79) as a complementary feature of our approach. Several repearchs have been conducted in the area of formal study of performances like in (GARC79)... where Ellis'protocol, among others, has been analyzed. Models which unify specification-validation-analysis are required to provide the designer with a complete tool.

ACKNOWLEDGMENTS :

A debt of gratitude is owed to Gerry POPEK (UCLA) for his invaluable discussions on this approach and to I.R.I.A. (SIRIUS project) which supported this research under contract ≠ 79038.

I am particularly grateful to G. LE LANN (SIRIUS) and C. ELLIS (XEROX) for their comments on an earlier draft of this paper, and to referees which recommanded several points of clarification and emphasis.

I would like to thank also J. GRAY (IBM San José) and G. BOCHMANN (University of Montreal presently at Stanford) for helpful suggestions and ideas.

REFERENCES :

(ALSB76) Alsberg, P.A. "Multi-copy resiliency techniques" University of Illinois research report, CCTC-WAD-6-505, May 76.

(ANDL78) Andler, S. "Synchronization primitives and the verification of concurrent programs" Workshop on operating systems, IRIA, Oct. 78

(BILL79) Biller H.,Eberhard, L. "On the evaluation of architectures and applications of distributed data base management system" Seminar on distributed data sharing, Aix en Provence, France, May 15-17 - 1979

ANNEX 1 : SPECIFICATIONS OF ELLIS' PROTOCOL

Let us express the specifications of SYNCM and SYNCS

```
SYNCM Specifications   <attached to the "ACTIVE"or "FREE" status >

OBJECT         SYNCM     <ith controller >

SORTS          LE, INT,BOOL,T,M,Q,P,S,GES

OPS            PREPAREG     :    M x GES          > GES
               SETG         :    M x GES          > GES
               UNSETG       :    M x GES          > GES
               ID           :    GES              > GES

  < We focus the syntax on the input state and input messages >

VARS           A(CTIV)      :    S; FREE : S;
               P : INT      <priority (p,i) will be noted Pi >
               i : INT      < controller number >
               INTREQ       : M <internal request >
               EXTREQ       : M <external request >
               UPDW         : M <update operation with local waiting list >
               UPDS         : M <simple update with no blocked transactions>

SPECS
<INTREQ reception >
 RECEIVE ( ( INTREQ,-),(-)  : = IF TEST (S,FREE) = TRUE
                                THEN PREPAREG  (INTREQ,(FREE,-,-))
                                ELSE<wait for the end of the session>
<EXTREQ  reception>
 RECEIVE ( (EXTREQ,Pk),(A,Pi,-)) : =
           IF    TEST (Pi,Pk)     = FALSE
           THEN IF SUP (Pi,Pk)    = TRUE
                THEN ENQ ((EXTREQ,Pk),Q) ; ID(A,Pi,-) ;
                ELSE ENQ ((INTREQ,Pi),Q) ; ID(A,Pi,Pk); PREPAREG'(EXTREQ,(A,Pi,
                                                         Pk));
           ELSE ID (A,Pi,-) ; SETG (EXTREQ,(A,Pi,-)) ;
              < The EXTREQ message completed a revolution in the virtual ring>

<UPDS reception>
 RECEIVE ((UPDS,Pi),(A,Pi,-)) : = UNSETG (UPD,(A,Pi,-))
<UPDW reception >
 RECEIVE ((UPDW,Pk),(A,Pi,-)) : = IF TEST (Pi,Pk) = FALSE
                                  THEN SETG' (UPDW,(A,Pi,Pk)) ;
                                  ELSE       DEQ(Q,(EXTREQ,Pj)) ; ID(FREE,-,-) ^
                                             PREPAREG'((EXTREQ,Pj),(FREE,-,-)) ;
```

```
PREPAREG (INTREQ,(FREE,-,-)) : = DEFINE (Pi) ; PREPAREL (LE): ID (ACTIV);ID(A,Pi,-);
                                 TRANSMIT((EXTREQ,Pi), (i+1)); WAIT (EXTREQ,Pi);

 SETG (EXTREQ, (A,Pi,-)) : = SETL(LE); PROCESS (T) ; ID(A,Pi,-) ;
                             IF EMPTY? (Q) = TRUE
                             THEN TRANSMIT ((UPDS,Pi),(i+1));WAIT(UPDS,Pi) ;
                             ELSE TRANSMIT ((UPDW,Pi),(i+1)) ; WAIT (UPDW,Pi);
 UNSETG (UPD,(A,Pi,-)) : = UNSETL (LE) ; ID (FREE) ; ID (FREE,-,-) ;
                        ⟨ UPD is a shorthand for the current UPDate request ⟩

 TCEJBO
```

SYNCS Specification

```
 OBJECT        SYNCS       (i^th controller)
 SORTS         LE, INT,BOOL,T,M,Q,P,S,GES
 OPS           PREPAREG'  : M x GES ------> GES
               SETG'      : M x GES ------> GES
               UNSETG'    : M x GES ------> GES
               ID'        : GES     ------> GES

 VARS         P(ASSIV): S; FREE : S;
               P : INT ; i : INT ;
               INTREQ : M  ; EXTREQ : M ;
               UPDW  :  M  ; UPDS   : M ;

 SPECS
⟨EXTREQ reception⟩
 RECEIVE ((EXTREQ,Pk), (FREE v P,-,-)) : = PREPAREG'((EXTREQ,Pk),(FREE,-,-)) ;

⟨UPDS reception⟩
 RECEIVE ((UPDS,-),(P,Pi,-)) : = SETG' (UPDS,(P,Pi,-));

⟨UPDW reception⟩
 RECEIVE ((UPDW,-),(P,Pi,-)) : = SETG' (UPDW,(P,Pi,-)) ;

 PREPAREG' ((EXTREQ,Pk),(FREE,-,-)) : = ID (P,Pk,-);
           PREPAREL (LE) ; TRANSMIT ((EXTREQ,Pk),(i+1)) ;
           WAIT (UPDS vUPDW,Pk) ;
 SETG' (UPDS,(P,Pi,-)) : = ID (P,Pi,-) ;  SETL (LE)⟨PROCESS (T)⟩ ;
       TRANSMIT ((UPDS,Pi),(i+1)) ;
       UNSETG' (UPDS,(P,Pi,-))  ⟨the session is over⟩ ;
 SETG' (UPDW,(P,Pi,-)v(A,Pi,Pk)) : = ID (P,Pi,-) ;   SETL(LE)  ⟨PROCESS (T)....⟩;
       TRANSMIT ((UPDW,Pi),(i+1)) ;
       WAIT (EXTREQ v UPDS v UPDW,-) ; ID (P,-,-) v ID (A,Pk,-) ;
      UNSETG'(UPDS,(P,Pi,-)) : = UNSETL(LE) ; ID' (FREE,-,-);
  TCEJBO
```

ANNEX 2: Mutual consistency proof in a concurrency-conflict environment (Ellis' protocol)

In this figure we represent the diagram commutations of the ith, j^{th} and k^{th} sites.

⟨ Q | EXTREQ | Pj ⟩

i^{th} (F,-) PREPAREG → (A,Pi) [EXTREQj] → (A,Pi) SETG → (A,Pi) PREPAREG' → (P,Pj) SETG' → (P,Pj) UNSETG' → (F,-)

j^{th} (F,-) → (A,Pj) → (A,Pj,Pi) (UPDW) → (A,Pj,-) [EXTREQj] → (A,Pj) SETG' → (A,Pj) UNSETG' → (F,-)

Identical to transactions without conflicts (with UPDS)

⟨ Q | INTREQ | Pj ⟩

Notation:
Mi :reception of message (M,Pi)

a) The kth controller is located between the jth and i^{th} on the ring

(F,-) PREPAREG' → (P,Pj) PREPAREG' → (P,Pi) SETG' → (P,Pi) UNSETG' → (P,Pj) SETG' → (P,Pj) UNSETG' → (F,-)

b) The kth controller is located between the ith and j^{th}

(F,-) PREPAREG' → (P,Pi) SETG' → (P,Pi) UNSETG'. PREPAREG' → (P,Pj) SETG' → (P,Pj) UNSETG' → (F,-)

ANNEX 3 : SPECIFICATION OF LE LANN'S PROTOCOL

SYNCM Formalization

```
OBJECT      SYNCM                       <For the i^th controller>
SORTS       LE,INT,BOOL,TQ,M,Q,CS,RS,OS,S
OPS         PREPAREG :                  M x GES ------> GES
            SETG     :                  M x GES ------> GES
            UNSETG   :                  M x GES ------> GES
            ID       :                  GES ------> GES
VARS        TQ : INT (ticket); i :INT ; CRED :S ; DEB : S ; EXEC : RS ; M : CS;
            S : CS ;
            NONEXEC : RS ; OVER : RS ; F : OS ; B : OS ; O : OS ;
            PERMIT  : M <sequencing permit> ; ACKPERMIT : M ; INTREQ : M ;
            EXTREQ  : M  ; ACKREQ : M ; UPD : M ; ACKUPD : M ; Q : Q ; GQ : Q;

            AT #  : INT  <number of allocated tickets>
            FAT   : INT  <first available ticket>
            ACK # : INT  <counter of received ACKREQ or ACKUPD>
            TQ    : INT  <ticket id>
            n     : INT  <number or duplicated entities for a given request>

SPECS
<Permit reception>

RECEIVE (PERMIT,CRED,i-1,i): = TRANSMIT (ACKERPERMIT,i-1) ;  ID(CS) = CRED ;
                              <eventually increment the cycle number> ;
                              <broadcasting of NILREQ corresponding to old
                               tickets> ;

                               DEFINE (AT #,FAT) <allocation of forecast tickets>;
                               TRANSMIT (PERMIT, i+1) ;<wait  for ACKPERMIT> ;
RECEIVE (PERMIT,DEB,i-1,i) : = TRANSMIT (ACKPERMIT,i-1) ;
                              <eventually increment the cycle number>

                               DEFINE (AT# ,FAT) ; SWITCH (DEB) ;
                               TRANSMIT (PERMIT,i+1) ; <wait for ACKPERMIT>;
                              <ticket allocation to blocked internal requests>;

                      LOOP     DEQ (INTREQ,GQ) ;
                               PREPAREG (INTREQ,(-,NONEXEC,-));

                    ENLOOP     WHEN (EMPTY ?(GQ) = TRUE v TEST(AT#,0) = TRUE)
                              <ENDLOOP when no more INTREQ in GQ or no available
                               ticket>
<INTREQ reception>
RECEIVE ((INTREQ,DEB,-,i), (-,-,F)) : = ID (RS) = NONEXEC ;
              < The NONEXEC status corresponds both to a blocked transaction in GQ
                and to a transaction which is not in front of Q >
```

```
   ENQ (INTREQ,GQ) ; WAIT (PERMIT) ;

 RECEIVE ((INTREQ,CRED,-,i),(-,-,)) : = PREPAREG (INTREQ, (-,NONEXEC,-)) ;

⟨ACKREQ reception⟩
 RECEIVE ((ACKREQ,-,-,i),(M,EXEC,0)) : = SETG ((ACKREQ),(M,EXEC,0) ;
⟨ACK UPD reception⟩
 RECEIVE ((ACKUPD,-,-,i),(M,EXEC,B)), : = UNSETG ( ACKUPD ,(M,EXEC,B)) ;

⟨EXTREQ reception will be treated in SYNCS⟩

 PREPAREG (INTREQ,(-,NONEXEC,FvB)), : = DECR (AT #,1); ID(OS) = 0 ; ID (CS) = M ;
                 ⟨ attach TQ to EXTREQ⟩ ;  ENQ ((EXTREQ,TQ),Q)  ;
                TRANSMIT (n (EXTREQ,TQ),-) ;
               ⟨broadcasting of a request to each controller involved in the
                synchronization⟩ ;
                IF TEST((EXTREQ ,TQ), FRONT (Q)) = TRUE ∧ ID(OS) ≠ B
                THEN ID (RS) = EXEC ; PREPAREL (LE) ; ID (M,EXEC,0) ;
                           ⟨ID ((FRONT(Q)-1)),RS) = NONEXEC⟩;

                ELSE ID(RS) = NONEXEC ;
                IF TEST (AT #,0) = TRUE THEN ID(S) = DEB   ELSE ID(S) = CRED
                WAIT (n.ACKREQ) ; ACK# = 0 ;
 SETG (ACKREQ, (M,EXEC,0)) : = INCR (ACK# ) ; ID (OS) = 0 ;
                IF TEST (ACK#,n) = TRUE
                THEN IF TEST (RS,EXEC) = TRUE ∧ FRONT (Q) = INTREQ
                THEN TRANSMIT (n. (UPD,TQ),-) ; ID (RS) = EXEC ;
               ⟨the(permanent) update request is broadcasted⟩

                SETL (LE) ;  PROCESS(T) ; ID(OS) = B ; ID(M,EXEC,B); WAIT(n.ACKUPD)
                ACK# = 0 ;
                ELSE ⟨wait for local INTREQ in front of Q⟩;

                ELSE WAIT (ACKREQ) ;

 UNSETG (ACKUPD,(M,EXEC,B)) : = INCR (ACK#) ;
                IF TEST (ACK#,n)   = TRUE
                THEN UNSETL(LE);ID(RS) = OVER ; ID(OS) = F ; ID(-,OVER,F) ; DEQ
                                                                      (T,Q) ;
                IF EMPTY ?(Q)  = TRUE
                THEN WAIT (INTREQ v EXTREQ) ;
                ELSE ID(FRONT(Q),RS)  = EXEC ; PREPAREL (LE) ;
                     IF(FRONT(Q)      = INTREQ ⟨corresponds to an internal REQ⟩
                     THEN ID (FRONT(Q),OS) = 0 ; ACK# = 0 ; WAIT(n.ACKREQ);
                                             ID (M,EXEC,0);
                ELSE ID (FRONT(Q),OS) = 0 ; TRANSMIT (ACKREQ,-) ; WAIT (UPD) ;

                ELSE WAIT (ACKUPD) ; ID (M,EXEC,B);
```

TCEJBO

Note : here ID(OS) = F corresponds to EMPTY? (Q) = TRUE

SYNCS formalization

```
OBJECT        SYNCS      ⟨for the i^th controller⟩
SORTS         LE,INT,BOOL,TQ,M,Q,RS,OS,S,GES

OPS           PREPAREG' :  M x GES ——→ GES
```

```
                SETG'          : M x GES ------> GES
                UNSETG"        : M x GES ------> GES
                ID'            : GES ----------> GES
VARS            TQ :INT ; j : INT ; EXEC : RS ; NONEXEC : RS ; OVER : RS ; F : OS ;
            O: OS; B : OS ; EXTREQ : M ; UPD : M ; ACKUPD : M ; Q : Q ; ACKREQ : M;
                ⟨O : reception of an EXTREQ⟩ ; ⟨B : reception of an UPD⟩

SPECS          ⟨ permit-reception semanties are identical to SYNCM ⟩
               ⟨  EXTREQ reception ⟩
                RECEIVE (EXTREQ,TQ),-,j,i),(-,-,-)) : = PREPAREG'(EXTREQ,(-,-,-)) ;
               ⟨ we may have several calls to PREPAREG' ⟩
               ⟨ UPD reception ⟩
                RECEIVE (UPD,-,j,i,),(S,EXEC,O)) : = SETG'(UPD,(S,EXEC,O)) ;
                PREPAREG'(EXTREQ,(-,-,F)) : = ENQ(EXTREQ,Q) ; ID (CS) = S ;
                ID (OS) = O;
                        IF (FRONT(Q) = (EXTREQ, TQ)) ∧ ID(OS) ≠ B
                         THEN PREPAREL (LE) ; ID(RS) = EXEC ;
                         TRANSMIT (ACKREQ,j) ; ID'(S,EXEC,O);
                         WAIT (UPD) ; ID ((FRONT(Q)-1),RS) = EXEC ;
                        ⟨if the queue was not initially empty⟩ ;
                         ELSE ID (RS) = NONEXEC ;
                        ⟨wait for EXTREQ in front of Q⟩


                SETG'(UPD,(S,EXEC,O)) : = SETL (LE)  ⟨ PROCESS (T).....  ⟩;
                                          ID(RS) = EXEC ; ID(OS) =B ; ID'(S,EXEC,B);
                                          TRANSMIT (ACKUPD,j) ;
                                          UNSETG' (UPD,(S,EXEC,B)) ;

                         ⟨ UNSETG'is not associated with the reception of a
                           synchronization message ⟩

                UNSETG'(UPD,(S,EXEC,B)) : = UNSETL (LE) ; ID (RS) = OVER ; ID(OS)=
                                            F ; ID'(-,OVER,F) ; DEQ (T,Q) ;
                                            IF EMPTY ? (Q) = TRUE
                                           THEN WAIT (INTREQvEXTREQ) ;
                                           ELSE ID (FRONT,Q),RS) = EXEC ; PREPAREL
                                           (LE) ;
                                               IF FRONT (Q) =    INTREQ
                                           THEN ID(FRONT(Q),OS) = O; ID(CS)=M ;
                                           ACK≠ = O ; WAIT (n.ACKREQ) ;
                                           ELSE ID(FRONT(Q),OS) = O; ID(CS)=S ;
                                           TRANSMIT (ACKREQ,-) ;WAIT (UPD) ;
```

TCEJBO

Notes : (1)
SYNCM and SYNCS are exclusive for a given controller in an environment without conflict ; they are merged otherwise in SYNC, the ADT associated with a given controller.

(2) We consider only the permanent update operation associated with the UPD reception (and n ACKREQ).

ANNEX 4

Mutual-consistency proof in a concurrency-conflict environment (Le Lann's protocol)

We have to verify the Σ- homomorphism among concurrent transactions.
Let us analyse what may occur in the ith, j^{th} and k^{th} controllers (with $k \neq (i,j)$).
We use sub-indices to associate the entity states to Ti and Tj which originate in sites i and j.

1) in the ith controller

Case a) the local INTREQi is taken into account after the reception of the UPD from the ith controller (UPDj); we have the following commutations:

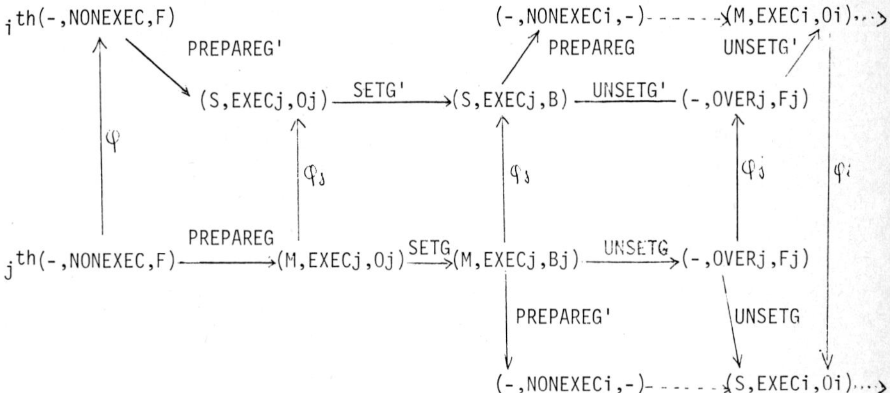

We return to the (2) step of functionning in a conflict-free environment

Case b) Now the INTREQi is taken into account before the reception of the UPDj

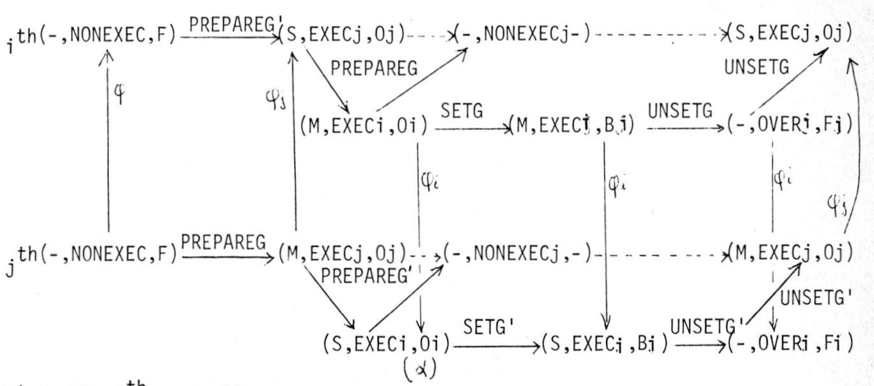

2) in the jth controller

We get exactly reverse situations than in 1)

3) in a kth controller ($k \neq i$ and $k \neq j$)

The following figures show that serialization of conflicting transaction is ensured.

Therefore Le Lann's protocol maintains strong mutual consistency in a concurrency-conflict environment.

<u>Figure 7</u> : Diagram commutations in the kth controller

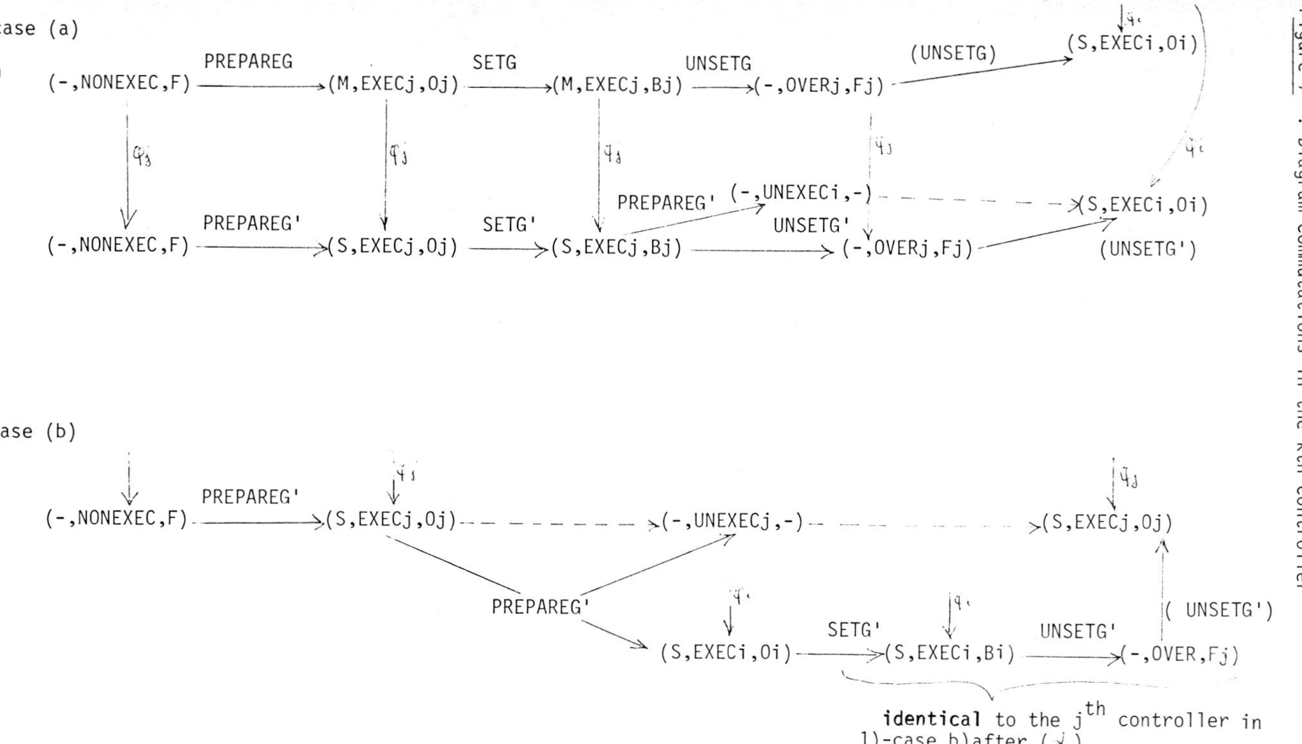

<u>Note</u> : Here we have two succesive PREPAREG' transitions

DISTRIBUTED DATA BASES
C. Delobel and W. Litwin (eds.)
North-Holland Publishing Company

QUALITATIVE AND QUANTITATIVE COMPARISON OF UPDATE ALGORITHMS IN DISTRIBUTED DATABASES

Paul WILMS

Laboratoire IMAG
B.P. 53X
38041 GRENOBLE Cedex (France)

Tél : (76) 54.81.45 ext 256

Several algorithms deal with the maintenance of consistency in distributed and duplicate databases. This paper aims to give some criteria in order to compare these different approaches. These criteria, quantitative and qualitative, form the basis for the elaboration of a valuable classification and comparison scheme. Finally we try to point out what essential needs and preoccupations of users and database managers could be when they use distributed and duplicate databases.

1. INTRODUCTION

1.1. The update algorithms

One of the most active areas in the field of distributed databases is the design of concurrency control mechanisms. In a previous report [WIL 79], we have described some algorithms for updating duplicate data, using a uniform formalization based on Nutt's evaluation nets.

These algorithms limit simultaneous execution of transactions in order to prohibit the mutual destruction of concurrent updates and to guarantee the consistency [ESW 76], [JOU 79] of the databases : each transaction, when completely processed, runs the system from a consistent state to another consistent state.

The main problems [MIR 77] involved in and connected to the management of distributed and duplicate databases are :

. the design of a concurrency control mechanism,
. the possibility of parallel processing,
. the resource allocation,
. the recovery after failures.

The databases we are interested in have the following characteristics :

. a copy of some data is duplicated on several sites : if the entire database is duplicated at all sites, the database is called a *fully redundant database* ;
. all information contained in the database is not concentrated on one site : the execution of a transaction will sometimes need the intervention of several sites in order to collect all the needed information : such a database is called a partitioned database ;
. more often, several reasons lead the database manager to duplicate some entities of the database while others can only be accessed on a specific site : it is a *mixed* or *partially redundant database*.

Most of the analyzed algorithms are concerned with fully redundant databases and maintain the *mutual consistency* of the *duplicate* databases.

A few of these algorithms also give an adequate solution to the problem arising in a partitioned *database*, which is the maintenance of the *internal integrity* of the database by an appropriate concurrency control mechanism ; in most cases, a specific dynamic resource allocation is also utilized.

1.2. Consistency and integrity

Mutual consistency is related to the existence of several copies of an information set, and implies an appropriate management of these copies to keep their logical unicity in spite of a physical multiplicity of copies. The goal of the mutual consistency is thus to keep all the copies identical in the absence of any update processing : in that case, all the copies possess the same version, i.e., all the same updates have been processed on all the copies. The updates must be broadcast to maintain mutual consistency of the copies ; nevertheless, such a broadcast is not always immediate or automatic after each update ; for that reason, two kinds of consistency are distinguished :

- a *strong* mutual consistency : between two updates, all copies belonging to running sites have the same version of the database ; a more formal approach is detailed in [GEL 79] ;
- a *weak* mutual consistency : different sites may possess different versions at a given time.

In any case, in absence of updating operations, the consistency is said to be maintained if all copies possess the same version of the database.

Internal integrity is concerned with the respect of constraints which are internal to the database and which are designed by the database manager ; this problem is not related to the existence of several copies. Mechanisms of mutual exclusion (using locks or semaphores) solve the concurrency problem and maintain the integrity : indeed, updates are always applied on non-obsolete information and the applied updates keep the database in a state for which all the constraints are respected. A formal approach is also detailed in [GEL 79] and [ESW 76].

The internal integrity will be achieved in a partitioned database [LEL 79] if only one of the following two situations can occur : either none of the data units manipulated by a transaction and to be updated is modified, or all these data units are modified.

1.3. The update algorithms in the hierarchy of network protocol levels

In the hierarchy of levels of computer network protocols, the algorithms for maintaining consistency and integrity of distributed databases may be viewed as follows :

(6)	application protocols
(5)	standard softwares
(4)	algorithms and protocols for distributed processing
(3)	end-to-end execution protocols
(2)	transport protocols
(1)	communication protocols

Upper levels are concerned with specific database management systems and application-oriented protocols.

The level (4) we are interested in provides some protocols for :

- . taking a distributed environment into account,
- . solving the problems caused by concurrent conflicting accesses,
- . allowing for a distributed processing in spite of the failure of some sites or communication links.

The algorithms dealing with consistency, integrity and resiliency are built under the assumption that a transport protocol is available which guarantees at least :

- . a sequential ordered transmission of messages between two communicating sites,
- . a correct transmission : the rate of non-detected errors due to transmission is negligible,
- . the effective transmission : messages are neither lost, nor duplicated if the liaisons between nodes are open.

In the case of a failure, this protocol does not permit a node to decide whether the last message has been lost or has been received and handled by a remote node whereas the acknowledgement has been lost.

Each controller which manages a copy is always notified of the opened and closed liaisons with remote controllers.

2. COMPARISON CRITERIA

The update algorithms can be compared at two levels :

- . a qualitative level : the algorithms are classified according to the kind of concurrency control mechanism used for the maintenance of consistency ;
- . a quantitative level : useful parameters are listed and results such as response time, number of needed messages, are computed.

2.1. Qualitative level

2.1.1. Concurrency control mechanism

A *centralized* locking strategy is a solution to the redundant update problem : one of the nodes is chosen as a "central" node and it is in charge of performing locking. This central node, however, is not necessarily a static property attached to a fixed node : each node initiating a transaction may become the central node for the current transaction.

In [ALS 76], this right to be the central node is attached to a fixed node called the "primary" : all transactions are transferred to this node in order to be processed ; the primary node is in charge of granting the transaction when the previous conflicting ones have been processed, i.e. when they have been acknowledged by a backup node. This solution is not always highly convenient because there is a risk of bottleneck at the primary node. The possibility of deadlock does not exist since the transactions acquire the needed locks at the primary node and they are handled in a sequential order.

In [SEG 79], this right is transferred after each transaction to the site which initiates a new transaction, when a transaction is in progress, the next ones cannot be started and they are queued at the primary node called "administrator". Deadlock is also prevented.

Acceptance or rejection of a transaction is not always based on the decision of a single site : the *concurrency control* mechanism is then *distributed* among several sites : this technique requires a *synchronization step* which lets the different sites to agree (or disagree) on the next transaction to be processed. After this synchronization step, the initiator of the transaction is allowed to broadcast the transaction : the update is then made permanent.

In [MUL 75] and [MIR 79], this approach is adopted : the site where the transaction is initiated broadcasts the transaction to the others ; if one of these sites detects a conflicting transaction, then the transaction with the highest priority is accepted while the other is rejected : thus, concurrent transactions can be initiated together, but only one of them is accepted. Under this approach, conflicts may occur and are detected.During the first synchronization step, some additional messages will be transmitted for rejecting a transaction in the case of a conflict.

Thomas [THO 77] develops a *distributed voting algorithm* : a majority consensus is required for the acceptance or rejection of a transaction. The nodes of the network form a daisy chain ; each transaction moves along this chain and each visited node votes in turn on the transaction until a majority consensus is reached. When a conflict is detected, the transaction is either deferred, either rejected depending on priority relationship between the conflicting transactions.

Many other algorithms [ELL 77], [LEL 78a], [ROS 78] associate a particular process to each transaction : in the first two algorithms, this process moves on a *virtual ring* and visits each site ; in [ELL 77], the transaction is stopped when it conflicts with an other of higher priority but a transaction is never rejected. On the other hand, in [ROS 78], the transaction visits each site in any order, and some sites may be visited again if necessary ; the conflicts are resolved on different ways depending on the priority of the transaction : either one of the conflicting transactions is rejected, either it is made to wait.

The concurrency control mechanism has an influence on the possible parallelism in the processing of requests and the kind of consistency.

2.1.2. Synchronization techniques

If the concurrency control mechanism is not based on a strategy with a centralized decider, synchronization techniques [LEL 79], [KAN 76] must provide for a uniform ordering of all the events arising somewhere in the distributed database and which have an impact on the maintainance of mutual consistency and/or internal integrity.

Therefore, Lamport [LAM 76] suggests to keep an individual clock on each site and to regularly exchange the local time ; so the different clocks could be readjusted if some derivation was detected among these clocks.

This idea of *individual clocks* readjusted when conflicts occur has been used for solving the synchronization problems in distributed systems [THO 77] : each transaction is given a timestamp (TS) ; the following rule is applied for the *timestamp* allocation :

$$TS := \max(\text{local time}, 1+\max\{TS(\text{base variables})\}).$$

With this rule, two different transactions emanating from the same processor are assigned distinct timestamps ; however, this does not guarantee that two transactions initiated by different processors receive distinct TS : the clock part of the TS is completed by the identification number of the site where the transaction is initiated.

So, a total ordering is obtained between the transactions and all these transactions can be processed in the same order by all sites.

In [ROS 78], the precedence relationship between transactions is based on a similar technique : at initiation, a process is given a unique number which may be a function of the time of day the process initially started, the identification number of its initial site and its priority ; this number is retained if the process is restarted. Physical clocks which deliver timestamps to transactions can be replaced by *logical clocks* for ensuring synchronization between transactions : indeed, the function of ordering carried out by a timestamp can be performed by integer counters, called *event counts* in [KAN 76], which simply count how long in terms of updates a node has been waiting since its last turn [ELL 77]. It is so possible and easy to evaluate the promptness [GEL 78], [GEL 79] of a system which is a measure of the number of transactions not yet processed in comparison with the ideal copy where the processing is instantaneous.

Logical clocks which provide a logical (or virtual) time are frequently used in update algorithms : in [ELL 77], transactions are ordered using a local counter incremented after each assignment ; the ordering between requests emanating from different sites still requires the introduction of the site identification number. In order to keep synchronization between event counts, on the reception of a transaction transmitted by a remote site, the local counter is adjusted to the value of the event count associated to this transaction if this value is higher than the local counter. An identical approach may be found in [HER 79].

However, there is a significant difference in the handling of transactions for the last two algorithms. In [ELL 77], the transaction circulates on a virtual ring from one site to another, and is transmitted as long as it does not conflict with a transaction of higher priority ; otherwise it has to wait for the completion of the conflicting transaction. In [HER 79], a transaction is allowed to be processed by a site if the following two conditions are satisfied : the transaction is the oldest one and the site has received from *each* other site a message (waiting queues should contain one message per site).

In [LEL 78b], transactions are identified by numbers called tickets ; these tickets are selected by the different sites in a distributed manner by reading the control token which moves from site to site on a virtual ring. The control token always contains the value of the first available ticket ; with this solution, a purely sequential identification of transactions is achieved. The property of sequential identification has a great importance since any site knows instantaneously if it has received and processed the previous transactions. This property is particularly interesting for recovery procedures.

A sequential identification is also used in [SEG 79] : each site keeps the transaction number, called actuality degree, of the last processed transaction. This actuality degree is checked in order to guarantee that all sites process the transactions in the same order ; it is also inspected when the primary site (administrator) has failed in order to install a new administrator with an up-to-date version.

2.1.3. Kinds of transactions

Concurrency control mechanisms serve the purpose of consistency maintainance ; partial or global locking techniques are designed. Do all kinds of transactions necessit the implementation of these mechanisms ? Different network architectures and different applications may require varying amounts and types of locks. Moreover, in applications where updates only consist of storing input values into the database, locking is unnecessary [JOH 75]. This is true whenever $f(g(x)) = f(x)$ for all update functions f and g : it is the case, for instance, when values are directly applied to variables : the result is not function of the previous value of the entity. For these applications, the concurrency control mechanism is reduced in verifying that an outdated update (g) is not performed but simply cancelled if a more recent one (f) has already been achieved.

In other applications, such as inventory files where the only updates are additions to and subtractions from entry values within the database, the ordering of updates can be ignored : these applications satisfy the relation : f(g(x)) ≡ g(f(x)) for all update functions : the linearization in the processing of transactions is not entailed, and locking is totally unnecessary. In SDD1 [BER 77], the problem of detecting conflicts between transactions has been deeply studied : several classes of transactions which do not conflict have to be pre-specified by the database manager ; for these classes, locking is avoided. This last approach, while being the most general one, maintains a high level of parallelism between transactions.

2.1.4. Kind of consistency

In the introduction, we have defined two kinds of consistency : a strong mutual consistency and a weak mutual consistency.

A strong mutual consistency is obtained with a centralized locking strategy ; some distributed concurrency control mechanisms also ensure the strong mutual consistency : it is the case if no overlapping in the processing of transactions is possible.

2.1.5. Granularity

The granularity is defined as the smallest entity which is locked during the processing of a transaction. Most of the algorithms do not clearly explicit this point : if a transaction only locks the accessed information (variables), the parallelism between several transactions can be sensibily improved ; in the worst case, the processing of a transaction requires the entire database to be locked. In [THO 77], the granularity is given by the set of variables involved in a transaction : these variables are called base variables. Concurrent transactions will be processed together if the intersection of their base variable sets and their update variable sets (variables the transaction modifies) is empty : indeed, in this case the concurrent transactions are not conflicting.

An analogous notion of conflicting transactions is developed in [ROS 78] : two requests handled by different processes and accessing a given entity are in conflict if one of the requests is a write request and the site(s) containing the entity has (have) not yet received a termination message or rollback message for either process.

In SDD1, the problem of granularity has been examined in depth : the transactions are divided into several classes. Transactions which belong to different classes will be processed simultaneously. Let us note that it is out of the scope of the update algorithms to analyze each transaction and to set each transaction into the appropriate class.

We are convinced that most of the algorithms could provide a much smaller level of granularity than the entire database. However the detection of conflicts becomes then longer since each granule of a transaction must be compared with each granule of the concurrent transaction.

2.1.6. Parallelism

Parallelism in the processing of transactions can be viewed in two different ways :
- the parallelism *internal* to each transaction ;
- the parallelism *between* transactions.

Internal parallel processing for a given transaction requires the possibility of running simultaneously different processes dedicated to the same transaction. This is not possible with the solution explained in [ROS 78] since a *unique process* is dedicated to each transaction. In general, a daisy chain structure [THO 78] or a virtual ring structure [ELL 77], [LEL 77] do not favour this kind of parallelism : indeed, when a node has performed its activity on a given request, it transmits a message to its successor (neighbour) which is then authorized to start its activity ; most of the time, the controllers have to acknowledge the received messages, before processing, for resiliency reasons [ALS 78].

Let us note that in [LEL 78a] the virtual ring configuration does not make any assumption on the kind of transaction processing : the virtual ring configuration is only relevant for the transmission of the token from a site to the next one ; this token lets transactions to be started ; after initiation, any technique (broadcast, point-to-point) may be used for the processing of the transaction on the different sites.

In some algorithms [MUL 75], [MIR 79], [SEG 79], [HER 79], [BER 77], messages are broadcast during the synchronization step : several processors simultaneously process the same transaction. The resulting parallelism will have an influence on the response time (better) for individual transactions.

Parallelism between transactions is meaningful if the granularity is not reduced to the entire database ; otherwise, a real parallelism is not possible since transactions are performed in a sequential order : at the utmost, the synchronization steps could be performed simultaneously as long as a conflict is not detected [MUL 75], [MIR 79]. If the parallelism between transactions is prohibited, the different copies of the database will remain strongly consistent.

Notwithstanding the absence of parallelism between transactions, it is important to note that with a point-to-point transmission, some sites may have already achieved a transaction while the others not, so that the different sites are handling different transactions : this phenomenon results in a shift in the execution time between the different processors [ELL 77], [LEL 78a], [THO 77].

2.1.7. Resource allocation

The processing of any transaction requires the allocation of some resources : if the database is fullyredundant, the allocation problem can be simply solved locally : the decision of any individual controller will satisfy the internal integrity rules and let the database in a consistent state. If the resources needed for the execution of a transaction are distributed among several sites, several controllers will participate in the allocation of the needed resources : mechanisms have to be devised for avoiding deadlocks, and infinite waiting. In [LEL 78a], the strategy of resource allocation is pseudo-dynamic since backout is acceptable. During a first step, resources are allocated ; these resources are still preemptible by sending a forcing request ; in a second step, these resources become confined, i.e. they are not preemptible anymore : the transaction can then be performed. The protocol provides controllers with the possibility to expand *dynamically* the set of resources needed by processes.

The algorithms developed in [ROS 78] are well-adapted for a dynamic allocation of resources since a process assigned to each transaction visits the different sites involved in the transaction and catches needed resources. If the process dies (WAIT-DIE) or is wounded (WOUND-WAIT), the acquired resources are deallocated. Processing of a transaction is started when the set of needed resources is obtained.

Miranda [MIR 79] also considers the case of remote entities which are semantically tied (partitioned databases) : during the first synchronization step, locally-locked objects can be preempted by an OINT message (order of interrupt). Whenever an object has been locked, it will accept only a message from its master controller and ignore any other request : so, inconsistency will be avoided.

These three approaches and SDD1 [BER 77] are concerned with the internal integrity of distributed entities : a solution to the update problem for partially redundant databases is provided.

2.1.8. Resiliency

It seems to be unrealistic to consider reliable systems only. Therefore it is important to assess the influence of a failure on the behaviour of any algorithm.

We first present some kinds of failures which could arise in a network ; we then evaluate the impact of failures on the different update strategies.

The failure of a host prevents the associated controller from participating in the update strategy. If a controller waits for the acknowledgement of the totality of remote controllers, the failure of any host causes the update technique to be stopped [MUL 75] if a mechanism of timeout is not implemented. If the running of the application is possible in spite of the failure of some hosts, the service provided is said resilient. To refine this concept, the notion of n-host resiliency has been introduced by Alsberg [ALS 76] : a service is n-host resilient if the service cannot be provided only when n hosts are simultaneously down during a critical phase of the service. Algorithms based on a majority consensus technique [THO 77], [SEG 79] need at least one half of the hosts to be connected. If a virtual ring structure is used, the service can be provided if a controller which terminates the critical phase of the service finds a successor for processing the transaction. This successor will dynamically change depending on hosts failing and recovering [LEL 77].

The occurrence of failures during the processing of a transaction could lead to inconsistencies if some controllers have not received some transaction while others have. Therefore two steps are necessary for the processing of a transaction : upon receiving an update message, the controller stores it on stable storage, but does not yet perform the update ; it sends the update message to a successor [ELL 77], [LEL 78b], or sends back an acknowledgement [MIR 79], [SEG 79], [BER 78]. When the initiator of the transaction receives this transaction again (virtual ring), or when the master has received all the acknowledgements, the commit point is reached : this point represents the instant at which the update moves from non effective to effective. The commit message means that the transaction has been completed and that the update is to take effect. In SDD1, a 3-phase commit procedure has been developed to avoid the risk of inconsistency [BER 78].

An other kind of failure consists in the disruption of communication links between two or several hosts : as a consequence, several subnetworks may appear : the independent functioning of these subnetworks will lead to inconsistencies. A solution has been proposed [THO 77], [SEG 79] to hinder the simultaneous processing of several independent subnetworks : a transaction can be processed only if a majority of controllers are connected. In other algorithms, when some subnetworks merge, a human intervention is required to recover a consistent database.

Automatic recovery procedures aim at providing host which recovers with an up-to-date version of the copy. This recovery requires sometimes an interruption in the processing of the current transaction : this interruption has an influence on the totality of sites in [THO 77], and on the two neighbours of the recovering site in [LEL 78b]. The recovery procedure is undertaken in parallel with the processing of other transactions in [HER 79]. In [SEG 79], the recovery procedure when the administrator has crashed necessits a polling for restoring an up-to-date controller, i.e. a controller for which actuality degree is maximal. The recovery mechanisms check the value of timestamps or tickets : a controller in [LEL 78b] must recover all the transactions for which the corresponding ticket is higher than the local one ; timestamps [THO 77] or actuality degrees [SEG 79] give the moment of the last transaction processed by any controller.

Many authors introduce the notion of journal of modifications : so, when recovering, a site performs all the transactions which were executed during its failure ; however, no comments are made on the management of these journals in order to avoid an infinite growth in the journal length.

Some algorithms could be simplified depending on the kind of transport service provided : a reliable broadcast ensures that the totality or none of the connected sites receive the message. This assumption is made in [HER 79]. In other algorithms [MIR 79], [SEG 79], the acknowledgement of the totality of sites is necessary to be sure that the broadcast has been correctly performed.

2.2. Quantitative level

In order to evaluate the individual performances of each algorithm, it is useful to list some general and typical parameters. This evaluation is restricted to the case of fully redundant databases. The selected *parameters* will serve for computing *results* concerning, for instance, the time delay needed to process an update transaction. An important work has been performed in this area by Garcia-Molina [GAR 78]. An other interesting work [PLA 79] is devoted to the evaluation of the performance of a specific algorithm (Ellis). A mathematical model of the distributed database management system in a fault-tolerant environment is proposed in [BOU 79] to evaluate its disponibility at the updating operations.

In this section, we first present a list of parameters and describe their potential influence on the algorithms ; we then propose some results which can be computed on the basis of the selected parameters.

2.2.1. Parameters

A. About transactions frequency

Mean interarrival time of update transactions at each node : Ar_u

It is supposed that the arrivals of update transactions are Poisson : so the transactions interarrival time is exponentially distributed with mean value Ar_u. The average update transactions arrival rate is noted by $\lambda_u = 1/Ar_u$: it represents the number of update transactions which arrive per second. The average update transactions arrival rate includes the transactions emanating from the local node and those transmitted by remote controllers. For a fully redundant database, this arrival rate is :

$$\lambda_u = \lambda_{u\ LOC} + \sum_j \lambda_{u,j} \qquad j \in [1,N],\ j \neq LOC$$

$$AR_u = [1/Ar_{u\ LOC} + \sum_j 1/Ar_{u,j}]^{-1}$$

For the sake of simplicity, Ar_u is assumed to be the same at each node ; in a more sophisticated model, a different value of Ar_u could be assigned to each node.

Mean interarrival time of read-only transactions at each node : Ar_r

The same exponential distribution is adopted with a mean value Ar_r.

$$\lambda_r = \lambda_r\ LOC$$

$$Ar_r = Ar_r\ LOC$$

Although some algorithms only consider update transactions, it is more realistic in the evaluation to integrate the read-only transactions. Let us note that these transactions only affect a site where they are initiated ; however these transactions must be processed when the state of the local database is consistent, thus in the absence of current modification of the local copy.

B. About transaction contents

Mean base set : Bs

It is the number of items referenced by a transaction ; this value is exponentially distributed with mean value Bs.
Some items can be accessed more frequently than other ones : a law of access distribution on the set of items has to be defined. This access distribution is highly correlated with the application.
The mean base set value is not very significant if not compared with the *total number of items* M which the database is composed of.
If the processing of a transaction causes the whole database to be locked, the two parameters Bs and M will lose their original interest : indeed, a conflict will arise whenever several transactions (at least one update transaction among them) are concurrently in progress. On the other hand, if granularity is refined to the item, then the probability of conflict (Pc) among concurrent transactions will depend on the total number of items and on the respective base sets. The probability of conflict among two concurrent transactions has been computed as :

$$P_c = \left(1 - \frac{C_{M-Bs1}^{Bs2}}{C_M^{Bs2}}\right) \quad \text{if } Bs1 + Bs2 \leq M$$

$$= 1 \qquad\qquad \text{if } Bs1 + Bs2 > M$$

C. About the network

Number of nodes : N

This number represents the number of nodes possessing the database in the system. In the case of a failure, all nodes do not participate in the processing of update transactions : so, the nodes are divided into two classes : the participating nodes (NP) and the nodes which are down (ND)

$$N = NP + ND.$$

If failures are not considered, then N = NP.
If we extend this study to distributed entities (no redundancy), then NP stands for the set of nodes which are concerned with the transaction and ND includes the down nodes and the nodes not implicated in the transaction.

Failure rate : F

Let UP describe the mean time period characterizing the normal running of the node (node Up) and DP the mean time period of the node failure (node Down).

$$F = \frac{DP}{DP + UP}$$

From this last value, it is possible to evaluate the probability of having NP nodes participating : the probability of a node being up is :

P(up) = 1-F ; the probability of Np nodes being up is then :

$$P(NP\ up) = \frac{N!}{NP!\ ND!}\,(1-F)^{NP}.F^{ND}$$

This formula is applicable if failures are independent.

Network transmission time : TT

As a first approximation, we assume the time it takes for any message to go from any node to any other node is a constant TT. This assumption is acceptable if the communication network is lightly loaded or if the load is uniformly distributed.

D. About processing and IO time

CPU item computation time : CIT

This is the time it takes to compute a new value for a given item ; if a transaction references x items on a given site, the total computation time is : x.CIT.

CPU time slice : ST

This is the time it takes to do a small computation such as comparing two values (timestamps, tickets, ...), checking or setting a lock, adding to or subtracting from a queue a given item.

IO time : IOT

The IOT is the time needed to read or write a value from or to an IO device. This value is either a lock, a timestamp or an item to be updated.

Retry delay time : RT

The retry delay time is introduced to take into account the time a node must wait before retrying a rejected transaction. This parameter is only significant if a rejection technique is adopted.

2.2.2. Measurements

Number of messages

We have considered the number of messages needed for an update to take place when no conflict occurs and the number of messages in the presence of conflicts. Even if the difference is sensible for some algorithms, it is not obvious that these ones are less powerful : indeed, the probability of conflict will then become an important point for further decision. Notice that messages to and from users are considered as internal messages to a node and not counted here. A broadcast message is counted as NP-1 messages. The number of messages required by a recovery procedure is also mentioned.

Load of a node

The load of a node will depend on the distribution law of the requests among the different nodes and the technique used for broadcasting an update : if a centralized mechanism is adopted, the load of the central node is much higher than the load of the other nodes : a bottleneck situation can result at the central node while the other nodes are lightly loaded. If control is uniformly distributed among the set of nodes, the resulting load at each node will be nearly the same. The IO and CPU utilizations can be computed at each node. This utilization is defined as the fraction of the available time that a server is busy and highly depends on the mean update transaction interarrival time.

Proportion of update transactions : K_u

Knowing Ar_u and Ar_r, it is easy to compute the proportion K_u of update transactions :

$$K_u = \frac{\lambda_u}{\lambda_u+\lambda_r}$$

Update response time : URT

The response time of an update transaction is defined as the difference between the finish time and the time when the update arrived at the initiating node. The update is finished when the initiating node has terminated all computations on the update and has notified the user that the update has been completed.

The URT is composed of :

- the initialization time, IT,
- the waiting time, WT, corresponding to the resolution of conflicting requests,
- the processing time, x.CIT,
- the time spent in the exchange of messages, y.TT.

The waiting time includes the retry delay time.

Mean throughput at a node

The mean throughput at a node is characterized by the number of transactions performed per time unit.

$$\text{THROUGHPUT} = \frac{1}{K_u.\text{URT} + (1-K_u).\text{RRT}}$$

where RRT is the response time of a read-only transaction.

Notice this last equation is only applicable if a read-only transaction is not performed during the processing of an update transaction.

Items locking rate : LR

The items locking rate is defined as the fraction of time an item is in the locking mode.

$$\text{LR} = \frac{\text{LT}}{\text{LT+NLT}}$$

where NLT is the time an item is not locked.

Queue sizes

If it is possible to detect the maximal values of parameters beyond which queue sizes continuously grow, then the domain of applicability of an algorithm can be delimited.

Impact of failures

The impact of failures on the behaviour of an algorithm can be evaluated in the following terms :

- resiliency,
- number of messages required by a recovery procedure,
- size of the stored information (i.e. management of journals),
- recovery time delay.

3. RESULTS OF THE COMPARISON

3.1. Number of messages

We distinguish the number of messages required by a simple update (NMSU) and the number of extra-messages resulting from a conflict (NMC).

The general equation of the average number of messages required by an update transaction is :

$$\text{NMU} = \text{NMSU} + \text{Pcc.NMC}$$

where Pcc is the probability of conflict :

$$\text{Pcc} = \text{Pc.Ps}$$

where Pc = probability of conflict in case of concurrent transactions (see 2.2.1. B.)

Ps = probability of concurrency (simultaneous processing of transactions).

$$\text{Ps} = f(\text{URT}, \frac{\text{Ar}}{\text{NP}})$$

Results for some update algorithms are summarized in the following table.

ALGORITHM	NMSU	NMC	PERF
MULLERY	7(NP-1)	[2NR,NR.NP]	0.14
ALSBERG	2NP+1	0	0.50
ELLIS	2NP	0	0.50
LE LANN	3(NP-1)+1	0	0.33
THOMAS	NP+N/2	[N/2,2NP-1].NR	0.67
SEGUIN	4(NP-1)+N/2	0	(0.22)
	2(NP-1)+N/2	0	0.40
ROSENKRANTZ	2NP-1	[2NR,NR.NP]	0.50
MIRANDA	5(NP-1)	[2NR,NR.(NP-1)]	0.20
HERMAN	[NP-1,(NP-1)(2NP-1)]	0	1.00

The number of messages transmitted during a no-conflicting update transaction grows linearly with the number of participating nodes. In the best case, i.e. when at least one transaction (read-only or update) per participating node is waiting for being processed at a given node, then the solution described in [HER79] is the most performant ; otherwise, if the transactions are unusual and if no service messages with the associated timestamp are regularly exchanged between nodes, then the number of messages needed by an update quickly grows in this approach.

For all the algorithms except in [HER 79], NMSU is a constant. Its value becomes higher in techniques using a total locking [MUL 75] and when each message is acknowledged [MUL 75], [MIR 79]. If failures are not considered [ELL 77], [ROS 78], the mechanism is not so sophisticated since several phases for the commitment are not required : the number of messages will therefore decrease. With a virtual ring structure [ELL 77], [LEL 78b], or if the master is unique during the whole transaction [ALS 76], [SEG 79], then the conflicting updates do not generate additional messages. On the other hand, in algorithms which adopt a rejection technique, NMC is not equal to zero.

The number of repeated rejections on a same transaction is noted NR.
This number can indefinitely grow if the rejected transactions do not acquire a higher priority when becoming older [MUL 75]. If the risk of starvation is avoided, the number of rejections has an upper bound. This number depends on the probability of conflict and of the rule of priority assignation (for rejected transactions). The rejection probability can be easily computed :

(1) $P_{rej} = Pcc.\frac{(NP-j)}{NP}$ in Mullery

(2) $P_{rej} = Pcc.f(ET)$ in the others

where . j is the identification number of the node ($j \in [1,NP]$)
. ET is the elapsed time since the transaction initialization
. $f(ET) \to 0$ with ET increase.

The probability for NR rejections can then be deduced from the previous equations :

(3) $P(NR\ rejections) = (Pcc)^{NR}.((NP-j)/NP)^{NR}$ in Mullery

(4) $P(NR\ rejections) = (Pcc)^{NR}.f(ET)$ in the others.

The maximal performance rate (PERF) is defined as follows : if NP copies of the database exist on NP sites, the PERF is equal to one if the number of messages needed for an update transaction to be processed is NP-1.

In general : $PERF = \frac{NP-1}{NMSU}$.

3.2. Load of a node per update transaction

The number of messages received and handled at each node has been evaluated ; we now deduce a compared load (CL), i.e. the load of any node (mL) in comparison with a central (master) node (ML) if it does exist. More distributed is the load on the different nodes, lower is the risk of bottleneck at a given node.

$$CL = \frac{mL}{ML} = \frac{\text{mean load}}{\text{maximal load}}$$

Let us remark that the value of ML represents the load of the central node in the absence of conflict.

CL = 1 <===> highly distributed control,

CL << 1 <===> presence of a fixed master controller during the processing of the transaction.

ALGORITHM	mL	ML	CL
MULLERY	4	3(NP-1)	4/3(NP-1)
ALSBERG	2	3	2/3
ELLIS	2	2	1/1
LE LANN	2	2	1/1
THOMAS	1	2	1/2
SEGUIN	3	NP-1+N/2	
	2	N/2	4/N
ROSENKRANTZ	2	2	1/1
MIRANDA	3	2(NP-1)	3/2(NP-1)
HERMAN	1	1	1/1

3.3. Update response time

ALGORITHM	Total transmission time	Waiting time
MULLERY	6TT	NR.RT
ALSBERG	2TT	2NHPT.TT
ELLIS	NP.TT	<(2NP-1)(NP-1).TT
LE LANN	NP.TT	NHPT.NP.TT
THOMAS	(N/2).TT	NR.RT
SEGUIN	2(1+Q).TT	NHPT.2(1+Q).TT
ROSENKRANTZ	NP.TT	NR.RT
MIRANDA	4TT	NR.RT
HERMAN	0	y.(CIT+IOT)+x.(ST+IOT)
	2TT	2TT+NHPT.(y(CIT+IOT)+x(ST+IOT))

The general formula for the update response time is :

$$URT = IT + WT + z.TT + y.(CIT+IOT) + x.(ST+IOT)$$

where . z.TT is the total transmission time,
- . z is the number of non simultaneous transmissions required by an update transaction,
- . y is the number of items implicated in the update transaction,
- . x is the number of elementary operations on locks, timestamps, ...

In the previous table, we have used the following symbols :

- . NR number of rejections,
- . RT retry delay time,
- . NHPT number of concurrent transactions of higher priority,
- . Q=1 if two consecutive transactions emanate from the same node,
  =0 otherwise.

If parallelism is authorized in the processing of an update, the total transmission time does not depend on the number of nodes ; it is not the case if only one process is attached to the transaction ; then the transmission time is proportional to the number of participating nodes since each node is visited in turn.

Waiting time is proportional to the time spent in processing transactions with higher priority (NHPT) ; if a rejection technique is adopted, then the waiting time depends on the number of successive rejections (NR) and the retry delay time (RT) chosen. It is important to remark that in [HER 79], URT is independent of the network transmission time if messages emanating from each node are waiting for execution.

3.4. Failures

Some of the presented algorithms are not very performant if the comparison criteria are the number of messages and the update response time in a reliable environment (no failure). This is often due to the fact these algorithms need extra-messages even in the absence of failure for robustness reasons. Resiliency has already been detailed in section 2.1.8. We now evaluate the number of messages (NMR) required by a recovery procedure, the time spent by this recovery (RTR) and the impact on the other nodes : i.e. how long current processing is suspended on the other nodes (INTERRUPT), and the number of nodes concerned by this recovery (NNCR).

ALGORITHM	NMR		INTERRUPT	NNCR
LE LANN	8	6(TT+ST)	3(TT+ST)	3
THOMAS	4(NP-1)	4(TT+ST)	2(TT+ST)	NP
SEGUIN (1)	2(NP-1)	2(TT+ST)	0	NP
(2)	4(NP-1)+N/2+1	4(TT+ST)	4(TT+ST)	NP
HERMAN	[3NP-1,5(NP-1)]	4(TT+ST)	0	NP

- . (1) if the administrator is up,
- . (2) if the administrator is down.

The recovery procedure alterates in various ways the normal functioning of the algorithm. In some algorithms, the whole system is suspended during a part of the recovery procedure [THO 77], and new failures or nodes recovery are prohibited during the critical recovery phase. In [LEL 78a], [HER 79] and in [SEG 79], the normal processing is not affected ; however in the last approach, the failure of a majority of nodes causes the application to be completely stopped.

As mentioned above (2.1.8.), the management of journals of modification is not sufficiently explained : indeed, it is important to know when some information contained in the journal could be deleted ; otherwise the stored information would continuously grow while storage capacity is limited.

4. ALGORITHMS CLASSIFICATION

In the next table, we summarize the essential characteristics of some update algorithms ; the associated reference is given in brackets. For Ellis, we have chosen to analyze the virtual ring structured algorithm. Some of these algorithms could be easily extended (EXT) in order to offer more general characteristics. Other algorithms could have been compared ; nevertheless, a large range of different techniques is covered with these ones.

More problems are solved if the algorithms take into account the concept of internal integrity in distributed databases because a very general architecture of the database (partial redundancy) is allowed without modifying the proposed mechanism. Moreover, if the service is resilient, the algorithm is able to run in a non reliable environment.

It is difficult (and perhaps meaningless) to give an accurate evaluation of these algorithms for any kind of application ; indeed, the interest of an algorithm depends on :

- the kind of transactions to be processed,
- the arrival rate of the transactions which influences the frequency of conflicts,
- the kind of database,
- the reliability of the communication subnetwork.

The degree of parallelism and the kind of transmissions will have an influence on the response time of a given transaction.

CHARACTERISTICS \ ALGORITHMS		MULLERY [MUL75]	ALSBERG, DAY [ALS76]	MIRANDA [MIR79]	ELLIS [ELL77]	LE LANN [LAN78a, c]	THOMAS [THO77]	SEGUIN [SEG79]	HERMAN, VERJUS [HER79]	ROSENKRANTZ [ROS78]	SDD-1 [BER77] [BER78]
CONSISTENCY	STRONG	X	X		X	X		X			
	WEAK			X			X		X	X	X
INTEGRITY	STRONG			X		X					
	WEAK									X	X
	NOT TACKLED	X	X		X		X	X	X(ext)		
SYNCHRONIZATION	TIMESTAMP			X			X			X	X
	EVENTCOUNT				X				X		
	TICKET					X		X(AD)			
	QUEUE	X	X						X		
RESOURCE ALLOCATION	STATIC	X	X		X	X	X	X	X		
	DYNAMIC			X		X(ext)				X	X
DATABASE	FULL REDUNDANCY	X	X	X	X	X	X	X	X	X	X
	DISTRIBUTED ENTITIES			X		X				X	X
	PARTIAL REDUNDANCY			X		X			ext	X	X
CONCURRENCY CONTROL	MASTER	X	X	X				X			X
	VOTE						X				
	DISTRIBUTED				X	X			X	X	
CONFLICT	REJECTION			X		X(ext)	X			X	X
	WAITING				X	X	X		X	X	X
	TOTAL LOCKING	X	X					X			
GRANULARITY (YES/NO)		N	N	Y	N	Y	Y	N	N	Y	Y
PARALLELISM	INTRA REQUEST	Y	N	Y	N	Y	N	Y	Y	N	Y
	INTER REQUESTS	N	N	(Y)	(Y)	(Y)	Y	N	Y	Y	Y
LOGICAL TRANSMISSION	VIRTUAL RING		(X)		X	X	X			X	
	BROADCAST	X		X			X	X	X		X
PHYSICAL TRANSMISSION	RELIABLE BROADCAST	X				X			X		
	NO-RELIABLE BROADCAST			X		X	X	X			X
	POINT-TO-POINT		X		X	X				X	
RESILIENCY		1	2,3,N	N	N(ext)	N	N/2	N/2	N	/	p
AUTOMATIC RECOVERY (YES/NO)		N	/	Y	Y(ext)	Y	Y	Y	Y	/	Y
RUNNING OF INDEPENDENT SUBNETS		/	Y	Y	/	Y	N	N	Y	/	Y
CURRENT PROCESSING INTERRUPT DURING RECOVERY		/	N	N	/	N	Y	N	N	/	N

5. CONCLUSION

A lot of update algorithms which deal with consistency of duplicate databases have been conceived in the recent years ; although these approaches always solve the same main problem, differences (sometimes important) appear in the kind of service offered to the user. In order to be able to compare these algorithms, we thought it was capital to define some criteria which should be fulfilled depending on the kind of the application under consideration. It is clear that as often as not, only a few of these criteria have to be fulfilled. So, we have listed and commented the criteria which seem to be essential and we have summarized the principal characteristics of each algorithm. We have also presented some parameters and distribution laws which could be taken into account for the quantitative comparison of these algorithms ; results concerning update response time and messages overhead have been established.

Further work in this area is still needed, especially :

- a practical simulation of these approaches,
- a detailed computation of results,
- the refinement of some parameters and laws,
- a quantitative comparison based on simulation results.

Finally we hope to reach the following objectives : for a given set of parameters and criteria, to indicate the "best" approach in terms of users requirements. Such a result should be valuable since it could have an industrial impact : for some given requirements, an "optimal" solution or a range of performant solutions could be proposed.

REFERENCES

[ALS 76] ALSBERG P., DAY J.
"A principle for resilient sharing of distributed resources". Proceedings of the Second International Conference on Software Engineering. Oct. 1976.

[BER 77] BERNSTEIN P.A., SHIPMAN D.W., ROTHNIE J.B., GOODMAN N.
"The Concurrency Control Mechanism of SDD1 : a System for Distributed Databases". Technique Report CCA-77-09. Dec. 1977.

[BER 78] BERNSTEIN P.A., SHIPMAN D.W., ROTHNIE J.B., GOODMAN N.
"A distributed database management system for command and control applications". Semi annual Technical Report 3.
Technical Report CCA-78-10. July 1978.

[BOU 79] BOUCHET P.
"Procédures de reprise dans les systèmes de gestion de bases de données réparties". AFCET, Journées "Bases de données cohérentes", Paris, Mai 1979.

[ELL 77] ELLIS C.A.
"Consistency and correctness of duplicate database systems". Proceedings of Sixth ACM Symposium on Operating Systems Principles. Nov. 1977, pp. 67-84.

[ESW 76] ESWARAN K.P., GRAY J.N., LORIE R.A., TRAIGER I.L.
"The notions of consistency and predicate locks in a database system". IBM Research Laboratory, San Jose, California, CACM Vol.19, n° 11, Nov. 1976.

[GAR 78] GARCIA-MOLINA H.
"Performance comparison of update algorithms for distributed databases". Progress Report 1 to 7 HHP Report, Stanford Univ., March 1978.

[GEL 78] GELENBE E., SEVCIK K.
"Analysis of update synchronization for multiple copy databases". IRIA, Rapport de recherche n° 332. Sept. 1978.

[GEL 79] GELENBE E., WILMS P.
"Note sur la cohérence, la promptitude et l'intégrité". Note interne, Orsay, Université Paris-Sud, Mai 1979.

[HER 79] HERMAN D., VERJUS J.P.
"An algorithm for maintaining the consistency of multiple copies". IRISA, Université de Rennes, May 1979.

[JOH 75] JOHNSON P., THOMAS R.
"The maintenance of duplicate databases". Network Working Group RFC677 working paper. Jan. 1975.

[JOU 79] JOUVE M., PARENT C.
"Qu'est-ce qu'une base de données cohérente ?". Journées AFCET "Bases de données cohérentes", Paris, Mai 1979.

[KAN 76] KANODIA R.K., REED D.P.
"Synchronization with eventcounts and sequencers". MIT Report, 1976.

[LAM 76] LAMPORT L.
"Time, clocks and the ordering of events in a distributed system". Massachussetts Computer Associates Report CA-7603-2911, March 1976.

[LEL 77] LE LANN G.
"Introduction à l'analyse des systèmes multi-référentiels". Thèse d'Etat, Université de Rennes, Mai 1977.

[LEL 78a] LE LANN G.
"Coherent data-sharing in failure-tolerant distributed processing systems". IRIA SIRIUS Project, Jan. 1978.

[LEL 78b] LE LANN G.
"Algorithms for distributed data-sharing systems which use tickets". Proceedings of the third Berkeley Workshop on Distributed data Management and Computer Networks. San Francisco, Aug. 1978.

[LEL 79] LE LANN G.
"An analysis of different approaches to distributed computing". First International Conference on Distributed Computing Systems, Huntsville, Alabama, Oct. 79

[MIR 77] MIRANDA S.
"Algorithms for distributed data-sharing systems which use tickets". Proceedings of the third Berkeley Workshop on Distributed data Management and Computer Networks. San Francisco. Aug. 1978.

[MIR 79] MIRANDA S., POPEK G.
"Specification and verification of a decentralized-controlled locking protocol (DLP) for distributed data bases". C.E.R.I.S.S., Université des Sciences Sociales de Toulouse. Feb. 1979.

[MUL 75] MULLERY A.P.
"The distributed control of multiple copies of data".
IBM Thomas J. Watson Research Center, Yorktown Heights, New-York, Aug. 1975.

[PLA 79] PLATEAU B.
"Evaluation des performances d'un algorithme de contrôle de la cohérence d'une base de données répartie".
AFCET, Journées "Bases de données cohérentes". Paris. Mai 1979.

[ROS 78] ROSENKRANTZ D.J., STEARNS R.E., LEWIS P.M.
"System level concurrency control for distributed database systems".
ACM Transactions on Database Systems, Vol. 3, N° 2, June 1978, pp. 178-198.

[SEG 77] SEGUIN J., SERGEANT G., WILMS P.
"Cohérence et gestion d'objets dupliqués dans les systèmes distribués".
RR n° 77, CICG/ENSIMAG, Mai 1977.

[SEG 79] SEGUIN J., SERGEANT G., WILMS P.
"A majority consensus algorithm for the consistency of duplicated and distributed information".
First International Conference on Distributed Computing Systems. Huntsville, Alabama, Oct. 1979.

[THO 77] THOMAS R.H.
"A majority consensus approach to concurrency control for multiple copy data bases".
Bolt Beranek and Newman Inc., Report 3733. Dec. 1977.

[WIL 79] WILMS P.
"Etude d'algorithmes de cohérence d'informations dupliquées et réparties. Formalisation à l'aide de réseaux de Nutt".
Rapports de Recherche 160 et 160 bis. IMAG. Fév. 1979.

DISTRIBUTED DATA BASES
C. Delobel and W. Litwin (eds.)
North-Holland Publishing Company

AUTOMATA MODELS OF COMPUTER NETWORKS

A. Baczko, F. Seredyński

Institute of Computer Science
Polish Academy of Sciences
Warsaw, Poland

Two basic problems related to the utilization of distributed network resources are discussed. The first part presents a model of operative, decentralized control of computing resources distribution among the network customers. The optimalization criterion of computer network resources utilization is related not to the technical network parameters but to its customers. The second part presents a concept of a hybrid switching method in a network node. Basing on a synthetic indicator of a network node functioning quality determined with the help of an abstract model, a data switching method preferred under given condition is obtained.

1. INTRODUCTION

As the basic problems connected with the design and construction of computer networks are being gradually solved, the problem of creating mechanisms permitting more effective utilization of the potential and possibilities of those networks becomes more and more important, as far as the distributed data bases are concerned. Significant domain in this field may be encouraged, it seems, by further automation of network processing and information transmission mechanisms. This automation should be adapted to the distributed character of network computer resources and also, while these mechanisms are being investigate, should take into account the requirements of the network customers. The present paper reflects both these tendencies.

The first part of the paper, based on 8 , concerns the organization of operative, decentralized control of the distribution of the computer network computing resources among its customers. This part of the paper is founded on the ideology of collective behavior and game theory of stochastic automata 9, 10 . The second part of the papers, based on 1 concerns the organization of a hybrid switching method in a node of a data transmission network. The investigation method assumed in the paper is the experimental study employing the computer simulation method.

2. A MODEL OF OPERATIVE DECENTRALIZED DISTRIBUTION OF COMPUTING RESOURCES OF A COMPUTER NETWORK

2.1. STATEMENT OF THE PROBLEM

In the majority of papers dealing with the organization of the computer systems control, considering problems of optimal utilization of the resources of both the computing system and the computer network, these systems are usually treated as queueing systems. The traditional characteristics of these queueing systems are usually optimalized, such as the mean waiting time, storage size, capacity, etc. It is well known that through applying this methodology - improving the indicated model parameters - the general functioning quality of the considered system can be improved. Such an approach to the problem of the optimalization of computer network resources utilization does not, however, take into account many important problems related to the functioning of computer networks.

An approach to the problem of the optimalization of computer network resources utilization should be based on an ideology whose aim is to fulfil the criteria involving the very nature of computer network functioning. It is obvious that the aim of constructing and functioning of a computer network is the satisfaction of the network users' needs - these being, generally speaking, the performance of their own computing tasks.

However, a computing task is not, in its turn, an aim in itself for the user but is related to the accomplishment of more general tasks connected with economic management, new apparatus design, etc.

It is natural to think that performing a given computing task brings the user some profit. It is therefore easy to assume that for every user we can define a function of dependence of his profit on the amount of computing resources of the network allotted to him. Moreover, it is natural to assume that the most sensible distribution of the computer resources of the network is a distribution according to the criterion of maximal summary users' profit from utilizing the computer network.

Thus, possessing information about local functions of users profits and actually existing computing resources, we can solve the standard problem of optimal resources distribution (a nonlinear programming problem) and basing on the obtained solution we can organize control in the network. Still, considering possible real situations, we can discuss a different approach to the problem.

If the local profit functions are unknown or vary in time in an unpredictable manner, and each time only the current values of these functions are known, then there arises a problem of operative redistribution of the computing resources of the network adapting themselves to the real profit functions. Taking into consideration the isolation of the network users and the aspiring to decentralize network control, we can attempt to organize in the network a decentralized control of the computing resources based on the results presented in [11]. The suggested solution of the problem of optimal resources distribution does not, however, solve the problem of operative distribution of computing resources among the network users.

The solution of the problem of operative distribution of computing resources of the network among the network users can be achieved through the organization of the interaction of the network computers in order to divide among them the input streams of users' tasks.

The presented arguments lead us to a model of operative distribution of the network's computing resources. A detailed description of that model is given below.

2.2. A DESCRIPTIVE MODEL OF A COMPUTER NETWORK

It is assumed that the considered computer network consists of geographically dispersed computers connected by a communication network. It is a general use network destined to fulfil the computing needs of all the users having access to it. All these computers of the network are computer systems of varying output. Every computer of the network has a storage buffer intended to store the incoming tasks as well as other input/output devices.

The functioning process of a computer network is described by a two-level model consisting of the network users model (first level) and computer network model (second level). On the first level the distribution of some conditional resource between the network users is performed and on the second level the computing resources of the network are distributed among the users as a result of an interaction between them and the network. Since a specific case was investigated, where it was assumed that a computer network is a homogeneous network with a ring communication net, the subsequent description of the model is conducted from that point of view (Fig. 2.1).

2.3. A MATHEMATICAL MODEL OF A COMPUTER NETWORK

In a mathematical network model it is assumed that a computer network consists of N one-channel queueing systems with a finite queue having maximal length L. All the computers of the network are connected by a ring communication network with ideal channels. The task transmission time between two neighboring nodes of the network is neglectably small in comparison with the time of processing the message in a network node. It is assumed that all the queueing systems possess identical probability distribution of service time with the same parameter μ. At the input of the i-th $(i = 1,2,\ldots,N)$ queueing system arrives, from the i-th customer, transaction stream to be processed. We take that the input tasks streams possess identical probability distributions with parameter Λ_i.

All queueing systems are able to regulate the load of their buffer storage space. The control of the input transactions stream is performed through a service price mechanism. Every system, periodically and independently from all others, establishes a price $C_i(t)$ (where t - discreet time) of servicing one transaction.

A transaction coming from the i-th customer to the i-th queueing system is placed in the queue if there is room in the system buffer. When the transaction is accepted the system obtains from the user a payment $C_i(t)$. The accepted transaction will be processed according to the existing discipline.

During the functioning of the network the queueing systems can cooperate. If the i-th system receives a transaction from the customer and the system's buffer is full the system can transmit the transaction to a neighboring one. The transmission can take place if the service price in the (i-1)-th or (i+1)-th system is smaller than in the system i. The transaction arriving from the i-th system to the (i+1)-th system is placed in the queue if, of course, there is any buffer storage place. If this transmission ends with the acceptance of the transaction then the (i+1)-th system receives payment equal to its established price $C_{i+1}(t)$. Moreover, the i-th and (i+1)-th systems receive a so-called transaction transit fee $0.5[c_i(t) - c_{i+1}(t)]$. If the (i+1)-th system did not accept the transaction because of a buffer overflow then the transaction transit in the network can go on, but only if on the transit path there exists a price gradient. The transit ends in a j-th ($j \leqslant N-1$) node of the network. The transaction is placed in the queue of the j-th system and then accounts are cleared between all the systems taking part in the transit according to the above rules. If the j-th node was full and the condition $C_{j+1}(t) < C_j(t)$ was not satisfied, the transaction is liquidated.

When the transaction of the i-th user has been processed, it is transmitted back to him.

2.4. A MATHEMATICAL MODEL OF THE COMPUTER NETWORK USERS

In the mathematical model of the computer network users it is assumed that to every user who has access to network computing resources through its i-th node is related a concave utility function $\Psi_i(\lambda_i)$. This function depends on the mean number λ_i of transactions of this user processed during a given time interval.

At the disposal of every i-th user there is a quantity resource $R_i(t)$ which is distributed among the users at discreet moments of time t. The user who obtained the resource $R_i(t)$ can send to the network, during a given time interval, a number of transactions to be processed equal to

$$\Lambda_i(t) = R_i(t)/C_i(t) \qquad (2.4.1)$$

The resource $R_i(t)$ can be interpreted as the quantity of some conventional money assigned to the user by the network administration from a general fund R at the administration's disposal. The fund R is distributed among the network users according to their requirements $p_i(t)$. The requirements of the users with respect to the resource R are received by the network administration and subsequently, this resource is divided proportionally to the submitted requirements, i.e.

$$R_i(t) = Rp_i(t)/\sum_{i=1}^{N} p_i(t) \qquad (2.4.2)$$

The users form their requirements with respect to resource R in the following way

$$p_i(t) = \begin{cases} p_i(t-1) + k_o \dfrac{\Delta\psi_i(\lambda_i)}{\Delta\lambda_i} - \dfrac{p_i(t-1)}{R_i(t-1)}, & \text{if} \quad {}_i \neq 0 \\ \\ p_i(t-1) + k_o\left[\Psi_i(\lambda_i) - \dfrac{p_i(t-1)}{R_i(t-1)}\right], & \text{if} \ \Delta\lambda_i = 0, \end{cases} \qquad (2.4.3)$$

where $k_o > 0$.

Such a forming of requirements with respect to resource R, corresponds, according to the solution of the known problem of resource distribution [11], to the users' tendency to maximalize their local profit. It also permits to distribute the network computing resources in a way maximalizing the expected value of the summary profit obtained from utilizing these resources, i.e.

$$\max M\Big[\sum_{t=0}^{T}\sum_{i=0}^{N}\Psi_i(\lambda_i)\Big] \tag{2.4.4}$$

with a limitation of network computing resources

$$\sum_{i=1}^{N}\lambda_i \leqslant N\mu \ , \tag{2.4.5}$$

where T is the time of computer network functioning. Observe that the users may not know the form of their profit function and be guided only by its current values. Besides, the functions themselves may change in time in an unpredictable manner.

2.5. COMPUTER NETWORK CONTROL

The presented method of distribution of the resource R between the users of the network does not solve the problem of operative distribution of the network's resources among them. In order to solve this problem, a decentralized procedure was suggested. This procedure would divide the incoming transaction streams between the network's computers.

During the network functioning process, as shown above, the queueing system accumulate a profit in each time interval. The value of that profit $d_i(t,t+1)$ obtained by the i-th system during the time interval $(t,t+1)$ can be determined in the following way (Fig. 2.2)

$$\begin{aligned} d_i(t,t+1) = {} & \Lambda_i(t)[q_i^1 C_i(t) + 0.5\, q^1_{i,i-1}\,(C_i(t) - C_{i-1}(t)) + \\ & + 0.5\, q^1_{i,i+1}(C_i(t) - C_{i+1}(t))] + \\ & + 0.5\,\Lambda_{i-1,i}(t)[q^1_{i-1,i}(C_i(t) + C_{i-1}(t)) + \\ & + q^2_{i-2,i}(C_{i-1}(t) - C_{i+1}(t))] + \\ & + 0.5\,\Lambda_{i+1,i}(t)[q^1_{i+1,i}(C_i(t) + C_{i+1}(t)) + \\ & + q^2_{i+1,i}(C_{i+1}(t) - C_{i-1}(t))]\ , \end{aligned} \tag{2.5.1}$$

where $\Lambda_{i-1,i}(t)$, $\Lambda_{i+1,i}(t)$ - the number of transactions arriving by transit to the i-th system, from the (i-1)-th, (i+1)-th systems respectively, during the time interval $(t,t+1)$; q_i^1 - the

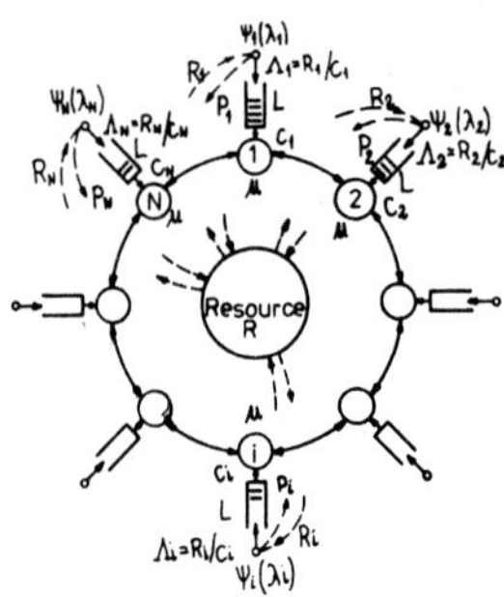

Fig.2.1 A model of operative distribution of computing resources in computer network

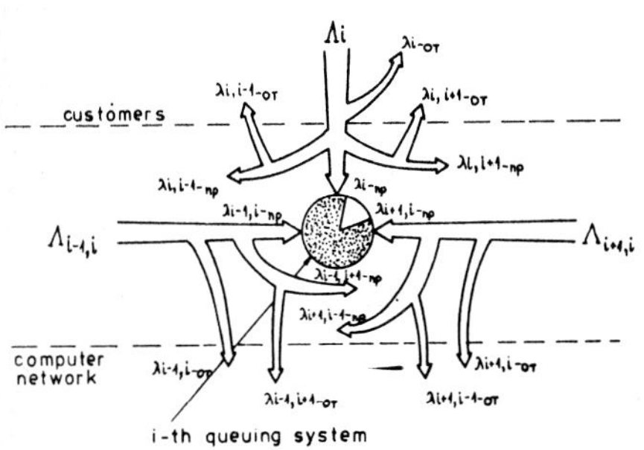

Fig.2.2 Transaction streams in network node

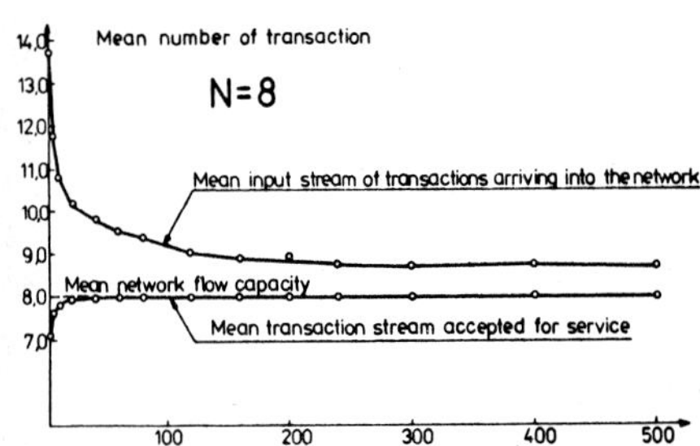

Fig.2.5 Mean values of input streams depending on buffer capacity

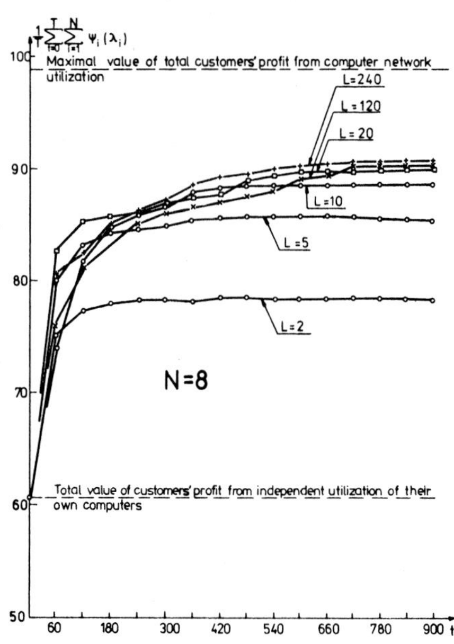

Fig.2.3 Mean value of total network customers' profit dependent the number of divisions of resource R

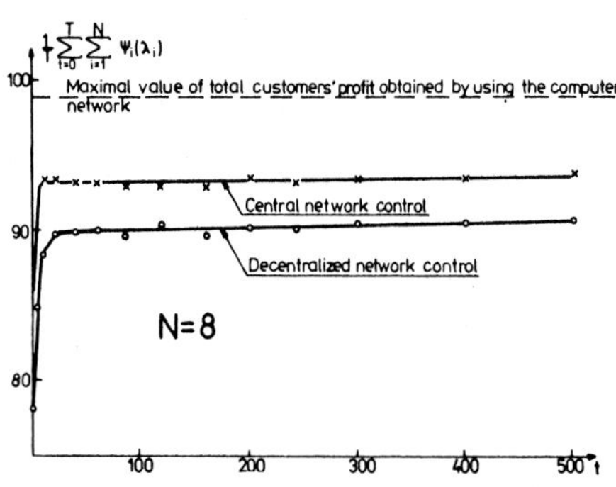

Fig.2.4 Mean value of total network customers' profit dependent buffer capacity

part of the i-th user's transactions accepted for processing by the i-th system during the time interval (t,t+1); $q^1_{i,i-1}, q^1_{i,i+1}$ - the part of the i-th user's transactions sent by the i-th system to the (i-1), (i+1) systems respectively, and accepted for processing by the network during the time interval (t,t+1); $q^1_{i-1,i}$, $q^1_{i+1,i}$ - the part of transactions which arrived from, respectively, the (i-1), (i+1) systems and accepted for processing by the i-th system during the time interval (t,t+1); $q^2_{i-2,i}$, $q^2_{i+1,i}$ - the part of transactions which arrived respectively, to the (i-1)-th, (i+1)-th systems, passing in transit through the i-th system and accepted for processing by the network during the time interval (t,t+1).

The aim of functioning of the i-th queueing system during the work of the network will be the maximalization of the expected value of its own profit, i.e. achieving

$$\max M\left[\sum_{t=0}^{T} d_i(t,t+1)\right]. \tag{2.5.2}$$

As an algorithm permitting such a maximalization we can employ the gradient algorithm of establishing the price of processing by the i-th system

$$C_i(t+1) = C_i(t) + k_1 \frac{d_i(t,t+1) - d_i(t-1,t)}{C_i(t) - C_i(t-1)}, \tag{2.5.3}$$

where $K_1 > 0$, $C_i(-1) = 0$, $d_i(-1,0) = 0$. The variation scope of the price C_i can be limited by the following inequality

$$0 < C_{min} \leqslant C_i \leqslant C_{max} = R. \tag{2.5.4}$$

The application of the above algorithm of establishing the service price in an unlimited variation scoped of the values of the incoming streams may lead, however, to uncontrollable tie-ups of the service systems or to uncontrollable transaction streams not accepted for service. Thus, if in the i-th service system the value of the tie-up coefficient x_i measured in the system, is greater than some given value a_p then the following control is used:

$$C_i(t+1) = C_i(t) - C_i(t) - C_{min} \quad (1-e^{-k_2(x_i-a_p)}), \tag{2.5.5}$$

If in the (i-m)-th service system the value of the measured in the system, coefficient of unaccepted transactions y_i is greater than some given value b_{np}, then the following control is used

$$C_i(t+1) = C_i(t) + R - C_i(t) \quad (1 - e^{-k_3(y_i-b_{np})}), \tag{2.5.6}$$

where $k_2 > 0$, $k_3 > 0$.

2.6. A MODEL OF AN OPERATIVE DISTRIBUTION OF THE COMPUTING RESOURCES OF A COMPUTER NETWORK AND HOMOGENEOUS AUTOMATA GAMES

The functioning process of the above model of a computer network can be interpreted in the language of game theory, in particular in the language of the theory of games with limited interactions [10]. Let us observe the basic moments of consistence between the functioning process of a ring computer network and the class of games with limited interaction - homogeneous games of stochastic automata on a circle. Note that the profit d_i obtained by the i-th system depends on a limited number of variables: on its own price C_i and on prices C_{i-1}, C_{i+1} of its neighbors. The function determining the profit of the i-th system does not at all depend on the number N of systems of the network and is actually given by one functional relationship for all systems.

When considering the behavior of a collective of queueing systems we can expect that the profit obtained by this collective will be determined by the equilibrium situations existing in the game.

It is known [10] that in homogeneous games, in the case of existence of an equilibrium situation, the players achieve the equilibrium points according to Nash. In particular, if the Nash equilibrium points correspond to maximal price, then the players are playing a Moore game - a game when a collective of players achieves the possible maximal value of the game. There exist, however, examples of games when the games of maximal price are not stable games according to Nash. In such games the prize of the players' collective is much smaller than the price of maximal price games.

It is shown in [12] that the introduction of a conjugate exchange process into homogeneous games transforms the maximal price games into stable games according to Nash and, thus, ensures the achievements of the maximal prize in the game by the players' collective. Under the conditions of the functioning of the above presented model of a computer network the accomplishment of the conjugate exchange process takes place through organization of the interaction of the network systems. This guarantees that the systems collective achieves maximal profit (resource R) and thus guarantees the fulfilment of the assumed criterion of optimal (equation 2.4.4) functioning of a computer network.

2.7. EXPERIMENTAL TESTING OF THE MODEL

The presented model of an operative distribution of computing resources of the computer network was tested on a computer by a simulation model. The investigated network consisted of $N = 8$ nodes. It was assumed that the input transaction streams are Poisson streams and that the queueing systems are characterized by an exponential distribution of the length of service time intervals with parameter $\mu = 1$. A service regulation of the "first in - first out" type was used. The network users were defined by the following profit functions:

$$\left.\begin{aligned}
\Psi_1(\lambda_1) &= 6.66(-2\lambda_1^2 + 9\lambda_1 - 7);\\
\Psi_2(\lambda_2) &= 4.13\sqrt{-\lambda_2^2 + 10\lambda_2};\\
\Psi_3(\lambda_3) &= 9.04(1 - 2e^{-\lambda 3});\\
\Psi_4(\lambda_4) &= 8.72\sqrt{e(1- e^{-2\lambda_4})};\\
\Psi_5(\lambda_5) &= 12.72 \sin(\pi/3\lambda_5);\\
\Psi_6(\lambda_6) &= 5.49 \ln(1 + \lambda_6) + 4.38\sqrt{\lambda_6};\\
\Psi_7(\lambda_7) &= 6.66(-13\lambda_7^2 + 40\lambda_7 + 27);\\
\Psi_8(\lambda_8) &= 8.02 \ln(-\lambda_8^2 + 5\lambda_8 + 1);
\end{aligned}\right\} \quad (2.7.1)$$

For the above system of user profit functions and deterministic parameters of the model, the maximal value of the target function (2.4.4) is obtained for the stream vector of the processed user transactions $\lambda^* = (\lambda^*_1 = 2.00, \lambda^*_2 = 0.75, \lambda^*_3 = 1.00, \lambda^*_4 = 0.50, \lambda^*_5 = 1.00, \lambda^*_6 = 0.50, \lambda^*_7 = 1.50, \lambda^*_8 = 0.75)$. Here the value of the target function amounts to 98.78. In comparison we can remind that the value of the total user profit when their own computers are independently employed and with deterministic parameters amounts to 60.5.

Below we present the results of the experimental model testing. These results were obtained with the following coefficient values: $k_o = 0.1$; $k_1 = 0.05$; $k_2 = 2.00$; $k_3 = 0.125$. The coefficient values were determined experimentally and chosen from the point of view of maximalization of the network customers' total profit. The results obtained during the testing of a model with a decentralized behavior of service systems were compared with the results of a test performed on the same model with central control of the work of the queueing systems.

We shall start the review of test results from the consideration of Fig. 2.3 representing the dependence between the mean value of total customers' profit and the number of distributions (iteration number) of resource R. Two values of the total customers' profit were distinguished: the value of total customers' profit when their computers were used independently and the maximal possible total customers profit when they used the computer network. The two values of total customers' profit correspond to the situation when the model parameters: the input transaction stream and time of transaction service are deterministic values. Fig. 2.3 shows that when the number of distributions of resource R increases, the network control, based on a decentralized behavior of the queueing systems, accomplishes such a distribution of the network computing resources among the customers which is nearly optimal. The total

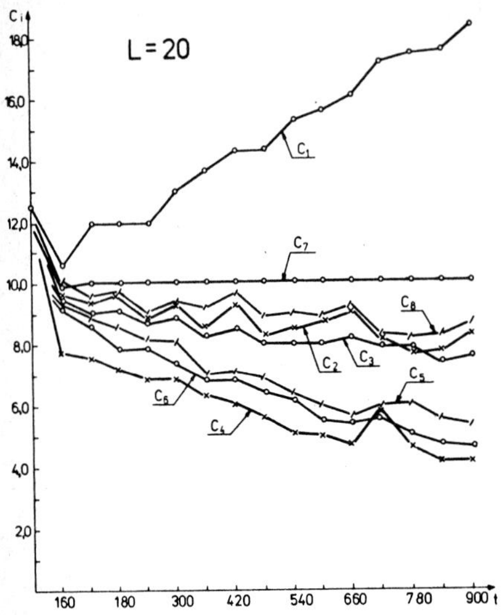

Fig.2.6 The mean value of service price during the time interval Δt

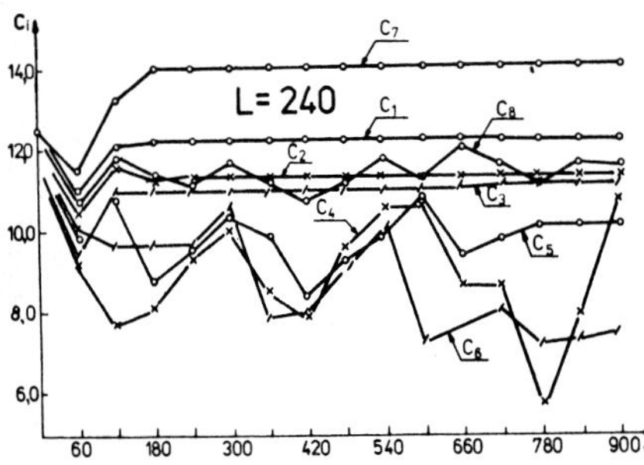

Fig.2.7 The mean value of service price during the time interval Δt

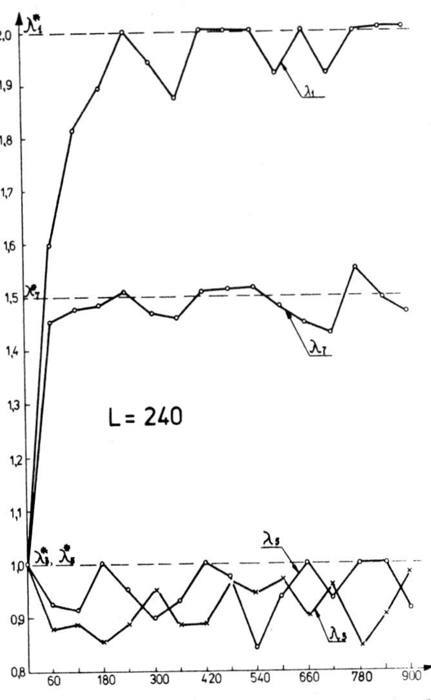

Fig.2.8 The mean value of the serviced transaction stream during the time interval Δt

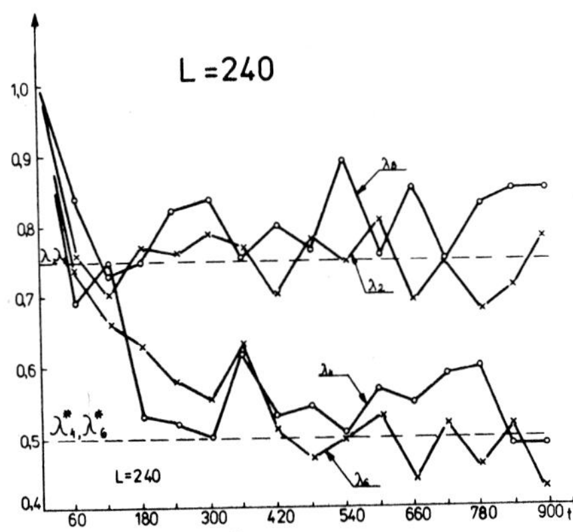

Fig.2.9 The mean value of the serviced transaction stream during the time interval Δt

customers' profit value, which is a measure of the effectivity of the network computing resource distribution, depends on the storage capacity of the queueing system buffers. This dependence, however, is significant only for a small buffer storage capacities (Fig.2.4) and, starting from $L \approx 20$, the value of total customers' profit does not, in fact, depend on buffer capacity.

In Fig. 2.4 we compared the mean values of total customers' profit with a decentralized and centralized network control. The value of total customers' profit in conditions of centralized control determines the upper limit of the effectivity of network functioning under the assumptions about the stochastic character of model parameters. As we can observe (Fig. 2.4), a decentralized network control ensures high effectivity of network computing resources distribution, only slightly giving way to the effectivity of network computing resources distribution accomplished through centralized control.

Fig. 2.5 shows the curves of the mean value of the input transactions stream and of the mean value of the transactions stream accepted for service by the network, dependent on the buffer capacity of the service systems. As we can see, under a steady-state regime of network functioning, the mean transaction stream accepted for service reaches the value equal to the mean throughput of the network for buffer capacity as small as $L \approx 20$. At the same time, the mean input transaction stream is sufficiently large and relatively decreases while the capacity of service systems increases, finally achieving a constant level.

The service prices established during the network functioning process form a price gradient allowing the transactions to flow through the network and relieving the increasing load. When the buffer capacity of service systems is small the price changes possess (Fig. 2.6) sufficiently great dynamics. However, together with the increase of buffer capacity, the dynamics of price changes decreases in time (Fig. 2.7). When the buffer capacity attains sufficient size, the prices stabilize themselves and, moreover, the price gradient remains unchanged.

Figs. 2.8 - 2.9 illustrate the dependence of mean values of network customers' transaction streams undergoing service in the time interval t for $L = 240$. The presented dependence illustrates the fact that network control sufficiently quickly accomplishes such a distribution of network computing resources among the customers, which is near to the optimal distribution.

The results of experimental studies of the model confirmed the accepted idea. They offer a possibility of applying this model to the actual task of operative control of computing resource division of a computer network.

3. THE METHOD OF HYBRID SWITCHING IN A NODE OF A DATA TRANSMISSION NETWORK

The main factor influencing the work effects of a distributed data base is its data transmission network. Below we consider one of the most important problems in the optimalization of work of a data transmission network (DTN) - the choice of switching methods in the network nodes.

In the already working or constructed various data transmission networks different switching methods are used, such as circuit switching (CS), message switching (MS), virtual circuit-packet switching (VCPS), packet-datagram switching (DGPS) as well as leased circuits (LS). A feature characteristic of data transmission network is the accomplishment of connections and information exchange between terminals varying with respect to transmission rate, work mode, codes, formats and service repertoire, from the conversational access mode to transmission of large amounts of data. During the network utilization and as a result of research, it was found that every one of the switching methods has its disadvantages and merits and is therefore more convenient for some applications than others. Research on the properties of data switching methods conducted in many scientific centres showed that there exist preference application regions of each data switching method [2, 3, 4, 5, 6, 7 and others]. The preference regions are obtained in many research centres for the set of different network parameters.
Research indicating the existence of preference regions of applying each switching method led to the construction of networks employing hybrid method (the application, according to a definite procedure, of two or more data switching methods with the use of the same exchange and common circuits).

Initially, the hybrid character of the switching method made the connection of terminals with different technical characteristic possible. A typical example is the Japanese experimental network DDX-1 [3], where the customer terminals are connected by circuit switching when they have compatible technical parameters, and by packet switching when a change of code, speed or format is demanded or for specific applications. According to the a priori analytically determined preference regions of applying switching methods, a division of subscriber stations and services was introduced.

Such hybrid methods did not, however, totally remove the non-adjustment of the network to the variable load and requirements of customers. The main reason for this was not taking into account the variable characteristic of traffic streams, conditions in the network and requirements of communication administration and customers. The problem discussed in this paper is making the work of the data transmission network node more flexible by adaptative adjustment of the data switching method.

3.1. ASSUMPTIONS

In our consideration we limited ourselves to the data switching system of the exchange, assuming that in the data transmission network its configuration and data stream size for internodal relations are known (determined) as well as the systems of data stream control, connection path choice, signalling, concentration and multiplexation. We also assumed that the switching exchange makes the accomplishment of simplex connections and of more than one data switching method possible.

A data transmission network can be treated as a technical device used to create connections between terminals. At a given moment we can distinguish in the network connections which exist, are being accomplished, or disconnected. Assuming that the network is synchronic, the created connections can be compared to the hypothetical reference connection normalized in the recommendation X. 92 CCITT

[1]. The recommendation concerns service with circuit, packet and leased circuit switching, but its structure can be applied to other DSM. We additionally assumed that we consider simplex connections. A duplex connection can be obtained using two simplex connections.

Under the above assumptions the analyzed object was reduced to a segment of a simplex communication channel. The composition of such segment makes the creation of a reference connection possible. Besides the segment diagram, Fig. 3.1 also shows the influence of the remaining connections and disturbances on the transmission process.

3.2. AN ABSTRACT NODE MODEL

In order to start the research of the node work optimalization it was necessary to introduce evaluation criteria and functioning indicators.

To do this we expressed the abstract node model (I_W) as an ordered 8-tuple consisting of: the parameter weight vector ($\underline{P}$), the parameter characteristic functions vector ($\underline{Q}$), the external variable vector ($\underline{Z}$), the set of state dynamics ($\overline{X}$), the set of output states ($\overline{Y}$), the set of quality indicators (W), the set of operating functions (F) and the set of constraints (O) on the remaining elements of model (I_W). In a model of type:

$$I_W = (P,Q,Z,X,Y,W,F,O);$$

$Z = \underline{Z}^t = (z_1^t,\dots,z_{IZ}^t)$ the vector of the characteristics of the data stream incoming to the node at the moment t, e.g. traffic intensity, connection duration length, length of data blocks, inter-transaction time and others, IZ - the number of external variables;

Y - the set of characteristics of the output stream,

$P = \underline{P} = (p_1,\dots,p_M)$ - the vector of weights of node work quality evaluation parameters. The parameters of node work quality evaluation may, for example, include utilization of the circuit, channel, transmission devices, the delays connected with switching, storage connection losses, transmission reliability, adequate time and others. The weight of node evaluation parameters determines the degree to which it influences the work of that node.

$Q = \underline{Q} = (q_1,\dots,q_M)$ - a vector describing the variation of node work quality as a function of the variation of the characteristics of the incoming data streat, M - the number of parameters

W - the set of synthetic indicators evaluating node work quality for each switching method,

$F = \left\{SM_1,\dots,SM_m,\dots,SM_K\right\}$- the set of data switching methods possible to accomplish in the node, K - set magnitude,

O - the set of constraints on the remaining elements of the model caused by the surroundings of the technical structure of the node.

In the model we have the following relations:

$$\underline{Q} = \underline{Q}(\underline{Z}^t) = (q_1(\underline{z}_1^t),\dots,q_M(\underline{z}_M^t)),$$

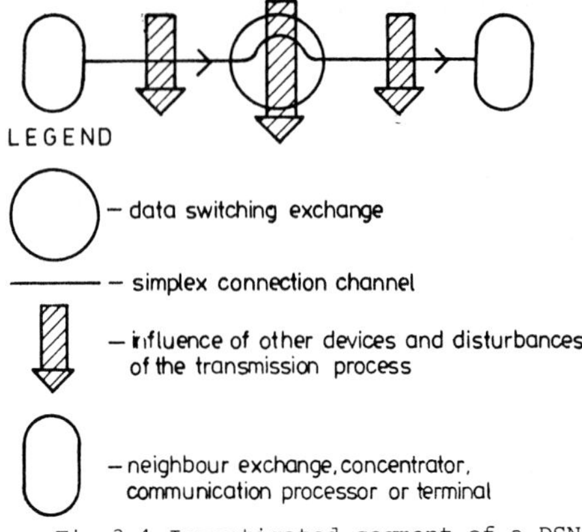

Fig.3.1 Investigated segment of a DSN simplex connection channel

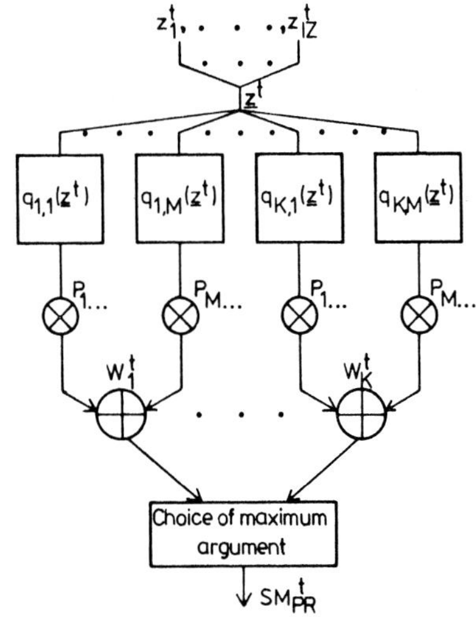

Fig.3.2 Choice of preferred data switching method

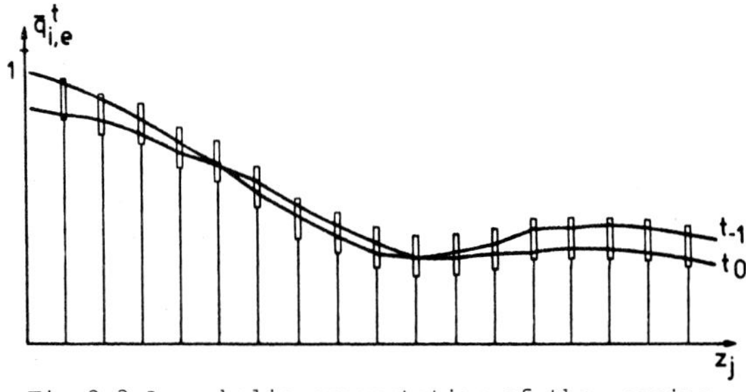

Fig.3.3 A symbolic presentation of the meaning of introducing a fuzzy function $\bar{q}_e^t$

$$W = \left\{ W_m : W_m \longrightarrow SM_m \right\},$$
$$Q = \left\{ \underline{Q} : Q \longrightarrow SM_m \right\}.$$

The choice of external variables and parameters depends on the specific features of the network and on its administration. With the help of this abstract model synthetic indicators from the set W were determined, serving to measure the quality of data exchange functioning for individual accessible switching methods from the set F. The synthetic quality indicators take the form of a scalar product of vectors $\underline{P}$ and $\underline{Q}_m^t$, where the weight vector P is identical for each switching method and the characteristic function vector is different:

$$W_m^t = \langle \underline{P}, \underline{Q}_m^t \rangle = \sum_{i=1}^{M} p_i \cdot q_{m,i}(\underline{Z}^t) .$$

Every synthetic quality indicator takes into account the requirements of customers and administration with the help of technical and utility parameters. These parameters depend on external variables describing the characteristics of traffic streams at a given moment of time t. The influence of these variables for a given switching method is represented by characteristic functions of every parameter. These functions can be determined by analysis, simulation or during the work of the exchange.

3.3. DETERMINATION OF A PREFERRED DATA SWITCHING METHOD

Now we will present a procedure determining the preference domains and the preferred available data switching method.

For lack of space we do not present the analysis and proofs concerning the existence and choice of the domains preferred for application of each DSM. We will limit ourselves to the results of research described in [1].

1) In the first step we determined the external variables describing the data stream arriving at the node at the time moment t.

2) Next we determine the characteristic functions of the considered parameters for every data switching method. Estimate parameters are also considered.

3) The norming of the characteristic functions with the help of external values from the set of constraints

$$q_{m,i}^t \in Q; \quad ||q_{m,i}^t|| = \frac{q_{m,i}^t}{\sup_Z (q_{m,i})} . \qquad (3.1)$$

4) Determination of parameter weights $p_i \in P$; $p_i \in R_o^1$.

5) Determination of node work quality indicators for every data switching method according to formula (3.1).

Determination of these values helps, as we have shown in [1], to define the preference regions of application of each switching method as the ranges of external variables, where the indicator of a given switching method has a value greater than the others.

6) Determination of a switching method preferred at a given moment. If by SM we denote the switching method and by PR - the preferred one, then

$$SM^{t}_{PR} = \arg\max_{m} \langle \underline{P}, \underline{Q}^{t}_{m} \rangle .$$

A diagram of the procedure is presented on Fig. 3.2.

3.4. DETERMINING THE CHARACTERISTIC FUNCTIONS OF ESTIMATE PARAMETERS

In the sequel we shall consider a way to determine characteristic functions of estimate parameters, which include, for example: conservation and construction facility, flexibility and modularity, easy of cooperation with a computer, service offered to the customers, code-format transparency, general access to subscribers and system utilization ease.

An adequate apparatus for a precise, mathematical description of the group of estimate parameters is provided by the fuzzy set theory. This theory, founded on the works of Łukasiewicz on multivalued logic and formulated by Zadeh is applied in many fields of knowledge. It serves as a tool in the analysis of problems which are hard to define or problems defined only partly.

While trying to determine the variability of characteristic functions $q_i(\underline{z})$ we can find ourselves in three of the following decision situations:

a) full fuzziness or lack of information about the dependence $q_i(\underline{z})$ for a given i-th parameter; this makes impossible considering it in the model,

b) lack of fuzziness or full information about the dependence $q_i(\underline{z})$; this is the case when parameters are easy to determine by analysis or simulation,

c) partial information about the dependence $q_i(\underline{z})$, defined as fuzzy, is the most typical situation in real systems; here it is related to the group of estimate parameters.

Following Zadeh we adopt the definitions concerning the fuzzy set theory and some of the notation. Let P be the space of interest and R - a finite subset of space P.

$$p_i \in P; \quad i \in N_1^n ;$$

$$R = \left\{ p_1, p_2, \ldots, p_n \right\}.$$

Definition 3.1 [14]

A finite fuzzy subset defined on the space P has the form:

$$E = \left\{ (\mu_1\ p_1), \ldots, (\mu_n\ p_n) \right\},$$

where $(\forall i \in N_1^n)(\mu_i \in R_0^1)$.

In the first expression μ_i denotes the degree in which p_i belongs to the set E, where 0 denotes not belonging and 1 - full belonging. Values from the interval (0,1) denote partial belonging.

More generally, a fuzzy subset E of set P can be expressed in the form

$$E = \int_P \mu_E(p)/p \ ,$$

where $\mu_E : P \longrightarrow [0,1]$ is the membership function and $\mu_E(p)/p$ is the so-called fuzzy singleton.

Let us now turn to the problem of determining characteristic functions of estimate parameters employing fuzzy set theory.

Let us define the considered set $Z = \left\{ z_1^t, \ldots, z_{IZ}^t \right\}$, where "t" denotes that moment of time, when, according to our assumption, the values of external variables take on a determinate character. We shall call $\bar{q}_e{}^t$ of the form:

$$\bar{q}_e{}^t = \left\{ (b_1\ z_1^t),\ (b_2\ z_2^t)\ , \ldots,\ (b_{IZ}\ z_{IZ}^t) \right\};$$

a fuzzy subset of set Z, where b_i, $i \in N_1^{IZ}$, are the membership functions of element z_i^t to the fuzzy subset, conforming to the definition 2.5; $b_i \in R_0^1$ and the fuzzy subset $\bar{q}_e{}^t$ can be expressed in the form:

$$\bar{q}_{m,e}^{\ t} = \int_Z b_m(z^t)/z^t .$$

For every $DSM \in SM_M$ from set F' a fuzzy subset Z of external variables is defined; this is marked by an index. The lower index "e" means that we are considering one of the estimate parameters.

Initially we assume that we are considering the membership function "b_j" for one external variable "z_j^t", the values of the remaining variables remaining fixed. Similarly, we can consider membership functions for all elements of the space of interest Z such that information can be obtained about the characteristic function variability of a given estimate parameter as a function of system external variables. Now we shall define a function described on the membership functions of the elements of fuzzy set $\bar{q}_{m,e}^{\ t}$. The arithmetic average of the membership function we shall express by:

$$f(\bar{q}_e{}^t) = \frac{1}{IZ} \sum_{i=1}^{IZ} b_i \ .$$

Hence we have the relation $f:(R)^{IZ} \longrightarrow R_0^1$. The value of the algebraic average of the membership functions we shall express by $f(\bar{q}_{m,e}^{\ t}) = q_{m,e}^t$.

The above relation presents a constructive way of obtaining the characteristic function values, since it is a form of linear approximation. When we want to take into account estimate parameters, the linguistic approach to fuzzy sets proves useful. This approach is closer to the intuitive notion of fuzziness. In comparison to the algebraic approach, it makes more distinct the extension of possibilities of considering uncertainties obtained by probabilistic methods. We shall define the linguistic variable according to Zadeh:

Definition 3.2

A linguistic variable B is a variable whose values are words or sentences in a natural or artificial language. The variable can assume linguistic values from the set of expressions T(B), where each of the terms in T(B) is a label of a fuzzy subset $q_{m,e}$ of the universe of discourse Z.

A linguistic variable is associated with two rules:

a) a syntactic rule, which defines the well-formed sentences in T(B), and b) a semantic rule, by which the meaning of the terms in T(B) may be determined.

We consider the primary terms big, average, small, whose meaning might be defined by their respective compatibility functions b_{big}, b_{qverage}, and b_{small}. For these, the meaning or, equivalently, the compatibility functions of non primary terms may be computed by the application of a semantic rule. For example: if

$$T(B) = \underline{\text{big}} + \underline{\text{average}} + \underline{\text{small}} + \underline{\text{not big}} + \underline{\text{more or less average}} + \underline{\text{very small}} + \underline{\text{rather big}} + \ldots$$

then, following Zadeh:

$$b_{\underline{\text{very big}}} = (b_{\underline{\text{big}}})^2 ,$$

$$b_{\underline{\text{more or less average}}} = (b_{\underline{\text{average}}})^{1/2} ,$$

$$b_{\underline{\text{not very big}}} = 1 - (b_{\underline{\text{big}}})^2 \qquad \text{etc.}$$

If functions $q_j(z_i)$ have a variable character (a part can have a constant value or have no semantic meaning) then, following Zadeh, we can employ approximation functions. These functions can take the form:

for a decreasing dependence

$$s(v, \alpha, \beta, \gamma) = \begin{cases} 0 , & v < \alpha \\ 2\left(\frac{v-\alpha}{\gamma-\alpha}\right)^2 , & \alpha \leqslant v \leqslant \beta \\ 1 - 2\left(\frac{v-\gamma}{\gamma-\alpha}\right)^2 , & \beta \leqslant v \leqslant \gamma \\ 1 , & v > \gamma \end{cases} ;$$

for an increasing-decreasing dependence

$$\pi(v,\beta,\gamma) = \begin{cases} s(v,\gamma-\beta,\gamma-\frac{\beta}{2},\gamma), & v<\gamma \\ 1 - s(v,\gamma,\gamma+\frac{\beta}{2},\gamma+\beta), & v>\gamma \end{cases} ;$$

for an increasing dependence $s' = 1 - s(v,\alpha,\beta,\gamma)$, where $\beta = (\alpha+\gamma)/2$ is the graph inflexion point.

The function shapes are presented in Fig. 3.5.

Thus, we can define the set of expressions as follows:

$$T(B) = \underline{small} + (\underline{small})^2 + (\underline{small})^{1/2} + \underline{average} + (\underline{average})^2 + \\ + (\underline{average})^{1/2} + \underline{big} + (\underline{big})^2 + (\underline{big})^{1/2},$$

where the respective functions can be expressed in the following way:

$$b_{\underline{big}} = s(v,\alpha,\beta,\gamma);$$

$$b_{\underline{average}} = \pi(v,\beta,\gamma);$$

$$b_{\underline{small}} = s'(v,\alpha,\beta,\gamma) = 1 - s(v,\alpha,\beta,\gamma).$$

Such a set of approximation functions appears sufficient, but, nevertheless, it may be extended. Employing the linguistic approach to fuzzy set theory, we obtain the required characteristic functions of estimate parameters in the form

$$(\forall m \in N_1^K)(q_{m,e}(z^t) = f(\int_Z b_m(z^t)/z^t) = \frac{1}{IZ}\sum_{i=1}^{IZ} b_i); \; IZ \in N_0^{IZ} ,$$

where IZ' denotes the number of considered variables of the DSN. A graphic illustration of the meaning of fuzziness is presented in Fig. 3.3, where the size of the opening can be interpreted as the interval containing the real function value.

It is worth observing that according to the presented approach the form of DSN quality indicators remains unchanged, and the preferred DSM can be expressed by the formula

$$SM_{PR}^t = \arg\max_m \sum_{i=1}^{M} p_i \quad q_{m,i}(\underline{Z}^t)$$

only the method of determining the elements of the vector $\underline{Q}_m(\underline{z}^t)$ undergoes change.

The presented application of fuzzy set theory to the treatment of estimate parameters is, as we have seen, an effective, although rather arbitrary, method of considering such parameters. It appears that for many subjective parameters it will be sufficient to consider only two or three variables, since the obtained dependencies possess an informal character and the variables are intercorrelated.

3.5. DESCRIPTION OF SIMULATION STUDIES

In order to analyse and verify the results, simulation testing was conducted for a model of an isolated segment of a simplex connection containing those parts of the switching exchange which served that connection as well as two channels. The influence of other connections in the network and transmission distortions was also taken into account.

With the help of this model we investigated the proposed hybrid method utilizing circuit switching (CS), message switching (MS) and virtual circuit-packet switching (VCPS). To ensure the comparability of results identical external conditions were maintained for all runs.

During the simulation the external variables describing the traffic stream undergoing switching were assumed and then the characteristic function changes of model parameters were investigated. This made obtaining the preferred DSM possible after the weights of individual parameters were considered according to Fig. 3.2.

In the simulation experiments the external variables were: the mean information length (z_1) in a semirandom Poisson traffic stream, the number of data in a connection (z_2) and the activeness of a traffic stream in a channel (z_3). In the investigations six parameters were considered: channel utilization, answer time, effective transmission speed, flexibility of cooperation with a computer and ease of system utilization. The two last parameters have an estimate character.

Weight coefficient were arbitrarily assigned to the above parameters. The division of importance measure of the hardware group, (i.e. a group important for the network administration) with respect to the service group (i.e. important for the users) was assumed as 0.25 : 0.75. The individual parameters were given weights listed in table 4.2.

The accepted values were based on known results of research concerning the influence of individual parameters on DTN functioning.

Table 4.2. The weights of parameters of model functioning quality

Denotation	Hardware	Weights	Denotation	Service	Weights
P_1	Storage units utilization	0.06	P_4	Answer time	0.19
P_2	Channel utilization	0.13	P_5	Effective transmission time	0.50
P_3	Flexibility of cooperation with computer	0,06	P_6	Ease of system utilization	0.06
$\sum$		0.25			0.75

The experiment was conducted in two stages. In the first, characteristic functions of the considered parameters were determined and preference regions of applying individual data switching methods were applied. In the second, the hybrid switching method was tested with respect to the external variables estimation method.

Hybrid switching methods achieved according to three different rules were compared: rigid preference regions, changing preference regions determined for external variables average with respect to time and chosen switching method preferred for every information.

The determination of characteristic functions of estimate parameters is emphasized; it is an exemplary accomplishment of the outlined above application of the linguistic approach to the fuzzy set theory.

Thus, a simulation model of a connection segment (Fig. 3.1) contained a model of a fragment of the hypothetical switching exchange where the switching took place. A flow diagram of a data exchange making the accomplishment of, among others, HDSM possible, is presented in Fig. 3.4. It was assumed that this exchange enables us to accomplish the investigated DSM's and simplex connection switching.

Detailed data concerning the simulation testing are presented below.

Transmission speed in channels C_1, C_2 : v = 4800 bits/sec,

Storage units capacity: LB_1, LB_2 - 3 pieces of information or packets each BLS_1 and$_2$ - 20000 bits,

Information processing in CU and SK: up to 7 pieces of information or packets simultaneously,

Connection time for CS and VCPS: 400 ms ,

Delay related to processing in LB 1 and $_2$: 300 ms ,

Delay related to processing in CU: $d_1/30$ ms ,

Processing in LP with a go-through connection: 20 ms ,

Packet size for VCPS: 1000 bits,

Message or packet header size: 80 bits,

Mean information length: $z_1 \in (700, 8000)$ bits,

Number of data in a connection: z_2 = 10000 bits or 25000 bits,

Traffic stream effectiveness in a channel: $z_3 \in (0.4, 0.7)$,

Error rate dependent on information length z_1 detected in the protection system: $1 \cdot 4 \cdot 10^{-4} - 1 \cdot 4 \cdot 10^{-5}$,

Effective transmission speed of exogenic traffic: 720 bits/sec.

The choice of channel transmission speed v_1 = 4800 bits/sec and error rate of order 10^{-5} correspond to the average technical parameters of the data transmission channel accomplished with the help of isolated telephone circuits. The chosen transmission speed was taken into account. The variability range of z_3 is a result of the assumed concern about normal, not overloaded functioning of the system.

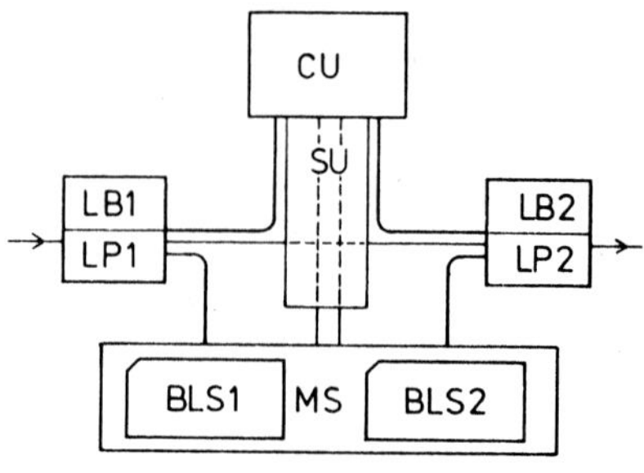

Fig.3.4 Scheme of hipothetical data switching exchange

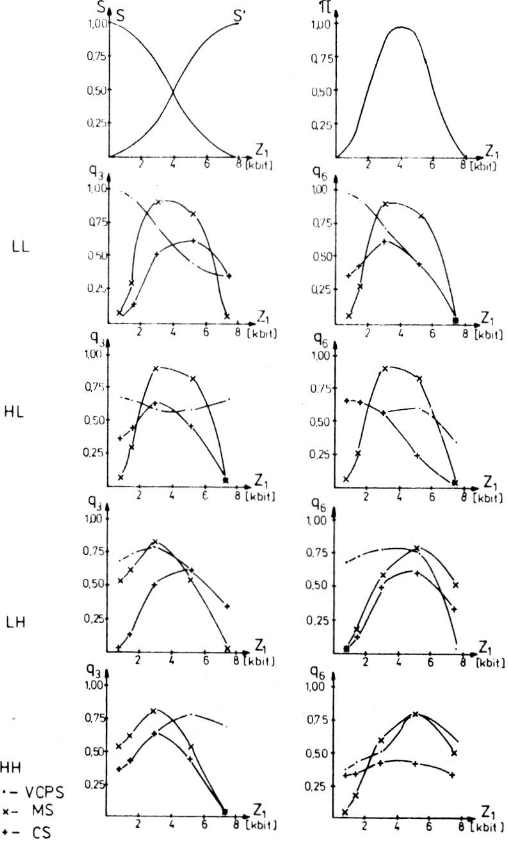

Fig.3.5 Graphs of characteristic functions of parameters P_3 (flexibility of cooperation with computer) and P_6 (ease of system utilisation)

Characteristic functions of measurable parameters were directly determined in the simulation process. As function shape we assumed the mean values of results obtained from different pseudorandom number generators employed to generate Poisson data streams incoming to the exchange. Individual characteristic functions were normalized according to the following expressions:

q_1 - storage units utilization (utilization of memory BLS $_1$ and $_2$)

$$\|q_1\| = 1 - q_1 ,$$

q_2 - channel utilization (utilization of channel C_1)

$$\|q_2\| = q_2 ,$$

q_4 - answer time

$$\|q_4\| = \frac{q_4 - d_1/4800}{20} \text{ bit/sec} ,$$

q_5 - effective transmission time

$$\| q_5 \| = \frac{q_5}{4800 - 720} \quad \frac{\text{bit/sec}}{\text{bit/sec}} .$$

Characteristic functions of estimate parameters are determined for the case of fuzziness with the application of linguistic variables and Zadeh approximation functions. The linguistic expressions assumed basing on the available publications, approximate the characteristic functions of estimate parameters. The linguistic variables of individual estimate parameters dependent on a given external variable are presented in Table 4.3.

Table 4.3. Linguistic variables approximating the characteristic functions of estimate parameters

DSM / Parameter	Level	VCPS z_1	VCPS z_2	VCPS z_3	MS z_1	MS z_2	MS z_3	CS z_1	CS z_2	CS z_3
P_3 Flexibility of coopera-tion with computer	L	B	B	B	A	-	A	S	S	A
	H	S	S	A	A	-	B	B	B	A
P_6 Ease of system utilization	L	B	B	B	A	-	A	S	A	B
	H	A	S	A	A	-	S	B	B	S

z_1 - mean information length; z_2 - number of data in a connection; z_3 - traffic stream activeness

L - low; H - high; B - big (S); A - average; S - small (S′)

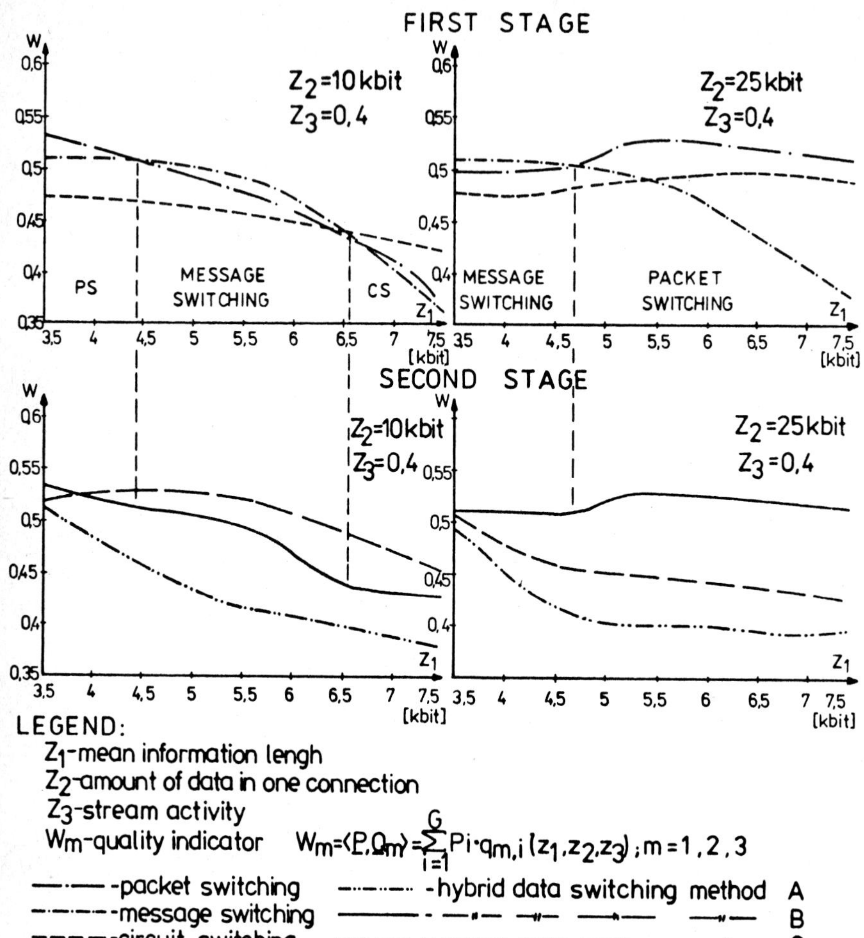

Fig.3.6 Results of simulation studies of a hybrid switching method

The legend explains the meaning of individual symbols and the division of external variables scope into high (H) and low (L) levels. The values of linguistic variables were presented in a graphic form with the use of functions S,π , S' (Fig. 3.5).

The results, chosen as examples are presented in the graphs of indicator value variation as a function of variable mean information length, other variables remaining fixed. Two upper graphs illustrate the first stage of simulation testing - the determining of preference regions of individual switching methods. The lower graphs present respective results of the second stage - a comparison of system quality indicators for the three rules of HDSM functioning: rigid preference regions (A), regions determined basing on an average with respect to values of external variables (B) and choice of a DSM preferred for each information (C) (Fig. 3.6).

The significant results of simulation testing include, among others: confirmation of work effectiveness of the suggested DSM (estimate parameters taken into account) and proof of the superiority of adaptative methods) (B) and (C), Fig. 3.6) over traditional non-adaptative methods.

4. CONCLUSIONS

In our paper we presented two problems related to the optimalization of computing resources utilization and transmission computer networks. During the analysis of both problems we gave attention to make the adaptation ability of the solutions and to the directing the network functioning towards the accomplishment of customers' requirements expressed employing synthetic quality indicators (taking the form of money or other conventional units).

In the model of operative distribution of the network computing resources, as a result of the interaction of the two model levels (customer level and network level) in the network functioning process the computing resources are distributed among its users. This is done conforming to the criterion of maximal total customer profit from the computing resources utilization. The computing resources possess an adaptation ability, i.e. they can be redistributed among the customers according to the variable in time functions of customer profit in order to fulfil the assumed optimalization criteria. The accepted organization of decentralized network control, based on the concept of collective automata behavior, permits great effectivity of computing resources distribution, whereas the control algorithms are relatively simple.

In the past concerning the hybrid switching method in the node of a data transmission network we applied the synthetic quality indicator, included in the abstract node model, to determine the preference regions of the utilization of each method. Estimate parameters were considered basing on the fuzzy set theory. In the dynamic version of the hybrid method, preference region changes ensure an adaptative choice of a switching method optimal under given conditions. This makes better satisfaction of customer requirements and better resource utilization possible.

The conducted simulation studies are a stage of a complete system simulating the control of the distributed network resources' utilization. After this stage is accomplished, the application of the system to a real computer network is planned.

REFERENCES

[1] Baczko A., The Analysis of Hybrid Data Switching Method in the Node of a Public Data Network, Ph.D. Dissertation, Referaty Nr 66, Wydawnictwa Instytutu Telekomunikacji Politechniki Warszawskiej, Warsaw 1979 (in Polish).

[2] Bocker P., Data Traffic in Communication Networks. WTF, Geneva 6-8 Oct. 1975, p. 2.3.1.1-2.3.1.8.

[3] Hashida O., Kodaira K., Digital Data Switching Network Configurations. Review of the Electrical Communication Laboratories, vol. 24, No 1-2, 1976, p. 85-96.

[4] Jenny Ch.J., Kümmerle K., Distributed Processing within an Integrated Circuit/Packet - Switching Node. IEEE Transactions on Communications, vol. com-24 No 10 Oct. 1976, p. 1089-1100.

[5] Kümmerle, P.K., Rudin H., Jenny C., Zafiropulo P., Network Architecture for the Integration of Circuit and Packet Switching. ICCC, Toronto, 3-6 Aug. 1976, p. 505-514.

[6] Rosner R.D., Packet Switching and Circuit Switching: A Comparison. NTC, New Orleans 1975, p. 42-1-11.

[7] Séminaire de téléinformatique. Colloques IRIA, Rocquencourt, 6-10 Sept. 1976.

[8] Seredyński F., Some Problems of Decentralized Control of Computer Networks, Ph.D. Dissertation, Leningrad Electrotechnical Institute, Leningrad 1978 (in Russian).

[9] Tsetlin L., On the Behavior of Finite Automata in Random Media, Automation and Remote Control, 22, p. 1210-1219 (1961).

[10] Varshavskii V.I., The Collective Behavior of Automata, Moscow, "Nauka", 1973 (in Russian).

[11] Varshavskii V.I., Meleshina M.V., and Perekrest V.T., Use of Model of Collective Behavior in the Problem of Resources Allocation, Automation and Remote Control, 7, p. 1107-1114 (1968)

[12] Varshavskii V.I., Zabołotnyj A.M., Seredyński F., Homogeneous Games with Conjugate Exchange Process, Proceedings of Academy of Sciences USSR Technical Cybernetics, No 6, p. 132-134 (1977) (in Russian).

[13] Zadeh L.A., The Concept of a Linguistic Variable and its Application to Approximate Reasoning. American Elsevier Publishing Co., New York 1973.

[14] Zadeh L.A., A Fuzzy-Algorithmic Approach to the Definition of Complex or Imprecise Concepts. System Theory in the Social Sciences, Birkhäuser 1976, p. 202-282.

DISTRIBUTED DATA BASES
C. Delobel and W. Litwin (eds.)
North-Holland Publishing Company

PROBLEMS OF DEVELOPING LARGE REGISTRATION SYSTEMS BASED ON DISTRIBUTED DATA BASE

Eszter KERTÉSZ - Judit POLGÁR

Data Management Department
SZÁMKI Research Institute for Applied Computer Sciences - Budapest
HUNGARY

The authors present a demonstration system based on distributed data base technics, which gives a starting basis for the computerization of concrete nation-wide large registration systems. First the major features of large registration systems are discussed, then a concrete solution of this type of systems is shown, which is based on distributed data base technics. The demonstration system uses the available homogenous hardware-software resources. The possibilities of the extension of the applied design method are analysed in an arbitrary hardware-software environment.Finally the paper mentions the technical problems, which raise using the existing hardware-software possibilities and keep back the development of general distributed data base systems.

INTRODUCTION

In the last few years the computer-aided solution of large registration systems is getting greater importance in Hungary, because several registration systems give the basis of information for the state administration. Though developing this kind of information systems, discovering and co-ordinating the relationships between the different registration systems and computerizing them have already traditions in our country, the recent results of computer technics, hardware and software possibilities available for managing large volume of data make the development and increase of efficiency of the mentioned computer-based information systems possible.

We present in our paper a demonstration system based on data base technics, that gives a starting basis for the design and implementation of nation-wide large registration systems. We have carried out this experiment at the Research Institute for Applied Computer Sciences - SZÁMKI in Budapest within the scope of a series of experiments on data base application during the last few years. In addition to the presentation of results we wish to call the attention to such questions, which arise during the implementation of a distributed data base system and the solution of these problems would be very advantageous for the general use of this technique.

THE CHARACTERISTICS OF LARGE NATION-WIDE REGISTRATION SYSTEMS

From the aspect of computer-based realization the most important characteristics of large registration systems helping the solution of the state administration's tasks are the following:

- It is necessary to built, store and maintain a large quantity of data. The order magnitude of data is a few thousand millions characters;
- Data are extremely wide spread according to their contents and there are relations among data at various levels of hierarchy;
- The same data or a portion of it should be made accessible and usable for several users classified on the basis of codes and analysed by several users;
- The places of origin of data are dispersed in the country. In the greater part of cases the regional processing of elementary data and passing of summarized data to country and county level is unsatisfactory, since the user requirements neede for organization, design and computer based realization of system in advance cannot always be determined;
- It is necessary to insure the possibility of so-called "ad hoc" enquireing with quick answer;
- Systems have specific demands on data security and control.

On the basis of characteristics listed above it can be said, that the volume of data as well as specific use of it demands hardware and software requirements of higher level than the traditional data processing tasks.

Developing of large registration system is a long process. Their owners are nation institutes, ministries and their systems are based on data referring to the entire population, the whole land, all the companies of the country. This type of data processing with traditional file management methods can use only batch mode by reason of predefined requirements, which is not suitable for users of the state management systems.

For the solution of large registration systems we have to pay attention to existing systems. The experiences gained with these systems make it possible to develop planning and methodical tools, which help to solve further registration systems in an efficient way. Besides existing systems the experiences of different experimental and demonstration systems are noteworthy.

THE POSSIBILITIES OF COMPUTERIZED SOLUTION

The appearance of different data base management systems made it possible the efficient manipulation, maintenance and questioning according to different point of view with quick answers of complicated structured data.

On the other hand the complication of above-mentioned systems necessitates sharing the data base systems in accordance with further functional, geographical position, etc. This recognition led to distributed systems and within it to distributed data base systems and analization of problems connected with them.

Studying the main features of large registration systems we can say, that these systems are shared according to processing logic, logical functions, data, data protection, security and control, namely they have exactly the same main characteristic as the distributed systems have.

In that case for developing computer-based solution of large registration systems the methodical reflection discovered at distributed systems can be adopted and managing of data in the system is converted into possible using distributed data base systems.

HARDWARE-SOFTWARE RESOURCES

Our experiments and research works were based on Honeywell-Bull 66/60 main computer and its terminals in time sharing and batch mode using IDS I. /Integrated Data Store/ and MDQS IV. /Management Data Query System/ software.

TASK OF DEMONSTRATION DATA BASE

The task was to develop a large registration system in which the primary data are manipulated by the offices in the counties. On the other hand these primary data are used and analysed by the registration systems in nation-wide institutions. The logical connection and hierarchical level of data in the system are shown on the conceptual schema in Figure 1.

There are connections between the primary and higher-level data and these have an affect in both directions, namely the usage of data registered in district level may be modified by changing of nation-wide data which are connected with - for example - alteration of administrative borders. On the other hand some kinds of changes in primary data have effect on data of nation-wide registration.

In the demonstration system case we can speak about common manipulation of different hierarchical levels data bases; two of them consist of nation-wide data and one data base is for storing primary data. The latter, logically unified, analitical data base is shared physically bearing in mind the quantity and geographical placing of data. Such a physical data base includes data of one county.

The connection of functional and physical data bases is shown in Figure 2. It is apparent that we have three different functional data bases, which means physically two nation-wide and 19 county-level data bases. At the determination of physical division the point of view was in addition to keeping the administrational units together that the size of one data base should not have more than one 100 Mbyte disc capacity.

THE METHOD APPLIED FOR THE DESIGN OF A DEMONSTRATION SYSTEM

There are two basic methods which are applicable for planning distributed data base: compositional and decompositional. These two kinds of methods at distributed data base correspond to two kinds of views, which are the same from the user's point of view, but in the course of developing the system it is necessary to have different procedures.

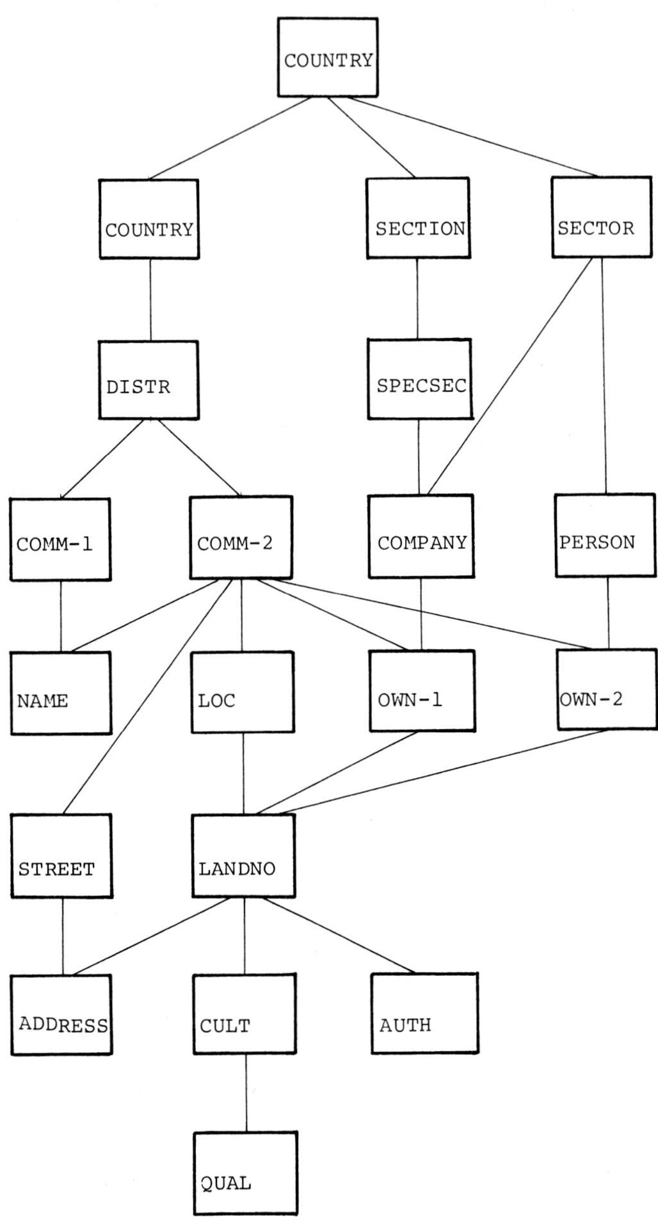

Figure 1: Conceptual schema

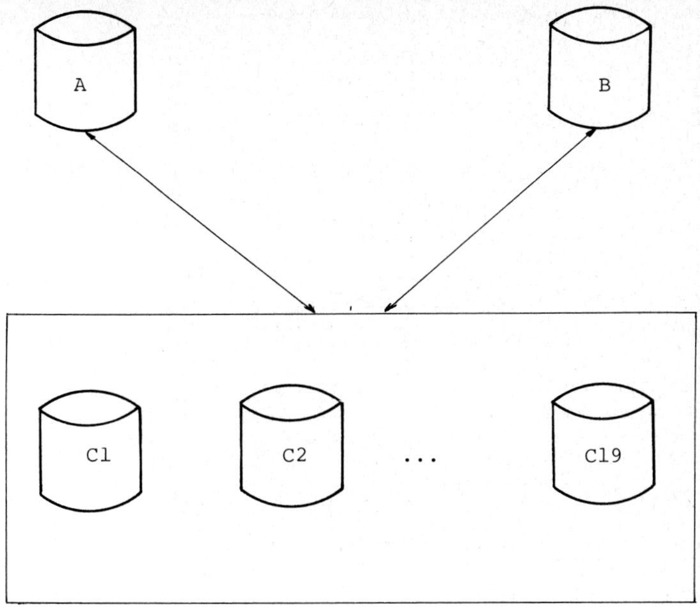

Figure 2: The connection of functional and physical data bases

We established our distributed data base with decompositional method, which means that first we defined all data and logical interrelations of data which are important in the system as well as we developed the conceptual schema of logical data base. Therefore the conceptual data base of the system is homogenous, only one data base, which is shared according to user-functions and modes, geographical position and storage capacity.

THE SOLUTION OF THE COMPUTER-BASED SYSTEM

In our demonstration system we established and manipulated the different types of data bases in a central computer. The data bases consist of IDS complex-structured files and for producing some tables and enquiries we used IS organisation file, too.

We do not make a digression on the detailed contents of the data bases, because that is only a concrete example of a complex problem. The same features and problems present themselves in case of similar kind of registration systems which can be noticed in this system.

All three data bases are network structured and their schema are shown in Figure 3.4.and 5. using IDS short-hand description mode.

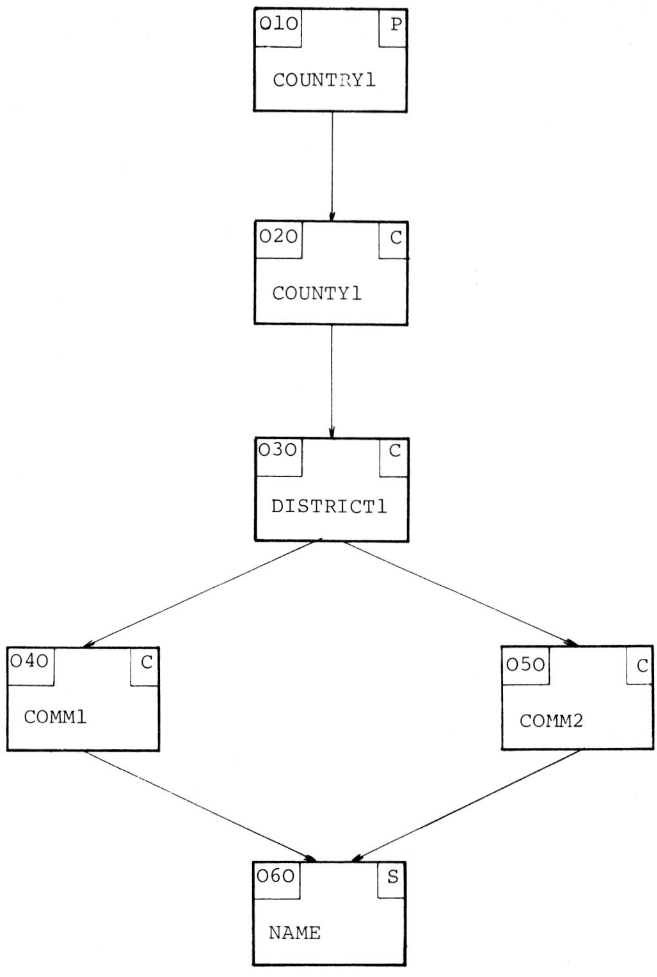

Figure 3: Structure of data base A

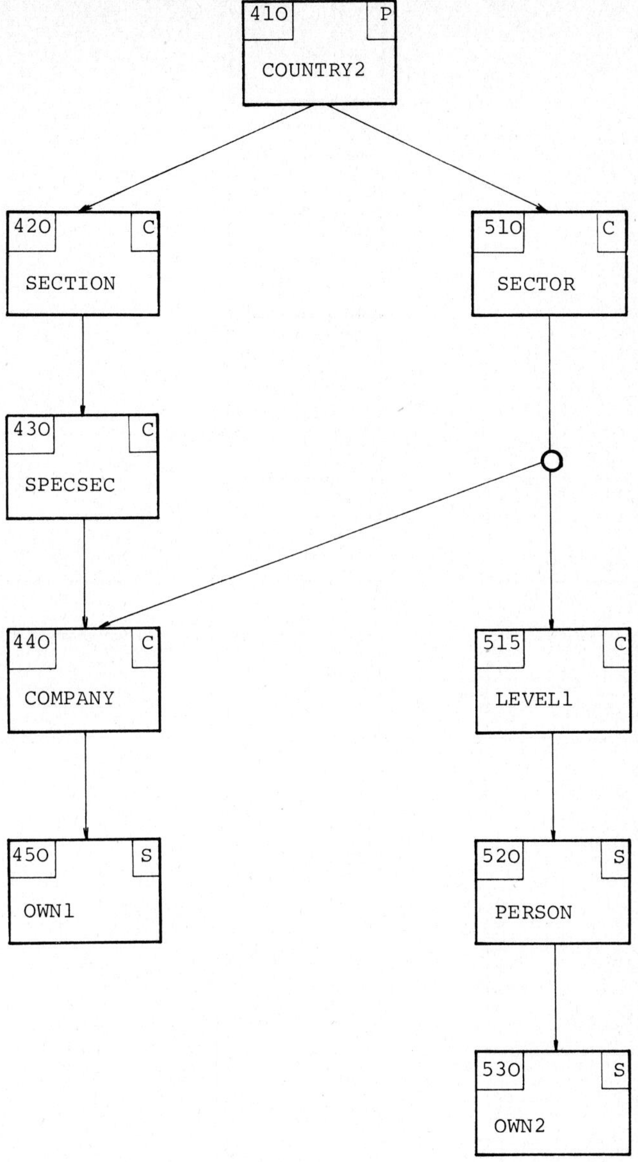

Figure 4: Structure of data base B

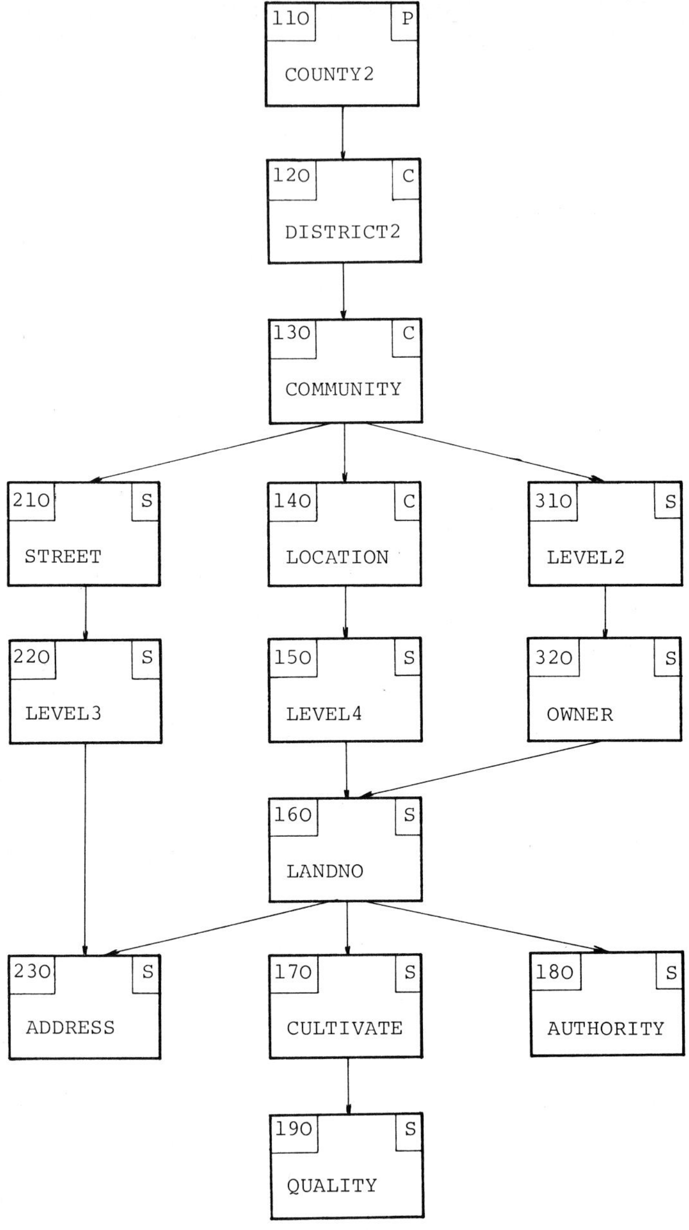

Figure 5: Structure of data base C

The volume of data stored in the demonstration data base was determined so, that the data should be easy to survey for analysing the experiment but they should demonstrate the problems related to the large amount of data as well. The following table shows the numbers of occurences within each type of record.

DB	Record					Total
	name	type	loc.[+]	length[++]	occurance	characters
	COUNTRY1	010	P	16	1	16
	COUNTY1	020	C	38	2	76
	DISTRICT1	030	C	49	5	245
	COMM1	040	C	23	14	322
	COMM2	050	C	22	14	308
	NAME	060	S	1477	14	20678
A						21645
	COUNTRY2	410	P	20	1	20
	SECTION	420	C	18	12	216
	SPECSEC	430	C	20	26	520
	COMPANY	440	C	168	143	24024
	OWN1	450	S	27	143	3861
	SECTOR	510	C	18	10	180
	PERSON	520	S	27	7562	204174
	OWN2	530	S	27	14387	388449
B						621444
	COUNTY2	110	P	38	2	76
	DISTRICT2	120	C	45	5	225
	COMMUNITY	130	C	57	14	798
	LOCATION	140	C	45	42	1890
	LANDNO	160	S	49	19527	956823
	CULTIVATE	170	S	28	28763	805364
	AUTHORITY	180	S	33	4134	136422
	QUALITY	190	S	25	31152	778800
	OWNER	320	S	31	14530	450430
	STREET	210	S	36	268	9648
	ADDRESS	230	S	14	9849	137886
C						3278362

\+ P=Primary, C=Calculated, S=Secundary

++ The lengths are specified in characters

The demonstration system functionally - in respect of the data base management - consists of three subsystems:

- Creation of data base, that performs the establishment and control of the physically separate and independent data bases;

- Data base maintenance, that performs the updating of data of data bases;
- Data retrieval, that contains the permanent tables generated from the data bases and the interrogations.

DATA BASE CREATIONS

Creation of distributed data bases can be performed in several ways depending on the fact, whether they are independent of each other or the content of a data base depends on another data base from a certain point of view.

Generally the creation of single independent data bases do not indicate a particularly new problem, because in this case the files can be established independently of each other. Here the analitical data bases C can be regarded as single data base files, for which input data were provided partly by the previous computer registration systems partly by new data located in the district offices, and the same loading algoritm should be used for every physically separate file. Creation of the nation-wide data bases meant a more complicated problem.

In the case of data base A the data concerned are developed jointly by two institutions with nation-wide competence and later they use them jointly, too, and contain statistical data from the regional data bases for the sake of providing efficient management information. So the creation of the data base occurs in two steps, first loading of administrative data forming the skeleton and identification system of data base can happen, then loading of statistical data is based on the first step after creations of single territorial data bases with inserting interworking data bases.

In the case of data base B the creation can be implemented also in two steps. First a reorganization of a previous independent registration file occurs into data base structure, then the loading of identifiers follows providing for the relationships between the data bases B and C.

DATA BASE MAINTENANCE

We can distinguish two categories at the maintenance of a distributed data base system from the point of view of data management. The first one is a simple case, when update of such data is performed, that appear only in one data base, or the update does not affect data of other data bases. In this case the problem is a conventional data base maintenance task together with the related questions. We do not wish to discuss it in our presentation, because here no new problem appears in the case of distributed data base system.

More exciting questions arise from the concurrent update of more data bases. Here the basic question is from the point of view of the users assuring the consistency among the data of the data bases, and from the technical side the conditions of this type of update are established by the interconnection or rather the interconnectibility of data bases.

Assurance of the consistency appears in two directions in the case of the demonstration system. The simpler case is when we study the question of how a change occuring in a higher level data base affect the analitical data base. Since in the nation-wide data bases data related to the state administration and other high administrational decisions can change that are planned in advance and they come into force from a given date, here the problem is only organizational, and this kind of update can be executed for example at night before it comes into force, when the on-line interrogations is not allowed anyway. This way it can be assured that in the moment of coming into force the data being interrelated with each other should be consistent in all the data bases.

In the other case when for example the update in the analitical data base calls for the change of the statistical data or changes occur in the identifiers assuring the relations, we face an essentially more complicated problem. This type of change is not foreseeable in advance. In this case it is only assurable that the modification of the secondary affected data base should occur immidiately after the modification and during the modification the data of the affected records should not be accessible.The data base management systems generally provide for this fact.

Under the circumstances of operational processing a procedural solution must be worked out for this case so, that the information retrievals from the different levels of data bases should not result in different data.

Another technical condition of the quasi-concurrent maintenance of more than one data base is the realization of the interconnection of data bases. The interconnection of data bases is the primary condition of providing for interrogation, but we deal with this question here in detail.

The content and relationships of the entire data base system are specified in the so-called conceptual schema, the physical locations and characterizations of each data bases are specified in the internal schemas. The specifications of data and relationships belonging to a given application, which concern different parts of the entire conceptual schema are contained in the external schemas. For the sake of an operating data base system proper connections must be established among the three level of schemas, and certain hight level data base management softwares provide for these connections automatically.

In our demonstration system we applied MDQS data management software for connecting the data bases. This general data management system is suitable for managing more than one IDS files and other traditional files concurrently. In the management system the role of the conceptual schema was performed functionally by the Data Definition specification of MDQS, and the internal schema corresponded essentially to the Data Directory. The appropriate Application Definition specifications contain the required information for the individual applications. It follows from the above-mentioned, that in this system the different levels of specifications assure at the same time, that it would be possible to access a certain part of the data base only under the control of the data base administrator. Every user can have access only to the data modifiable by him. If the connection of data bases can be solved in this way, the updating problem including more than one data base does not seem to be a particular problem.

DATA RETRIEVAL

Retrieval of data can also be divided into two categories from the point of users; producing permanent catalogues and tables defined in advance, and interrogations with requirement for immediate answer. In the latter case the answer can be retained, that is assuring hard-copy or interrogation can be requested onto a screen.

Requirements for large volumes of tables specified in advance were satisfied by parametral batch programs. In this case there was not any requirement for concurrent retrieval from more than one data base, so we solved this problem with COBOL-IDS programs. The Report Writer option of COBOL language was very useful.

The interrogation in on-line system was implemented by the aid of MDQS. In this case we performed concurrent retrievals from more than one data base, with the use of connection of discussed in the section of Data Base Maintenance. In this case it was not a restriction for the user, which data should be retrieved from which data base. In our demonstration system we programmed the most frequent questions from the user requirements in parametral form, for certain questions we worked out very user-oriented, interactive, easily handled forms. These questions were stored in a library, so they became usable in a very simple way for the users. In addition to the prepared types of questions any type of question can be programmed concerning the data stored in the data bases, but it depends on the availability of a previously established proper Application Definition for the given interrogation, it requires 1-2 hours or 1-2 days programming and testing work depending on the complexity of the question.

QUESTIONS AND PROBLEMS DURING THE IMPLEMENTATION OF THE DEMONSTRATION SYSTEM

In the last part of our presentation I wish to talk about the problems which have arisen during the implementation of the discussed system, and I hope to contribute to further examinations of distributed data base systems from the users point of view.

The demonstration system implemented by us - fitting into the objective basis environment available for the experiment - is a distributed data base system, that assures the distributed and concurrent use of data bases with different purpose and hierarchical levels on homogenous hardware-software resources, that is besides the higher hierarchical level data bases which belong to the system and which are stored reasonably on the central computer, the analitical data bases containing the territorial data are located also on the central computer. In this case the territorial distribution suggests the physical distribution of data, and the on-line access of them can be implemented from the district offices only through a network.

ADVANTAGES AND DISADVANTAGES OF THE SOLUTION

Though the solution was affected by objective circumstances, it is worth to analyze, to discover its advantageous and disadvantageous features, because this type of solution of distributed data base systems is an exepted alternative according to the technical literatures.

Advantages:

- The concurrent use of the different hierarchical level

data bases was implementable with the help of an existing software;
- The problem of consistency in the data of the different hierarchical level data bases was solved relatively more easily;
- It became possible to apply and analyse MDQS IV. data management software, which made an efficient solution possible at the interrogations and maintenances of different data bases even in the case, when beside more IDS files it had to work with files of other structures. In the majority of cases these interrogations and maintenances could be realized in more than one step, in a more complicated way for the users, maybe with no immidiate answers;
- It is easy to solve the central management and control of the system;
- At the implementation of the unified information system in consequence of the central storage and operating it was possible to work out an unified computer system for the management of territorial data bases, too;
- The compatibility, fitting problems derived from inhomogenous hardware-software resources do not occur.

Disadvantages:

- Users can access directly the territorial data bases only through a network, and this fact involves significant costs;
- The access of territorial data bases is affected by the loading of the central computer;
- In a lot of cases the data base management must be performed in batch mode /costs, network problems/, that, however, does not allow the expansion of the advantages of data base management;
- The control of territorial data is complicated for the territorial offices;
- The spontaneous development of the centrally operated territorial systems is pushed into the backround, consequently after a while the territorial information supply will not be satisfactory.

CONSIDERATIONS RELATED TO OTHER SOLUTIONS

Besides the discussed solution we studied, what kind of problems would have been raised by making both territorially and functionally distributed system, which were more suitable for the user's system.

First let us set out from the simpler case, that the earlier specified computer system must be produced so, that from amoung the data bases corresponding to the logical data structures the nation-wide data bases locate on a central computer and the territorially distributed data bases are in the territorially competent computer centers. In this case we cannot start from the assumption, that the question is connected with homogenous hardware-software resources, because the territorial computer centers may be different in the type and size of computers, the configuration of computers and last but not least in the available software, namely the data base management systems.

Such a model contains a lot of alternative possibilities. Assuming that the file structures defined in the centrally designed computer system can be implemented uniformly in every computer center, that is there is a possibility for example to manage complex file structure containing Codasyl structure elements. In that case at the development of the individual territorial systems such kind of computer systems must be implemented parallel, which have the same functions and operational factors, and which can manage same structures but use different data base systems. The connection of the territorial and central data bases is not so simple, because in this case the problem is to establish interfaces between the different data base management systems.

Even the internal storages of the different Codasyl-type data base management systems are not uniform, so identification and development of several interworking data bases are needed for the operation of the system.

It is visible, that in the case of these complicated distributed data base systems it is very difficult to satisfy the different online maintenance and enquiry requirements with the existing data base management systems.

Finally, let us consider the case, when we use different hardware-software resources and they do not make it possible to establish the same data base structure-type. In this case the territorial data bases have the same functional features, but the concrete computerized solution will be so different in the programming methods and storing structures that in fact the distributed data base systems appear as a set of different separated computer systems, and their concurrent usage and combination with the central data base can be done with individual analysis and design.

In the case of such an inhomogenous system the question arise which standardizational requirements and restrictions are necessary to speak about a real distributed data base system. For that reason we have to analyse the users' requirements needed from a higher level data management system in order to be suitable for the existing data base management systems.

REFERENCES:

1. Distributed Systems - International Computer State of the Art Report
   Infotech Information Limited, Maidenhead, Berkshire, 1976.

2. ANSI/SPARC Data Base Management System Study Group Interim Report
   American National Standards Institute, Washington,D.C., 1975.

3. MDQS IV. User's Guide
   Honeywell Bull Series 60 /Level 66/ /6000
   Honeywell Information Systems Inc., 1975.

4. MDQS IV. Administrator's Guide
   Honeywell Bull Series 60 /Level 66/ /6000
   Honeywell Information Systems Inc., 1975.

DISTRIBUTED DATA BASES
C. Delobel and W. Litwin (eds.)
North-Holland Publishing Company

INTEGRITY, CONSISTENCY, CONCURRENCY, RELIABILITY IN DISTRIBUTED DATABASE MANAGEMENT SYSTEMS

Georges GARDARIN

IRIA SIRIUS and INSTITUT DE PROGRAMMATION
BP 105 78150 LE CHESNAY

This paper presents an overview of the major results and algorithms which have been proposed in order to maintain consistent a distributed database. These algorithms try to solve three types of problems : user errors, concurrency conflicts and site crashes. The contributions in these generally distinct but related areas are studied. In addition, we survey the major algorithms for updating replicated databases. A modelization by extended PETRI nets is suggested. Finally, a new algorithm for reliably and consistently updating replicated data is introduced.

1. INTRODUCTION

A distributed database satisfies a set of assertions called integrity constraints [LITW79]. Integrity constraints should be enforced to guarantee the consistency of the data seen by user programs. In a centralized as in a distributed system, consistency is threatened by three factors :

1) User update errors which can introduce inconsistent data in the database.
2) Concurrency conflicts which can induce improper sequences of operations leading to inconsistencies.
3) Site crashes which prevent the completion of certain programs having partially but not totally updated a database.

Various solutions have been proposed to avoid or detect inconsistencies. In the following, we examine the main proposals.

First, to allow detection of inconsistencies due to incorrect updates, user programs are divided in steps of consistent processing called transactions. A transaction must keep the database consistent. This can be verified at the compilation time by inserting consistency tests in the transaction, or at the execution time by verifying the integrity constraint. We present a survey of the main results in that area.

Second, to avoid inconsistencies induced by concurrency conflicts, the simultaneous execution of transactions must be restricted. Only equivalent to serial schedules should be permitted. Conflict avoidance algorithms based on locking is a classical solution to maintain serializability. On the other hand, conflict detection associated with transaction rollback seems to be a promising methodology. We summarize the distributed avoidance and detection algorithms which have been proposed.

Third, site crashes entail inconsistencies which are solved by ensuring transaction atomicity. This is generally performed by a two step commit protocol which can have several forms. The basis and limitations of the two step commit are analysed.

Finally, correct maintenance of replicated data is the crossing line of two important problems : concurrency conflicts and crash recovery. We present a survey and some comparisons of the major algorithms proposed to maintain replicated data.

2. USER ERROR DETECTION AND AVOIDANCE

2.1. User Error Types

There exists at least two types of user errors which can threaten the database consistency. First, user programs can be incorrectly programmed. Such errors are generally detected at debug time. However, it is current that some of them remain. Therefore, the database management system should prevent incorrect database updating due to incorrect programming. Second, user program input data can be incorrect. That is often the case when end users performing data entry are not specialized persons. To prevent such errors, the user program should verify the input data as completly as possible. However, it is not possible to avoid some typing errors, such as 3,000 in place of 3,200 for a salary. Even if all verifications are not possible, it is desirable that tools be supplied in order to detect and correct or to avoid user errors.

2.2. User Error Detection

The method utilized to perform user error detection is integrity constraint monitoring. Integrity constraints are defined by the database administrator and are verified by the database management system whenever the database is modified. More precisely, user programs are divided in consistent steps of processing called transactions [ESWA76]. At the end of a transaction, all integrity constraints should remain satisfied. However, some of them can be verified after performing a database update [BADA79]. That is the case for integrity constraints where only one data item or an individual record is involved. All other integrity constraints are checked at transaction end, before commiting updates. For this purpose, the database which would be obtained with the transaction updates is considered and integrity constraints are evaluated. If one of them is false, the transaction updates are canceled and the transaction is rolled back. It is not necessary to examine all integrity constraints but only those whose value (true or false) could be modified by the transaction updates. Generally, such integrity constraint verifications are very expensive and user error detection by integrity constraint monitoring appears as an inefficient mechanism.

2.3. User Error Avoidance

Some efficient integrity constraint verification methodologies have been proposed [HAMM78, GARD79c]. In these approaches, integrity constraint maintenance is prepared at compilation time rather than at execution time, and therefore we can say that user error are avoided. More precisely, tests are inserted in the transaction in order to verify that modifications introduced in the database cannot violate the integrity constraints. Generally, just some inexpensive tests are necessary. Therefore such approaches should be very efficient but it is rather difficult to find out the tests to insert.

The first approach [HAMM78] is based on an analysis of operations performed by a transaction at compilation time. The integrity constraints studied are restricted to those constraining an individual object.Considering a pair operation - integrity constraint, an assertion processor performs an analysis that produces an efficient test for the assertion under the operation. This process begins with perturbation analysis, which determines the effect that execution of the operation can have on the truth of the assertion. The informations thus derived permit to determine a set of conditions under which the assertion can remain true after executing the operation. If the conditions are suspicious, then the assertion processor generates an efficient test that will be performed at the time the operation will be invoked and which will determine the assertion value. Moreover, wherever possible, the generated test can be evaluated before executing the operation, thus allowing to avoid the execution and roll back of the operation. In addition, several equivalent tests can be generated. The test that should actually be used by the database system at run-time is the one that is expected to incur the lowest cost in its execution. Finally, this approach allows user error avoidance by perturbation analysis at compilation time and prompt efficient test evaluation at run time, but only for a restricted class of integrity constraint.

The second approach which has been proposed [GARD79c] is based on program correctness proof [HOAR69]. Transactions are written in PASCAL like programming language. A data manipulation language based on predicate calculus is embedded in the programming language. An axiomatic definition of both PASCAL and the embedded data manipulation language is utilized in order to show that integrity constraints are invariants for transactions. The proof technique consists in pushing the integrity constraint through the statements of the transaction with the Hoare axiomatic and predicate calculus theory. The formal proof success requires inclusion by hand of correct tests in the transaction program. Finally an automatic transaction consistency verifier is proposed which will definitely permit to avoid inconsistencies induced by incorrect programming and/or incorrect data entry. However, to build such a transaction consistency verifier remains a difficult program proving task.

3. CONCURRENCY CONFLICT AVOIDANCE AND DETECTION

3.1. Concurrency Conflict Types

When simultaneously accessed by transactions, a database can become inconsistent. Let us call an entity the unit of data which is individually controlled by the data base management system. Each modification of an entity creates a new version of that entity. There exists two types of concurrency conflicts which can appear when transactions simultaneously create new versions [ENGL76] :

1) Lost operation occurs when a new version of an entity is created by a transaction which utilizes obsolete versions of entities to produce the new one.

2) Inconsistency appears when an integrity constraint is violated.

Simultaneous executions of transactions must be limited in order to prevent lost operations and inconsistencies.

3.2. Sufficient Condition For Correctness

It is possible to characterize a sub-set of possible simultaneous executions of a finite family of transactions (T1,T2,...,Tn) which does not involve lost operation or inconsistency [GARD77].For this purpose, we need first to introduce some definitions. A transaction is considered as a sequence of atomic actions which performs a set of operations on the entities of a database. An operation on an entity is formally defined as a sequence of actions which performs a consistent function on an entity, that is which enforce the internalintegrity of an entity. Two operations Oi and Oj are compatible iff, for any instance of the entity(ies) acted upon, any simultaneous execution of these two operations gives the same result as the execution of either Oi followed by Oj or Oj followed by Oi. Two operations Oi and Oj are permutable iff, for any instance of the entity(ies) acted upon, the execution of Oi followed by Oj gives the same result as the execution of Oj followed by Oi. A sequence of actions which corresponds to a simultaneous or a sequential execution of a family of transactions is called a schedule of that family. The problem is to find a sufficient condition for a schedule to be correct, that is without lost operation and inconsistency.

In that section, we would like to introduce two sufficient conditions [ESWA76, GARD78a] which have been proposed for assuring schedule correctness. It is first obvious that serial schedules, that is schedules without simultaneity between transactions(one at a time) are correct. An equivalent to serial schedule [ESWA76] is a schedule which processes entities in the same transaction order that a serial schedule. A sufficient condition for a schedule to be correct is that it be equivalent to a serial schedule [ESWA76]. This condition known as serializability is not necessary. Let us define two transformations of a schedule [GARD78a].

1) Separation of operations : The separation of operations in a schedule is obtained by replacing each simultaneous execution of compatible operations by the sequence giving the same result.

2) Permutation of operations : The permutation of operations in a schedule consist in changing the order of two successive permutable operations.

Then, a less restrictive condition than serializability is extended serializability, that is that the schedule can be transformed by separations and permutations of operations into a serial schedule. In [GARD78a] even a less restrictive condition than extended serializability is proposed and it is shown that this condition is not necessary. Some work has still to be done in order to find a necessary and sufficient condition for a schedule to be correct.

In practice, possible schedules are restricted to correct ones by two types of mechanisms : conflict avoidance and conflict detection. The first method is based on a locking scheme which permits to avoid conflicts before executing an operation. The second one is based on a time-stamping scheme which permits to detect existing conflicts which are then solved by transaction roll back. With these two methods which are illustrated below, the set of possible schedules is only a restricted subset of correct schedules. Some nice but complex algorithms have been proposed to extend these subsets [BERN77,GARD78b].

3.3. Avoidance by Locking

Locking is the most utilized strategy to avoid conflicts. With such a strategy, operations are grouped in operation modes. Two operation modes are incompatible if they cannot be utilized simultaneously on the same entity without conflict risk. Before performing an operation on an entity, a transaction should request to lock that entity in the corresponding mode. If the entity is already locked by another transaction in an incompatible mode, then the requesting transaction must wait until the entity be unlocked by the conflicting transaction. For this purpose, there exists a special unlock primitive. Therefore, locking is performed by the way of a locking protocol generally composed of two primitives :

LOCK (entity, operation mode)
UNLOCK(entity).

It has been shown that in order to maintain consistency, a transaction must be two phase, that is cannot utilize the lock primitive after unlocking an entity [ESWA76].

In a distributed environment, lock requests must be transferred through the network from the user program to the systems managing the utilized entities. That increases communication costs. In addition, locking introduces the deadlock problem [COFF71, CHU74, GOLD77, GARD78b]. In a distributed data base management system, deadlock can be detected by an algorithm looking for cycles in the waiting graph between transactions. Some problems arise because the waiting graph is distributed. Even if complex deadlock detection algorithms have been proposed, the most efficient solution seems to be grouping the waiting graph on a unique site when a transaction has been waiting for a long period of time. Finally locking appears as a conceptually simple method to avoid concurrency conflicts whose efficiency remains challenged [RIES77,GARD78b].

3.4. Detection by Time-Stamping

A promising methodology for solving concurrency conflicts is based on detection of lost operations and inconsistencies with time-stamps. When such a problem is detected, one of the two conflicting transactions is rolled back. In order to detect lost operation, it is sufficient to detect when an updating transaction utilizes an obsolete version of an entity [GARD79a,ROSE78]. Detection of inconsistencies is a little more complex. For this purpose, it has been proposed [GARD78b] to give a unique serial number to each transaction and to time-stamp an entity with the serial number of the last transaction which has updated it. When a transaction is started, we associate it a stable number which is the lowest serial number of the transaction currently in execution. Then a potential inconsistency is detected when a transaction accesses an entity which has a time-stamp greater than its stable number. In summary, a transaction is rolled back when :

1) The transaction updates an entity while processing an obsolete version of the same or of another entity.

2) The transaction reads an entity which has a time-stamp greater than its stable number.

Such a strategy can be extended to a distributed system. However, that requires :

a) a unification of serial numbers in the network;

b) a starting dialogue in order to determine the stable time for a transaction. Step a can be done with a global definition of serial numbers in the network ; a simple strategy consist in using the local time of the site initiating a transaction compacted with the site number in low digits as serial number of this transaction [LAMP78].An alternative strategy consists in using a circulating ticket [LELA78]. Step b can be performed by an algorithm initiated at the beginning of a transaction collecting all local stable times and determining the minimum of them which is the global stable time [GARD79b].

4. SITE CRASHES AND RECOVERIES

4.1. Transaction Atomicity

In order to keep the database integrity when a site crashes, it is necessary to guarantee transaction atomicity, that is to be sure that either all the updates of a transaction are committed on all sites, or not at all are. For this purpose, the two step commitment protocol has been proposed [LAMP77]. Let us call master the site which runs the user program of a transaction and slaves the sites which perform the remote updates. The first step of the two step commit consist in submitting all slaves to the master decision [GARD79e]. This is done by broadcasting a ready to commit request from master to slaves. If all slaves answer ready, then the master can initiate the second step by broadcasting a real commit message. The important point is that after acknowledgment of a ready to commit, a slave is completly dependent on the master and cannot decide to abort or commit a transaction alone. This assures that all slaves perform in the same way the unique master decision, and therefore guarantees transaction atomicity.

4.2. Site Recovery

The first type of recovery is the quick recovery [JOUV77] when only the central memory has been lost. In that case,it is sufficient to cancel transactions which has not been declared ready to commit and to ask the master for what to do with transactions which have reached the ready to commit state.

The second type is the long recovery which is performed when the database has been dammaged [JOUV77]. In that case, it is not sufficient to restore the local database with an old dump and to apply the modifications recorded in a local journal up to the last checkpoint, but it is also necessary to synchronize the local recovery with other sites. For this purpose, either synchronized checkpoint can be set or the distributed system can undo the modifications performed at other sites by cancelled transactions. Such procedures have still to be precised.

5. AN OVERVIEW OF ALGORITHMS FOR UPDATING REPLICATED DATA

5.1. Objectives and Model

In order to achieve a good degree of reliability and availability in a distributed data base management system and to improve access time to a data set from a given computer, it is necessary to allow multiple copies of portions of the database. This complexifies the consistency problem : the distributed system must guarantee mutual consistency of the copies, that is the convergence of all copies toward an identical unique state if the production of transactions in the system is stopped. For this purpose, it is necessary to control that all updates are applied to all copies in the same order. Several algorithms have been proposed. In the following, we examine the main proposals.

In addition, we present an illustration of the principal algorithms based on extended Petri nets. A net portrays the control messages which are required in order to authorize an update. A procedure is represented by a transition with input nodes and output nodes. A message is represented as an arc joining an output node to an input one (see figure 1). A procedure is executed when one of its input nodes has received the associated messages. The execution of a procedure generates the messages corresponding to one of the input nodes. Such an illustration is given for three node networks. It is assumed that the net is cleared after each execution. Such modelisations could be utilized to prove algorithm properties.

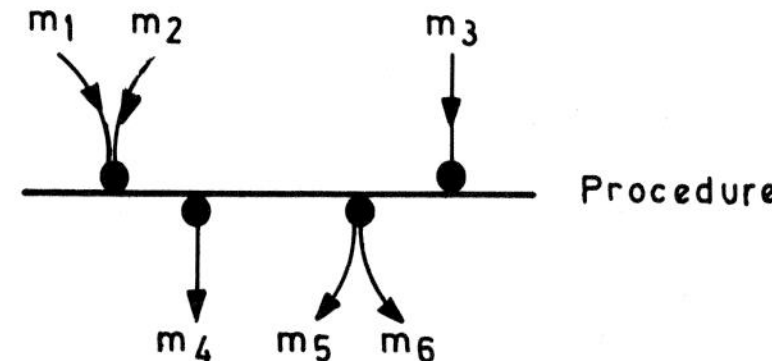

FIGURE 1 - REPRESENTATION OF PROCEDURE AND MESSAGES

5.2. The Centralized Locking Algorithm [ELLI77,MENA78]

The simplest method to avoid interference is to lock each resource being read or written by active transactions by the way of a central controller, which is generally a chosen local controller but which can be a specific communication controller [HOLL77]. This central controller is specialized to perform locking and unlocking of resources.

The centralized locking algorithm proceeds as follows :

a) before performing an operation on a resource, a transaction requests for locking the resource in the desired operation mode [GARD76] to its original controller.

b) one message is then sent by the original controller to the central controller requesting for the locking of all the copies of the resource.

c) the central controller checks the requested lock ; if it can be granted, then a grant message is sent back to the original controller ; if not, a reject message is sent back to the original controller which returns a reject response to the transaction.

d) once the original controller has received the grant message, the operation can be performed ; if it is an update operation, it is performed by sending simultaneously the result of the update operation to all the sites which manage a copy and by waiting for an acknowledgment message from each of them.

e) at the end of the transaction, after the two step commitment, all the resources used by the transaction are unlocked.

The main disadvantage of this solution appears with the inoperability of the central controller : it causes the inoperability of the whole distributed database system. In [MENA78] a solution has been proposed to this problem. However, it requests that a copy of the global lock table be managed by each site. Then, it is possible to change the central controller when a failure of the previous one has been detected ; but, it has the serious disadvantage of multiplying the number of transmitted messages.

Figure 2 gives an illustration of the execution of a lock request under the centralized locking algorithm for a three sites network. T portrays the requesting transaction. A site is represented by a circle. CLOCK is the basic central locking algorithm. LOCK is the local algorithm executed by a site when receiving a lock request. It then generates a RLOCK message, that is the request message for locking all the copies. If all the copies are free, then the requested lock is granted, otherwise it is rejected.

5.3. The Decentralized Locking Algorithm [ELLI77,STON78]

The decentralized solution partially presented in [ELLI77] and [STON78] avoids the failure problem and is able to continue updating the database when one or more sites are inoperative. It proceeds as follows :

a) as in step (a) of the previous algorithm, before performing an operation on a resource, a transaction requests for locking the resource to its original controller ;

b) one message is then sent by the original controller to each controller which manages a copy of the requested resource ; simultaneously, a time-out is unlatched superior to the longest reasonnable transmission plus response time ;

c) when receiving an external request, each controller checks the requested lock ; if it can be granted, then a grant message is sent back to the original controller ; if not, a reject message is sent back to the original controller ;

d) when the original controller receives a reject message, it must sent a cancellation of all the locking requests it has sent in step (b) even if they have been granted, and return a reject response to the transaction ;

e) when the original controller receives a grant message or detects a time-out, it must check if each invoked site has granted the lock request or is inoperative ; if yes and if at least one site is operative, the operation can be performed ; if it is an updating operation, it is performed by sending simultaneously the result of the updating operation to all the sites which manage a copy and by waiting for an acknowledgment or a time-out response ;

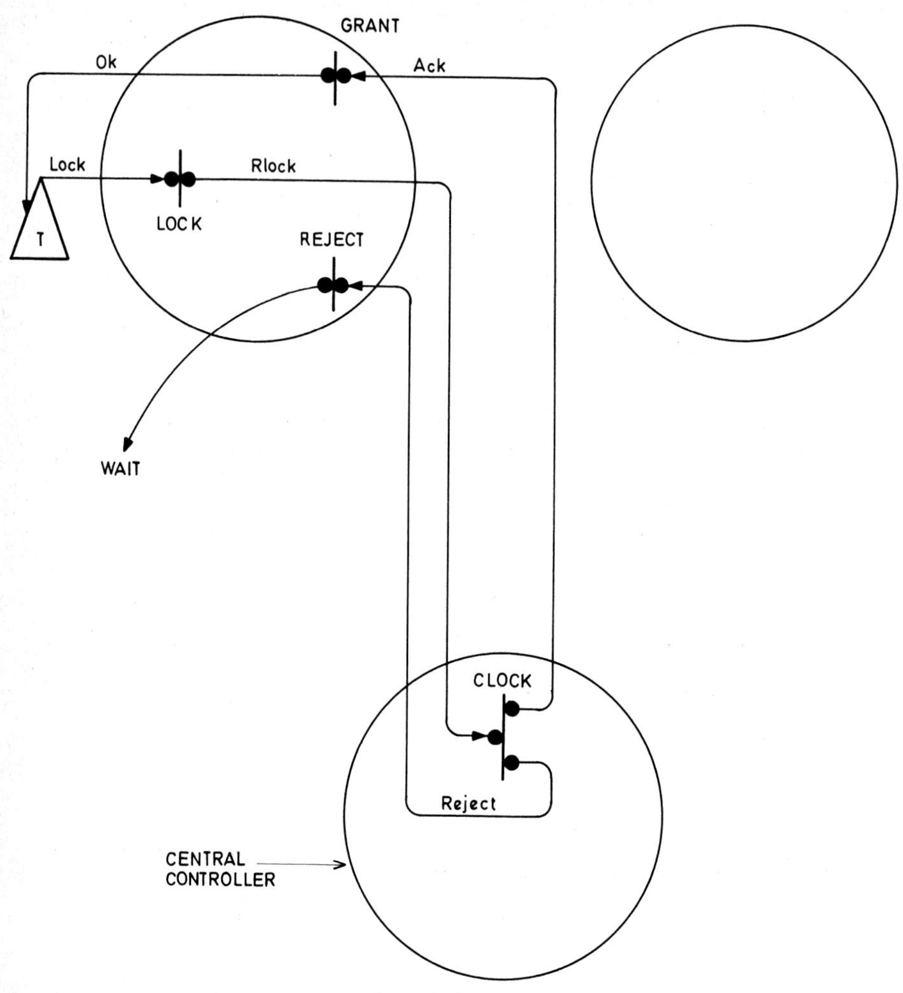

FIGURE 2 - THE CENTRALIZED LOCKING ALGORITHM

f) at the end of the transaction, after the two step commitment, all the resources locked by the transaction must be unlocked ;

g) a special procedure is needed for recovering a site which has been repaired ; such a procedure needs the history of the database ; it can be performed by the way of asking any operational site for it [JOUV77] or by the persistent communication feature [SUTH74]. Thus, the philosophy of ignoring sites which are inoperative leads to robust operations [ELLI77].

Figure 3 represents the execution of a lock request under the decentralized locking algorithm for a three site network. The notations are those introduced for the centralized algorithm. In addition, a time-out is portrayed as a ground connection.

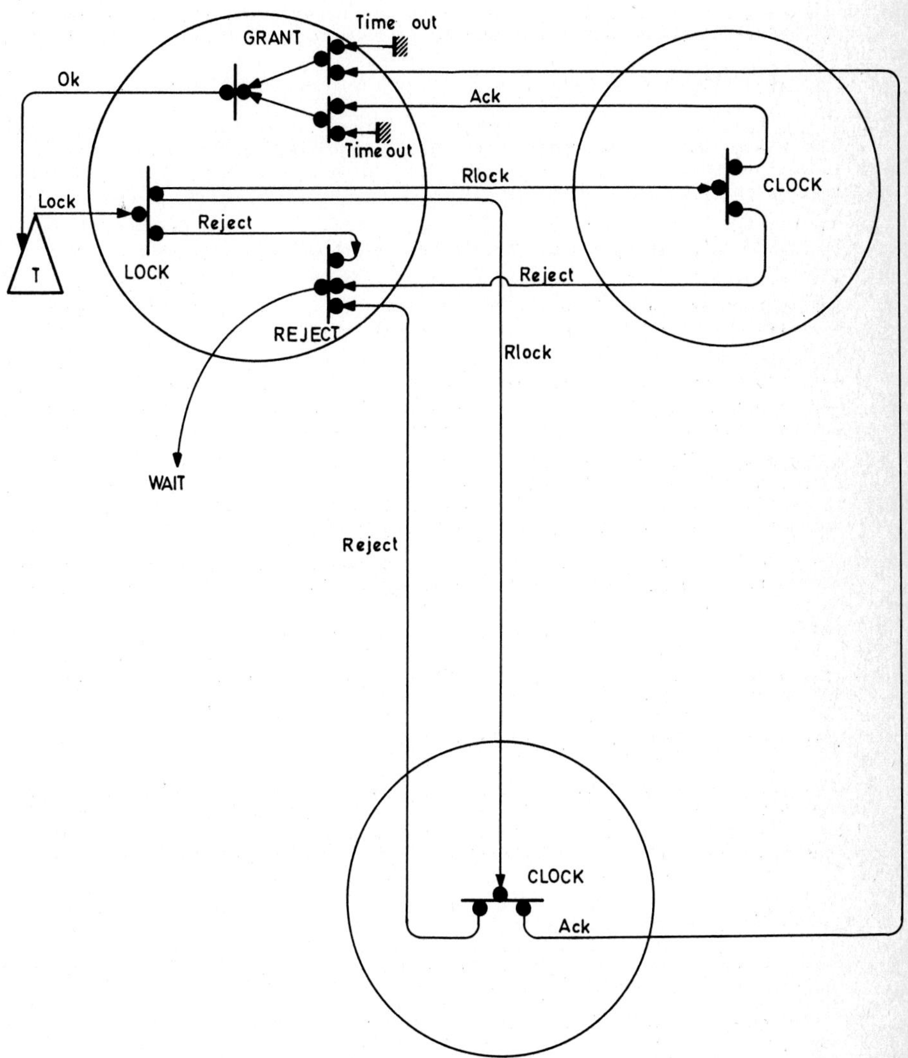

FIGURE 3 - THE DECENTRALIZED LOCKING ALGORITHM

5.4. The Primary Site Methodology [ALSB76,STON78]

Between a centralized and a decentralized control,a method have been proposed which requires that all update activity for a given resource be funneled through a set of computers called the primary sites. In [STON78], two implementations of this methodology has been introduced. We present here an algorithm derived from the second one. For simplicity , an up-list of the whole network is assumed to be maintained on each site and no care is taken with network partitions [ROTH77].

The algorithm proceeds as follows :

a) when a transaction submits a request for performing an operation, its original controller examines the up-list and calculates the k primary sites for the resource ; they are the k first sites in the up-list which manage a copy of that resource ;

b) one message is then sent by the original controller to each primary site controller ; this message requests the locking of the copies of the resource ;

c) each primary controller checks the requested lock ; if it can be granted, then a grant message is sent back to the original controller ; if not, a reject message is sent back to the original controller which returns it to the transaction ;

d) once the original controller has received the k grant messages, the operation can be performed ; if it is an updating operation, all the copies of the resource must be updated ; it is performed as in the centralized algorithm ;

e) a reconfiguration procedure is needed to maintain the up-list ; execution of such a procedure is performed as soon as a site fails ; it can be performed as in the daisy chain algorithm ; moreover, each operative site must known the new up-list in order to maintain a unique set of primary sites ;

f) the recovery procedure when a site has been repaired is identical to that of the centralized algorithm with in addition the inclusion of the repaired site in the up-list.

Let us point out that, by varyingk from 1 to the number of operational sites, this locking algorithm goes from the centralized one with a different site controlling each resource to the decentralized one.

5.5. The Decentralized Voting Algorithm [THOM76]

Another solution to the interference problem is a distributed voting algorithm suggested by THOMAS. Like in [GARC78], we only consider the daisy chain version of the algorithm. Such an algorithm is based on the association of a time stamp to each resource. This time stamp reflects the time at which the resource was assigned its present value.

The algorithm proceeds as follows :

a) when a transaction submits an update request to its original controller, it includes as part of the request :

   - a unique priority number as the request priority together with the site number,
   - the name of the resource to be updated and its new value,
   - a list of the resources upon which the update is based, called the base resources,
   - the list of time stamps corresponding to the base resource values used to perform the updating ;

   this request is then passed around the daisy chain of all active sites ;

b) a controller, when it receives the request must perform one of the following action :

- vote reject if one or more of the base resource time stamp is obsolete,
- vote accept only if the base variable time stamps are current and the request does not conflict with another current request ; it conflicts if one active request (one which is not accepted and not rejected) is trying to modify one base resource or if the resource to be updated is a base resource for another active request,
- vote deadlock reject if the base resources are current but the request conflicts with an active request of higher priority,
- defer voting if the base resources are current but the request conflicts with an active request of lower priority, or if the base resource time stamps of the request are more current than the corresponding local resources time stamps ;

c) when a controller notes that a majority consensus has been reached on a request it must perform the request and notify all other controllers to accept and perform it ; moreover, the different active requests must be examined at each site, in order to reject those which are conflicting with the accepted request ; the original controller must return an acceptation to the transaction as soon as it has been informed of it ;

d) when a controller rejects a request, it must notify each other controller that the request has been rejected ; the transaction must be informed of this rejection ; moreover, when a controller is informed of a rejection, it must examine again deferred request and vote on it if it is possible ;

e) the recovery procedure when a site has been repaired is the same as in the decentralized locking algorithm ; it is important to note that the number of sites considered in the voting procedure includes the inoperative ones. Thus, the resynchronisation after repairing is facilitated.

Let us point out that the algorithm considers only updating requests : another algorithm is needed to insure consistency for readers. Such an algorithm can be found in [GARD78b].

Figure 4 represents the execution of an update request under the decentralized voting algorithm for a 3 sites network. The notations are the same as for the centralized algorithm.

5.5. The Preanalysis Methodology [BERN77,BERN78]

The previously presented algorithms do not use an apriorist knowledge of the transaction behaviour. The SDD.1 updating methodology is quite different. Interferences resolution is performed by the way of preanalysing the whole set of accesses with the help of a conflict graph. When the database is designed, classes of transactions are defined by the database administrator. Each class corresponds to a read set and a write set of resources. Write sets and read sets may overlap between different classes. To analyse this overlappings, a conflict graph is constructed as follows : each node corresponds to a read or write set of resources ; an undirected edge links two nodes belonging to a same class or two nodes representing non disjoint set of resources.

Four different synchronisation protocols are available. By the way of the conflict graph, a protocol is chosen for every transaction. More precisely, when a transaction is activated, a protocol selection function operates by mapping the transaction entered into a class in regard to its read and write preview. According to the class and the preanalysis of the conflict graph the adequate protocol is chosen. Protocol P1 specifies no inter-computer synchronisation at all. It is utilized when the class is not involved in a cycle in the conflict graph. A transaction

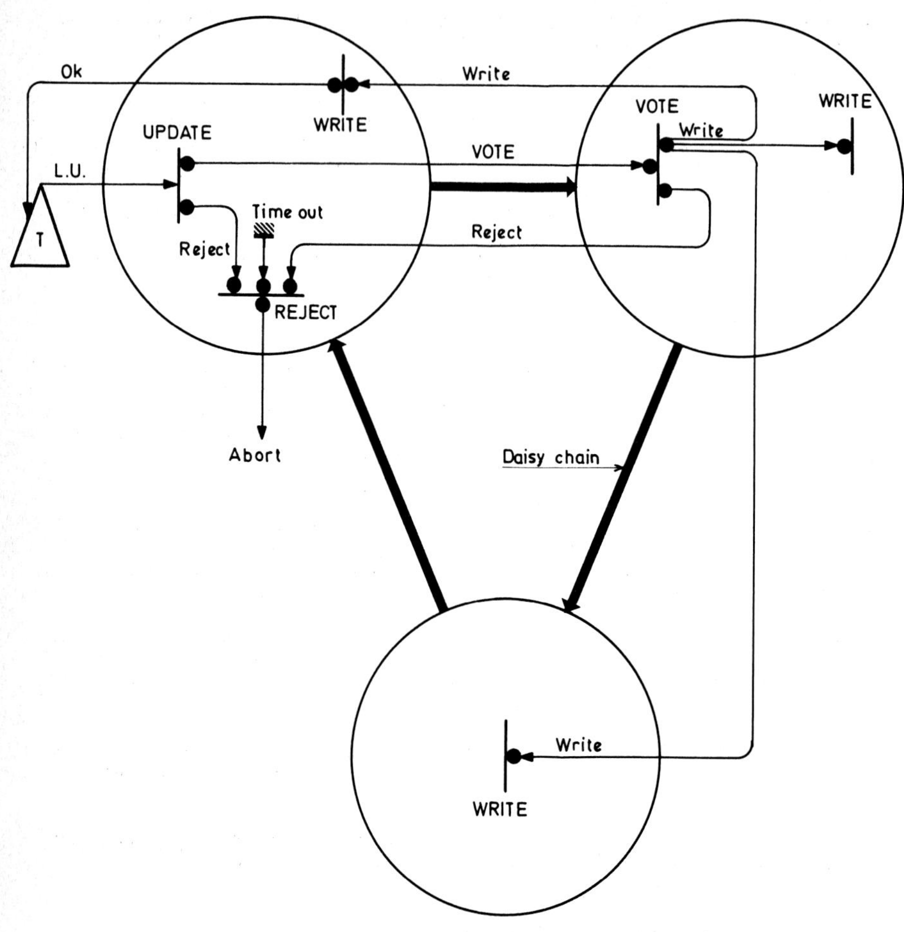

FIGURE 4 - THE DISTRIBUTED VOTING ALGORITHM

which runs under this protocol only performs local locking in order to ensure the convergence of the distributed database. Three other protocols are available P2, P3 and P4. The less efficient protocol requires some kind of global locking of all the resources.

The more representative and interesting protocol is P3. In order to explain it, it must be said that in SDD-1 every resource is time stamped by the time of the last write performed on it. Moreover a time stamp is associated to every transaction : that is its starting time. A write is only performed if the time stamp of the initiating transaction is superior to the resource one. Protocol P3 is run when a cycle envolving a write set to write set edge is detected in the conflictgraph. In this case, read and write messages of the conflicting classes must be serialized in the transaction time stamp order. For this purpose, a conditional read is forced to the transaction. Such a read must wait until no message can come from the conflicting class initiated by a transaction having a time stamp inferior to the requesting transaction one. Moreover, the read is accepted only if the resource has a time stamp inferior or equal to the transaction one. Otherwise the transaction is roll-backed. Finally, the ultimate goal of the SDD-1 strategy is to reduce the number of messages interchanged to synchronize the transactions and to avoid global locking when it is possible.

Figure 5 portrays an execution of P3 for a three site network. The transaction is executed on site 1. It is assumed that only site 3 runs a conflicting class of transactions.

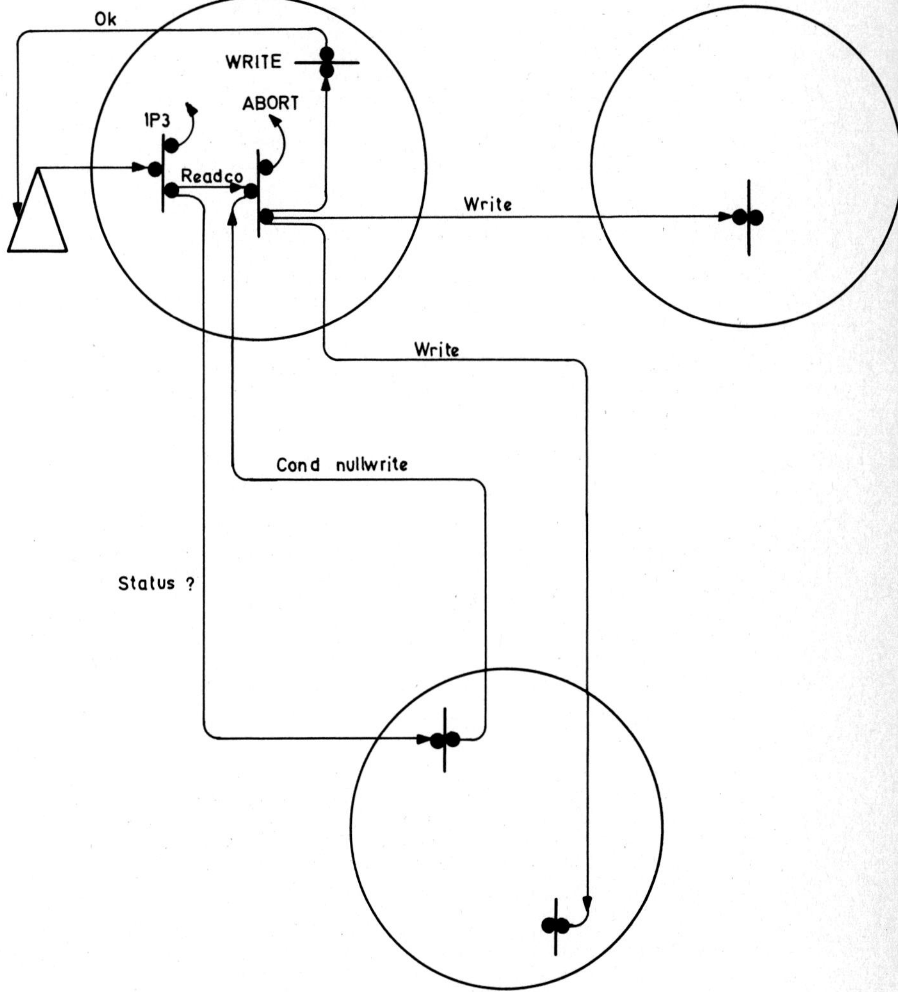

FIGURE 5 - THE P3 PROTOCOL IN SDD-1

5.6. A distributed control algorithm for reliably and consistently updating replicated databases [GARD79d]

The algorithms proposed for updating replicated databases can be separated into two classes : global locking and time stamping. For the global locking scheme, either centralized control [MENA78,STON78] or distributed control [ELLI77] can be implemented. However, both cases require many control messages. For the timestamping method [THOM78,BERN78] timing information permits the ordering of transaction updates. However, the addition of a time stamp to every data element in the database significantly increases the storage cost. To reduce storage and communication costs for updating replicated data bases, we propose the following new algorithm that uses local locking and time stamps on lock tables (the set of record identifiers and the description of the operations performed corresponding to a transaction) rather than on every record. Local locking is utilized to maintain internal consistency of the file copy that is being updated or modified, and time-stamping of lock tables permits enforcement of mutual consistency among the replicated databases. Mutual consistency is checked after every consistent step of local processing. In other words, global locking is postponed until the commitment of the transaction is executed. This allows us to group the control messages at the end of a transaction and thus reduces overhead in control message.

In summary, the proposed algorithm achieves a set of objectives which are highly desirable for reliably and consistently updating replicated databases :

1) It maintains internal consistency for each local database, that is it assures that no simultaneous execution of well programed transactions can violate the local integrity constraints.

2) It maintains mutual consistency, that is it guarantees that after stopping transaction production in the distributed system, all the copies will converge toward an identical state.

3) It entails transaction atomicity, that is it assures that the updates of a transaction are either all completed or not at all executed.

4) It allows updating with only one operational site ; this objective does not permit a majority consensus updating policy which does not provide a high degree of availability, particularly for two site networks where updates cannot be performed when one site is down.

5) It provides low interprocess communication cost.

The reader will find a precise description of this algorithm in [GARD79d].

6. CONCLUSION

In this paper, we have presented algorithms to detect or avoid user errors, concurrency conflicts and inconsistency due to site crashes. Most of these algorithms are developped separately. A unified approach to all these problems is needed in a distributed system. Such a global approach is today in progress in the SIRIUS-DELTA project [LEBI79].

On the other hand, consistency maintenance is not a trivial aspect and a lot of progresses are still to be made in several areas, among them integrity constraint monitoring, site recovery, evaluation and proof of correctness.

7. REFERENCES

[ALSB76] P.A. ALSBERG, G.G. BELFORD, S.R. BRUNCH - "Synchronization and Deadlock" CAC Document Number 185 - University of Illinois - March 1976.

[BACH77] C.W. BACHMAN - "Advances in Database Technology" - Infotech State of the Art Tutorial - LONDON December 1977.

[BAD79] D.Z. BADAL, G.J. POPEK - "Cost and Performance Analysis of Semantic Integrity Validation Methods" - SIGMOD 1979, pp. 109-115, BOSTON, Ma

[BERN77] P.A. BERNSTEIN, N. GOODMAN, J.B. ROTHNIE, C.A. PAPADIMITRIOU - "Analysis of serializability in SDD.1 : a system for distributed databases" - Computer Corporation of America - Technical report N CCA-77-05

[BERN78] P.A. BERNSTEIN, D.W. SHIPMAN - "A formal model of concurrency control mechanisms for database systems" - 3 rd Berkeley Workshop on Distributed Data Management and Computer Networks, pp. 189-205, August 78 - BERKELEY

[CHU74] W.W. CHU, G. OHLMACHER - "Avoiding deadlock in distributed databases" - ACM National Conference - pp. 156-160, november 1974.

[ELLI77] C.A. ELLIS - "A robust algorithm for updating duplicate databases" - 2rd Berkeley Workshop on Distributed Data Management and Computer Networks, pp. 146-158, May 1977 - BERKELEY.

[COFF71] E.G. COFFMAN, M.J. ELPHICK, A. SHOSHANI - "System Deadlocks" - Computing Surveys - Vol. 3 n° 2, 1971, pp. 67-78.

[ENGL76] R.W. ENGLES - "Currency and concurrency in the cobol database facility"- Modelling in DBMS - North Holland Pub Co. Ed. by J. NIJSSEN, pp. 624-633, 1976.

[ESWA76] K.P. ESWARAN, J.N. GRAY, R.A. LORIE, I.L. TRAIGER - "The notion of consistency and predicate locks in a database system" - Comm. ACM - Vol 19/11 - November 1976, pp. 624-633.

[GARC78] H. GARCIA MOLINA - "Performance comparaison of two update algorithms for distributed databases" - 3rd Berkeley Workshop on Distributed Data Management and Computer Networks, pp. 108-122, August 1978, BERKELEY.

[GARD77] G. GARDARIN, P. LEBEUX - "Scheduling algorithms for avoiding inconsistency in large databases" - 3rd International Conference on Very Large Databases, TOKYO, october 1977.

[GARD78a] G. GARDARIN - MFCS - Lecture Notes in Computer Science n° 64 - Sept.1978, pp . 201-212.

[GARD78b] G. GARDARIN - "Résolution des conflits d'accès simultanés à un ensemble d'informations. Applications aux bases de données réparties". Thèse d'Etat, Université de PARIS VI, Avril 1978.

[GARD79a] G. GARDARIN, B. PIOT - "Detection and Frequency Evaluation of Concurrency Conflicts" - Ist European Conference on Parallel 2 Distributed Processing, Février 1979, Toulouse, pp. 236-241.

[GARD79b] G. GARDARIN - "Problems and Solutions for Updating Multiple and Distributed Copies of Data" - 5th Conference on the Theory of Operating System VISEGRAD, Jan. 1979.

[GARD79c] G. GARDARIN, M. MELKANOFF - "Proving Consistency of Database Transaction" 5th Very Large Databases, Rio, Oct. 1979

[GARD79d] G. GARDARIN, W. CHU - "A Reliable Distributed Control Algorithm for Updating Replicated Data" - 6th Data Communication Symposium, Pacific Grove, California, Nov. 1979, pp. 42-51.

[GARD79e] G. GARDARIN, M. JOUVE - "The Execution Kernel of a Distributed Database Management System" - IFIP Conference on Data Base Architecture, North Holland ed., pp. 3 à 21, Venise, June 1979.

[GOLD77] B. GOLDMAN - "Deadlock detection in computer networks" - Thesis Mass. Institute of Technology June 1977.

[HAMM78] M.M. HAMMER, S.K. SARIN - "Efficient Monitoring of Database Assertions"- ACM/SIGMOD 78, Int. Conference on Management of DATA, DALLAS,June 1978.

[HOAR69] C.A. HOARE - "An Axiomatic Basis for Computer Programming" CACM, Vol. 12/10, Oct. 1969, pp. 567-580.

[HOLL77] E. HOLLER, O. DROBNIK - "Implementation of decentralized coordination mechanisms in distributed mini-micro computer system". Technical Report-Institut fur Datenverarbeitung in der Technik- KARLSRUHE RFA, 1977.

[JOUV77] M. JOUVE - "Reliability aspects in a distributed database management system" - AICA'77 Proc. Data Bases, pp. 199-209.

[LAMP77] B. LAMPSON, H. STURGIS - "Crash recovery in a distributed data storage system" - Internal report, Computer Science Laboratory, XEROX PALO ALTO Research Center - 1976.

[LAMP78] L. LAMPORT - "Time, clocks and the Ordering of Events in a Distributed System" - Comm. ACM July 1978 V21/7, pp. 558-565.

[LEBI79] J. LEBIHAN, C. ESCULIER, G. LE LANN, L. TREILLE-"SIRIUS-DELTA : Un prototype de gestion de bases de données réparties" - Colloque International sur les Bases Réparties, Versailles, mars 1980.

[LELA78] G. LE LANN - "Algorithms for distributed data-sharing which use tickets" 3rd Berkeley Workshop on Distributed Data Management and Computer Networks, pp. 259-272 August 1978, BERKELEY

[LITW79] W. LITWIN - "A Model for a Distributed Data Base" - Internal Report IRIA to be published

[MENA78] D.A. MENASCE, G.J. POPEK, R.R. MUNTZ - "A locking protocol for resource coordination in distributed databases" - SIGMOD Austin TEXAS to be published in TODS.

[RIES77] D.R. RIES, M. STONEBRAKER - "Effects of Locking Granularity in a Database Management System" - ACM TODS, Vol 2/3, Sept. 1977, pp. 233-246.

[ROSE78] D.J. ROSENKRANTZ, R.E. STEARNS, P.M. LEWIS - "System level concurrency control for distributed database systems" - ACM TODS Vol. 3/N3,June 1978 pp. 178-198

[ROTH77] J.B. ROTHNIE, N. GOODMAN - "A survey of research and development in distributed database management" - 3rd International Conference on Very Large Databases TOKYO, Oct. 1977

[STON78] M. STONEBRAKER - " Concurrency control and consistency of multiple copies of data in distributed INGRES" - 3rd Berkeley Workshop on Distributed Data Management and Computer Network, pp. 235-258, August 1978, BERKELEY.

[SUTH74] W.R. SUTHERLAND - "Distributed Computation Research at BBN" Vol. III - BBN Technical Report N 2976 - Dec. 1974.

[THOM76] R.H. THOMAS - "A solution to the update problem for multiple copy database which use distributed control" - BBN report N 3340 July 1975.

DISTRIBUTED DATA BASES
C. Delobel and W. Litwin (eds.)
North-Holland Publishing Company

THE ETOILE PROJECT

L. DARGENT, C. GODART
SIRIUS-CRIN NANCY

ABSTRACT : "ETOILE" manages replicated data distributed on a star (in french : étoile) system consisting of a central node coordinating regional nodes. Each node contains all the data to be accessed by the users of this node ; these data are therefore replicated. The consistency of the global database is maintained by a set of Distribution and Consistency Management Modules (DCMM), a DCMM is implemented on each node. In the demonstration, "ETOILE" manages a distribued database composed of one central and two regional databases.

RESUME : Le système "ETOILE" gère des données réparties selon le modèle étoilé, constitué d'un site central coordonateur et de sites régionaux. Chaque site possède toutes les données nécessaires aux utilisateurs de ce site, ce qui introduit des duplications. La cohérence globale des données est assurée par un ensemble de logiciels de Répartition et de Cohérence (LRC), chaque site possèdent un LRC. Dans la démonstration, "ETOILE" gère une base de données répartie entre un site central et deux sites régionaux.

"ETOILE" deals with a top-down conception approach of a distributed database, i.e for a distributed application, a single conceptual schema is described. This schema is distributed on each node. This top-down approach is opposed to the bottom-up approach consisting of the cooperation of existing local conceptual schemas. We take care of a particular organization kind : the starred organization. Such an organization consists of a central node (supporting a central database) and regional nodes (each supporting one regional database). The regional nodes are autonomous and equivalent the one to the another. Each regional node has a functional relationship with the central node (there is no direct relationship between the regional nodes). This two-leveled hierarchy is available for a lot of entreprises (administrations, banks, establishments with sub-offices...). This organization allows the distributed database to be momentally inconsistent, but each update must be reverberated in a determined time. The developments of every database are independent the ones from the anothers during a working session, and periodically, consistency sessions are established to transmit updates between the nodes. The periodicity of these sessions is given, depending on the application. There is no network connection during working sessions (the nodes are autonomous) this allows to spare communication costs. The "ETOILE" system could deal with heterogeneous DBMS, but in the case, the presented realization is homogeneous. A user's action on a local database starts a sequence of secondary actions on distant nodes.

All the data needed by a local user are stored on his node (autonomousness principle). Therefore replications of data are needed between different nodes. With each kind of data described in the global conceptual schema a distribution character is associated.

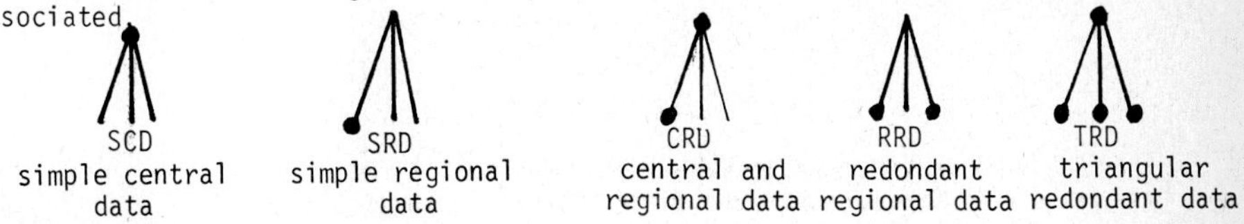

SCD
simple central data

SRD
simple regional data

CRD
central and regional data

RRD
redondant regional data

TRD
triangular redondant data

An object would have a central description and a regional description depending on the distribution character of each data compounding this object. We would extract from the global conceptual schema (including distribution characters of data) two local conceptual schema a central and a regional one. Each regional node has the same logical description of the datas (but the data are different). That shows the equivalency between the regional nodes. All the data of the distributed database are accessed by a set of precompilated programs. A distributed action is composed of a chain of precompilated programs. The user initiates the chain starting the first program during the working session. The other programs of the chain will be started by the system during the next consistency session. Note that only the first chain's programs are conversational. These precompilated programs use macro-statements of the system. These macros allow to point and to follow up the updates done by the program. The macro-statements manage particular objects (objects used by the system) of the database, of which objects keep "marks" of the updates.

During a working session, all the nodes are running independently.

During a consistency session, all the nodes have to be present and each regional node must communicate with the central node.

On each node, a Distribution and Consistency Management Module (DCMM) takes the updates' marks in the database, communicate with the distant node (central for the regional nodes, regional for the central node). This distant node can then start the precompilated program which is corresponding to the following of the distributed action. These DCMM allow in a similar way to transmit the updates and to make the database consistent.

A reliability mechanism have been proposed (breakdowns during a consistency session-Cf 3) but is not implemented.

DEMONSTRATION

STEP I : Presentation :

- Implementation choices.
- Datastructure.
- Example of Precompilated programs.

STEPS II : Working session example :

- Conversational utilization of precompilated programs to create, modify and suppress occurencies of objects.

STEP III : Recovery of the updates done during the step II.

We will especially point out the building by the DCMM of the file of messages to be transmitted to the distant node. An update is represented by a message.

STEP IV : Corresponding execution on the distant node :

Using the messages defined in step III, the distant DCMM will start the corresponding precompilated program of the chain.

STEP V : Complete consistency session :

Tree nodes will be simulated on a computer. At the end of the session, we will point out the consistency of the distributed database.

1. D. MEYER "How to get a distributed database from a local one" D.F.U. Congress Karlovy-Vary, Czéchoslovakia, 1976.

2. D. MEYER, J.M. DEFEUILLET "Comment passer d'une base locale à une base répartie; Exemple de la gestion comptable et financière du CNRS", Congrès AFCET, 1977.

3. D. MEYER "Transformation d'une base de donnée contralisée en une base de données répartie sur un réseau d'ordinateurs". Thèse Docteur Ing. Université de Nancy I, 1977.

4. D. MEYER, L. DARGENT "Une base de donnée répartie pour une organisation étoilée". Congrès AFCET, 1978.

5. C. GODART "Le modèle de répartition ETOILE". Rapport de DEA, 1979, Université Nancy I.

DISTRIBUTED DATA BASES
C. Delobel and W. Litwin (eds.)
North-Holland Publishing Company

Technical outline of the POLYPHEME demonstration prototype.

Authors : P. Decitre°, J. Andrade°°
° CII-Honeywell-Bull research center (Grenoble)
°° Laboratoire IMAG Universite de Grenoble.

Abstract:
Developed at GRENOBLE University by a joint effort of the University database group and the network group of CII-Honeywell-Bull research center. The POLYPHEME prototype will be presented at the Versailles symposium on distributed databases.

This paper is a short description of the distributed database example used in the demonstration followed by some technical aspects of systems involved in the prototype.

This work was partially supported by IRIA-SIRIUS project under contracts N° 77-076 and N° 78-008.

The POLYPHEME group is composed of the following persons M. Adiba, J. Andrade, E. André, G. Bogo, Y. Caleca, P. Decitre, C. Euzet, C. Delobel, F. Fernandez, Paik in sup, Nguyen Gia Toan, A. Stiers

The POLYPHEME prototype <ADI80> demonstration was recorded at Grenoble at the end of 1979. We describe here the distributed database used for that demonstration, the architecture of the global machine and local machines <ACE78>, the distributed execution layers involved <DEC80> and some numerical information concerning the prototype.

The demonstration database.

The distributed database chosen for the demonstration is far from being a real railway system database, although it is derived from a railway management system. It is composed of two local databases and one global database. The site RENNES manages wagons and goods using the two relations:

Wagons (W , Line, tonne, orig-station, goods, Date-of-load)
Goods(Code , Descript, type, customer, date)

The site TOULOUSE manages railroads and marshalling yards with these two relations:

Railway-line (Line , source, sink, type, status)
Marshalling-yard (Name , caracl, carac2)

The global site GRENOBLE manages wagons, railway roads and trains using the four relations:

Wagons (W , Line, tonne, orig-station)

Railway-lines (Line , source, sink, type, status)
Trains(T , Line)
Wagon-train(W,T)

The global operations available are the following: create a train, insert a wagon in a train, extract a wagon from a train, cancel a train, move a train from one railway line to another. The local operators available from the global machine are create a wagon, create a railway road.

Architecture of the global machine.

The global machine runs on an IRIS80 computer of CII-Honeywell-Bull. It is an interactive batch task, under the SIRIS8 operating system, made up of 4 main components (see fig1).

DEM, the distributed execution monitor, plays the distributed O.S. role: starting the applications, offering distributed execution services (remote process start, messages exchanges, error detection,...), managing local terminal I/O. This monitor is described in <DEC80> and its main synchronization mechanism (remote triggering of PL1 procedure) is described in <AND78>.

To communicate with remote DEM monitors of local machines it uses the DEP (distributed execution monitor) described in <NTP28>. This protocol is implemented as an interface between a DEM layer and a DEP layer.

The DEP layer uses the VCAM communication access method of SIRIS8. This access method (see fig2) allows various message exchanges between SIRIS8 tasks. It may be used in the same way to communicate between local SIRIS8 tasks or remote SIRIS8 tasks. The communication means are:

- A front-end processor giving access to:
  - º DSA network developed by CII-HB,
  - º TRANSPAC, the French public packet switching network,

or:

- CYCLIRIS, a CYCLADES transport station running as a SIRIS8 task and giving access to:
  - º CYCLADES network developed by IRIA,
  - º TRANSPAC via a black box adaptator.

The demonstration was recorded using CYCLIRIS and the CYCLADES network.

The GEX layer ensures the chaining of global user's requests, their transfer to the global DBMS URANUS <NGU77>. It receives from URANUS a localized binary tree as the result of a user's request transformation. It extracts and sends in parallel each subtree to the corresponding local machines receiving and storing tuples in response from each subtree evaluation. When all subtree results have been completely received it calls URANUS to interpret the global relational operators of the tree and to compute the global user's reply. In its current state GEX can manage only one global user at a time.

The URANUS layer used in the POLYPHEME prototype is an extension of URANUS as described in <NGU77>. It handles the global and local DDL and DML of POLYPHEME machines. The main new feature is the decomposer-localiser <NGU79> which transforms a user's relational request in a binary tree whose nodes are relational algebra operators and whose leaves are relations or parameters. Each node and leaf is localized.

In its current state URANUS is able to interpret such a tree when all the leaves are locally available. It uses a virtual memory to store relations and relation descriptions. It is able to map relations on SOCRATE <CII74> databases.

Architecture of a local machine.

A local machine is composed of DEM, DEP, URANUS and LEX layers. The three first layers are very similar to the same layers of the global machine described above. The LEX layer corresponds to GEX. It receives subtrees, reformats them for submission to the URANUS DBMS, activates the URANUS interpreter, takes each resulting relation and sends it tuple by tuple to the calling global machine. A local machine can manage a queue of global requests in a pipe-line mode from several global machines. It is however impossible to verify the consistency of global databases and we have left aside problems of concurrency control and error recovery.

Main figures.

- DEM is coded in about 600 lines of PL1; DEP in 200 PL1 and 300 assembly language instructions.
- GEX is coded in about 400 PL1 lines written using DEM conventions.
- URANUS is coded in about 4000 PL1 lines plus some assembly language instructions.

A simple request as "project (Line,state)" with one subtree to be sent and 10 resulting tuples is executed in about 5 seconds using a global and local machine on the same IRIS80 connected through VCAM.

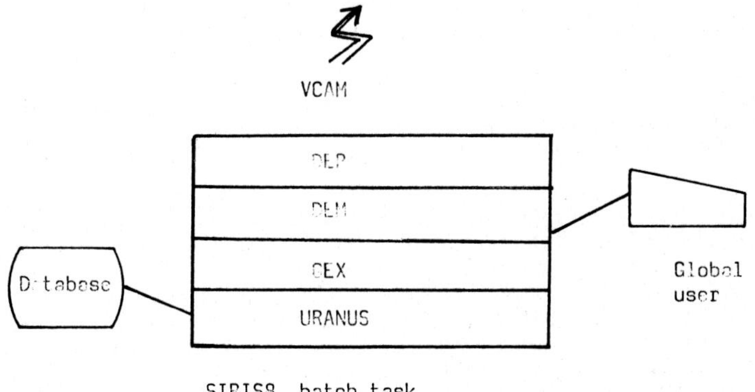

Figure 1 : Architecture of the global machine.

Figure 2 : VCAM communication access method.

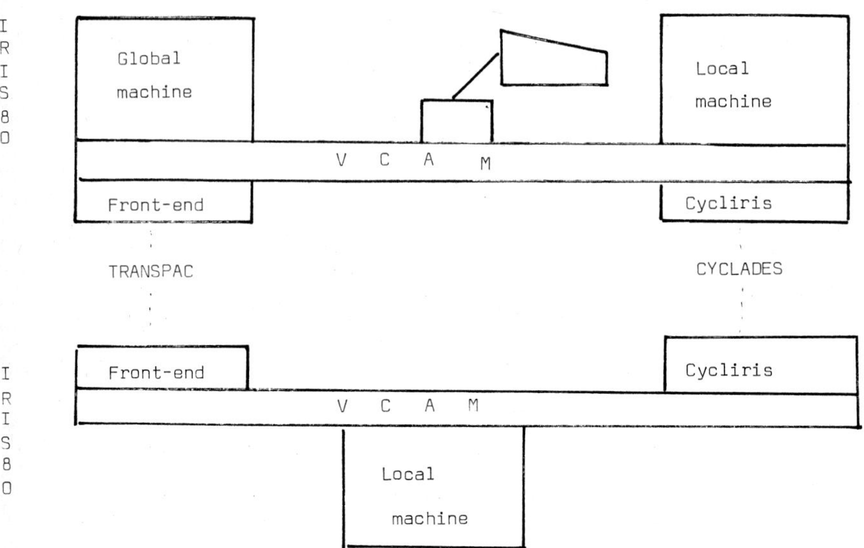

ACE78 M.ADIBA, J.Y. CALECA, C. EUZET, "A distributed database system using logical relational machines". VLDB conference, Berlin Sept. 78.

ADI80 M. ADIBA, J.M. ANDRADE, P. DECITRE, F. FERNANDEZ, NGUYEN GIA TOAN, "POLYPHEME an experience in distributed database design and implementation". To be published at Versailles symposium on distributed databases.

AND78 E.ANDRE, P.DECITRE "On providing distributed application programmers with control over synchronization" Computer network protocols, Liège 1978.

CII74 SOCRATE SIRIS7/SIRIS8 Manuel d'utilisation, CII-Honeywell-Bull 4338E1FR Oct. 1974.

DEA80 P. DECITRE, E. ANDRE, "POLYPHEME project: the DEM distributed execution monitor" To be published at Versailles symposium on distributed database, 1980.

NGU79 NGUYEN GIA TOAN, "A unified method for querry decomposition and shared information updating in distributed system". 1st international conf. on distributed computing systems. Huntsville Oct 1979.

NGU77 NGUYEN GIA TOAN "URANUS, une approche relationnelle à la coopération de bases de données". Thèse de 3ième cycle, Université de Grenoble 1979. (In French).

NTP28 E. ANDRE, "PERE protocole d'exécution répartie", note technique POLYPHEME 1978, Université de Grenoble. (In French).

DISTRIBUTED DATA BASES
C. Delobel and W. Litwin (eds.)
North-Holland Publishing Company

THE DISTRIBUTED INTERROGATION SYSTEM FRERES

Patrick BOSC
IRISA-UNIVERSITE DE Rennes
Campus de Beaulieu
35042 RENNES CEDEX
FRANCE

Le systéme FRERES, développé à l'IRISA, permet l'interrogation d'une base de données répartie de structure hiérarchique composée de bases de données existantes hétérogènes, réparties sur le réseau CYCLADES. Chaque base locale (base de données ou fichiers) est supposée contenir un sous-ensemble d'occurrences de la hiérarchie globale (partitionnement de base répartie). La démonstration concernera l'utilisation de FRERES dans le domaine de la documentation pour effectuer l'interrogation d'un catalogue collectif réparti de périodiques. On pourra rechercher les périodiques présents dans une bibliothèque donnée ou les caractéristiques d'un périodique de titre donné , etc...

The FRERES system, developped by IRISA, provides the capability for the interrogation of a hierarchic distributed database whose components are heterogeneous databases, distributed on computers connected by CYCLADES network. We assume each local database (real database or set of files) contains a subset of instances of the global hierarchy (partition of the distributed database). The demonstration will concern the use of FRERES in the documentation area : the periodicals-interrogation of a distributed collective catalog of. It will be possible to search periodicals belonging to a given library or characteristics of a periodical whose title is known, etc...

1. INTRODUCTION

Development of communication networks led many people to work in distributed applications area, and researches were undertaken for designing distributed database management systems (DDBMS). Thus, in 1974, a project began in IRISA whose goal was the design and implementation of a very simple version of a DDBMS, called FRERES(*). A first version of the prototype was completed in July 1977 and demonstrated at IFIP Congress which took place at Toronto. Here, we shall describe very briefly this system and people will find more detail in [BOSC 78a], [BOSC 78b][CHAU 78] and [BOSC 79].

2. OBJECTIVES AND ASSUMPTIONS

The primary objective of FRERES was to build an interrogation system for a distributed database whose components, called local databases, were existing and heterogeneous databases, including files, managed by their own system. So, we had to provide users located anywhere on a network, with an homogeneous schema or global view and a language which hide the heterogeneousness of local databases.

Since, we desired to build a prototype, we decided to limit to scope of our work. We only consider the case where local databases were "Semantically close", it means concerning a same universe : employers or cars or books by example. Moreover, we chose the global database to be described by a hierarchy whose root it called the individual. Thus, we fall in a very simple case of distributed database, a partionned one, in which each local database is an element of the partition. In this context, it is obvious that a user query applies to all (or a subset of) local

---

* supported by DRME and SIRIUS pilot project.

databases and there is no query decomposition problem. The remaining problem concerns the way of processing a given query, expressed in the user language, on several heterogenous databases or files.

3. PRINCIPLES OF FRERES

The user language, LGI, is based on SOCRATE data manipulation language but much more simple. We can briefly describe it as follows :

<query> ::= RETRIEVE (<list of attributes>) FOR

$\left\{ \begin{matrix} \text{ONE} \\ \text{ALL} \end{matrix} \right\}$ <individual-name> SUCH AS <condition>

<condition> ::= <predicate>{<op> <predicate>}*

<op> ::= AND|OR

Any predicate contains quantifiers, data names and values.

As we said before, a LGI query must be processed on several local databases. To achieve this goal, a way consists in the translation of the LGI query into the data manipulation language of each local database management system. Such a solution does not seem very judicious for files and problems arise for language translation with databases. So, we defined another solution based on a normalized description of each local database and the expression of query in an intermediate language.

Each local database is described as a tree (the global hierarchy) which is split, for efficiency purposes, into subtrees called logical files. Each logical file possesses an access function which delivers a logical record. The decomposition into logical files is placed under the responsibility of the administrator and he has to write the corresponding access functions. The set of logical files, their access functions and the description of each logical record constitute the local view of a local database.

For query processing, the basic idea is to use the local DBMS's to get data from the database and to process queries inside FRERES. Any LGI query is first translated into a low-level intermediate language, called LI, without regard to local views. This step, done once for concerned local databases translates the semantics of the query. Then, the LI program is adapted, according to each local view. This step is essentially devoted to the generation of access functions calls. After this adaptation processing, a final program is got and interpreted. Finally, produced results are converted into a same format according to the global view.

4. DISTRIBUTION OF FRERES

Consedering network aspects, the objective was to define a one-user server on CYCLADES. Moreover, we desired to detect failures as soon as possible, to inform the user of unfortunate events and when possible, the system to recover by itself its initial state. The system is composed of a master subsystem (MSS) and as many slave subsystems as concerned local databases. The MSS handles the dialog with the user according to the VTP protocol and communications with the SSS's according to an internal protocol. Moreover, it processes syntactical analysis of LGI queries, translation into LI, broadcasting of LI program to the SSS's, synchronization of the answers. Each SSS is responsible of the receving of orders sent by the MSS and processes adaptation and interpretation of the program and conversion of results which are sent back to the MSS.

5. THE DEMONSTRATION

The demonstration will concern the use of FRERES in the documentation area. With the help of SIRIUS coordination group, we decided to apply the system to the interrogation of a distributed collective catalog of periodicals about informatics, electronics and telecommunications.

The global database, whose individual is a periodical, is composed of two files, located at Rennes (IRISA) and Paris (IRIA) respectively, containing subsets of periodicals. The schema of the global database is drawn below :

PERIODICAL

ISSN NUMBER — EDITOR's NAME — CITY EDITION — PRESENT TITLE — PREVIOUS TITLE — NEXT TITLE

COLLECTION (1 TO 31 INSTANCES)

LIBRARY NUMBER — STATUS OF COLLECTION (Open, Closed or unknown) — LACKS (Yes or No) — BEGINNING YEAR — BEGINNING NUMBER — END YEAR — END NUMBER

The two local databases are files whose records structure correspond the global schema. More precisely, a record contains all informations about a periodical. In such a case, the local views will contain only one logical file which maps the real file. The access function is a short program written in FORTRAN, that accesses sequentially the periodicals.

As we shall see during the demonstration, it is possible to ask many questions, such as :

- retrieval of attributes of a periodical whose present title is known
- retrieval of attributes of a periodical whose one title is known
- retrieval of attributes of periodicals belonging to a given library
- retrieval of attributes of periodicals belonging <u>only</u> to a given library
- retrieval of attributes of periodicals for which at least one collection began before a given year.
- retrieval of attributes of periodical whose present title is known and at least one collection has no lacks.
- retrieval of the number of periodicals for which all collections have the status : closed.

FOOT-NOTES

The following persons work in this project : M. BENMAIZA, C. BOUCHON, P. BOURRET, A. CHAUFFAUT, J. LE PALMEC, H. RICHY, R. TREPOS, J.M. VILLARD.

REFERENCES

[1] Bosc 78a : P. Bosc, A. Chauffaut, R. Trépos : FRERES System ; User's manual. IRISA. May 1978.

[2] Bosc 78b : P. Bosc : Contribution to distributed data interrogation. Functional architecture of FRERES. Thesis. IRISA. November 1978.

[3] Chau 78 : A. Chauffaut : Contribution to distributed data interrogation. Distribution of FRERES. Thesis. IRISA. November 1978.

[4] Bosc 79 : P. Bosc : An overview of FRERES : a system to interrogate distributed data. IGDD/IRIA Seminar on distributed data sharing systems. Aix en Provence. May 1979.

DISTRIBUTED DATA BASES
C. Delobel and W. Litwin (eds.)
North-Holland Publishing Company

SYSIDORE : SYSTEME DE SELECTION D'INFORMATION DOCUMENTAIRE REPARTIE

A. KARMOUCH SIRIUS-CERISS *

Universite des Sciences Sociales
Place Anatole France
31070 TOULOUSE CEDEX
France

SYSIDORE est un système expérimental d'accès conversationnel à une base documentaire répartie. La base est interrogée en un langage dérivé du langage du système MISTRAL (CII-HB) et consiste en un ensemble de bases locales gérées par MISTRAL. Les bases locales peuvent être implémentées sur un même ordinateur ou sur plusieurs ordinateurs géographiquement répartis. L'utilisateur peut choisir parmi plusieurs bases réparties ; la recherche dans une base s'effectue par une équation primaire et/ou secondaire de mots clés. L'utilisateur dispose aussi d'outils d'aide à la recherche : liste des thesaurus, des domaines, etc..... et d'outils d'apprentissage du fonctionnement du système.

SYSIDORE : Distributed Information Retrieval System

SYSIDORE is an experimental system for interactive retrievals in a distributed Information Database. Queries are formulated in a language derived from the language of the MISTRAL system (CII-HB). The distributed data base consists of a set of local data bases managed by MISTRAL. The local data bases may share the same computer or may be distributed on several distant computers. The user may choose between several distributed data bases ; primary and/or secondary equations of keywords are used in the retrieval in each data base. The system provides tools to help the user in retrievals (lists of thesaurus, domains, etc...) and in SYSIDORE manipulations.

INTRODUCTION :

Dans un environnement réseau on considère une base documentaire répartie comme étant un ensemble de bases locales. Ces bases peuvent être soit implantées sur une seule machine (cas des serveurs) soit réparties sur plusieurs machines (ou sites). La gestion locale est assurée par les centres documentaires propriétaires de ces bases. Le logiciel d'accès à chaque base est MISTRAL conversationnel (CII-HB).

Dans ce cadre SYSIDORE est un système expérimental qui permet d'interroger (à partir d'un point quelconque du réseau) à l'aide d'une requête unique, tout ou partie des bases locales.

FONCTIONS DE BASE

Pour pouvoir dialoguer avec l'utilisateur le système SYSIDORE dispose d'un langage procédural proche de celui utilisé dans MISTRAL. Les procédures sont décomposées en cinq grandes classes. Chaque classe de procédures permet d'obtenir un des services offerts par le système.

* les personnes suivantes ont participé à la réalisation de ce système : B.MOUSSAOUI, A. ST UPERY.

Une interrogation peut donc s'effectuer en cinq phases successives :

Information et apprentissage : cette fonction s'adresse aussi bien aux utilisateurs occasionnels qu'à ceux qui utilisent le système de manière habituelle. Elle constitue, pour ces deux sortes d'utilisateurs, un répertoire classé par groupe de procédures et suivant une liste de sujets susceptibles de les interesser.

Sélection de la base répartie à exploiter :l'utilisateur qui désire interroger une base répartie, formule une requête de sélection au système puis fournit à celui-ci le nom de la base répartie. Il convient de signaler que l'utilisateur ne connaît ni la localisation physique des bases locales qui composent la base répartie sélectionnée, ni les noms de ces bases qui ne sont connus que par le système.

Aide à la recherche documentaire : pour mieux bâtir une stratégie de recherche documentaire, on peut exprimer le besoin de s'informer sur les éléments à l'aide desquels la recherche est effectuée dans la base. On peut également obtenir des informations sur la structure et les relations qui lient ces éléments entre eux.

Recherche documentaire proprement dite : elle est effectuée à partir de deux équations de recherche : primaire et secondaire. L'équation primaire est composée de termes d'un thésaurus ou lexique, reliés par les opérateurs logiques OU, ET, SAUF. L'équation secondaire s'applique aux résultats obtenus par l'équation primaire. Elle est limitée aux critères de date de parution et/ou nombre de pages des documents. La syntaxe des deux équations est nécessairement conforme aux règles imposées par le système MISTRAL.

Edition des résultats de la recherche : il s'agit des résultats obtenus par l'équation de recherche primaire et/ou secondaire. Ils sont communiqués à l'utilisateur par site d'origine et suivant un format unique. Les caractéristiques éditées pour un document sont limitées aux champs : auteur, titre et mots-clés.

MODULES GENERAUX :

La structure fonctionnelle du système SYSIDORE est composée de trois modules généraux : 1 - l'interface utilisateur chargée d'assurer le dialogue avec l'utilisateur pour l'aider à définir ses besoins d'informations;
2 - le système d'accès local qui, à partir d'une requête-utilisateur, engage un dialogue avec le système MISTRAL pour réaliser cette requête ;
3 - le système d'accès distant chargé d'assurer les échanges inter-sites. Ces échanges sont synchronisés à l'aide d'un protocole de haut niveau défini à cet effet.

Ce papier n'est qu'une description sommaire du système SYSIDORE, pour plus de détails on pourra se reporter aux documents cités en références.

BIBLIOGRAPHIE :

[1]- A. KARMOUCH, Exploitation en conversationnel (sous temps partagé) de bases documentaires réparties sur un réseau général d'ordinateurs § Thèse de 3èmeCycle UPS - TOULOUSE - Juin I979.

[2]- A. KARMOUCH, étude du système : Accès réparti à MISTRAL conversationnel - Rapport de fin du contrat n°78-188 - CERISS U.S.S. Toulouse.

[3]- CII - HB - ; MISTRAL III/IV Réf. 00F375 11 REV0, 00F37465 REV0 et 00F37509 REV0.

ANNEXE : Exemple d'utilisation de SYSIDORE

! SYSIDORE Commande d'activation du système sous temps partagé.

BONJOUR SYSIDORE A VOTRE SERVICE

COMMANDE PRINCIPALE :

? P : IN [FORMATION]

COMMANDE PRINCIPALE/SECONDAIRE :

? S : CO [MMANDE] Listage des commandes principales et secondaires.

LES COMMANDES SUIVANTES SONT A VOTRE DISPOSITION :
INFORMATION, SYSTEME, COMMANDE, SITE, BASE, SELECTION,
AIDE, DOMAINE, CHAMPS, ARBRE, LEXIQUE, THES, RECHERCHE,
EDITION, STOP.

COMMANDE PRINCIPALE/SECONDAIRE :

? S : CO [MMANDE] BASE

LA COMMANDE SECONDAIRE "BASE" PERMET D'OBTENIR DES
INFORMATIONS SUR UNE OU PLUSIEURS BASES REPARTIES.

SYNTAXE : S : BA [SE] $\{$BASE 1,BASE$_i$, ..BASE$_n\}\{$Tout$\}$

COMMANDE PRINCIPALE/SECONDAIRE

? S : BA INFORMATIQUE

NOM BASE	SITE	ORGANISME PROTECTEUR DU SITE	ORGANISME PROPRIETAIRE DE LA BASE
INFORMATIQUE	GRENOBLE	CICG	IRIA
	TOULOUSE	CICT	USST
	TOULOUSE	CERT	CERT
	LOUVECIENNES	CII-HB	IRIA

COMMANDE PRINCIPALE/SECONDAIRE :

? P : SE [LECTION] Demande de sélection d'une base répartie

NOM DE LA BASE ? INFORMATIQUE
MOT DE PASSE ?

COMMANDE PRINCIPALE/SECONDAIRE :

? P : RE [CHERCHE]

EQUATION PRIMAIRE/COMMANDE

? (RESEAUX OU NETWORK) ET (-) → caractère suite

? COMMUTATION

EQUATION SECONDAIRE (O/N)

? N Résultat = 3 DOCUMENTS

COMMANDE PRINCIPALE/SECONDAIRE :

? P : EDIT

....
....